# The Flowering Thorn

## International Ballad Studies

*edited by*
Thomas A. McKean

A project of the Kommission für Volksdichtung
and the Elphinstone Institute

Utah State University Press
Logan, Utah

Utah State University Press
Logan Utah 84322–7800

Cover and book design and typesetting by Thomas A. McKean.
Cover photograph: Hawthorn (*Cratægus monogyna*), Schivas,
Aberdeenshire, Scotland, June 2003, Thomas A. McKean.

Library of Congress Cataloging-in-Publication Data

The flowering thorn : international ballad studies / edited by Thomas A. McKean.
        p. cm.
"A project of the Kommission für Volksdichtung and the Elphinstone Institute."
Includes bibliographical references (p.     ) and index.
        ISBN 0-87421-568-4 (alk. paper)
    1. Ballads—History and criticism. 2. Folk literature—History and criticism. I.
McKean, Thomas A., 1961-
        ML3545.F596 2003
        782.4'3—dc22

2003018611

# CONTENTS

# Introduction

## Thomas A. M<sup>c</sup>Kean

Thou'll break my heart, thou warbling bird,
That wantons thro' the flowering thorn:
Thou minds me o' departed joys,
Departed never to return.

Robert Burns[1]

The flowering thorn expresses the dual nature of the ballad: at once a distinctive expression of European tradition,[2] but also somewhat tricky to approach from a scholarly perspective, requiring a range of disciplines to illuminate its rich composition. Much of this latter quality has to do with the very features that characterize ballads, *erzählenden Lieder*, or narrative songs.[3] These include an appearance of fragmentation, a wide range of cultural and social referents, complex, evocative symbolic language, and variation.

The notable multiformity of meaning, text, and tune is mirrored in scholarship, too. *The Flowering Thorn* is therefore wide ranging, with articles written by world authorities from the fields of folklore, history, literature, and ethnology, employing a variety of methodologies—structuralism to functionalism, repertoire studies to geographical explorations of cultural movement and change. The twenty-five selected contributions represent the latest trends in ballad scholarship, embracing the multidisciplinary nature of the field today. The essays have their origins in the 1999 International Ballad Conference of the Kommission für Volksdichtung (KfV), which focused particularly on ballads and social context, performance and repertoire, genre, motif, and classification. The revised, tailored, and expanded essays are divided into five sections—the interpretation of narrative song; structure and motif; context, version, and transmission; regions, reprints, and repertoires; and the mediating collector—offering a range of examples from fifteen different cultures, ten of them drawing on languages other than English, resulting in a series of personal journeys to the heart of one of Europe's richest, most enduring cultural creations.

While articles are tightly focused on their central themes, they naturally create cross currents that enrich the entire book. Some of these common themes, seen from very different perspectives, include gender issues, collecting and editing as cultural translation, the vigorous life of literary ballads in the oral tradition, the reemergence of class as a significant aspect of both text and performance, and the long-running dynamic relationship between oral and printed sources. On a fundamental level, though, each article explores the creation of meaning: semantic meaning based on close textual analysis; structural and thematic meaning emerging from study of commonplaces, verse form, and characterization; cultural meaning as embodied in performance and transmission; and meaning as created through the mediations of collection, edition, and translation. To a great extent, the essays collectively address questions of cultural stability, often at the heart of any discussion of tradition, showing the multifaceted, and subjective, nature of meaning, function, and significance in the ballad world. What is it, then, about ballads, some of the "finest specimens of human creativity" (Dundes 1996: xi), that allows such diversity of interpretation?

Ballads—"as hard to define as they are easy to recognize," in Hodgart's memorable phrase (1962: 10)—survive through varying fashions and cultural changes, moving back and forth between oral and written traditions, and maintain a fierce existence in the modern world, coming again into bloom when sung (see Bronson 1959–72: ix). In surviving through change, they achieve a kind of cultural stability, a phrase which may, in some ways, be thought of as synonymous with tradition. Paradoxically, if there is one characteristic shared by traditional songs throughout the world, it is variation (see Coffin 1977: 1–19), but variation and change that takes place within a particular, relatively stable framework. While the "popular ballad" may no longer be popular in literal terms, nor in school curricula as frequently as it once was, it remains one of the most intriguing of all artistic expressions.

The narrative song tradition, wrote David Buchan, "gives expression to the cultural preoccupations of—and sometimes the sense of identity of—a given group" (1994: 377), and more than that, as Brendáin Ó Madagáin has shown in Ireland, song can function as emotional release "on occasions when feelings were such that ordinary speech was inadequate" (1985: 143). For the Inuit, "songs are thoughts, sung out with the breath when people are moved by great forces and ordinary speech no longer suffices" (Rasmussen 1931: 321). In Romanian and Slovenian tradition, an entire world of legend is played out through the medium of these songs (see, for example, Constantinescu in this volume; Ispas 2000; and Kumer 1988). In Germany, songs can combine the real and the historical to yield a rounded vision of human experience (Dittmar 1985: 531; also compare Vargyas 1979; Buchan 1976). In Spain, Mexico, Hungary, and Italy, to name just a few countries with strong traditions, ballads can become "the substance of social commentaries" (Hay 2000: 159; also Brednich et al. 1979: 44–137). In Portugal, "ballad singing only attains its full intensity at harvest time, when its full power is unleashed in the open air. In this setting, the ballad is quite remarkable and striking since it is sung according to a strictly ritualized time-table, in the heat of work, several times a day, by the whole of the agricultural community" (Caufriez 1995: 253).

These are just a few of the ways that ballads, along with other forms of traditional song, offer us intimate access to culture and individual worldview, enabling a richer understanding of ourselves. Though now subterranean in many European societies, the narrative song tradition, in particular, addresses and relates to universal issues. A look at any daily newspaper will confirm our endur-ing concern with issues of power, hegemony, and injustice, death and vengeance; cultural identity, and gender rivalries, all themes found in abundance within the ballad tradition.

Regardless of where one stands on "the ballad wars" between the individualists and the communalists,[4] ballads undoubtedly arise, like any other song, from social interaction—family and community contact where song is both the cata-lyst and the product (McKean 1997a: 97–98, 142–48; also see Glassie 1995: 398–99). Song transmission has, consequently, long been associated with small social units, but where scholars used to consider a song corpus to exist at a community, or even regional, level, it turns out that this body of tradition is really built out of a series of one-to-one relationships between a singer and an interested learner, what might be called "tradition as personal relationship" (McDonald 1997). Such a relationship of song exists between Scottish Traveller Elizabeth Stewart and her late aunt Lucy, from whom she learned her huge repertoire of songs, ranging from music-hall ditties to classic ballads (McKean 2003). She also acquired other skills, of course, such as dealing in secondhand goods, musicianship, and do-mestic crafts from both Lucy and her mother, Jean. It is well to remember, then, that singers are not exclusively singers but rounded individuals, who also learn a wealth of other cultural information and forms of artistic expression over and above their song traditions. These relationships of cultural acquisition can be contemporaneous, creating a synchronic community of song and singers (a horizontal tradition), or a series of them can link together hierarchically through time, making a diachronic lineage of song (a vertical tradition).[5]

Survivalist, antiquarian, and romantic collectors of the eighteenth and nine-teenth centuries concentrated almost entirely on the vertical tradition and its transmission, inter- rather than intra-generationally (see Bell 1988; and Wilgus

1959: chap. 4). In recent decades, this has changed in two significant ways. First, there has been an expanded exploration and appreciation of the workings of horizontal tradition. And second, perhaps more importantly, it has become accepted that the term *oral* tradition must be used with care and that it is not exclusively oral. Some traditional songs are recast by literary artists, and, conversely, ballads of literary origin, especially those emerging from the Romantic tradition—that of Bürger, Goethe, and Schiller, for example—are made traditional through oral transmission and memory (see, for example, Marjetka Golež Kaučič's paper in this volume). There has been a symbiotic relationship between the oral and the print worlds for centuries, with songs moving flexibly back and forth between the two, each doing little harm to the other's function.[6]

There have probably always been those who are more comfortable with verbal communication and aural memory, while others (since the advent of writing) think in visual, orthographic terms. Where one singer may remember songs through sounds, emotions, and moving images or sequential tableaux, another may actually visualize the words themselves, either with letters, or in the words of the Gaelic bard Màiri ni Lachainn, "A' feitheamh na bardachd a' ruith air na glasfhadan" [Awaiting the poetry running atop the walls] (MacInnes 1968: 41).

Some singers think in oral terms, others in nonoral ones;[7] the two skills, the two patterns of mind, coexist, sometimes within the same person, though one usually takes precedence. It seems likely that in today's essentially literate, multimedia world of sound bites and three-second jump cuts, orality exists in smaller, shorter units than it did in preliterate times. A song may pass into the oral tradition for more than a generation, or, perhaps, for only a few weeks or months, before the mediation of print, recording, or broadcast lends its own particular effects to the process. This does not negate the importance of orality as an agent of polishing and honing language over time but rather, simply points the way toward a greater complexity, which is surely to be expected from a human cultural product.

The complexity of the aural and written worlds demands that we ask what we really mean by tradition itself. While leaving detailed definition aside (see note 2), I maintain that a peculiarly oral cognitive process can surely coexist with the skills of reading and writing and also within a society that is culturally literate, that is, one under the influence of print but where each individual does not necessarily read or write. Within one person's tradition, performance, and wider cultural milieu, then, the two traditions graze each other along their entire length, and yet their separate workings are clearly identifiable, as Hamish Henderson said of ballad Scots, the "flexible formulaic language of the older Scottish folksong" (1990: 82). Orality and literacy are, "at least in such an environment, better considered not as mutually exclusive cultures but as mutually supportive mental habits" (Atkinson 2002: 18).

Elucidating how these two cultures coexist demands wide-ranging contextual study, such as that pursued by the influential Carl von Sydow throughout his work. "Investigators have, to far too great an extent, been content with extracts," he wrote in 1934, "instead of seeing their information as part of a natural, living whole" (1977: 44). Folklorists embraced the call with alacrity; the seven hundred pages of Henry Glassie's monumental *Passing the Time in Ballymenone* (1982), so the story goes, were written as context for two fiddle tunes. Ballad scholars have also taken up the challenge (for example, Bronzini 1981: 84), with contextual and performance information increasingly seen as essential to interpretation. In theory, then, extrapolations from this perspective have a validity unperceived by outside observers immersed in their own aesthetic, using their own cultural vocabulary. The process is essentially one of transforming an outsider observer into a special kind of insider, or, in the context of balladry, part of what Barre Toelken describes as the "performative interaction between people who understand each other" (1995: 33). "By and large we are not studying the accumulated texts of a few educated poets but the dynamic record of a general vernacular capacity to use the poetic power available in the song traditions and in the contexts of everyday life in order to foreground and articulate central features of shared human concern" (Toelken 1986: 50).

Ballad scholars have been fruitfully examining performance traditions ever more closely in hopes of illuminating the almost alchemical process whereby a static, rhythmic accretion of words becomes a living song through the addition of melody, a dynamic of performance, and a personalized, internalized emotional expression. According to Scottish singer Jane Turriff,

> If you're no in the mood, ye winna mak a job o't. I go by the air, the sad air, an it carries me away.... Well ye see, if ye haven't got the air of the song, you're nowhere.[8] Fin I sing, I pit ma hert intae ma singin. An I get carriet away wi the song.... You've got a wey o singin the old songs. An ma granfather wis the same, an ma mother wis the same. She aye took oot the song well. It's jist like watchin television! Ye jist think that ye're there an you picture the song in yer hert and ye're singin.[9]

As numerous studies have shown, the acquisition of a song repertoire is often not a matter of happenstance; most singers deliberately seek out and learn songs from well-regarded singers of their acquaintance.[10] Most singers also possess a depth of cultural background, personal experience and history, an understanding of the dynamics of tradition, and an acute awareness of technique and style (conscious, unconscious, or both), which inform their performance. Nowhere is Lynwood Montell's advice to treat people "as a living force" (1970: viii) more justified than when examining ballad traditions, for within their experience, their "hert feelin," lies the key to understanding texts and meanings and their cultural concerns at the time of performance (Buchan 1994: 378).

But listeners, what Barre Toelken calls the "pro-active ballad audience,"[11] must also have these layers of experience and knowledge to enable them to understand a performance on the terms in which it is presented. "Any traditional listening audience," writes Toelken, "actively seek[s] out meaning.... Traditional listeners do more than just hear a ballad: they 'glean' it" (1999). The interplay engendered through the reciprocal relationship between the text and audience can no longer be perceived as a static entity: when engaging any text the audience becomes embroiled in an interactive game that can be played over and over again. This process takes place with differing results for each individual and for each contact with that specific text. Just as the success of any game depends upon the involvement of the participants, the success of any "reading" of a text depends not only upon that text but upon the audience. Gaps in texts not only provoke but necessitate audience interaction (Neal and Robidoux 1995: 224).

Tradition itself, then, may be said to exist in the ethereal, transient performance space between singer and listener. If this is so, and we add notions of re-creation derived from oral-formulaic theory,[12] then we must surely also ask the extent to which the *listener* recreates the song in the listening, as much as the singer does in the performing. Just how proactive is the ballad audience?

Clearly, the listeners' range of cultural background, experience of the song tradition, and, indeed, personal experience radically affect their relationship with the song and the singer. Even a passing acquaintance with plot, a few verses, or even fragments enables listeners to fill in lacunae in the sung narrative, extend metaphor and symbolism, feel the implications of the melody line, and engage in many other forms of internalized interpretation. Indeed, in recent years, some scholars have argued that "fragments" do not exist as such and each verse, couplet, line, or even phrase should be considered as a signifying unit in light of its own cultural evocations of meaning, implication, and connotation (see G. Porter 2000; and Porter and Constantine 2003). The song—melody, performance, and text, of whatever length—combine to involve the listener's intellectual and emotional armory in the act of conscious or unconscious understanding.

Toelken's proactive ballad audience and Gerald Porter's "collaborative role of the listener" (G. Porter 2000: 340) are really, in the end, about homing in on the way meaning is derived from cultural communication, a question which ballad scholarship has fruitfully begun to address over the last decade or so. Reception theory tells us that a text is, in itself, inherently indeterminate in meaning (Atkinson 2002: 8; also see Iser 1974; and Jauss 1974, 1982), but, "for folklorists at least, there is still a constraint upon indeterminacy in ballad texts deriving from the perceived authority of the singer" (Atkinson 2002: 139). Such authority allows the singer, in the Romanian tradition, for example, to "fill the epic schemas...with realistic details that reflected the life experience and the expectations of their listeners" (Constantinescu 2000: 61–62). Singers are loading the dice, so to speak, imposing their own, heavily implied lines of interpretation.

So where exactly does authority lie? Perhaps in the singer's mind, in the performance, the performance context, in the audience's, community's, and fieldworker's perceptions, or in a recorded or transcribed version that is heard or read, or perhaps in all of these loci, the shared space where these different manifestations of a song intersect. Meaning is best accessed, then, "through the study of relationships" (J. Porter 2000: 367), such as that between text and tune, text and context, or singer and audience. That is not to imply that meaning can ever be deduced absolutely: "the conflict of interpretations is insurmountable and inescapable. Between absolute knowledge and hermeneutics, it is necessary to choose" (Ricouer 1981: 193). Siding with the latter, then, interpretation takes place anew at each intersection of time, performance, and reception. Meaning, therefore, is as multiform as the ballad and the audience itself (see Toelken 1986).

One of the key places to look for meaning has always been the text itself. Nevertheless, in light of years of contextual and performance analysis, some scholars have seen a need to reaffirm the centrality of the text and textual meaning. D. K. Wilgus, for one, did so thirty years ago (1973). But, as James Porter points out in this volume, Wilgus's appeal did not exclude other areas of study; he said only that we should "take the songs as a whole, their singers, their performances, their contexts, and yes, also their texts."

To textualists, "folk songs and ballads do comprise a 'literature' of a rather particular kind, from which an approach to 'meaning' (in the literary sense) can be teased out" (Atkinson 2002: x; see also Toelken 1995: 29–30). Richard Bauman calls for "a perspective on context from the inside out, using the text itself as the point of departure" (1992: 142). Roger Renwick, in turn, sees this kind of interpretive work as the only truly empirical foundation to build upon (again, as with his mentor Wilgus, without *excluding* other fruitful avenues of enquiry):

> I urge only that we take as our mission the task of explaining, not "expressive enactments," not "cultural processes," but *folksong*. To do so in an effective, convincing, and collective way we must "recenter" our studies in the materials that once gave us great strength but that we self-defeatingly abandoned in an obsessive search for new ideas at the expense of seeking truly to understand our subject matter. (2001: vii; xi–xii)

Textual study works best, it seems, on individual versions, though some generalizations can surely be drawn from families of variants as well. It still has much to tell us about meaning and structure, without doubt, but through the study of repertoire, it also can reveal a great deal about the singers themselves. That said, one must proceed with caution because, after all, a repertoire—bringing us back to contextualism—so strongly reflects the time it was collected, who collected it, and why and how they did so (see Renwick 2001: 142–50, and his article in this anthology; Atkinson 2002: 244–50; Porter and Gower 1995: 269–72, 280–86; also Goldstein 1989).

Thematic study is perhaps the last key area of ballad research to touch upon here. As a tool for accessing ballad structure and meaning, it is largely derivative of the quest for an internationally applicable system of classification.

In 1966, a group of scholars, under the auspices of the Deutsche Volksliedarchiv (DVA) in Freiburg, gathered for a conference, Über Fragen des Typenindex der europäischen Volksballaden [On the Question of a Type Index of European Ballads]. This led to the foundation of the Kommission für Volksdichtung (KfV),[13] which still runs an annual conference and is the most active working group of the Société Internationale d'Ethnologie et de Folklore (SIEF).

The first question was definition, and the one proposed at that first meeting ("ein Lied das eine Geschichte erzählt mit dem Schwerpunkt auf einer dramatischen Konfliktsituation"; see note 3) was soon seen as flawed, notably in the area of religious ballads, "weil ihnen ein wichtiger Bestandteil der eigentlichen Ballads, nämlich die dramatische Konfliktsituation, fehlt" [because an important component of the ballad is missing, namely, the dramatic conflict situation] (Brednich

1973: 11). Scholars soon realized that definitions should be broader to deal with the range of subject matter and approach central to the ballad genre across cultural lines. In the end, "a song that tells a story" is perhaps the simplest, most usable definition (certainly in the context of this introduction).

A universally applicable classification system for the European ballad has proven no more tractable. The first proposal, the 'Freiburg System,' emanated from the DVA, home to the earliest plans for a practical type index along the lines of the Aarne-Thompson folktale index (Aarne 1961).[14] A few years later, emerging from seminars at UCLA in the 1970s, the Wilgus-Long proposal concentrated on narrative or thematic units (see Wilgus 1978, 1970). Naturally, each approach has its advantages: The former brings a helpful categorization of related story lines, or song families, the latter allows tracing individual themes through a range of realizations, making functional analysis of a given theme a realistic possibility. Zmaga Kumer, for one, recognized that the two methods were symbiotic and that pursuing both was essential—"das eine tun, das andere nicht lassen" [do the one thing, but not neglect the other], according to the proverb (1976: 51 and see Engle 1985: 143)—but she was keen to emphasize that the main aspiration and method of the ballad researcher must always be "die innere Struktur einer Ballade kennenlernen...aus welchen Bestandteilen und auf welche Weise sie gebaut ist" [to get to know the internal structure of a ballad, how it is constructed, and of what components] (49).

The main emphasis of the KfV has shifted over the years, following (and indeed setting) trends in European and American folklore studies towards contextual and interpretive work. Nevertheless, while a universally applicable system is perhaps unachievable, much good work has advanced our thinking about ballad structure, which has, in turn, fed into periodic reshapings of classification strategies (see Waltz and Engle 2003: frontmatter). The recently developed capability to search an entire database electronically, including metadata, offers obvious advantages over conventional indexes and methods. Such an integrated solution has been doggedly pursued by Robert B. Waltz and David Engle, whose catalog is available online (2003).[15] Now, in the digital age, the creation of usable and useful indexes drawing on type and thematic research is, at last, a realistic possibility.

And what of future research? I end with a perennial question, always asked by those concerned with the future of balladry: "Where are all the young ballad singers?" Equally, we may ask, "Where are all the ballad listeners?," for ballads, like other traditional songs, are a communal art form. That is not to side with those who advocate theories of communal composition but rather, to emphasize that song must not only be performed but heard and felt by an audience, yielding transient moments of shared experience and created meaning. Of course, singers often learn, preserve, and enjoy songs entirely for themselves, becoming both performer and audience; I do not mean to imply that these performances do not create meaning as well, though it is a qualitatively different process. In addition, our definition of tradition as a relationship, or as the process of passing on material, relies on communication between at least two people. Within these ideas, and in the complex, multilayered interplay between melody and text, lies the future of ballad studies.

Being an informed ballad listener is a learned art, learned by some in the context of their family, community, or peer group, and by others through actively seeking out today's performance environments, which can range from intimate family settings to commercial broadcasts. This book holds a key to many aspects of that art; those who read on will glimpse something significant about the flowering thorn. Having been part of such a learning process myself—raised in a singing environment and later taking up another culture's songs as performer and scholar—I can attest to its value, for within balladry there is complex human emotional interaction, combined with striking imagery polished by use and memory. In balladry you will find artistry, as Hugh MacDiarmid wrote of the little white rose of Scotland, that "smells sharp and sweet—and breaks the heart" (1967: 248).

*For Barre Toelken*

*Notes*

1.  "Ye Banks and Braes o' Bonnie Doon" (Kinsley 1971: 456).
2.  "Tradition" and "traditional" are used throughout this book in their habitually accepted sense. I certainly agree that only a minority takes part in perpetuating a given tradition (von Sydow 1977: 12, 48), and, while I am cognizant of long-running debates on the "breadth of its semantic extent" (Glassie 1995: 395), tradition is too useful a word to avoid in this context simply because of its many layers of meaning. For just a few of the debates and definitions, see Glassie 1995; Vansina 1985; Cohen 1989; Finnegan 1991; Newall 1987.
3.  These three terms are used as equivalents throughout this book; *Volksballad* ("folk ballad") is also in common usage. The inaugural meeting of the Kommission für Volksdichtung (KfV) in 1966 defined the genre this way: "Eine Ballade [ist] ein Lied...das eine Geschichte erzählt mit dem Schwerpunkt auf einer dramatischen Konfliktsituation, mit anderen Worten, daß ein zentrales Erzählthema abgehandelt wird" [a ballad is a song

that tells a story, with the main focus on a situation of dramatic conflict, in other words, one that deals centrally with a narrative theme] (Brednich 1973: 11). See Bec 1977 for a treatment of the word "ballade."

The KfV's work now includes a wider range of traditional song, but still, for the most part, deals with songs that tell a story. More exact definitions are myriad and problematic, in some cases not transferring internationally with great success, so it is hoped my general, broad usage will be acceptable in this context. Traditional singers themselves generally do not use these terms (Brown 1998: 47–48).

4.  There is a long-running controversy over whether individual ballads were the product of communal composition or an individual composer (see Wilgus 1959, chapters 1 and 2).

5.  David Atkinson uses the terms transient and transcendental (2002: 248), the second borrowed from Barry McDonald (1997: 58), to represent two ends of a continuum, though I feel these terms lend an extreme air to both types of tradition, evanescence and apotheosis, respectively.

6.  For a series of papers discussing the broadside traditions of Slovenia, Belgium, Bulgaria, Hungary, Italy, Finland, Germany, Ireland, and the Netherlands, see Top and Tielemans 1982. See Atkinson 2002: 18–19 for a discussion of the impact of broadside print on British song tradition. David Buchan also addresses this question for the Scottish context (1972: chapter 18). For the interrelationship between print and oral narrative traditions in Scandinavia, see von Sydow 1977: 37–38; in Scotland and Ireland, see Bruford 1969, part 3. For a general discussion, see Ong 1982.

7.  I take "oral" to include the visualization of ballad action and plot while singing, as opposed to the visualization of actual texts, written or printed. For a discussion of visualization in storytelling, see Macdonald 1978. The same phenomenon is generally accepted to take place for many ballad singers; I am currently researching this phenomenon with singers in North East Scotland.

8.  Tape SA1973/71 B1 in the School of Scottish Studies Archives, department of Celtic and Scottish Studies, University of Edinburgh, recorded by James Porter and Hamish Henderson. Extracts appear with the School's kind permission.

9.  These Jane Turriff interviews are on tapes 1994.50–51, North East Folklore Archive, Mintlaw, Aberdeenshire, Scotland. Transcripts are available on the web at <http://www.nefa.net> (click on the Banff and Buchan Collection). See McKean 1997b: 242 for more along these lines.

10. See Kumer 1981: 53–54, and, for example, Abrahams 1970; Top and Tielemans 1981; Top 1981; Top and Tielemans 1982; Fowke 1994; Porter and Gower 1995; Goldstein 1968; Ó Cróinín 2000; and McKean 2003.

11. Like Toelken, I have reservations about the word "proactive," but I think it is useful in this context.

12. The theory proposes that singers of the south Slavic epics, which sometimes run to many thousand lines, recreate the songs each time using only a remembered skeletal plot structure and a range of formulaic word combinations, phrases, and couplets (see Lord 2000, and Lord 1995: chapter 7). This premise has been applied to European balladry— as distinct, that is, from the south Slavic epic—with widely varying care and success— German: Roth 1977; Cheesman 1994: chapter 3; Spanish: Beatie 1964; Webber 1995; Scandinavian: Holzapfel 1978; Richmond 1963; Anglo-Scottish: Jones 1961; Buchan 1972; Andersen 1985; McCarthy 1990. Albert Friedman has produced several probing, detailed responses to these ideas (1961, and especially 1983).

13. <http://www.kfvweb.org/>.

14. For a thorough example of this type, see Jonsson et al.1978.

15. For applications to German balladry, see Engle 1979. For an exploration of classification problems in the pan-Hispanic tradition, see Hay 1993.

## References

Aarne, Antti. 1961. *The Types of the Folktale: A Classification and Bibliography.* Translated and enlarged by Stith Thompson. 2d rev. ed. FF Communications, vol. 75, no. 184. Helsinki: Suomalainen Tiedeakatemia / Academia Scientarum Fennica.

Abrahams, Roger D., ed. 1970. *A Singer and Her Songs: Almeda Riddle's Book of Ballads.* Music editor, George Foss. Baton Rouge: Louisiana State University Press.

Andersen, Flemming G. 1985. *Commonplace and Creativity: The Role of Formulaic Diction in Anglo-Scottish Traditional Balladry.* Odense University Studies from the Medieval Centre, vol. 1. [Odense]: Odense University Press.

Atkinson, David. 2002. *The English Traditional Ballad: Theory, Method, and Practice.* Ashgate Popular and Folk Music Series. Aldershot and Burlington, Vt: Ashgate.

Bauman, Richard. 1992. "Contextualization, Tradition, and the Dialogue of Genres: Icelandic Legends of the Kraftaskad." In *Rethinking Context: Language as an Interactive Phenomenon,* edited by Charles Goodwin and Alessandro Duranti, 125–45. Cambridge: Cambridge University Press.

Beatie, Bruce A. 1964. "Oral-Traditional Composition in the Spanish *Romancero* of the Sixteenth Century." *Journal of the Folklore Institute* 1: 92–113.

Bec, Pierre. 1977. *La lyrique française au Moyen Âge (XIIe–XIIIe siècles): Contribution à une typologie des genres poétiques médiévaux. Études et textes.* Publications du Centre d'Études Supérieures de Civilisation Médiévale de l'Université de Poitiers, nos. 6, 7. Paris: Éditions A. and J. Picard.

Bell, Michael J. 1988. "'No Borders to the Ballad Maker's Art': Francis James Child and the Politics of the People." *Western Folklore* 47: 285–307.

Brednich, Rolf W. 1973. *5. Arbeitstagung über Fragen des Typenindex der europäischen Volksballaden...in Škofja Loka, Jugoslawien,* edited by Heinke Binder und Rolf W. Brednich. Veranstaltet von der Kommission für Volksdichtung der Société Internationale d'Ethnologie et de Folklore (SIEF). Freiburg: Deutsches Volksliedarchiv.

Brednich, Rolf W., Jürgen Dittmar, David G. Engle, and Ildikó Kriza, eds. 1979. *Arbeitstagung über Fragen des Typenindex der europäischen Volksballaden...in Esztergom/Ungarn.* Veranstaltet von der Kommission für Volksdichtung der Société Internationale d'Ethnologie et de Folklore (SIEF). Budapest: Ethnographisches Institut der U.A.d.W.

Bronson, Bertrand Harris. 1959–72. *The Traditional Tunes of the Child Ballads, with Their Texts, According to the Extant Records of Great Britain and America.* 4 vols. Princeton: Princeton University Press.

Bronzini, Giovanni Battista. 1981. "Form, Ideologie und Funktion der erzählenden Volkslieder des Salent unter Bezugnahme auf das salentinische Griechenland." In *11. Arbeitstagung über Probleme der europäischen Volksballade...in Jannina/ Griechenland,* edited by Rolf W. Brednich, 81–103. Veranstaltet von der Kommission für Volksdichtung der Société Internationale d'Ethnologie et de Folklore (SIEF). Jannina: University of Jannina.

Brown, Mary Ellen. 1998. "Ballad." In *Encyclopedia of Folklore and Literature,* edited by Mary Ellen Brown and Bruce A. Rosenberg, 47–48. Santa Barbara, Denver, Oxford: ABC-Clio.

Bruford, Alan. 1969. *Gaelic Folk-tales and Medieval Romances.* Dublin: Folklore of Ireland Society.

Buchan, David. 1972. *The Ballad and the Folk.* London: Routledge and Kegan Paul. Reprint, Phantassie, East Lothian: Tuckwell Press, 1997.

———. 1976. "History and Harlaw." In *Ballad Studies,* edited by E. B. Lyle, 29–40. Cambridge: D. S. Brewer.

————. 1994. "The Historical Balladry of the North East." *Aberdeen University Review* 192 (autumn): 377–87.

Caufriez, Anne. 1995. "The Ballad in Northeastern Portugal." In *Ballads and Boundaries: Narrative Singing in an Intercultural Context*, edited by James Porter, with Ellen Sinatra, 251–64. Proceedings of the 23rd International Ballad Conference of the Commission for Folk Poetry (Société Internationale d'Ethnologie et de Folklore). Los Angeles: Department of Ethnomusicology and Systematic Musicology.

Cheesman, Tom. 1994. *The Shocking Ballad Picture Show: German Popular Literature and Cultural History*. Oxford: Berg.

Coffin, Tristram Potter. 1977. *The British Traditional Ballad in North America*. Bibliographical and special series published through the cooperation of the American Folklore Society. Rev. ed. with a supplement by Roger deV. Renwick. Austin and London: University of Texas Press.

Cohen, D. W. 1989. "The Undefining of Oral Tradition." *Ethnohistory* 36: 9–18.

Constantinescu, Nicolae. 2000. "Ballad and Intercultural Communication." In *Bridging the Cultural Divide: Our Common Ballad Heritage/Kulturelle Brücken: Gemeinsame Balladentradition*, edited by Sigrid Rieuwerts and Helga Stein, 60–69. Hildesheim, Zürich, New York: Olms.

Dittmar, Jürgen. 1985. "Das Geschichtliche Ereignis im Deutschen Erzählied. Ein Gattungsvergleich." In *Ballata e Storia. 14. Arbeitstagung der Kommission für Volksdichtung der Société Internationale d'Ethnologie et de Folklore (SIEF)* (also published in *Lares* 51), 527–38. Firenze: Olschki.

Dundes, Alan. 1995. "How Indic Parallels to the Ballad of the 'Walled-Up Wife' Reveal the Pitfalls of Parochial Nationalistic Folkloristics." *Journal of American Folklore* 108, no. 427: 38–53.

Dundes, Alan, ed. 1996. *The Walled-Up Wife: A Casebook*. Madison: University of Wisconsin Press.

Engle, David G. 1979. "Ballad Classification and Social Criticism." In *9. Arbeitstagung über Fragen des Typenindex der europäischen Volksballaden...in Esztergom/Ungarn*, edited by Rolf W. Brednich, Jürgen Dittmar, David G. Engle, and Ildikó Kriza, 156–73. Veranstaltet von der Kommission für Volksdichtung der Société Internationale d'Ethnologie et de Folklore (SIEF). Budapest: Ethnographisches Institut der U.A.d.W.

Engle, David G. 1985. *A Preliminary Catalog and Edition of German Folk Ballads: The Test of a Thematic Classification System on 187 Narrative Folksong Types*. Ph.D. dissertation, University of California, Los Angeles.

Finnegan, Ruth. 1991. "Tradition, but What Tradition, and Tradition for Whom." *Oral Tradition* 6: 104–25.

Fowke, Edith. 1994. *A Family Heritage: The Story and Songs of LaRena Clark*. With Jay Rahn. Calgary: University of Calgary Press.

Friedman, Albert B. 1961. "The Formulaic Improvisation Theory of Ballad Tradition— A Counterstatement." *Journal of American Folklore* 74: 113–15.

————. 1983. The Oral-Formulaic Theory of Balladry—A Re-Rebuttal." In *The Ballad Image: Essays Presented to Bertrand Harris Bronson*, edited by James Porter, with a foreword by Wayland D. Hand, 215–40. Los Angeles: Center for the Study of Comparative Folklore and Mythology, University of California.

Glassie, Henry. 1982. *Passing the Time in Ballymenone: Culture and History of an Ulster Community*. Publications of the American Folklore Society, no. 4. Philadelphia: University of Pennsylvania Press.

————. 1995. "Tradition." *Journal of American Folklore* 108: 395–412.

Goldstein, Kenneth S. 1989. "The Collector's Personal Aesthetic as an Influence on the Informant's Choice of Repertory." In *Ballades et chansons folkloriques*, 367–71.

Actes de la 18th Session de la Commission pour l'Étude de la Poésie de Tradition Orale (Kommission für Volksdichtung) de la Société Internationale d'Ethnologie et de Folklore (SIEF). Actes de Célat, no. 4. Québec: Célat, Université Laval.

Hay, Beatriz Mariscal. 1993. "Cataloguing Open-Structured Narratives: The General Catalogue of the Pan-Hispanic Romancero." In *The Stockholm Ballad Conference 1991: Proceedings of the 21st International Ballad Conference, 19–22 August 1991*, edited by Bengt R. Jonsson, 43–51. Skrifter utgivna av Svenskt Visarkiv, no. 12. Stockholm: Svenskt Visarkiv. Also published in *ARV: Scandinavian Yearbook of Folklore* 48 (1992), 43–51.

———. 2000. "From Chanson to Romance: Notes on the Spanish Carolingian Ballad Tradition." In *Bridging the Cultural Divide: Our Common Ballad Heritage/ Kulturelle Brücken: Gemeinsame Balladentradition*, edited by Sigrid Rieuwerts and Helga Stein, 152–60.

Henderson, Hamish. 1990. "The Ballad, the Folk and the Oral Tradition." In *The People's Past*, edited by Edward J. Cowan. Edinburgh: Polygon, 1980, reprint 1990.

Hodgart, M. J. C. 1962. *The Ballads*. 2d ed. London: Hutchinson University Library.

Holzapfel, Otto. 1978. "Scandinavian Folk Ballad Symbols, Epic Formulas and Verbal Traditions." In *Ballads and Ballad Research*, edited by Patricia Conroy, 113–21. Seattle: University of Washington Press.

Iser, Wolfgang. 1974. *The Implied Reader: Patterns of Communication in Prose Fiction from Bunyan to Beckett*. Baltimore: Johns Hopkins University Press.

Ispas, Sabine. 2000. "Struggle with the Dragon." In *Bridging the Cultural Divide: Our Common Ballad Heritage/Kulturelle Brücken: Gemeinsame Balladentradition*, edited by Sigrid Rieuwerts and Helga Stein, 162–75.

Jauss, Hans Robert. 1974. "Literary History as a Challenge to Literary Theory." In *New Directions in Literary History*, edited by Ralph Cohen and translated by Elizabeth Benzinger, 11–41. London: Routledge; Baltimore: Johns Hopkins University Press.

———. 1982. *Toward an Aesthetic of Reception*. Translated by Timothy Bahti. Vol. 2 of *Theory and History of Literature*. Minneapolis: University of Minnesota Press.

Jones, James H. 1961. "Commonplace and Memorization in the Oral Tradition of the English and Scottish Popular Ballads." *Journal of American Folklore* 74: 97–112.

Kinsley, James, ed. 1971. *Burns Poems and Songs*. London: Oxford University Press.

Kumer, Zmaga. 1976. "Einige Gedanken zur Di[s]kussion um die Balladen-klassifikation." In *7. Arbeitstagung über Fragen des Typenindex der europäischen Volksballaden vom 10. Bis 12. Juli 1975 in Breukelen/Niederlande,* edited by Jürgen Dittmar, 49– 55. Veranstaltet von der Kommission für Volksdichtung der Société Internationale d'Ethnologie et de Folklore (SIEF). Freiburg: Deutsches Volksliedarchiv.

———. 1979. "Singers' Repertories as the Consequence of Their Biographies." In *Lore and Language* (special issue) 3, nos. 4–5 (January/July 1981): 49–54. Proceedings of the 10th Symposium on European Ballad Research, Edinburgh, edited by Rolf W. Brednich. Kommission für Volksdichtung der Société Internationale d'Ethnologie et de Folklore (SIEF).

———. 1988. "Die Ballade im Volksleben der Slowenen (Zur Frage des Verhältnisses zu anderen Gattungen)." In *Ballads and Other Genres/Balladen und Andere Gattungen*, edited by Jerko Bezić et al., 21–26. Proceedings of the 17th International Ballad Conference in Rovinj, 1987. Zagreb: Zavod za istrazivanje folklora.

Lord, Albert. B. 1995. *The Singer Resumes the Tale*. Edited by Mary Louise Lord. Myth and Poetics. Ithaca and London: Cornell University Press.

———. 2000. *The Singer of Tales*. Edited by Stephen Mitchell and Gregory Nagy. 2d ed. Harvard Studies in Comparative Literature, no. 24. With audio and video CD. Cambridge: Harvard University Press, 1964. Reprint, Cambridge: Harvard University Press.

MacDiarmid, Hugh. 1967. *Collected Poems of Hugh MacDiarmid*. Edited by John C. Weston, Rev. ed. with enl. glossary. New York, London: Macmillan, Collier-Macmillan

MacDonald, Donald A. 1978. "A Visual Memory." *Scottish Studies* 22: 1–26.

MacInnes, John. 1968. "The Oral Tradition in Scottish Gaelic Poetry." *Scottish Studies* 12, no.1: 29–44.

McCarthy, William Bernard. 1990. *The Ballad Matrix: Personality, Milieu, and the Oral Tradition*. Bloomington and Indianapolis: Indiana University Press.

McDonald, Barry. 1997. "Tradition as Personal Relationship." *Journal of American Folklore* 110: 47–67.

McKean, Thomas A. 1997a. *Hebridean Song-maker: Iain Macneacail of the Isle of Skye*. Edinburgh: Polygon.

———. 1997b. "Gordon Easton and 'The Beggarman' (Child 279/280)." In *Ballads into Books: The Legacies of Francis James Child*, edited by Thomas Cheesman and Sigrid Rieuwerts, 237–48. Bern: Lang.

———. In press. "The Stewarts of Fetterangus and Literate Oral Tradition." In *The Singer and the Scribe*, edited by Philip Bennett. *Internationale Forschung zur Allgemeinen und Vergleichenden Literaturwissenschaft*, edited by Alberto Martino. Amsterdam: Rodopi.

Montell, Lynwood. 1970. *The Saga of Coe Ridge: A Study in Oral History*. Knoxville: University of Tennessee Press.

Neal, David, and Michael Robidoux. 1995. "Folklore: 'Phenomenologically' Speaking: Filling in the Gaps." *Southern Folklore* 52: 211–29.

Newall, Venetia J. 1987. "The Adaptation of Folklore and Tradition (Folklorismus)." *Folklore* 98, no. 2: 131–51.

Ó Cróinín, Dáibhí, ed. and comp. 2000. *The Songs of Elizabeth Cronin, Irish Traditional Singer*. Dublin: Four Courts Press.

Ó Madagáin, Breandán. 1985. "Functions of Irish Song in the Nineteenth Century." *Béaloideas* 53: 130–216.

Ong, Walter J. 1982. *Orality and Literacy*. London: Methuen.

Porter, Gerald. 2000. "The Intertextuality of the Song Fragment: Dickens and Popular Song." In *Bridging the Cultural Divide: Our Common Ballad Heritage/Kulturelle Brücken: Gemeinsame Balladentradition*, edited by Sigrid Rieuwerts and Helga Stein, 338–53.

Porter, Gerald, and Mary-Ann Constantine. 2003. *Fragments and Meaning in Traditional Songs*. Oxford: Oxford University Press.

Porter, James. 2000. "Ballad Singing, Fieldwork, Meaning." In *Bridging the Cultural Divide: Our Common Ballad Heritage/Kulturelle Brücken: Gemeinsame Balladentradition*, edited by Sigrid Rieuwerts and Helga Stein, 356–74.

Porter, James, and Herschel Gower. 1995. *Jeannie Robertson: Emergent Singer, Transformative Voice*. American Folklore Society Publications, New Series. Knoxville: University of Tennessee Press.

Rasmussen, Knud. 1931. *The Netsilik Eskimos: Social Life and Spiritual Culture*. Report of the fifth Thule expedition 1921–24,... vol. 8, nos. 1–2. Translated by W. E. Calvert. Copenhagen: Gyldendalske Boghandel.

Renwick, Roger deV. 2001. *Recentering Anglo/American Folksong: Sea Crabs and Wicked Youths*. Jackson: University Press of Mississippi.

Richmond, W. Edson. 1963. "'Den Utrue Egtemann': A Norwegian Ballad and Formulaic Composition." *Norveg* 10: 59–88.

Ricouer, Paul. 1981. *Hermeneutics and the Human Sciences: Essays on Language, Action and Interpretation*. Edited by John B. Thompson. Cambridge: Cambridge University Press.

Roth, Klaus. 1977. "Zur Mündlichen Komposition von Volksballaden." *Jahrbuch für Volksliedforschung* 22: 49–65.

Toelken, Barre. 1986. "Context and Meaning in the Anglo-American Ballad." In *The Ballad and the Scholars*, 29–52. Los Angeles: Clark Memorial Library.

————. 1995. *Morning Dew and Roses: Nuance, Metaphor, and Meaning in Folksongs.* Folklore and Society, Publications of the American Folklore Society, New Series. Urbana and Chicago: University of Illinois Press.

————. 1999. "Abstract" submitted to the International Ballad Conference, Aberdeen.

Top, Stefaan. 1981. "Studien zum Repertoire einer 88jährigen flämischen Volksliedsängerin: Zielsetzung, Problematik und erste Ergebnisse." In *11. Arbeitstagung über Probleme der europäischen Volksballade...in Jannina/ Griechenland,* edited by Rolf W. Brednich, 187–198. Veranstaltet von der Kommission für Volksdichtung der Société Internationale d'Ethnologie et de Folklore (SIEF). Jannina: University of Jannina.

Top, Stefaan, and Eddy Tielemans. 1981. *Meen van Eycken: Een Gezongen Biografie* [Meen van Eycken: A Biography in Songs]. Brussels: Centrum voor Vlaamse Volscultuur en de Koninklijke Belgische Commissie voor Volkskunde.

Top, Stefaan, and Eddy Tielemans, ed. 1982. *12 de Internationale Volksballadentagung. Aspects of the European Broadside Ballad and Other Problems of Actual Song Research.* Brussels: Centrum voor Vlaamse Volkscultuur.

Vansina, Jan. 1985. *Oral Tradition as History.* Madison: University of Wisconsin Press.

Vargyas, Lajos. 1979. "The Ballad as a Source for History." In *9. Arbeitstagung über Fragen des Typenindex der europäischen Volksballaden...in Esztergom/Ungarn,* edited by Rolf W. Brednich, Jürgen Dittmar, David G. Engle, and Ildikó Kriza, 44–60. Veranstaltet von der Kommission für Volksdichtung der Société Internationale d'Ethnologie et de Folklore (SIEF). Budapest: Ethnographisches Institut der U. A. d. W.

v[on] Sydow, C[arl] [W]ilhelm. 1977. *Selected Papers on Folklore, Published on the Occasion of His 70th Birthday.* (A selection of papers written from 1932–45.) Copenhagen: Rosenkilde and Bagger, 1948. Reprint, New York: Arno Press.

Waltz, Robert B., and David Engle. 2003. "The Traditional Ballad Index: An Annotated Bibliography of the Folk Songs of the English-Speaking World." Online electronic database. Available at <http://www.csufresno.edu/folklore/BalladIndexTOC.html>

Webber, Ruth House. 1995. "Ballad Language: Repetition and the Formula." In *Ballads and Boundaries: Narrative Singing in an Intercultural Context,* edited by James Porter, with Ellen Sinatra, 156–64. Proceedings of the 23rd International Ballad Conference of the Commission for Folk Poetry (Société Internationale d'Ethnologie et de Folklore). Los Angeles: Department of Ethnomusicology and Systematic Musicology.

Wilgus, D. K. 1959. *Anglo-American Folksong Scholarship Since 1898.* New Brunswick, N.J.: Rutgers University Press.

————. 1970. "A Type-Index of Anglo-American Traditional Narrative Songs." *Journal of the Folklore Institute* 7: 161–76

————. 1973. "The Text Is the Thing." *Journal of American Folklore* 86: 241–52.

————. 1978. "Remarks." In *8. Arbeitstagung über Fragen des Typenindex der europäischen Volksballaden...in Kopenhagen/Dänemark,* edited by Rolf W. Brednich and David G. Engle, 12–26. Veranstaltet von der Kommission für Volksdichtung der Société Internationale d'Ethnologie et de Folklore (SIEF). Freiburg: Deutsches Volksliedarchiv.

## Recordings

Goldstein, Kenneth S., ed. 1968. *Sara Cleveland of Brant Lake, New York.* Sharon, Conn.: Folk Legacy Records 33. Recording with notes.

# Now She's Fairly Altered Her Meaning: Interpreting Narrative Song

# Now She's Fairly Altered Her Meaning:
## Interpreting Narrative Song

Songs have an infinite range of potential symbolic and functional meanings to both their singers and listeners. Scholars, like any other proactive ballad audience, bring a world of unique referents and a range of individual background information to the study of traditional song. Through a synthesis of internal and external evidence, the essays in this section tell us much about various song traditions but also about the methodological, and indeed the human concerns, of their authors. We prefer, incidentally, to use terms such as "interpretation" and "meaning" in relation to traditional song, rather than "decoding," which suggests a studied obscurity (see Toelken 1995: 33). Meaning in folk tradition is complex, rich, and rewarding to study. It is, however, undoubtedly obscure at times. As Barre Toelken (1995) said, "Perhaps we can feel lucky to be pursuing such a topic at a time in cultural history when we can discuss this imagery more openly and no longer feel inclined to think that rural and 'primitive' people are too dull to create intentional poetic ambiguity" (2).

These textually and culturally centered studies look at repertoire, symbolic language, motifs, linguistic structures, and character roles internal to the songs. Connecting these in many of the essays are gender issues, which are addressed through interpreting ballads as indicators of sexual, economic, and cultural freedom, and from the perspective of singers' choice of song in relation to the male and female roles embodied in the texts. From symbolic evidence, Pauline Greenhill infers a range of nonheterosexual meanings, particularly relating to women's economic freedom versus their usual stereotyped roles. These veiled, often subconscious, meanings allow women unobtrusively to subvert standard assumptions about gender roles in traditional song. In the Scottish context, Lynn Wollstadt looks at the implications of songs that can be described as gender typed by content and investigates whether this differentiation is reflected in male and female singers' repertoire choices.

Also touching upon gender roles, and their swirling interaction with spiritual, religious, and medical practices, is Luisa Del Giudice's "Healing the Spider's Bite." The intriguing phenomenon of *tarantismo*, a compelling synthesis of movement, music, and medicine which encapsulates the magical elements of all three, goes some way toward explaining the elemental power of ballads, the most visceral of traditional songs. This same primeval energy is seen, too, in Vic Gammon's brief look at the "Lamkin" ballad (Child 93), part of his survey of music, charm, and seduction in British balladry, drawing on a wide range of examples. Here we come face to face with the fine line that separates comfortable, safe domesticity (the singing of a lullaby by a domestic servant) from what we like to imagine is inhuman violence (the same servant's complicity in the murder of a baby). This is just one example of the visceral, elemental nature of the ballad tradition.

In "The Servant Problem in Child Ballads," Roger deV. Renwick looks more closely at the master-servant relationship, a common thread in many ballad stories:

> But standin by was a little foot page,
> To the lady's coach he run,
> Although I am the Lady's page
> I am Lord Barnard's man. (Child 81)

Loyalty, duty, and morality are laid bare by reading between the lines of classic texts to elucidate traditions of servant authority and disobedience within the context of the ballad world.

Reading between the lines is precisely the method pursued in much of Gerald Porter's work, especially his recent collaboration with Mary-Ann Constantine, *Fragments and Meaning in Traditional Songs* (2003). "Jesting with Edge Tools," in this volume, is one of a suite of papers (for example, 1997, 2000) examining specific trades and ethnic types in the broadside tradition of the British Isles. Through songs of the popular press, he maintains, it is not only possible to deduce something about attitudes to the working classes but also, by drawing on a type of reception theory, to interpolate something about the cultural assumptions that singers and songmakers would expect their listeners to have about ethnicity and profession, in this case, the carpenter.

Finally, in a wide-ranging study of "De May Bush," Cozette Griffin-Kremer shows how song—content, use and function, symbolism—fits sycretistically into wider forms of cultural expression, in this case the calendar customs of Beltane, the Celtic midsummer festival. Like many festivals, an eighteenth-century Dublin May Day was associated with misrule, chaos, and inversion. Griffin-Kremer relates the song to the enactment of cultural ritual, cosmological thought and symbolism, and the expression of local political rivalries, breaking down narrow genre contraints to show how different iterations of the same tradition can permeate many levels of society. In such a case, a song can acquire meaning and function unique to each element of the society of which it is a part, an idea implied by Willa Muir's well-known phrase "living with ballads" (1965).

*References*

Muir, Willa. 1965. *Living with Ballads*. London: Hogarth Press.

Porter, Gerald. 1997. "Telling the Tale Twice Over: Shakespeare and the Ballad." In *Ballads into Books: The Legacies of Francis James Child*, edited by Thomas Cheesman and Sigrid Rieuwerts, 165–78. Bern: Lang.

———. 2000. "The Intertextuality of the Song Fragment: Dickens and Popular Song." In *Bridging the Cultural Divide: Our Common Ballad Heritage/Kulturelle Brücken: Gemeinsame Balladentradition*, edited by Sigrid Rieuwerts and Helga Stein, 338–53. Hildesheim, Zürich, New York: Olms.

Porter, Gerald, and Mary-Ann Constantine. 2003. *Fragments and Meaning in Traditional Songs*. Oxford: Oxford University Press.

Toelken, Barre. 1995. *Morning Dew and Roses: Nuance, Metaphor, and Meaning in Folksongs*. Folklore and Society, Publications of the American Folklore Society, New Series. Urbana and Chicago: University of Illinois Press.

# Healing the Spider's Bite:
## "Ballad Therapy" and *Tarantismo*

Luisa Del Giudice

In 1959, Ernesto De Martino, ethnologist and scholar of comparative religion, led what has become a near-legendary expedition to the Salento (southeastern-most tip of the heel of the Italian boot) to study the phenomenon of *tarantismo*.[1] The book which resulted from this experience, *La terra del rimorso*, is considered the summa on *tarantismo* but remains, as yet, unpublished in English.[2] It takes its place in the centuries-old current of writing (medical, philosophical, and ecclesiastic) about this form of music and dance therapy, beginning in the fourteenth century. The phenomenon engaged major thinkers, including Leonardo da Vinci, in debates which pitted magic against scientific thought, and pre-Christian ecstatic religious traditions against the church's attempts to eradicate them.

De Martino describes *tarantismo* as a traditional ritual practice, involving music, dance, and color, used to cure (especially) peasant women of a mythic spider's bite. The *taranta* (vernacular for *tarantola*) was not a "tarantula," as we understand it, but could include a spider, snake, or scorpion, that is, various creatures with a venomous bite. Those afflicted were called *tarantati*[3] —literally "tarantulated." Why was this a *mythic* spider? Because in only rare cases was any victim actually bitten by a spider, although most insisted they had been. The ritual system may have originally arisen from observing actual cases of lactrodectism resulting from the bite of a *Lycosa*, but it soon evolved into a complex set of symbolic practices that went far beyond any clinical disease.[4] Those affected were mostly women, but who were they? De Martino's fieldwork identified many *tarantate* as young women in situations of forbidden or unrequited love, or unhappily married women, spinsters, and widows. The first bite usually occurred during summer harvest, under the hottest sun of the day— which is also when spiders are most apt to bite. Thereafter, it recurred annually, marking the anniversary of the first bite (hence, *rimorso* with reiterative prefix, in De Martino's title above, which in Italian means both "remorse" and "rebitten").[5]

Musicians were central to this form of therapy and were well paid for their services. Once the disorder had been attributed to a spider's bite, experienced musicians were called to the victim's home, and a musical diagnosis of the disorder began. The musicians' role was to find the *correct* rhythm to awaken the spider and make it dance, in order to destroy it. Indeed, a belief connected to the tarantula's musical sensibilities held that the spider emitted a certain melody when it bit, which was transferred to its victim (De Martino 1976: 132–49). Through music and dance, musicians elicited deep and unresolved aspects of the victim's malaise: from repressed or problematic sexuality to depression, anxiety, and so forth. The question of what the "bite" represented was always an individual matter, but it is important to note that *tarantati* were among the poorest of the poor so that afflictions resulting from socioeconomic hardships might be considered one of their common denominators, even though historically, it was not always so; noblewomen and even ecclesiastics danced to expunge their spider.

The *tarantata* and her tarantula came to be on intimate terms; each tarantula answered to a pet name (Caterina, Rosina, Maria Antonietta, etc.), had its specific personality, and could only be aroused by a certain rhythm. There were lustful spiders which induced erotic dance movements. Aggressive spiders could call for a sword dance, while melancholic ones might prefer funeral laments. There were, however, depressed and mute *tarante* which did not respond to music and did not cause their victims to dance nor sing. Each whim of the tarantula had to be fulfilled, or it could cause more suffering and refuse to die. The spider could be annoyed by, or respond to, color, as well. Indeed, normally a range of colored ribbons or scarves were shown to the *tarantata,* and she might be aroused by one color and throw herself on the object, tearing it to shreds. If some hapless onlooker was wearing that color, he or she was in danger of attack. When a tarantula died, a daughter or granddaughter of the spider might take its place, so that generations of spiders might afflict one victim over decades. Some *tarantate* have danced for more than thirty years. In one case, a woman bitten at the onset of puberty, as many seemed to be, danced for sixty years.

The therapy varied, and the dance movements, which were not highly codified, normally involved two phases, first one on the floor, where the dancer more or less imitated the movements of the spider; then rising, she often ran in a circle, pounding and stamping the spider into the ground (De Martino 1976: illustrations). These cycles alternated from morning till night, with brief rest periods between, punctuated by the literal vomiting up of the spider's "venom"; together they ultimately brought on physical and psychological catharsis.

In the Salento, one could witness the ritual of *tarantismo* either in the private domain, where musicians played in the homes of the *tarantate,* or in the town of Galatina on June 28–29. During the domestic enactment, in fact, onlookers were important participants in this ritual, lending emotional and financial support to the family. Substantial sums of money were required to pay two or three musicians to play continuously for three to seven days, or even more. In Taranto, during the seventeenth century, such musicians were actually subvened by the municipal authorities to play in the piazza as a public service. In Galatina by contrast, during the night of June 28 and on June 29, the feast of Saint (Peter and) Paul, patron saint of *tarantismo*, the rituals were closed to the public by the *tarantate*'s families, but the curious could see them before they entered the chapel. Here the *tarantate* assembled each year to spend the night in the chapel, dance, pay homage, and be released from the spider's web and the saint's curse. Inside the chapel, however, ecclesiastical authorities allowed no music, thereby maiming the ritual at its core.[6] The *tarantate* screamed in agonies of despair or rage, climbed onto the altar, hung from rafters. The saint's statue was put behind a grate to save him from their assaults; *tarantismo* was not a pretty sight.

Tarantate no longer assemble in Galatina and have not since the mid-1970s, when the chapel was closed and the miraculous waters running under it were declared contaminated. So the last remnants of "classic" *tarantismo* have been dispersed.[7] This is not to say there are no more *tarantati,* even though a communally shared ritual no longer seems viable. We suspect they are there, although no longer a public presence, for the votive candles to the saint are still lit in a small roadside shrine to St. Paul near Muro Leccese. Today, instead, we find a new generation of euphoria-seeking youth who have transformed this cultural practice of suffering into public celebration. The *pizzica*, the predominant music of *tarantismo*, has become the Salentine New Age rage, as followers quest for mystical union in a magical "cosmic" dance. How this generation is re-using *tarantismo* is a question I began investigating in August 1997, through interviews with musicians and dancers of *pizziche*.[8] These issues will not be pursued here, however.

My focus in the remainder of this essay will be somewhat narrower as I turn to a specific case where balladry, and especially its erotic metaphorical language, seems to intersect with the core of the *tarantismo* phenomenon. Here is a description of the scene: a night in the mid-1970s, in a private setting (just as the public ritual is being condemned and the Galatina chapel is closing); upon returning home, Luigi Chiriatti finds his parents awaiting him in the kitchen, where they have been trying to console and calm 'Ntoni (derived from Antonio), a man in his sixties who is described as being particularly sensitive to the *pizzica* rhythm, easily moved by this music, and something of a "closet" *tarantato*:

> Si trasformava, si scazzicava, entrava in tremolío. 'Ntoni non
> "ballava" nel senso classico del termine, si muoveva su due

mattonelle, dando nel contempo un senso di movimento generale.
Dondolava la testa, pestava i piedi e soprattutto agitava, faceva
tremolare le mani e le dita. Se lo guardavi ne rimanevi incantato.
[He would be transformed, he'd get agitated, he'd tremble. 'Ntoni
didn't "dance" in the classic sense of the term, he'd move as
though on two floor tiles only.... He'd swing his head, stamp his
feet, and he'd especially move his hands and fingers, making them
tremble. If you watched him you'd be transfixed.]

(Chiriatti 1995: 23)[9]

Chiriatti's parents had been unsuccessfully trying to get 'Ntoni to dance; they
had therefore promised 'Ntoni that their son would soon arrive to play the tam-
bourine so that 'Ntoni could get whatever was troubling him out of his system.

But Chiriatti would not participate in the ritual, for reasons he discusses,[10]
and his parents instead resorted to singing songs (accompanied by a harmonica),
songs traditionally unrelated to the ritual. What they sang were lyric songs and
ballads of implicit and increasingly explicit erotic content to *scazzicare* 'Ntoni.
This highly codified term within the culture of *tarantismo* is intimately linked to
the power of music (particularly the *pizzica*) to excite or stimulate a person through
movement and dance.[11] Among the songs they sang to 'Ntoni were ballads: first
"La mia mamma la l'è vecchiarella," a variant of "La bevanda sonnifera" (The
Sleeping Potion; Nigra 77[12]), where a mother sends her daughter to fetch water;
along the way she is propositioned by a knight; her mother gives her permission
to make love with the knight in exchange for a payment, stating that it is a good
way to raise a dowry. Normally, in this ballad type, mother and daughter devise
the ruse of giving the knight a sleeping potion, whereby the daughter takes his
money but retains her honor. The second song, "La cerva" (The Doe), is an
extended metaphor describing lovemaking and loss of virginity in terms of the
hunt: A doe is decapitated in a dark wood; she is wounded but does not die,
blood flows, she protests.[13] Finally, the third song, "Zio 'Tore" (Uncle
Salvatore)—serving as something of a decoding of the second song—is a frank
description of an aggressive and direct sexual encounter where no words are
exchanged and no foreplay is attempted (see Appendix for texts).

Therefore, we have a sexual act merely alluded to or anticipated in the first
song, poetically veiled through extended metaphoric language in the second,
and explicitly described in the third. The texts all acknowledge and seem to
sanction the sexual act, it is important to note. We deduce from the choice of

song texts that the singers had obviously diagnosed the sixty-year-old bachelor 'Ntoni's malaise as sexual in nature. 'Ntoni repeatedly approached the singers, listening attentively to capture their words (replicating the way *tarantati* typically approached musicians to "seize" the instruments' sounds, the music's rhythms; for an example, see the film *Taranta*) and danced obsessively for a long time. Thus, concludes Chiriatti, he witnessed his first domestic *tarantismo* ritual in his own home and there came to understand that sexuality was at the center of the phenomenon. What, after all, was the meaning of the most-often-repeated *pizzica* strophe: "na, na, na, beddhu l'amore e ci lu sape fa" [na, na, na, beautiful is love and the one who knows how to make love], Chiriatti asked himself. He then understood it to mean that one becomes a *tarantata* because one does not know how to make love; to be cured from love's bite, one must learn how to do just that.[14]

The crescendo of sexual explicitness in these texts is complemented by the *pizzica* rhythm and dance movement. Indeed, *tarantismo*'s canonic song texts could not be more explicit in referring to sexual organs and St. Paul's role in the ritual. St. Paul both causes and cures the spider's bite; he both stimulates and quenches sexual desire (De Martino 1976: 105–7). This "floating" stanza used repeatedly, even today, states,

> Santu Paulu miu delle tarante
> pizziche le caruse mienzu all'anche;
> Santu Paulu miu delli scursuni
> pizzichi li carusi alli cujuni.
> [Saint Paul of the tarantulas
> Prick (bite) the young girls between the thighs;
> Saint Paul of the scorpions
> Prick (bite) the young boys in the balls.][15]

But what does 'Ntoni's case have to do with classic *tarantismo*? It does not involve a woman (as the vast majority of cases did) but rather, an older bachelor; not professional musicians, but rather ordinary singing members of the community. Furthermore, it was largely improvised on the spot and did not use canonical *pizzica* texts. I would argue that the case is significant for precisely these reasons, inasmuch as it sheds light on intertextuality in a song community and the cultural worldview which shapes song and ritual. It also attests to the power of the *tarantismo* matrix to assimilate texts outside its, by then, reduced canon (which, historically, was much wider). Further, it provides a clear case of the way a community may read the *deep* meaning of texts and perceive them to be connected and flexible, thereby rendering them applicable to a range of life's vicissitudes, needs, and contexts. Historically, we know that ballads have frequently served a variety of functions: They have been sung as lullabies (Del Giudice 1988), been enacted dramatically, and served ritual functions, as well. Elsewhere I have reported on carnival ballad theater in northern Italy (Del Giudice 1986). Here, instead, singer-healers provide an effective example of balladry as folk medicine in a ritual healing practice. Call it "ballad therapy." We are thus in the presence of yet another eloquent example of applied balladry which speaks to the genre's vitality and remarkable flexibility.

As so forcefully argued by Toelken (1995) for various other music and song communities, here, too, in the Salento, a common poetic heritage, rich with polysemous metaphoric possibilities embedded in song, may be tapped by its versatile and knowledgeable singers in performance in response to the immediate needs of singer, audience, and context. In 'Ntoni's dance, "performed" to ballad texts, we witness an enactment of many possible latent meanings at once—shared, though unarticulated, by the small kitchen gathering. Together they interpret and transform the texts, transmuting the ballad genre's "deep" meanings into praxis. Somewhere in that shared traditional knowledge of song, several erotic metaphoric equations may have registered: the metaphor of the dance as sexual activity, and the metaphor of sexuality as pathology, both well codified within Italian balladry (see Del Giudice 1989).

The metaphor which equates sexuality with a pathologic state, with swooning and trembling, occurs in Western tradition since at least Ovid's time, where love is considered an illness which invades and convulses the mind and the body. Swooning, trembling, and convulsions form the very substance of *tarantismo* if we review the symptomology of the sufferers, as reported by *tarantati* themselves and fieldworkers (see De Martino 1976: 113–16, Chiriatti 1995).[16] The phenomenology imputed to both the spider's bite and love's bite is not merely analogic (see Chiriatti 1995: *morso d'amore* = "love's bite"). St. Paul *becomes* the spider which invades and torments victims like a god possessing an ecstatic novice; he makes them ill, but this poison itself makes them well. Like cures like. He is an erotic saint; he initiates and then commands the dance. The *tarantate* are his "brides" *(le spose di S. Paolo).*

And it is the dance itself, the dance of the little spider (or "the little dance of the *taranta*," the *tarantella*),[17] which cures the *tarantata*'s afflictions. It may not be a coincidence after all that the dance—a prevalent image in Italian balladry as elsewhere—likely provided the ballad genre's unconscious point of entry into the cathartic ritual of *tarantismo*. The creative reuse in Chiriatti's kitchen refunctionalized the ballad at its level of underlying structure since none of the ballads sung contain dance metaphors per se as do, for example, "La bella al ballo" (Nigra 99); "Ratto al ballo" (Nigra 16; see Del Giudice 1989). Dance imagery in balladry and other folk songs and the dance itself, through just such ecstatic rituals, apparently satisfy primary urges and help heal psychic or mythic spider "bites," as well as more concrete ones. Is it far-fetched to suggest that ballads may serve a similar psychological function for communities unacquainted with such codified ritual healing practices as *tarantismo* in the Salento?

A rationalist view may hold that the social management of sexuality is at the heart of balladry, and much folklore besides—Italian and otherwise. Setting this consideration aside, what most intrigues us here is *how* the versatile figurative codes are used in real-life situations, through music and song events, spontaneous, as well as ritually recurring. The cultural matrix of autochthonous *tarantismo* in the Salento, profound, encompassing, and durable, has assimilated even narrative song texts into its powerful system. In 'Ntoni's case, balladry's marked erotic metaphorical language accessed one of the nerve centers of *tarantismo*. The Chiriatti kitchen enactment is emblematic. Salentine song tradition could provide an entire medicine cabinet of love potions and *remedia amoris*, metaphorically speaking, the most potent of which seems to be the *pizzica* itself. These songs can cure love's bites: the languishing variety, the violent and uncontrollable passions, the comic and lighthearted, even vengeful hatred (the reverse of love's coin) against lovers or their scornful parents.

Although I cannot discount the fact that the choice of songs for any collection may reflect the predilections of anthologists, editors, and individual singers (rather than accurately representing the tradition itself), a recent compilation of Salentine traditional song (*Bonasera a quista casa*), and the experience of translating its texts into English, gave me the opportunity to become more acutely aware that the *language* and content of Salentine songs—from *pizzica* to lyric, narrative, and work songs—resonates forcefully with the theme of sexuality. Fully eleven of the collection's sixteen songs featured erotic love as their prime focus. The range of attitudes ranged from lyrical to cautionary to crude and explicit.[18] Most frequently, however, they speak of frustrated and unrequited love, forbidding parents, and thwarted desire. Love in these songs seems not to be celebratory but problematic and conflicted.

This is not surprising if one recalls that, until recently in conservative traditional Salentine society, familial and social patriarchy heavily managed and curtailed individual desire and made youthful sexual expression next to impossible.[19] A commonly recurring *pizzica* phrase in these songs: "I want to make love with someone who understands it / who hears my voice and can recognize it," expresses the frustrated search for understanding and sexual satisfaction.[20] Indeed, sexual repression (and oppression), practised with greatest force against women, was precisely one of the causes which led many women to the outer social fringe, to desperate measures, to break temporarily with the social order through the ecstatic dance of *tarantismo*—one of the few avenues culturally available for healing a broken spirit—or a spider's bite.

## Appendix

The following texts are taken from Chiriatti 1995: 24–25 (my translations).

1.  La mia mamma la vecchiarella (Nigra 77)   [My Mother [is] a Little Old Woman]

    La mia mamma la vecchiarella        [My mother is a little old woman
    e mi manda a prender l'acqua         and she sends me to fetch water
    per bere e cucinar.                  to drink and for cooking.
    Allu mienzu de la via                Midway down the road
    lu ccuntrai lu cavalier              I meet a knight
    e mi disse: "O damigella             and he asks me, "O maiden,
    se vuoi fare l'amore con me."        will you make love with me?"
    "Lassa vau alla mamma mia            "Let me go and ask my mother
    e se la mia mamma vole               and if mother agrees
    presto presto ritornerò."            I'll return quick as a wink."
    "Vanne fija, e fija vanne            "Go daughter, and [surely] daughter go
    e questa sarà la dote che ti         for this will be the dowry that your
    fa la mamma a te.                    mother gives you."]

2.  La cerva                           [The Doe]

    Nu giurnu sciia a 'ncaccia alla foresta    [One day I went to hunt in the forest
    intra lu boscu de Ninnella mia,            In the woods of my Ninella;
    'ncontrai na cerva e li truncai la testa,  I met there a doe and I cut off its head;
    morta nu bbera e lu sangu scurria.         It was not dead and blood flowed.
    Se 'nfaccia la patruna a lla finestra:     The [land] lady came to the window:
    —Nu m'mmazzare la cerva ca è la mia.       —Don't kill the doe, for it is mine.
    —Nu su venutu pe ammazzare la cerva,       —I have not come to kill the doe;
    ieu su venutu per amare a tie.             I have come to love you.]

3.  Dimmela ziu Tore, dimmela

    Dimmela ziu Tore, dimmela
    dimmela se l'hai tuccata:
    —Sine, l'aggiu pizzicata sulla chianta te la manu.

Sta fatiava sutt'all'alberi quandu iddha s'ha presentata,
mancu tempu cu la guardu ca l' ia già mezza spojata.
Cu lu mele e cu la manna parìa fatta dha carusa,
mancu tempu cu li parlu mienzu l'erba l'aggiu stisa.

[Tell Me, Uncle Salvatore, Tell Me]

[Tell me, Uncle 'Tore, tell me
tell me, did you touch her?
—Yes, I pricked her on the palm of her hand.
I was working under the trees when she came around;
I didn't even look at her but what I had already half undressed her.
That young girl seemed to be made of honey and cream.
I didn't even talk to her and in the grass laid her down.]

## Notes

1. I use the Italian term untranslated because "tarantulism" does not connote this quite specific cultural phenomenon.
2. I have been informed that Dorothy L. Zinn has translated *La terra del rimorso* into English and awaits its publication.
3. *Tarantati* is the generic plural, but *tarantate* is the feminine plural and, hence, the more frequent term since the vast majority of them were female.
4. Indeed, the spider to which the symptoms of *tarantismo* were commonly attributed was the relatively harmless European wolf spider, or *Lycosa tarentula*, although the real culprit causing clinical lactrodectism in the area was the *Lycosa tredecimus gottutus*, a black spider with thirteen red spots.
5. The term oddly also seems to be orally connected to *rimosso*, the "repressed past," in pyschoanalytic terms.
6. The disintegration of the ritual is, in large measure, generally attributed to the Catholic Church's intervention in this belief system and its superimposition of the confused and contradictory figure of St. Paul as patron saint of *tarantismo* (De Martino 1976: 106). One may consider this choice of saint ironic since St. Paul both experienced ecstatic religion— on the road to Damascus—and fought this tradition as a newly converted Christian.
7. On late *tarantismo*, see Chiriatti 1995. An exhibit of related photographs taken during the 1970s in Galatina (and through to the 1990s), documenting the public ritual: *Il luogo del culto: Galatina: Immagini del tarantismo 1970–1992* [The Cult's Site: Galatina: Images of *Tarantismo* 1970–1992] was on view during a conference in Los Angeles (see note 8).
8. An international, interdisciplinary conference on such phenomena, entitled *Performing Ecstasies: Music, Dance, and Ritual in the Mediterranean*, took place in Los Angeles, 18–22 October 2000, organized by the author; proceedings are forthcoming (Del Giudice and Van Deusen 2003). My contribution, "Folk Revival and the Culture of *Tarantismo* in the Salento," represents a continuation of the present essay.
9. Translations from the Italian are mine.
10. "...non volevo 'entrare' nel rito, volevo restare cosciente, conservare razionalità e 'vedere' cosa stava accadendo, che tipo di struttura assumeva il tarantismo con un personaggio come 'Ntoni" [I didn't want to 'enter' into the ritual; I wanted to remain conscious, maintain rationality, and 'see' what was happening, what sort of structure *tarantismo* would take with a character such as 'Ntoni] (Chiriatti 1995: 23). Chiriatti discusses his conflicted attitudes toward the ritual and St. Paul during his childhood years and later in his encounters with the saint and this culture, about which he felt both insider and outsider.

11. It is unclear to me whether the term may not suggest sexual stimulation as well: Although grammatically one may more readily accept *s* + *cacciare* (derived from *ex-captiare*, "to chase out, to chase away"), an association with *cazzo* ("penis"), may impact the term's meaning, folk etymologically speaking.

12. The number refers to the standard collection of Italian (largely Piedmontese) narrative songs: Nigra 1956 [1888].

13. An analogous and more-widespread Italian song makes the equation of hunter=male seducer, prey=female seduced, quite explicit. It is commonly known as "Il cacciatore del bosco" [The Hunter of the Woods].

14. Many *tarantate* in the literature, in fact, were accused of using *tarantismo* as an alternative for lovemaking (see *tarantismo* as a *carnevaletto delle donne*, "a little carnival for women"). As Chiriatti was told by women of a certain age: Many people danced, not only *tarantati*; those who could find other ways to make love didn't need *tarantismo*! This is a rather cynical and reductionist view of the victim's motives, but one which finds voice throughout the history of *tarantismo* literature.

15. Variants of this stanza are quite common. See, for example the variant in De Martino 1976: 361.

16. See also Luigi Stifani's description of the symptomology of *tarantismo,* as he understands it, in the film, *San Paolo e la Tarantola* by Edoardo Winspeare and Stefanie Kremser-Koehler. He was a violinist and musician to *tarantate* for many decades.

17. The diminutive may betoken more than cheerful familiarity and respond to apprehensions by lightening or deprecating.

18. E.g., "do not heed men / they are all traitors" ("Fifteen Years"); "Love me, my beauty, for I have things [for you] / I have a little basket of cherries" ("Carter's Song," a floating stanza which finds its home in many songs); "How I love you and desire you, my beauty, how I love you / Sunday, Sunday, I will take you into my garden. // I'll show you the plant, I'll show you the plant of the green branch / and its little apples of pure gold" ("Bitter Water"); to the frankly crude and physical: "Mother, if I don't marry / I'll cut it [the penis] off / And I'll hang it, and I'll hang it / And I'll hang it by the fireplace. / / And I'll beat it so hard with the sledgehammer / to reduce it / to [seem like] rabbit's hair. / Love me, my beauty, for I have things [for you] / I have a little basket of cherries" ("Stornello"; the "basket of fruit" is yet another motif which frequently occurs in these songs). These songs may be found on the compact disk, *Bonasera a quista casa.*

19. Winspeare's feature film, *Pizzicata*, indeed tells the story of a young peasant girl "bitten" by the spider. When she must choose between an Italian American Second World War pilot shot down over the Salento and the son of a wealthy landowner to whom she has been betrothed—between obedience to her father and the dictates of her heart—the curse of *tarantismo* descends. Note that here the erotic conflict is exacerbated by grief and entrapment when the American is killed by his rival.

20. In at least two of the songs cited, this phrase is preceded by the more explicit, "I want to make love with a girl / throw her on the bed, and make her cry 'mother.'"

## References

Chiriatti, Luigi. 1995. *Morso d'amore: viaggio nel tarantismo salentino.* Lecce: Capone.

Del Giudice, Luisa. 1986. "Ballad Theater: Carnival Dramatization of Narrative Ballads in Brallo (Pavia): Cecilia, Ratto al Ballo, Isabella, Fernanda e Bortolino." In *Tod und Jenseits im Europäischen Volkslied*, edited by Walter Puchner, 337–60. 16th Internationale Balladenkonferenz, Kolympari, Kreta, 19–22 August 1986. Publications of Folklore Museum and Archives (University of Jannina), 6. Ioannina: University of Jannina.

————. 1988. "Ninna-nanna-nonsense? Fears, Dreams, and Falling in the Italian Lullaby." *Oral Tradition* 3: 270–86. Also published in *La ricerca folclorica*, edited by Leonardo Piasere, 105–14. Vol. 22 of *Europa zingara*. Brescia: Grafo, 1991.

————. 1989. "Erotic Metaphor in the Nigra Ballads." In *ARV: Scandinavian Yearbook of Folklore* 45, 17–41.

Del Giudice, Luisa, and Nancy Van Deusen, eds. Forthcoming 2003. *Performing Ecstasies: Music, Dance, and Ritual in the Mediterranean*. Claremont, Calif.: Claremont Graduate University Press.

De Martino, Ernesto. [1961] 1976. *La terra del rimorso*. 3$^{rd}$ ed. Milano: Il Saggiatore, 1961.

Nigra, Costantino. [1888] 1956. *Canti popolari del Piemonte*. Reprint, Turin: Einaudi.

Toelken, Barre. 1995. *Morning Dew and Roses: Nuance, Metaphor, and Meaning in Folksongs*. Folklore and Society, Publications of the American Folklore Society, New Series. Urbana and Chicago: University of Illinois Press, 1995.

## Recording

*Bonasera a quista casa: Antonio Aloisi, Antonio Bandello ("Gli Ucci"): Pizziche, stornelli, canti salentini*. 1999. Lecce: Edizioni Aramirè EA01. Recording.

## Films

*Taranta*. Gian Franco Mingozzi. 1961. Film.

*Pizzicata*. Edoardo Winspeare. 1996. Film.

*San Paolo e la Tarantola*. Edoardo Winspeare and Stefanie Kremser-Koehler. 1991. Film.

# Music, Charm, and Seduction
# in British Traditional Songs and Ballads

## Vic Gammon

In this essay, I want to explore certain themes and intertextual elements in popular and traditional songs that circulated in Britain and Ireland, and wherever people from these islands went, roughly in the period from 1600 to 1850. I make no particular distinction between songs that traveled orally and those that circulated in print. Certainly these two media produce different characteristics in the material, but the distinction is largely an aesthetic one, and pieces regularly crossed between the two.[1]

Using the myth of the siren in Homer's *The Odyssey* as a starting point,[2] I explore popular images of music, particularly vocal music.[3] These are the elements and interrelated themes of the siren myth as I see them:

- The irresistible power of music—its magical, "enchanting," "charming" nature;
- The potentially evil nature of music (or its possibilities for evil uses);
- The sensual and sexual nature of music—a dangerous pleasure that should be resisted or indulged only with powerful protection;
- The loss of self-control and judgment induced by music—music as the enemy of reason, with the power to drive people mad;
- Sirens tend to be animal in form or have something of an animal nature; they are creatures of air or sea, not like earthbound humans. (In postclassical times, they have been depicted as a sort of mermaid; older representations give them birdlike features.)[4]

I will use the adjective "sirenic" to describe songs that contain these elements in any significant way. I will show that the themes and ideas of the siren myth were commonplace in British popular and traditional song and that they overlap and interrelate. I will finish by looking at pieces that deal explicitly with mermaid-type creatures and consider the ways the themes are worked into them. There are, of course, many ways of studying song texts, and this is but one: the search for common or related themes across an extensive range of material.[5]

*"Charmed by the Notes"—Birds, People, Encounter, and Separation*
Typically, many traditional lyrics open on a bright morning with birds singing.
Some simply celebrate the scene itself, as does "The Birds in the Spring," when
"the voice of the Nightingale re-echoes all round" (Stubbs 1970: 10). Or the
beauty of birdsong may be an incentive to come away with a lover, as in the Irish
song "Kellswaterside":

> "For in sweet Ballybogey, where I will you bring,
> You'll hear the birds whistle and nightingales sing;
> Your heart will be glad and no tears need you weep,
> And the birds in the evening will sing you to sleep."
>
> (Huntington 1990: 466)

In some songs the erotic connotation of birdsong is made explicit, as in "The
Bonny Hawthorn":

> "O hark bonny Bess, hear the birds in the grove,
> How delightful their song, how inviting to love."

Another version has "how in tissing [enticing] to love" (Bodleian Library, University of Oxford, Harding b25 [255]; 2806 c.18[42][6]). A morning meeting among
singing birds is a commonplace setting for an amorous encounter, as in "A Sweet
Country Life":

> No fiddle nor flute or haughtboy or spinet,
> Can ever compare with the lark or the linnet.
> Down as I lay among the green bushes,
> I was charmed by the notes of the blackbirds and thrushes.

This idea of the superiority of the natural song of the birds is overturned in the
next verse by the sweetness of the song of the young woman:

> Johnny the ploughboy was walking alone,
> To fetch up his cattle so early in the morn,
> He espied pretty Nancy among the green rushes,
> Singing more sweet than the blackbirds and thrushes.
>
> (Bodleian Library, University of Oxford, Harding B 25(1857);
> see also Broadwood 1843: 11)

Nature scenes with singing birds and the comparison of the female voice to birdsong crop up in some Scots songs: "Her voice is like the ev'ning thrush / That sings on Cessnock banks unseen" (Burns 1995: 669–70). Singing young women are a commonplace of the popular idiom in such songs as "On a Tuesday Morning" (Palmer 1979: 149) and "Green Bushes."[7] To "The Shepherd of the Downs," the sound of a female voice is paralyzing:

> As he was a walking one evening so clear
> A heavenly sweet voice sounded soft in his ear
> He stood like a post, not one step could he move
> He knew not what ailed him, but thought it was love.
>
> (Copper 1971: 258–59)

The female with a beautiful voice is common in popular and traditional song: Characters like "Long Preston Peg," "that sings with a voice so soft and so sweet," abound (Dixon and Bell 1857). Sometimes the motif is used in an interesting way that contrasts the positive and the negative. In "The Poor Man's Labour's Never Done," the contrast is between early and later marriage:

> First when I married my wife, Janet,
> Out of her company I couldna stay
> For her voice it was sweeter then the lark or the linnet,
> Or the nightingale at the break o' day
>
> Now she's fairly altered her meaning
> Now she's fairly altered her tune
> Nothing but scoldings comes up her throat
> So the poor man's labour's never done (Shuldham-Shaw 1966: 80–81).

The process of the marriage going sour is depicted through the change in the wife's voice. A similar sentiment is expressed in the song "The Joyful Widower," when the bereaved husband muses

> I rather think she is aloft
>     And imitating thunder
> For why, methinks I hear her voice
>     Tearing the clouds asunder (Johnson 1771: 99).

The motif of the beautiful-voiced female has plenty of life in it and runs through nineteenth-century popular song, sometimes in a comic way, undermining or parodying the older conventions. In Stephen Foster's "minstrel" song, Nelly Bly has a voice "like a turtle dove" (Bodleian Library, broadside ballad collection: Firth b. 27 [153], often reprinted on song sheets without crediting the writer). Even in the mock pastoral of the music-hall tradition, found in oral circulation by Alfred Williams, "Pretty Polly Perkins" has "a voice like a blackbird, so mellow and clear" (Williams, MS No.Mi.680).

The arresting quality of the voice, sometimes male, sometimes innocent, sometimes knowing, is affirmed in a number of pieces, such as "Just as the Tide Was Flowing," where the woman, an object of male fantasy if ever there was one, "so sweetly sang a roundelay." Because of her dress, her musical taste, and money, she is presented as a woman of higher social status than the sailor who encounters her (Karpeles 1974: 558–59). In "Bushes and Briars," the song which reputedly changed Vaughan Williams's life, the female sings out her feelings—"her voice it was so clear"—in an English song that comes close to the blues in its feeling (Palmer 1983: 27–28).

The narratives of these encounter songs range through the possible outcomes of such events: marriage, rejection, and misalliance (I will deal with seduction later). Invert these encounters, and you have leave taking and separation. Here again we find birds singing, as in the ubiquitous "Pleasant and Delightful":

> The blackbirds and thrushes, sang on every green spray,
>     And the larks they sang melodious, at the dawning of the day.

The related song "Jimmy and his True Love" is a song of parting set against a backdrop of birdsong (Mackenzie 1928: 125; Laws O30[8]).

In these types of song, the beauty of the surroundings heightens the pain of parting and loss. One is reminded of Burns:

> How can ye chant, ye little birds,
> And I sae weary, fu o' care.
> Thou'll break my heart, thou warbling bird,
> That wantons thro' the flowering thorn:
> Thou minds me o' departed joys,
> Departed never to return. (Kinsley 1971: 456)

So birdsong and human song can be associated with negative experiences and emotions. In "Banchory's Land," a song from Aberdeenshire, Scotland, the effect of singing fails to attract the disenchanted female; the effect is opposite to what happens with the arresting voice:

> It was on a mid-Lanterns as Phoebus left the sky
> While I did sing with all my might my true love passed by
> While I did sing with all my might my true love passed home,
> And mony an anxious look she gave to see fin I would come.
>
> (*Greig-Duncan Collection*, 4: no. 707A)

Singing is also used other ways in popular and traditional songs: The lover stricken by his condition can lose his voice, and singing can function as consolation and remembrance, as an expression of merriment and celebration, as a cause for anger and violence, and as a warning.

Perhaps the most extreme contrast in singing in a narrative occurs in "Lamkin" (Child 93). The eponymous main character, in some versions an unpaid mason, enters the civilized home of a lord while he is away and, with the help of a treacherous nurse, murders the lord's baby and wife. After stabbing the child, the murderers engage in a travesty of infant care:

> Then Lamkin he rocked,
>     and the fause nourice sang,
> Till frae ilka bore o' the cradle
>     the red blood out sprang.

Nursing and singing a lullaby are allied to a gruesome act of murder. But these villains get their just desserts and are executed—to the accompaniment of a different sort of singing:

> O sweetly sang the blackbird
>     that sat upon the tree;
> But sairer grat Lamkin,
>     when he was condemned to die.
>
> And bonny sang the mavis,
>     out o' the thorny brake

But sairer grat the nourice,
    when she was tied to the stake.

We are back with the birds, this time providing an ironic counterpoint to retribution (Child 93A).[9]

*"His Intentions Were to Court a Pretty Maid"—Singing and Seduction*
To see singing as a means of seduction is only an extension of its power to charm and enchant. In "Jack the Jolly Ploughboy," the singing has a clear intention:

Jack, the jolly ploughboy, was ploughing up his land;
His horses lie beneath the shady tree.
He did whistle, he did sing, caused the valleys for to ring;
His intentions were to court a pretty maid.

                                    (Mackenzie 1928: 130; Laws M24)

In the related song "The Nut Girl" (or the "The Nutting Girl"), the ploughman's voice has an intense effect on the young woman:

There was a brisk young damsel,
    A nutting in the wood,
His voice was so melodious,
    It charmed her as she stood.
She had no longer power,
    In the lonely wood to stray,
But what few nuts she had poor girl,
    She threw them all away.

She went unto her Johnny,
    As he sat on his plough,
Says she young man I feel myself,
    I'm sure I can't tell how;
He said my pretty fair maid,
    I'm glad to meet you here,
Come sit you down beside me,
    I will keep you out of fear.

Young Johnny left his horses,
    Likewise he left his plough,
He took her to a shady grove,
    His courage for to show.
He took her by the middle so small,
    And then he set her down
She said young man I think I see,
    The world go round and round.
          (Bodleian Library, broadside ballad collection: 17252)

We notice similar elements in the ballad of "Hind Etin":

Lady Margaret sits in her bower door,
    Sewing at her silken seam;
She heard a note in Elmond's wood,
    And wishd she there had been.

Significantly, when Margaret gets to the wood, she starts gathering nuts:

She hadna pu'd a nut, a nut,
    Nor broken a branch but ane,
Till by it there came a young hind chiel,
    Says, Lady, lat alane. (Child 41A)

The "young hind chiel" abducts her and takes her to live in a hidden place in the greenwood, a cave in some versions, where she bears him children. It seems likely that "The Nutting Girl" is a come-down version of a much more ancient and mysterious song, and the "young farmer" is the descendant of the fairylike Hind Etin. In both songs, it is the power of sound that attracts the women.

Songs like "The Nut Girl" are rich in a kind of simple metaphor: Young women throw their nuts away, an encounter takes place "Just as the Tide Was Flowing," and "The Lark in the Morning" is both the bird singing and a suggestion of what the idealized pastoral figures in the song are up to.

The lark in the morning she rose from the west
And mounts in the air with the dew upon her breast;

And with the pretty ploughboys she'll whistle and she'll sing,
And the ploughboy is as happy as a prince or a king. (Palmer 1983: 164)

The idea that singing can be consciously manipulated to seduce is quite old in the English tradition. The old carol of the clerical seducer Jankyn and his victim Aleyson (punning with Kyrieleyson) appears in the fifteenth-century Sloan manuscript. Jankin's voice has "a merry tone," he reads the epistle well, he "cracks a merry note" and uses extreme decoration in his singing:

Jankyn crakit notes, an hundred on a knot,
And yyt he hakkyt hem smallere than wortes to the pot
[He chops them smaller than vegetables for the pot].

The voice has done its seductive work; all Jankyn needs is to wink and tread on Aleyson's foot, and she is his; unfortunately, the result is pregnancy (Greene 1977: 278–79).

This song runs in the same tradition as others making fun of clerics, such as the "Friar in the Well," where the protagonist declares he wants sex with a young girl. She fears going to hell, but he reassures her that if she were in hell, he could sing her out. She agrees but asks him to bring her ten shillings. He returns from getting the money, and she tricks him into falling into the well:

You said you could sing my soul out of hell,
Well, now you can sing yourself out of the well. (Purslow 1965: 33)

This song has been in existence since the later seventeenth century. A piece of similar vintage, from the pen of that period's most significant dirty and salacious songwriter, Thomas D'Urfey, makes a case for using singing to seduce:

Would you have a young virgin of fifteen years,
You must tickle her fancy with sweets and dears,
Ever toying, and playing, and sweetly, sweetly,
Sing a love sonnet, and charm her Ears. (D'Urfey [1719–20] 1959: 1, 133)

Of all the songs about the sexual attractiveness of the singing voice, the most widespread has to be "The Gypsie Laddie" (Child 200) in its various guises. In this celebrated ballad, a lady forsakes her husband, home, and children to live with the gypsies. Most versions celebrate the gypsy's singing:

> Three gypsies came to our good lord's gate
>> And wow but they sang sweetly!
> They sang sae sweet and sae compleat
>> That down came the fair lady.

Many versions, like this one, make it clear that there is more to the magic of the gypsies than just their singing:

> And she came tripping down the stair,
>> And a' her maids before her
> As soon as they saw her well-far'd face
>> They coost the glamer o'er her. (Child 200A)

Child glosses "glamer" as "charm;" other versions have it as "glamourie." Clearly, our modern vocabulary of attraction owes much to an older vocabulary of magic.

The music of the gypsies changes between different versions. In "The Whistling Gypsy Rover," the hero is described thus:

> He whistled and he sang till the greenwoods rang,
> And he won the heart of a lady.[10]

In an American version, "Black Jack Davy came a-singing through the woods" (Mellinger 1938: 110–12). In another, "He came walking o'er the hill singing loud and gaily" (Older 1963). And in yet another, "Gypsy Davie," the husband approaches the encampment:

> And he heard the notes of the big guitar
> And the voice of the gypsy singing
> The song of the Gypsy Dave.[11]

In some versions the abducting gypsies are executed. In others, generally the more-modern versions, the woman asserts her independence and refuses to return to her husband. (For an important study of this ballad, see Rieuwerts 1991.) Singing, whistling, or guitar playing, most versions stress the winning musicality of the gypsies.

*"He's Harped Them All Asleep": Soporific Music, Seduction, and Destruction*
Instruments appear widely as erotic symbols in the traditional songs of the
British Isles. I do not have space here to explore the rich body of material that
uses the fiddle, the German flute, and the bagpipe as sexual symbols, but a few
comments are in order.[12] Usually in such songs, playing music is a metaphor for
the act of sex. Sometimes dance tunes attest to the desire for sexual activity with
titles like "Do It Again" and "The Reel of Stumpie" (Madden Ballads, vol. 2, 17,
Cambridge University Library; Kinsley 1971: 678). These erotic songs are interesting and often inventive, but I do not feel they are deeply sirenic. They do
attest to the sensual and sexual nature of music and sometimes relate to the loss
of self-control while experiencing musical activity. However, a body of song
material features instruments being used in a deeply sirenic way, inducing sleep.
Most often, this happens by playing an instrument, usually a harp. However, in
an interesting early sixteenth-century song, "With Lullay, Lullay, Like a Child,"
attributed to John Skelton, the woman (sirenlike) is able to sing her unwanted
lover to sleep and escape to a preferred man who kisses and embraces her:

> With lullay, lullay like a chylde
> Thou slepyst so long; thou art begylde.
> * * *
> With "ba, ba, ba," and "bas, bas, bas,"
> She cheryshed hym, both cheke and chyn;
> That he wyst neuer where he was;
> He had forgotten all dedely syn.
> He wantyd wyt her loue to win
> He trusted her payment and lost all hys pray
> She left hym slepyng and stale away. (Greene 1977: 279–80)

However, it is the Scottish tradition and its diaspora that display this motif
most strongly, and it is usually the harp which is most potent in producing a
soporific effect (perhaps not surprising when the most likely alternative is the
bagpipe). "Glasgerion," or "Glenkindie," presents a Scottish harper with truly
sirenic power:

> He could harpit a fish oot o' saut water
>     or water oot a' a stane;
> He could harpit the milk fae a maiden's breist
>     Wha' ne'er gi'ed souk tae wean.

Glenkindie turns his harping to his own inclinations:

> He's harpit in the King's castle,
>> He's harpit them a' asleep;
> A' but the bonnie young countess
>> Wha' love did wauken keep.

> First he harpit a dowie air
>> And syne he harpit a gay,
> And many a sigh between the hands
>> I wat the lady gie (Child 67B)

However, his musical power is shared by his apprentice boy, Jock, which leads to tragic consequences for all concerned, a clear example of such power.

The motif of sleep-inducing harp music crops up in a number of other ballads: in some versions of "The Outlandish Knight" (Child 4B, stanza 2), in the jocular "Lochmaben Harper" (Child 192), and in "Fair Annie" (Child 62E, stanza 14). There is a strange verse in one of Motherwell's versions of "The Cruel Brother":

> She put the small pipe to her mouth,
>> And she harped both far and near,
> Till she harped the small birds off the briers,
>> And her true love out of the grave. (Child 49B, stanza 10)

Does the verb "to harp" simply mean "to play," or are two instruments involved? The end of this particular version seems to have picked up parts of other ballads, particularly "The Unquiet Grave," but the stanza above is testimony to the potency of musical power.

*"The Song She Sang She Sang so Sweet": Sirens and Mermaids*
It is, in part, the power of the voice itself that arrests "George Collins" on his morning walk:

> George Collins walked out one May morning
> When May was all in bloom.
> There he espied a fair pretty maid
> A-washing her marble stone.

She whooped, she holloed, she highered her voice,
She held up her lily-white hand.
"Come hither to me, George Collins," she said,
"For your life shall not last you long."
(*Journal of the Folk-Song Society* 1909: 301–2, version d; Child 85)

The stark warning is mysterious, but perhaps there is a connection, through the act of washing, with the mermaid that Clerk Colville finds at the symbolically titled "wall o' Stream":

"Ye wash, ye wash, ye bonny may,
    And ay's ye wash your sark o' silk";
"It's a' for you, ye gentle knight,
    My skin is whiter than the milk."

He's taen her by the milk-white hand,
    He's taen her by the sleeve sae green,
And he's forgotten his gay ladie,
    And away with the fair maiden. (Child 42A, stanza 6)

We are reminded at once that "…but hear the call / Of any Siren, he will so despise both wife and child." Colville, like George Collins, ends up dead.[13]

In "Clerk Colville," we have the merging of some of our themes. Child's C version even has this stanza:

And she took harp into her hand
    And Harped them a' asleep
And she sat down at their couch side
    And bitterly did weep. (Child 42C, stanza 7)

The maid who has diverted Colville from his prior love is described as a mermaid, and I will conclude this discussion with a look at some songs that deal with mermaids and mermaidlike creatures. It is clear that the mermaid in "Clerk Colville" takes human form when on land. The same is true of the man/seal in "The Great Silkie" (Child 113), but he appears not to have any musical attributes.

"I am a man, upo the lan,
    An I am a silkie in the sea;

> And when I'm far and far frae lan,
>> My dwelling is in Sule Skerrie."

The silkie fathers a child with an "earthly nourice" (who, interestingly, "sits and sings" as the song opens). But such an ill-matched union cannot end happily:

> "An thu sall marry a proud gunner,
>> An a proud gunner I'm sure he'll be,
> An the very first schot that ere he schoots
>> He'll schoot baith my young son and me." (Child 113)

Wimberley points to a Danish ballad where a human woman bears seven children to her lover under the sea:

> Her ears he stopp'd, and her mouth she stopp'd
> And down to the bottom of the ocean dropped. (Wimberley 1965: 135)

The function of stopping the ears is different from *The Odyssey*, but the existence of this detail in such a context is suggestive.

Some comic songs of nineteenth-century origin deal with encounters between humans and mermaids, sometimes leading to reproduction or exile to an alien watery home, but the sirenic lure of the mermaid does not seem to be significant in these pieces.[14]

There is a reasonably widespread song, recorded in England and North America, about a young woman by the seashore lamenting the loss of her drowned lover. It is variously known as "I Never Shall Marry" or "The Drowned Lover," on English broadsides as "The Lover's Lament for Her Sailor" and, sometimes, "The Mermaid." In some versions the woman throws herself into the sea in grief and is thus reunited with her lover:

> And now every night at six bells they appear,
> When the moon it is shining and sky it is clear,
> Those two constant lovers with all their young charms
> Rolling over and over in each other's arms. (Spicer 1995)

Is this the way people believed mermaids were made? In spite of the magical quality of this verse, and the fact that the song is sometimes called "The Forsaken Mermaid," this is not a mermaid song as we generally understand it. In one version, learned from the late Ron Spicer, the woman is described thus:

> She'd a voice like a nightingale, skin like a dove
> And the song that she sang it was all about love.

Another version runs,

> I heard a shrill voice make a sorrowful sound
> Midst the winds and the waves and the waters all round.
>
> (Purslow 1969a: 38)

This is more of a lover's ghost song that happens to have an oceanic setting, but we notice that the woman's birdlike voice has a siren quality.

In the classic ballad "Sir Patrick Spens," some versions feature a mermaid appearing before the storm:

> Then up and raise the mermaiden,
>     Wi the comb and glas in her hand
> "Here's a health to you, my merry young men,
>     For you never will see dry land." (Child 58J, stanza 18)

None of these mermaids sing, although they do converse. Given the low number of versions in which they appear (four out of eighteen in Bronson 1959–72, two of which are fragmentary), it is possible that this element is an import from other songs or stories that connect mermaids with storms. One is never quite sure, with the fluid nature of oral tradition; perhaps the next song discussed is actually a descendent of "Sir Patrick Spens."

The most widespread mermaid song, which some may remember from school, is again called "The Mermaid." Bronson prints forty-two versions of it (1959–72). It was circulating on broadsides in the mideighteenth century and seems to have gotten into many corners of the English-speaking world. The song is very simple: A ship's crew spies a mermaid, almost always "with a comb and a glass in her hand"; various members of the crew step up, and with typical balladic incremental repetition, foretell their deaths and the loss to their relatives; the ship is lost.

When I went through the texts of "The Mermaid," it seemed none of them mentioned singing until I came across a version collected in Twyford in Hampshire, England:

As I sailed out one day, one day
And being not far from the land;
   And there I spied a mermaid
   A sitting on a rock,
With a comb and a glass in her hand.

The song she sang she sang so sweet,
But no answer at all could us make;
   Till at length our gallant ship
   She tooked round about;
Which made our poor hearts to ache.

                       (Bronson 1959–72: no. 289, version 36)

In one other version of this song, I found implications that the mermaid sang:

   * * *

And her skin was like a lily so fair
Her cheeks were like two roses and her eyes were like a star
And her voice like a nightingale clear.

                       (Bronson 1959–72: no. 289, version 41)

Compare the mermaid in "Clerk Colville," whose "skin was whiter than the milk," and I need not highlight the recurring nightingale.

Perhaps the most interesting song of this sort is one often called "The Mermaid" as well, but more usually "The Maid on the Shore." There is nothing fishy about this woman, but elements of the siren are combined in a way both surprising and amusing:

'Twas of a young maiden who lived all alone
   She lived all alone on the shore, O;
There was nothing she could find for to comfort her mind,
   But to roam all alone on the shore, shore, shore,
   But to roam all alone on the shore.

It was of a young captain who sailed the salt sea,
   Let the wind blow high or low, O

"I will die, I will die," the young captain did cry,
    "If I don't get that maid on the shore, shore, shore,
    If I don't get that maid on the shore

"I have lots of silver, I have lots of gold,
    I have lots of costly wear, O
I'll divide, I'll divide with my jolly ship's crew
    If they'll row me that maid from the shore, shore, shore,
    If they'll row me that maid from the shore."

After long persuadance they got her on board
    Let the winds blow high or low, O
Where he placed her a chair in his cabin below,
    "Here's adieu to all sorrow and care, care, care,
    Here's adieu to all sorrow and care."

Where he placed her a chair in his cabin below,
    Let the winds blow high or blow low, O,
She sung charming and sweet, she sung neat and complete
    She sung captain and sailors to sleep, sleep, sleep,
    She sung captain and sailors to sleep.

She robbed him of silver, she robbed him of gold,
    She robbed him of costly ware O,
And she stole his broadsword, instead of an oar,
    And she paddled her way to the shore, shore, shore,
    And she paddled her way to the shore.

"My men must be crazy, my men must be mad,
    My men must be deep in despair, O,
To let her go 'way, with her beauty so gay,
    And paddle her way to the shore, shore, shore,
    And paddle her way to the shore."

"Your men was not crazy, your men was not mad,
    Your men was not deep in despair, O,
I deluded the sailors as well as yourself:

I'm a maiden again on the shore, shore, shore,
I'm a maiden again on the shore." (Bronson 1959–72: no. 43, version 29)

What fate would have befallen the woman if she had not sung the sailors to sleep? A. L. Lloyd had some additional verses in which the captain articulates his intention of spending the night with the woman and then passing her over to the crew. This idea seems to be welcome to the maid, who has "grown so tired of her maidenhead" as she walked all alone on the shore. I am not sure if Lloyd found these verses in a source unknown to me or made them up himself. If they are invented, I do not think the song needs them. The sexual implications are certainly there; not only does the captain fail to "get that maid on the shore" but she even paddles back with his broadsword! What the song represents is the adoption of siren qualities by a woman to assert her independence of action and resist male sexual violation and violence.

So the traditional and popular songs of the English-speaking world contain sirenic elements that we can connect back to ancient times and songs. These elements include the arresting, seductive, and soporific power of the voice and birdsong; the sexual potency of vocal, and sometimes instrumental, music; the danger of the loss of control that music can induce; and the portentous sight and sound of the mermaid. All these elements have been used and reused, divided and combined in countless songs and stories. They bear witness to a wide-spread and compelling notion that music, so "shrill and in sensual appetite so strong" (*The Odyssey*: book 12, line 65), is powerful and its influence is hard to resist.

*Notes*

Versions of this paper were given at the 1998 conference, The Siren in Music, at the University of Cambridge and at the 1999 Aberdeen conference. I thank all those who contributed comments. References to texts in the Child and Bronson collections are by number and version only.

1.  The study of what circulates and survives orally is of immense interest, but there is always a complex and fascinating interchange between literate and oral cultures. For a helpful overview of this area, see Ong 1982.

2.  Homer, *The Odyssey*, book 12. I particularly looked at versions by Chapman and Samuel Butler, both of which are easily available on the Internet.

3.  Music is always interpreted culturally; its meanings are never natural. This essay seeks to explore popular meanings, not criticize them. One of the inspirations for this essay is Robert Walker's *Musical Beliefs, Psychoacoustic, Mythical, and Educational Perspectives* (1990).

4.  I am suggesting that there is an aspect of bird song as experience or simile that has
    something of the siren quality about it. See the next section. Some fascinating aspects of
    anthropology suggest that the way we perceive and classify animals has important
    ramifications for our perceptions of the world. See, for example, Leach 1972.
5.  On related themes, using similar methods but in a historically more grounded way, see
    Gammon 1982.
6.  The Harding collection is available online at <http://www.bodley.ox.ac.uk/ballads/
    ballads.htm/>.
7.  Broadside printed by Wright and Co., Birmingham, entitled "The False Lovers," ca.1820–
    1827 (Birmingham Reference Library), but also collected many times.
8.  'Laws' refers to the standard reference work on *American Balladry from British
    Broadsides* (Laws 1957).
9.  For a fuller study of this ballad, see Gammon and Stallybrass 1983.
10. Remembered from a commercial recording heard in childhood, which, in retrospect, was
    obviously based on Bronson 1959–72: song 200, version 9.
11. Recalled from a long-lost recording of Woody Guthrie.
12. I have collected quite a lot of material on this subject and may cover it in a future essay.
13. See David Atkinson's essay in this book for a full discussion of versions of "George
    Collins" in Hampshire, England.
14. See, for example, "Married to a Mermaid" (Bodleian Library, University of Oxford,
    broadside ballad collection [sheet dated 1870], frame 17766) and "Paddy Miles and the
    Mermaid" (Bodleian Library, University of Oxford, Harding B11 [2920], frame 03825).

## References

Bodleian Library, University of Oxford, Harding broadside ballad collection,
    <http://www.bodley.ox.ac.uk/ballads/ballads.htm/>.
Broadwood, John. 1843. *Old English Songs, as Now Sung by the Peasantry of the Weald
    of Surrey and Sussex*. London: Balls and Co.
Bronson, Bertrand Harris. 1959–72. *The Traditional Tunes of the Child Ballads, with
    Their Texts, According to the Extant Records of Great Britain and America*. 4 vols.
    Princeton: Princeton University Press.
Burns, Robert. 1995. *Complete Poems and Songs of Robert Burns*. Glasgow:
    HarperCollins.
Child, Francis James, ed. 1882–98. *The English and Scottish Popular Ballads*. 5 vols.
    Reprint, New York: Folklore Press, 1956–57; New York: Dover, 1965. Corrected
    edition prepared by Mark and Laura Heiman. Northfield, Minn.: Loomis House Press,
    2002. Digital edition, with gazetteer, maps and audio CD. New York: ESPB Publish-
    ing, 2003.
Copper, Bob. 1971. *A Song for Every Season*. London: Heinemann.
D'Urfey, Thomas. [1719–20] 1959. *Wit and Mirth or Pills to Purge Melancholy*. Reprint,
    New York: Folklore Library Publishers (page references are to reprint edition).
Dixon, James Henry, and Robert Bell. 1857. *Ancient Poems, Ballads and Songs of the
    Peasantry of England*. London: John W. Parker. (Available, unpaginated, on the
    Internet at <ftp://uiarchive.cso.uiuc.edu/pub/etext/gutenberg/etext96/oleng10.txt>)
Gammon, Vic. 1982. "Song, Sex and Society in England, 1600–1850." *Folk Music
    Journal* 4, no. 3: 208–45.
Gammon, Vic, and Peter Stallybrass. 1983. "Structure and Ideology in the Ballad: An
    Analysis of Long Lankin." *Criticism* 26, no. 1 (winter 1984), 1–120.
Greene, R. L. 1977. *The Early English Carols*. 2d ed. Oxford: Oxford University Press.
Grieg, Gavin, and James B. Duncan. 1990. *The Greig-Duncan Folk-Song Collection*. Vol.
    4, edited by Patrick Shuldham-Shaw, Emily B. Lyle, and Andrew R. Hunter. Aberdeen:
    Aberdeen University Press (cited in the text as *Greig-Duncan Collection*).

Huntington, Gale. 1990. *Sam Henry's Songs of the People*. Athens: University of Georgia Press.

Johnson, James, and Robert Burns. 1771. *The Scots Musical Museum*. Edinburgh: Johnson.

*Journal of the Folk-Song Society*. 1909. Vol. 3 (1908–1909).

Karpeles, Maud. 1974. *Cecil Sharp's Collection of English Folk Songs*. 2 vols. London: Oxford University Press.

Kinsley, James, ed. 1971. *Burns Poems and Songs*. London: Oxford University Press.

Laws, George Malcolm. 1957. *American Balladry from British Broadsides: A Guide for Students and Collectors of Traditional Song*. Publications of the American Folklore Society. Bibliographical and special series, 8. Philadelphia: American Folklore Society.

Leach, Edmund. 1972. "Anthropological Aspects of Language: Animal Categories and Verbal Abuse." In *Mythology*, edited by Pierre Maranda, 39–67. Harmondsworth: Penguin.

Mackenzie, W. Roy. 1928. *Ballads and Sea Songs from Nova Scotia*. Cambridge: Harvard University Press.

Madden Ballads, Cambridge University Library.

Mellinger, Edward Henry. 1938. *Folk-Songs from the Southern Highlands*. New York: J. J. Augustin.

Ong, Walter J. 1982. *Orality and Literacy*. London: Methuen.

Palmer, Roy. 1979. *Everyman's Book of English Country Songs*. London: Dent.

———. 1983. *Folk Songs Collected by Ralph Vaughan Williams*. London: Dent.

Purslow, Frank. 1965. *Marrow Bones: English Folk Songs from Hammond and Gardiner MSS*. London: English Folk Dance Society.

———. 1969a. *The Wanton Seed*. London: English Folk Dance Society.

———. 1969b. "The Williams Manuscripts." *Folk Music Journal* 1 (1969), 301–15.

Rieuwerts, Sigrid. 1991. "The Historical Meanings of 'The Gypsy Laddie': Johnny Faa and Lady Cassillis." In *The Ballad and Oral Literature*, edited by Joseph Harris, 78–96. Cambridge: Harvard University Press.

Shuldham-Shaw, P. N. 1966. "The James Duncan Manuscript Folk Song Collection." *Folk Music Journal* (1966), 67–91.

Stubbs, Ken. 1970. *The Life of a Man: English Folk Songs from the Home Counties*. London: English Folk Dance Society.

Walker, Robert. 1990. *Musical Beliefs, Psychoacoustic, Mythical, and Educational Perspectives*. New York: Teachers College Press.

Williams, Alfred. MS No.Mi.680, Swindon Reference Library, England.

Wimberley, L. C. 1965. *The Folk Lore of the English and Scottish Popular Ballads*. New York: Dover.

## Recordings

Older, Lawrence. 1963. *Adirondack Songs, Ballads and Fiddle Tunes*. Sharon, Conn.: Folk Legacy Records FSA 15. Recording.

Spicer, Ron. 1995. *When the May Is All in Bloom*. Stowmarket, England: Veteran Tapes VT131CD. Compact disk.

# "Places She Knew Very Well":

# The Symbolic Economy of Women's Travels

# in Traditional Newfoundland Ballads

## Pauline Greenhill

My earlier work has focused upon "outings" as the recognition and examination of lesbian/gay/queer possibilities in traditional ballads in North America (1995, 1997a, 1997b). Here I will consider a rather different kind of outing, associated with individuals' movements from place to place: travel. The commonalities between these different forms of outings—as travel and "queering"—extend beyond their joking possibilities. Anything termed "queer" implies both oddity and suspiciousness, including its colloquial use to describe homosexuals and homosexuality. However, the noun queer's appropriation and rehabilitation by gays and lesbians for self-description allows its verb counterpart, "to queer," not only to recognize and allow for homosexual possibility but also signify various kinds of redirection.

Both forms of outings (homosexuality and travel related) and queerings (homosexuality and direction related) involve movement and change from a previous course. In their sexual contexts, outings and queerings require psychological maneuvering but may also have physical implications. After coming out or being outed, for example, an individual may move to a different community, either forced from a now-unwelcoming one or to identify with a more-queer positive one. With voyages, physical motion may involve psychological change; we often hear that travel broadens the mind. And these links continue in the songs I consider here. Most female journeys described in these ballads show fundamental differences from male ones in the same oeuvre, and certainly from conventional Euro-North American notions of travel; these outings, then, are queered, particularly by gender.

The ballads discussed come from Kenneth Peacock's three-volume Newfoundland collection (1965), distinctive not only for its wonderfully comprehensive texts—no fragments here (see Porter and Contantine 2003)—but also because it crosses song genres. Its contents include versions of classic ballads, traditional British ballads, popular and sentimental songs, and local songs (see Guigne: forthcoming). This variety represents both singers' repertoires and regional

oeuvres more accurately than do other collections from the same area (for example, Karpeles 1971; Greenleaf and Mansfield 1933). Peacock's texts broadly
represent the songs sung in those parts of Newfoundland where he collected
during the first years after the province's entry into the Canadian confederation.
My methods for considering this corpus began with a close analysis of each text,
including in my overall survey any ballads where a woman's movement from one
place to another was directly referenced. I then tried to locate patterns in the
kinds of travel, in their motivations, and in their outcomes. From these I found, in
short, that women's journeys primarily affect the "symbolic capital"[1] they hold in
these songs and Newfoundland society.

Women's travel, from conventional Euro-North American perspectives, raises
problems. James Clifford's work on what he calls "travelling cultures" (for example, 1992, 1997) argues that Euro-North American culture maintains a gendered,
ethnocentric understanding: "'Good travel' (heroic, educational, scientific, adventurous, ennobling) is something men (should) do. Women are impeded from
serious travel" (1992: 105). Representing gender, ethnicity, and travel as mutually
constitutive, as Clifford's work suggests, Newfoundland song texts involving
women's travel remove its direct associations with a particular series of "gendered,
racial bodies, class privilege, specific means of conveyance, beaten paths, agents,
frontiers, documents, and the like" (1992: 110). Even at the outset, it was clear to
me that Clifford's assertion that women are not seen as travelers applied most
accurately to the way the two—women and travel—are perceived and constructed
in elite and mainstream culture rather than everyday practice and nonelite cultural forms. And in Newfoundland ballads—definitely not elite cultural forms—
women and men sometimes travel in similar modes and to similar ends, and when
they do, their travel is usually of the conventional escape and discovery type.
But when men's and women's travels diverge, they become more clearly gendered.
Women are not restricted to the private sphere; we do not find men as travelers
and women as stay-at-homes.

Some women, of course, do travel at least partly in the mainstream male
format, generally dressing in men's clothing and seeking adventure in sailing,
soldiering, piracy, and highway robbery. But analysis of only those songs where
such bold females are found would eliminate the majority of women characters.
The limited—and, even in ballads, clearly male-gendered—concept of travel as
involving escape and discovery fails to illuminate the lives of less-unconven-
tional women. Male song characters are most often found on the road to unknown locations in the course of their occupations as soldiers, sailors, and

highway robbers. However, a woman song character often traverses familiar territory, or, as one song puts it, "places she knew very well" (Peacock 1965: 227).

My own work (Greenhill 1995, 1997a, 1997b) initially defined the many cross-dressing women of the originally British broadside ballads as generic travelers because, more than others of their sex who go on outings in Newfoundland songs, they epitomize the male concept of travel as seeking adventure and diversion. This is, of course, hardly surprising. Ballad and song texts usually operate within the realm of gender rather than sex; they are about culture, not biology. That is, in these songs women (like the female "Handsome Cabin Boy") can function within the male sphere.[2] Thus, the female—but male-identified—handsome cabin boy seeks adventure in male terms ("she had a mind to go roving where the foaming billows swell") but in addition engages in sexual activity ("For the captain with his cabin boy would often kiss and toy") (Peacock 1965: 280). Her resulting pregnancy unequivocally marks her as female, notwithstanding her clothes and roving mind:

> "Oh doctor, oh doctor" the cabin boy did cry,
> The sailors swore by all was good their cabin boy would die.
> The doctor ran with all his might, came smiling at the fun,
> For to think a sailor lad could have a daughter or a son.
>
> (Peacock 1965: 281)

Clearly, there are texts where women are the adventurous travelers (see Greenhill 1995: 158), but they are only a small minority of songs and women travelers in Newfoundland songs. The majority of women song characters go on journeys with quite different purposes. Men's occupational travel in ballads means that they are usually on the road accumulating material capital or objects for exchange. Sometimes they do the exact opposite of accumulating, as in murdered-girl ballads, when they divest themselves of an unwanted, implicitly pregnant fiancee. Women may also travel to accumulate: money, goods, supplies, objects, husbands, and sexual experiences. But they go on outings more often than missions or voyages. The accumulation and exchange in which women engage happens on a more figurative level. Covering territory, or even the simple acquisition of goods or objects, does not provide the ultimate purpose for their travels. They are shoppers rather than explorers. Shopping is serious business, though often dismissed, like so much other women's work in Euro-North American society, as mere play.[3] Remember that a good shopper uses her money wisely, ideally purchasing goods for less than their value, for a net gain. At the very least, she should get her money's worth. Of course, the opposite possibility, being ripped off or duped, also exists, as revealed in Newfoundland folk songs.

Newfoundland folk-song women may be on familiar roads seeking material capital, as does "The Rich Merchant's Daughter" (Peacock 1965: 226–27), going to market.[4] Outwitting the "young man" who tries to rob her and stealing his horse, she travels far. But she also accrues beyond all reasonable expectation:

> She rode over mountains and valleys,
> And places she knew very well;
> She left him a trifle in fortune,
> With about five shillings to tell....
>
> She put her thief's horse in the stable
> And in his portmantle she found
> Some hundreds of sparkling diamonds,
> The value of ten thousand pounds. (Peacock 1965: 227)

Certainly, other women folk-song travelers deploy material capital in the form of wealth, money, or property,[5] but pragmatically other forms of capital can be even more significant. Many folk-song women seek or acquire in travel what sociologist Pierre Bourdieu calls "cultural capital": "knowledge, skills and other cultural acquisitions, as exemplified by educational or technical qualifications" (defined by Thompson 1991: 14). "The Soldier Maid" learns valuable skills:

> With my feather in my hat I will have you all to see,
> My officer he taught me a stately man to be,
> The soldiers all admired me, my fingers were so small,
> And they learned me to beat upon the drum the best of all.
>
> (Peacock 1965: 347)

The drummer's value—her cultural capital—is so great that "I was guarded by my general for fear I would be slain" (347), and, upon discovering that she is a woman, her officer comments, "It's a pity we should lose such a drummer as a maid" (347). There are other examples, particularly from the cross-dressing ballads, of women's accumulation of special skills during and in the context of travel. Often these acquired abilities are associated with their chosen occupations (see also Greenhill 1997a: 117–18).

Most frequently, however, Newfoundland song women are after symbolic capital, "accumulated prestige or honour" (Thompson 1991: 14). They do not merely want a husband, any husband. They want homes, suitable mates, financial and emotional security, fitting circumstances in which to bear and raise children and attain social respectability, adult identity and status, and/or autonomy from the previous generation.[6]

The ways ballad women deploy their social and cultural assets indicate the vulnerability of their symbolic capital. They are cogently described by Polly Stewart: "as the plots of [Child] ballads unfold, we discover that the women in them are in agonistic situations—they have something to protect or something to gain" (Stewart 1993: 55). Stewart argues that women may achieve personal and/or cultural success and/or failure. Cultural success for women involves meeting the expectations of men; cultural failure means not doing so. Personal success "consists in averting harm...or in reaching a goal" and personal failure "in being subjected to harm...or in failing to reach a goal" (Stewart 1993: 57).

Consider, for example, the numerous murdered girls traveling from home with their lovers. In "Sweet Florella," the "jealous lover" invites her,

> Saying, "My sweet Florella
> Will you take a walk with me
> Down by the dark green river
> To fix our wedding day?" (Peacock 1965: 632)

Florella is not exploring or adventuring; she seeks to replace some of the symbolic capital she has lost by becoming pregnant out of wedlock. She fails, of course, and is instead murdered by her lover, but there are always risks in undertaking such travel and transactions with one's symbolic capital.

Women's travel, then, does not always succeed. But it can do so. The Turk's daughter who follows "Lord Bateman" (Peacock 1965: 210–13) wants him to fulfil his promise to marry her; eventually, she does supplant his new bride. Similarly, the raped "lady" in "Sir William" follows him, traveling in decidedly difficult circumstances:

> He mounted on his milk-white steed
> So fast as he could ride,

She tied a handkerchief around her middle
And she ran by the horse's side.

She ran till she came to the riverside,
And then she jumped in,
She swam till she came to the other side,
And then jumped out again.

She ran till she came to the king's fair court,
She dingled at the ring,
And who came out but the king himself
To let this fair maid in. (Peacock 1965: 230–31)

She tells the king that Sir William has robbed her not of her "store"—material capital—but her maidenhead—symbolic capital. The king calls Sir William, who offers her gold in recompense. However, she replies that she wants his "fair body." Of course, we find out in the end that

She proved to be a duke's daughter
And he but a tinker's son. (Peacock 1965: 232)

Perhaps because even at the outset she holds greater stores of cultural, symbolic, and economic capital than his, she bears considerable power. Yet she is willing to travel to avoid losing her capital, and she enhances it in marriage.

Often the economic and the symbolic/cultural are linked. "The Maid on the Shore" seeks to "comfort her mind" by "roam[ing] all alone on the shore" (Peacock 1965: 296); as travel may lead to psychological transformation, so may solitary reflection gain symbolic capital. But this maid also accumulates materially, turning the tables on the man who misinterprets her wandering (and her vulnerability!):

She robbed him of silver, she robbed him of gold,
She robbed him of costly ware-o,
And she stole his broadsword instead of an oar,...
And she paddled her way to the shore. (Peacock 1965: 297)

Sometimes traveling women have all the symbolic and cultural capital they want or need, putting them in a position of considerable power. In "Watercresses," the "brisk young damsel" who "come[s] tripping down this way" has clearly been to market:

> She had a bunch of early onions and a half a pint of beer,
> Some pickles and a bunch of watercresses. (Peacock 1965: 320)

The man she meets immediately offers her even more:

> "I got cows, I got sheep, I got pigs, I got geeses,
> Besides I have a dairy full of buttermilk and cheeses;
> If you'll consent to Missus, now, fair lady of all eases,
> We'll spend our time in love and watercresses." (320)

She asks for money for her wedding dress and bills. He gives her a sovereign but finds out by letter the next day that she is already married.

So while the road can be a dangerous place for women—they can be murdered, raped, or abandoned there—it can also be a power location for them to accumulate material, cultural, and symbolic capital. "The Foolish Shepherd" provides a resonant example:

> One day he wandered on the hill
> All looking for a sheep.
>
> He looked east, he looked west
> Then had another look,
> 'Twas there he spied a fair pretty maid
> All bathing in the brook. (Peacock 1965: 272)

Yet this maid's vulnerability is more illusion than reality. Threatened with rape in a "pook of hay," she offers an alternative:

> "Oh you come to my papa's house,
> You'll get a bed of down." (Peacock 1965: 273)

And so,

> They marched along together
> Till they came to her father's house.

"Now I'm a girl inside the gate
And you're a fool without." (273)

He curses her and threatens her with a knife. She counters with another curse and a threat with scissors.[7] She insults him:

"My father keeps a rooster
He lives amongst the hens,
He flitters his wings but he dare not strut,
And you're like one of them.

"My father keeps a dibby horse,
He lives in yonder barn,
He nods his head into the crib,
But he dares not touch the corn." (Peacock 1965: 275)

Clearly, then, Newfoundland songs show women moving freely and often powerfully in spaces beyond their domestic contexts and deploying material, cultural, and symbolic capital. As such, they can provide a useful corrective to the frequent overstatement of the binary gendering of space, and of women's and men's culture and travel. For example, Gerald Pocius's ethnography of the Newfoundland community of Calvert asserts a conventional gender spatial division, the semiotic linkage of male:female :: public : private :: wild space:domestic space:

If men generally know the wooded landscape, women find it
unfamiliar. Names may be known, but the experiential dimension is
lacking.... Women's space is the home, men's the woods and water.

(1991:92–3)

He explains this division in terms of exogamy and virilocality: "Females never know where they may live.... Even if they did acquire the spatial acuity of their brothers with regard to the larger landscape, it would not be of any use if they move somewhere else" (99).

Yet Newfoundlander Andrea O' Brien, born and raised in Calvert's neighboring community of Cape Broyle, shows that women and girls participate in a variety of economic and social activities, from berry picking and trouting to boil-ups and camping, which take them into the woods. They do not need male guides on these outings, and they certainly do not get lost any more frequently than men. O' Brien argues,

> Pocius should not assume that female cognitive maps are confined
> to dwellings, yard and other family units within the community.
> While their knowledge of the hinterlands may not be as extensive or
> utilitarian as men's, it exists, nonetheless, in varying degrees,
> according to the amount of acculturation a woman has had with the
> landscape. (1999: 82)

Any temptation to suggest that O' Brien's observations result from recent cultural change—that, like other women in their twenties, she and her peers are less socially and culturally restricted than were their foremothers—can be discounted by the fact that women have long participated as gatherers in the subsistence economy of Newfoundland outports. Men were often away on the cod and seal fisheries, sometimes for long periods. Women's independent knowledge of what O' Brien calls "the hinterlands" would then, as now, be necessary for survival. And so the textual configurations of these Newfoundland songs reflect a context in which women were and are by no means confined to the domestic context writ small.

Yet arguing that these songs "mean" in a literal sense, that they somehow directly reflect actual Newfoundland women's experience, fails to acknowledge their fundamental value. Instead, they reflect upon the way being female makes a character act and enact her life. Obviously, Newfoundland women travel to riverbanks—whether alone, with other women, or with men—on numerous occasions without fear of murder or attempted murder. They do not expect, when on the road, to encounter complete strangers who will propose marriage to them. Newfoundland ballads are not exhorting girls to dress as men and leave home. Yet in their workaday activities, urban and outport women must visit "places they know very well." Indeed, Newfoundland's marginalized economy often requires them to travel to even more remote locations, sometimes following after a man like the Turk's daughter in "Lord Bateman," sometimes at his side like the lady in "Sir William," and sometimes quite alone, as in "The Rich Merchant's Daughter" or "Watercresses." This sociocultural situation is not just an artifact of the current fisheries crisis but has happened throughout Newfoundland's history.

The songs I have discussed so far are not just from Newfoundland; like other traditional texts, they are found in many places. Yet more-localized Newfoundland texts reveal similar patterns and implications even more explicitly. Further, as women move into spaces previously unavailable to them, they transform them and their practices, for women and for men, just as the "girl" from Canada and the two "girls" from St. John's do in "The Jubilee Guild," composed by Arthur Keeping. Jubilee Guilds were formed to encourage instruction and collaboration in handicrafts, child care, domestic work, home nursing, and so on. Like much women's work, their activities tended to be devalued, but they brought considerable economic and social benefit to the communities where they operated. Such groups and their members are pretty universally considered in mainstream North America as petty, trivial, and useless. Thus, Arthur Keeping's song is unusual in recognizing and celebrating this aspect of women's work and its positive effects on both sexes/genders. Keeping's interpretation of women travelers strikingly mirrors those which preceded it.

"The Jubilee Guild"'s traveling women are outsiders (like the Turk's daughter in "Lord Bateman"); they bring knowledge to men (like "The Maid on the Shore"), and so on. But they are also catalysts; the change they enact is within the community, not themselves:

> ...A girl came down from Canada, McLellan was her name,
> She was a clever young girl, no need to be ashamed,
> And two more girls from St. John's town they joined her with a will,
> To go out to Burnt Islands and start our Jubilee Guild.
>
> When they came to Burnt Islands, 'twas welcome and good cheer,
> The people came both young and old to know what they might hear,
> They elected in the members belonging to this place,
> And the women sot with eager minds and smiles upon their face....
>
> Then the women all got together and a tea they did prepare
> They served it in the Island school where each might get her share.
> They said the boys were welcome up to their tea-and-chat
> But all the boys got frightened case they'd have to weave a mat.
>
> So now my song is ended, I'll have no more to say,
> But I could write a report, boys, to reach from Spaniard's Bay,

But that would take some paper and a time for me to write,

So wash your face and comb your hair, there's a meeting on tonight.

(Peacock 1965: 66–67)

Women's outings in Newfoundland folk songs, whether queered by gender ambiguity like the cross-dressing ballads or more apparently conventional like the example above, extend the range of "places she knew very well." Folk-song texts need not be taken as literal reflections of society to show how they can instantiate a wide range of possibilities. Women's outings, gendered and queered, whether in ballads or personal experience, provide a range of possibilities absent from other imaginative worlds.

## Notes

My thanks to Roger deV. Renwick for, as always, providing enthusiastic support tempered with cogent criticism.

1. Symbolic capital is sociologist Pierre Bourdieu's term and refers to "the acquisition of a reputation for competence and an image of respectability and honourability" (1984: 291).
2. Indeed, though much more rarely, men (like the sailor in "The Shirt and the Apron" [Greenleaf and Mansfield 1933: 222–23]), can function within the female sphere.
3. A feminist anthropologist cannot help developing an ironic stance toward the fact that when shopping attracts the attention of a prestigious male anthropologist (Appadurai 1997), it gains respectability and significance. Women (for example, Waring 1988, 1996) have previously recognized the economic centrality and meaning of such practices.
4. Similarly, the streetwalker in "The Shirt and the Apron" (Greenleaf and Mansfield 1933: 222–23) steals Jack's money and clothes.
5. Including, for example, "The Maid on the Shore," "The King's Daughter" (Peacock 1965: 206–7), "Watercresses" (Peacock 1965: 320–21), and many others.
6. As suggested by Roger deV. Renwick (personal communication, 1999).
7. Note that the woman chooses an object which parallels, but outperforms, the phallic choice of her male counterpart.

## References

Appadurai, Arjun. 1997. "Consumption, Duration, and History." In *Streams of Cultural Capital: Transnational Cultural Studies*, edited by D. Palumbo-Liu and H. U. Gumbrecht, 23–47. Stanford: Stanford University Press.

Bourdieu, Pierre. 1984. *Distinction: A Social Critique of the Judgement of Taste*. Cambridge: Harvard University Press.

Clifford, James. 1992. "Travelling Cultures." In *Cultural Studies*, edited by L. Grossberg, C. Nelson, and P. Treichler, 96–116. London: Routledge.

———. 1997. *Routes: Travel and Translation in the Late Twentieth Century*. Cambridge: Harvard University Press.

Greenhill, Pauline. 1995. "'Neither a man nor a maid': Sexualities and Gendered Meanings in Cross-Dressing Ballads." *Journal of American Folklore* 108: 156–77.

———. 1997a. " 'The Handsome Cabin Boy': Cross-Dressing Ballads, Sexualities, and Gendered Meanings." In *Undisciplined Women: Tradition and Culture in Canada*, edited by Pauline Greenhill and Diane Tye, 113–30. Montreal: McGill-Queen's University Press.

————. 1997b. "'Who's Gonna Kiss Your Ruby Red Lips?': Sexual Scripts in Floating
      Verses." In *Ballads into Books: The Legacies of Francis James Child*, edited by Tom
      Cheesman and Sigrid Rieuwerts, 225–35. Berne: Peter Lang.
Greenleaf, Elizabeth Bristol, and Grace Yarrow Mansfield. 1933. *Ballads and Sea Songs
      of Newfoundland*. Cambridge: Harvard University Press.
Guigne, Anna. Forthcoming. *Kenneth Peacock, the National Museum and the Politics of
      Newfoundland Nationalism*. Ph.D. diss., Memorial University of Newfoundland.
Karpeles, Maud. 1971. *Folk Songs from Newfoundland*. London: Faber and Faber.
O' Brien, Andrea. 1999. "'There's Nothing Like a Cup of Tea in the Woods': Continuity,
      Community and Cultural Validation in Rural Newfoundland Boil-Ups." *Ethnologies*
      21, no. 1: 65–84.
Peacock, Kenneth. 1965. *Songs of the Newfoundland Outports*. 3 vols. Ottawa: National
      Museum of Canada.
Pocius, Gerald. 1991. *A Place to Belong: Community Order and Everyday Space in
      Calvert, Newfoundland*. Athens: University of Georgia Press.
Porter, Gerald, and Mary-Ann Constantine. 2003. *Fragments and Meaning in Tradi-
      tional Songs*. Oxford: Oxford University Press.
Stewart, Polly. 1993. "Wishful Willful Wily Women: Lessons for Female Success in the
      Child Ballads." In *Feminist Messages: Coding in Women's Folk Culture*, edited by
      Joan N. Radner, 54–73. Urbana: University of Illinois Press.
Thompson, John. 1991. Introduction to *Language and Symbolic Power,* by Pierre
      Bourdieu. Cambridge: Harvard University Press.
Waring, Marilyn. 1988. *If Women Counted: A New Feminist Economics*. New York:
      HarperCollins.
————. 1996. *Three Masquerades: Essays on Equality, Work and Human Rights*.
      Toronto: University of Toronto Press.

# A Good Man Is Hard to Find:
# Positive Masculinity in the Ballads Sung
# by Scottish Women

Lynn Wollstadt

This essay looks specifically at the way ballads popular among female singers construct masculinity, focusing on the intersections of gender, class, and power. Since large-scale ballad collection began in the eighteenth century, at least, both men and women have learned and passed on these traditional songs, so we may consider the Scottish ballad tradition to be carried by both sexes. According to the recordings held at the School of Scottish Studies, University of Edinburgh, however, men and women do not necessarily sing the same songs.[1] The ten songs most often recorded from female singers, for example, have only two titles in common with the ten most often recorded from men. Analysis of the specific ballad narratives that were most popular among female singers in twentieth-century Scotland suggests that certain buried themes may underlie their choice.

The data discussed here regarding gender differences in ballad repertoires comes from the School of Scottish Studies Archives, department of Celtic and Scottish Studies, University of Edinburgh. I spent the summer of 1997 transcribing the catalogs of the school's archives into a computer database of approximately twenty-six hundred records that detail the recordings made between 1951 and 1997. I allowed only one instance of each ballad per singer (in other words, only one entry was made whether a singer recorded a particular song once or five times, unless the catalogs noted two unique, but same-titled, versions). This information reveals, among other things, how many times any one ballad was recorded by male and female singers. Although I have looked at some specific transcribed versions of songs, many recordings remain untranscribed. It is possible that certain recordings may contain variations that change the meaning of the song.

Three vital caveats must be borne in mind. First, it would be foolhardy to imply that any singer would never choose to learn a song whose lyrics did not appeal to him or her. Many other factors play into that decision, such as a pleasing melody or the social context with which the song is associated. Second, this discussion is based primarily on the number of times that a ballad was recorded and on the most common version of each ballad. Finally, it must be noted that the traditional songs that are most often recorded from any particular group of people are not necessarily the most popular among that group, or even the favorites of individual singers. Fieldworkers may request certain songs more than others, or singers may sing songs they think the fieldworker wants to hear. Nevertheless, the decision to learn and remember a song does require that a singer find the song appealing or meaningful in some way; the fact that a song *has* been learned means that that singer found it worth learning. Thus, it is significant that the songs that appear most often in the repertoires of women— those that significant numbers of women found worth learning—show similar patterns in their portrayal of gender roles. Moreover, these patterns are especially noteworthy because they are at odds with patterns in the larger corpus of traditional ballads in Scotland.

Among the men whom the ballads portray as "attractive"—sympathetic supporting characters as well as the male "love interests"—what are the qualities their women seem to value? Who are the "good guys?" Furthermore, what may the men in the ballad world tell us about the interests and lives of the singing women who kept the stories alive? While Scottish ballads generally take for granted a society where women function under male control, the most attractive, sympathetic male characters in the ballads popular among women are all in some way vulnerable or even victimized. The ballads Scottish women sing may recognize a cultural system of male hegemony, but they do not celebrate it.

This is not the case in the Scottish ballad tradition as a whole, however. The ballads that most often appear in the repertoires of twentieth-century women singers are much more critical of men who wield power than most Scottish ballads. Emily Lyle's collection of ballads, for example, contains forty-seven examples that include some sort of romantic male figure (1994). Almost three-quarters of these (thirty-five) show attractive, romantically desirable male characters in clear positions of power, often simply because of their social position. Close analysis of any of these narratives may reveal subtleties that make such broad generalizations dangerous, but the larger pattern is significant. Most of the time, male lovers are specifically identified as "gentlemen": lords, knights, earls, or perhaps squires, with the occasional elfin knight thrown into the mix. Of the twelve ballads that do not identify their male protagonists as noble, half omit any mention of the man's social class. Only six of these forty-seven ballads depict male protagonists who are clearly not of high social standing.[2]

More pertinently, the gentlemen lovers who pervade the tradition are "doers"; they *act*, and women must live with those actions. In "Burd Ellen" (Child 63), for example, Lord John leaves the pregnant heroine, and she follows his horse on foot, her tenacity finally rewarded when he marries her. The female protagonist of "Lord Thomas and Fair Annie"(Child 62) supports her well-born lover even when he brings home a wife, cleaning and cooking for the new bride's arrival. The heroine of "Lord Thomas and Fair Annet" (Child 73) must also deal with a romantic partner who chooses to marry a wealthier woman, and again the ballad does not condemn the lord for this decision. Lord Thomas remains a desirable figure; it is the rich, but homely, "nut-browne bride" who is the ballad's villain. "The Twa Sisters" (Child 10) fight over the knight who comes courting; "The Shepherd's Dochter" (Child 110) strives to marry, and teach a lesson to, the knight who has helped himself to her virginity. "The Shepherd's Son" (Child 112), on the other hand, is too nice for his own good. The ballad condemns his compassion, mocking the lack of personal power that this version seems to associate with his low social status. Because he does not force himself on a "lady fair" whom he finds swimming naked, instead helping her to the safety of her father's house, she taunts him:

> 'Pough! you're a fool without,' she says,
>     And I'm a maid within.

The lady's message is explicit:

> 'But had you done what you should do,
>     I neer had left you there.'

Rape, a display of male power, would have won him a well-born wife, but his courtesy only provokes ridicule.

These are only a few of the many ballad narratives that show women doing, and accepting, whatever it takes to win men who are individually and socially commanding and condemn men who are not. These narratives do not seem to be the ones that Scottish women have kept alive for generations, however. Of the ten ballads recorded most often by traditional women singers, none show women striving to marry the commanding, high-born men who are so often desired in the tradition as a whole. Rather, the attractive or sympathetic male characters in these ballads—when there are any—are in vulnerable situations; they have either lost their usual authority or never had it. Three of these ballads can be interpreted as cautionary tales which warn of the dangers of becoming romantically involved with men—"The Banks of Red Roses" (18 singers), "I Wish I Were a Maid Again" (21), and "Mary Hamilton" (20). As these three after-the-fact narratives do not contain any positive male characters, I will put them aside. Three ballads depict dying men or boys—"Barbara Allan" (15), "Lord Randal" (17), and "The Twa Brithers" (14)—characters who are sympathetic because of their vulnerability. Two others show women who suffer for being in love with men who are socially beneath them—"Andrew Lammie" (14) and "The Dowie Dens o' Yarrow" (28). These men are depicted positively but have no social authority. Only two of these ten ballad narratives show women who marry socially commanding men, and neither of these marriages is really the woman's desire—"The Laird o' Drum" (12) and "The Beggar Man" (18). Desirable romantic partners are not the men who wield the most power; on the contrary, well-born and authoritative men are often depicted most positively when they are on their deathbeds.

"Lord Randal" and "Barbara Allan" are both clear examples with male characters who seem attractive because of their powerlessness. Versions of the latter vary widely, but all involve a young man, often noble, dying for the love of a young woman.[3] Though she comes to his deathbed when called, Barbara Allan has the option to decide his fate; the love she withholds has the ability, in the ballad world, to restore her lover's health. Although reactions to this ballad do, of course, vary—Bertrand Bronson, for example, noted that it has demonstrated a "stronger will-to-live" than its "spineless lover had" (Lyle 1994: 284)—the narrative does makes clear which character is in the wrong. The ballad does not celebrate Barbara Allan's power over her lover but warns of its dangers. The audience's sympathies are likely to be with the helpless, dying man; Allan is cast as the villain: a selfish, shallow, grudge-bearing girl. That she realizes her fault and dies for her man redeems her only partially, for the ballad's focus is on the young man's death, and Barbara Allan dies offstage:

> Since my love died for me to-day,
> I'll die for him to-morrow.

"Lord Randal," collected by Emily Lyle as "Lord Ronald," also offers a noble, but helpless, male protagonist. The repetitive, suspenseful question-and-answer between the mother and the young lord gradually reveals the fact that Randal has been poisoned by his sweetheart. Thematically, the ballad is framed by the tension between the lord's normally commanding position and his current incapacity. The series of questions not only reveal the narrative situation but also emphasize the lord's noble position, its accompanying power, and the gradual loss of that power as he weakens. The last line of every stanza, "For I'm weary o huntin an fain wad lie doon,"[4] identifies him as well born (sport hunting was never a pastime of the poor) and associates him with the ultimate position of authority, that of predator. At the same time, though, it focuses on his weakening and vulnerability. The proof of the poisoning is evident when his bloodhounds, noble hunters that represent the lord himself, die. Their fate will soon be the lord's.

Some versions end when the lord tells his mother that he has been poisoned, but many draw out the death scene further, as the mother asks what he will leave to his father, brother, and sweetheart. These last three verses heighten the tension, focus the narrative on the absent and evil sweetheart, and also draw attention to the material goods left behind. Despite the young man's wealth and his social authority as a lord, he has been rendered powerless by a woman. However unacceptable this situation is, and however much a singer or listener may condemn the villainous sweetheart, hearing or singing the song must be, to some extent, a meditation on the loss of power and control.

"The Twa Brithers" is yet another meditation on the loss of control, this time involving a boy who has been, perhaps, accidentally fatally stabbed by his brother. A full third to a half of this ballad, too, consists of dialogue involving a dying person; here the murdering boy asks his dying brother, "What will I tell to your father dear," "sweetheart dear," and "stepmother dear" (as sung by Belle Stewart: SA1955/36 A3).[5] While the final verse of this ballad generally seems to be condemning the stepmother, who prayed the boy "might never come home" in the accidental stabbing versions, the focus is primarily on the pathos of the boys' plights. Both boys are sympathetic characters, victims of a situation that got out of control. Not only is the stabbed boy dying, an obvious situation of powerlessness, but the questions his brother asks force him to imagine how his loved ones will deal with his death. The stabber, on the other hand, must bear the burden of his accidental fratricide and take the news to his family.

Interestingly, this is the only one of the twelve ballads in the school's archive recorded by more than ten women that lacks a female main character. Only two men recorded it, and both sang only five-stanza versions (Donald Stewart: SA1955/67 B2; and Jimmy Whyte: SA1954/101 A10). One may only guess at the reasons for this surprising discrepancy. Why did so many women sing this ballad, and why did the few men not sing the whole story? It is not that men do not tend to sing tragic ballads. While many of the songs recorded by male singers are bothy songs, often humorous or bawdy, tragic ballads often appear in their repertoires as well. In fact, the tragic "Dowie Dens o' Yarrow" is the ballad most often recorded by singers of both sexes. While I must emphasize that individual singers choose songs for many reasons that may not necessarily have to do with the lyrics, such a marked discrepancy should be recognized, for it indicates that women found something appealing in "The Twa Brithers" that many male singers did not. It is not my aim to guess what this "something" is, but it is worth noting what this narrative has in common with the other ballads popular among women singers: the pathos of characters facing an out-of-control situation, doing the best they can to deal with the consequences.

"The Dowie Dens o' Yarrow" and "Mill o' Tifty's Annie" are also tragic ballads; both of them tell of young women who die because they cannot marry lovers who are socially beneath them. In both cases, the male lovers are clearly appealing but lack social authority. In "Mill o' Tifty's Annie," the young girl's love interest is Lord Fyvie's lowly trumpeter, Andrew Lammie. The ballad makes clear the young man's virtues:

> Proper he was, both young and gay,
> His like was not in Fyvie.

Even Annie's mother asks her,

> Did you ever see a prettier man,
> Than the trumpeter o Fyvie?
> (Mrs. Findlater and Mrs. Johnston: SA1966/44 A3)

Of the four male characters in the narrative, however, Andrew has the least authority. He answers not only to Lord Fyvie, his employer and lord, but also to Annie's father and, to a lesser extent, her brother, who must agree to her marriage. Andrew wields even less power in this situation than Annie, who predicts her own death when he announces his departure for Edinburgh:

> Ere you come back I will be laid
> In the green church-yard o Fyvie. (SA1966/44 A3)

Upon his return, Andrew even adopts the often-feminine role of declaring his imminent death, as Barbara Allan does:

> My love she died for me to-day;
> But I'll die for her to-morrow. (SA1966/44 A3)

While Andrew is portrayed as the most desirable man in the ballad, Lord Fyvie also comes across sympathetically in many versions. He is moved by Annie's tears and implores her father to allow the union, but Tifty remains steadfast, maintaining that his daughter must be wed to "some higher match." Lord Fyvie has less authority over Annie than her father does, and this impotence makes him a more sympathetic figure. The characters with power, Annie's father and the brother who beats her to death, are the ballad's villains.

The same is true in "The Dowie Dens o' Yarrow." In this case, the woman is courted by "nine noblemen" and a "plooman lad frae Yarrow" (*Greig-Duncan Collection*, 2: no. 215A).[6] When the nine armed noblemen come to fight him, the ploughman lad wins:

> Three he slew, and three withdrew
> And three lay deadly wounded,

only to be stabbed in the back by the girl's brother. The nobility, wielders of social authority, are not desirable partners; the ballad makes the unacceptability of their aggression clear, as the ploughman twice protests, "it's nae an equal marrow." His physical prowess seems to be an admirable trait, but it is clearly not enough. He is first a victim of their insistence on an unfair fight, and then at the mercy of the cruel brother's cowardly attack. The pathos intensifies when the focus turns to the ploughman's dead body, as his lover washes the face and combs the hair of the "bloody corpse" and "washed the reed blude [red blood] frae his wounds." While the ploughman's heroic fighting is summed up in two lines, his helpless dead body is the focus of three stanzas.

Two ballads, "The Laird o' Drum" and "The Beggar Man," do not appear, at first glance, to fit this mold of attractive male characters lacking social or personal power. Of the two, the latter is the easier fit. Though it exists in widely varying versions, its central plot tells of a farmer's daughter who runs away with a beggar man whom the family has lodged for the night. The couple's return some time later reveals the apparent beggar's true identity as a wealthy gentleman (often associated with James V). The daughter truly believes, however, that she is running off with a beggar or a Traveller. Indeed, many versions emphasize the desirability of the beggar by focusing on the dialogue between him and the daughter, where she implores him to take her along and he himself rebukes her:

> But lassie, lassie, ye're far too young;
> Ye hanae got the cant o' the beggin' tongue...
> Wi' me ye cannae gyaun. ("Auld Kirstie": SA1955/65 B18)

It is not the aristocrat to whom the girl is attracted and whom she wishes to follow; it is the social outcast, the poor Gypsy. Many singers even omit this traditional ending; the girl returns with young children, with no mention of the rich gowns that usually indicate the beggar man's true status. Even when this status is noted, the sight of the now-wealthy daughter is simply a consolation to the parents; the man portrayed as sexually desirable is still the beggar persona.

"The Laird o' Drum," on the other hand, explicitly tells of the marriage of a poor girl to a wealthy aristocrat, and thus seems to be a true anomaly among this group of ballads that women sing. But this is not the "happily ever after" marriage many ballads offer; the ballad refuses to romanticize its Cinderella theme, instead emphasizing the social realities of a marriage that crosses class lines. Both partners are in vulnerable situations. The woman is married against her will, in most versions, to a social superior who may regret his decision.[7] The laird, on the other hand, puts himself in a situation he cannot control when he insists upon marrying a girl who is beneath him socially. The girl has married gentry, but it is a marriage for which she did not ask. The laird is also dissatisfied; the authority of his position means that he can control circumstances to a certain extent and marry the woman he chooses. He cannot, however, have the marriage that he wants, for he cannot make his peers accept the marriage, and the couple are shunned when they arrive home. The final image is again one of death, as the girl asks who "wad ken they dust frae mine" when both are dead and buried (Mrs. Findlater: SA1967/110 A2). Identifying the reasons this ballad may have appealed to its many individual singers is, of course, guesswork, but despite its obvious differences, the narrative does contain elements of the themes found in the other songs popular among women singers. Both partners are in vulnerable situations, and a commanding social position fails to provide the control the laird would like. The ballad's final burial imagery underscores the poignancy of the couple's situation.

Such seems to be the fate of the men and women whom Scottish women have kept alive in their songs. The power of upper-class men is recognized and accepted but not celebrated. The narratives of the ballads most often recorded from women do not reward male hegemony, as so many other ballads do; good things do not happen to the men who rule society. The real heroes are the underdogs, the social outcasts, or aristocrats who have been rendered helpless.

While these characters may not be rewarded in the plots of the songs themselves, they are the ones with whom the songs seem not only to sympathize but
also admire and desire.

## Notes

1.  The ten most-recorded songs from male singers are "The Dowie Dens o' Yarrow" (41
    different singers), "Bogie's Bonny Belle" (27), "The Barnyards of Delgaty" (24), "Jamie
    Raeburn" (23), "The Ball o' Kirriemuir" (23), "The Beggar Man" (23), "Erin Go Braugh"
    (20), "The Road and Miles to Dundee" (20), "The Bonnie Lass o' Fyvie" (19), and "Jamie
    Foyers" (18).
    
    The ten most-recorded songs from female singers are "The Dowie Dens o' Yarrow" (28
    different singers), "I Wish I Were a Maid Again" (21), "Mary Hamilton" (20), "Banks o'
    Red Roses" (18), "The Beggar Man" (18), "Lord Randall" (17), "Barbara Allan" (15), "The
    Twa Brithers" (14), "Mill o' Tifty's Annie" (14), and "The Laird o' Drum" (12).

2.  These are "The Keach i the Creel" (Child 281), "Johny Faa, the Gypsy Laddie" (Child 200),
    "Bob Norris" (Child 83), "The Shepherd's Son" (Child 112), "The Dowie Dens o' Yarrow"
    (Child 214), and "Bog o' Gight" (Child 209). Furthermore, closer examination of these
    narratives reveals that of them, only "The Dowie Dens o' Yarrow" and "Bog o' Gight"
    actually offer romantically desirable heroes who are not nobly born or socially commanding,
    since "Bob Norris" is a tale of mistaken identity, Johny Faa is king of the Gypsies, and "The
    Keach i the Creel" is a comic ballad.

3.  Of the twelve versions of "Barbara Allan" transcribed by the School of Studies (not all
    recorded versions have been transcribed), only three, each sung by men, clearly identify the
    man as Sir John Graham. Four versions do not identify him as titled, calling him Jemmie
    Grove, Sweet William, or "a young man"; these were recorded by three women and one man.
    The five remaining versions, sung by four women and one man, all adopt a first-person
    narration and do not specifically identify the young man as a nobleman. In this small
    sample, it appears that women are less likely than men to sing versions of the ballad that
    identify the man as well-born, thus supporting my finding that the attractive or sympathetic
    male characters whom women more often sing about are unlikely to be in positions of
    personal or social authority.

4.  References to "Lord Ronald" are from Lyle's collected version, which she recorded in 1974
    from Mrs. Haman, née Minnie Duncan, originally published in *Tocher* 14 (1974): 222–23.

5.  SA numbers refer to tapes in the School of Scottish Studies Archive, department of Celtic
    and Scottish Studies, University of Edinburgh. Extracts appear with their kind permission.

6.  This version was collected about 1893 by James B. Duncan from Mrs. Margaret Harper in
    Cluny.

7.  In most, though not all, of the versions recorded and transcribed by the School of Scottish
    Studies, the woman's clearly expressed desire is to stay home, not to marry the laird. Ten
    transcribed recordings (with six female singers) show the woman telling the laird that she
    "widnae fancy" him. Seven (with three female singers) have the woman saying she may
    fancy him but she is of too low a degree to take his offer seriously. One male singer sings a
    version where she refuses to answer on the grounds that the question should not be asked
    because their classes are so disparate.

## References

Greig, Gavin, and James B. Duncan. 1983. *The Greig-Duncan Folk-Song Collection*. Vol.
    2, edited by Patrick Shuldham-Shaw and Emily B. Lyle. Aberdeen: University of
    Aberdeen Press (cited in the text as *Greig-Duncan Collection*).
Lyle, Emily, ed. 1994. *Scottish Ballads*. Edinburgh: Canongate Press.

# Jesting with Edge Tools:
# The Dynamics of a Fragmentary Ballad Tradition

Gerald Porter

Carpenters and Joiners are not hard to find in English traditional song. James Madison Carpenter is beginning to be recognized as one of the most significant collectors of English, as well as Scottish, song, while one of the best traditional singers at the beginning of this century was Mrs. Joiner of Chiswell Green in Hertfordshire (we do not know her first name) (Bishop 1998). Lucy Broadwood visited her on several occasions, and she sang a fine "Poacher's Song." This essay, though, is a search for the other carpenters and joiners, members of the occupations represented by those names. Although they were in other respects a militant and articulate group with a known singing tradition, there is no evidence that the songs they sang ever dealt with their work, and there are no songs with enough circumstantial occupational detail to suggest that it had a significant role. This contrasts, for example, with Germany, where collections of carpenters' songs were edited by firms that sold the special outfits that they wore.[1] There are only two examples of songs featuring carpenters in the oral tradition, "The House Carpenter" and "The Cruel Ship's Carpenter," and in both the occupation is purely incidental (Porter 1992: 13).

By the nineteenth century, the carpenters and joiners were one of the best organized and disciplined of all occupation groups. In the country they owned their own tools and were found in every village. In the towns they combined until 1850 with the millwrights (later the basis of the engineering industry) in a union that included cabinet-makers, pattern makers, and joiners. By 1812 the illegal carpenters' union in London had ten thousand pounds in the kitty. In 1825 they led a strike in the Potteries, the manufacturing district in the English Midlands. As a result, their pay rose by 1832 to nearly as much as an engineer's and three times that of a weaver. In the 1840s, as with the shoemakers, a distinction emerged between the "honorable" and "dishonorable" parts of the trade, much like the one between "first fixers," "second fixers," and "shop fitters" today.[2] In 1860, in response to the need for a more-powerful organization after losing a strike the previous year, the General Union of Carpenters was "battered into insignificance," and the Amalgamated Society of Carpenters and Joiners was formed (Cole and Postgate 1981: 406). It was one of the so-called Junta of unions, second only to the Amalgamated Society of Engineers (Morton 1974: 443).

The iconography of the union's membership certificate indicates its elite status: The design plays down the physical and dynamic presence of its members. They stand to the side, very much at ease with plane and saw resting on the ground, which is strewn with other tools. Only the carpenter on the left strikes a semiheroic pose. However, the workers' stature is achieved metonymically, by associating them with heroic signifiers drawn partly from the dominant discourse, partly from the neoclassical icons of the French and American Revolutions. These include plinths, columns, emblems of health and peace, and symbolic figures like Truth and Justice. However, they do not share the Romantic rhetoric of individualism espoused by those revolutions. Instead, the texts that are visible everywhere emphasize the power that comes from uniting and the humanity of collective action: The text on the architrave reads, "UNITED TO PROTECT NOT COMBINED TO INJURE," and the one beneath the columns says, "INDUSTRY AND BENEVOLENCE UNITE US IN FRIENDSHIP." The central panel is devoted to the key cooperative task of centering a bridge, one where many occupations are involved (see, for example, Michael Ondaatje's novel *In the Skin of a Lion)*. The foregrounding of a structure in this way is very common. From the early years of the century, "the various building trades offered the major outlet for skilled men" (Burnett 1974: 256), and the members identified increasingly with construction workers as a whole: The text beneath the seated figure at the top reads, "UNITED WE STAND."

The results were not long in coming. In the next London strike, in 1872, they were supported by other construction workers and won. As late as 1875, their union was still larger than that of the miners and the textile workers (Applebaum 1992: 416). In this company, the silence of the carpenters seems unaccountable. Perhaps the rarity of their songs is explained by a proverb that was common in the seventeenth century: "The best carpenter makes the fewest chips" (Wilson 1992: 47).[3] However, in the song record, it is precisely the chips that we must deal with: stray references, parodies, sexual metaphors that seem to stand apart from those who were following an occupation that, as part of the huge construction industry, still exists in virtually every street and village in the land.

*Ventriloquism*

There is some truth in the assertion by the Industrial Workers of the World that craft unionism undermines broader solidarity, and in the case of the song culture of the carpenters, there was certainly a situation where the songs all appear to derive from outsiders since their subjects are simplified and reduced. The fact that they were the subject of so many songs led to a situation of "speaking for the other," which, following Heidi Hansson and others, I characterize as a type of ventriloquism (Hansson 1998: 46–53). Hansson emphasizes that ventriloquism is an authoritarian position even when, as in this case, it is undertaken with the best of intentions: She gives the example of those feminists and postcolonialists who sometimes come perilously close to "inventing" those they describe (1998: 47). In this respect they are as reductive as the patriarchal and imperialist positions they seek to replace. In the field of ballads and folk songs, my starting point is a study by Mary-Ann Constantine, where she looks at the mediation of the events surrounding the wreck of the emigrant ship *Royal Charter* off the coast of north Wales during the last century. By setting the novelist, the religious homilist, and the journalist alongside the many sailors, passengers, and villagers of Moelfre that the songs and broadsides about the wreck attempt to foreground, she shows the impossibility of an unmediated voice, even in first-person narratives which supposedly documented the sailors speaking (1999: 65–85).

Since all narratives except some first-person ones are acts of ventriloquism, the same manipulation occurs in broadsides and sentimental and comic songs, from the seventeenth century to Bobby Darin. Paradoxically, such songs silenced the workers themselves by giving them a voice, one that was simplified and characterized by distance. However, because there is a dialectic between subject and object in the perception of other cultures, these outsider narratives can be read against the grain, in the light of what is known about the carpenters' own expressive culture, and I will attempt this in the second half of the paper.

## Speaking for the Other

When John Ruskin called carpenters in 1851 "the trade which of all manual trades has been most honoured,"[4] the "honour" to which he was referring must have been that of the craft unions. It can hardly have been found in the work of sociologists, poets, novelists, or singers since they regarded the status of carpenters as uniformly low. In 1577 the parson William Harrison placed carpenters in the lowest of his four groups, people "to be ruled and not to rule others.... These have no voice or authority in our commonwealth" (Briggs 1985: 113), and today the joiner is still the archetypal nongentleman,[5] as in Bobby Darin's hit song "If I Were a Carpenter":

> If I were a carpenter
> And you were a lady,
> Would you marry me anyway?
> Would you have my baby?

No carpenter, with one exception, has been the protagonist of a novel. The exception is *Adam Bede* (1859): George Eliot's grandfather was a carpenter, and it is relevant to the subject of this paper that the book opens with the carpenter singing at his work.

Although carpenters were a mobile group, it is evident that we are not looking for a countrywide tradition with universal features. The only common characteristics are found in songs written by outsiders who were speaking (or singing) for them, and this has sparked my interest in a nonexistent tradition. Outsider songs may stand in either a familiar or parodic relation to the trade itself. Millers and tailors clearly belong to the second group, but carpenters and joiners appear in all periods as part of the regular milieu, not usually either diminished or stereotyped. There is evidence that from an early date carpenters were fairly closely involved with the popular song market as consumers, something one would expect from tradesmen known as readers of popular texts (Porter 1992: 32–36). This is seen from the way they often appear in roles, usually minor, in the broadsides. In a Bath and London broadside of about 1850, "The Carpenter, or, The Danger of Evil Company," the hero comes under the influence of a drunken cooper, whose particular depravity seems to be his singing:

> This Man [the Cooper] could tell a merry tale,
>     And sing a merry song;
> And those who heard him sing or talk,
>     Ne'er thought the ev'ning long.
>
> But vain and vicious was the song,
>     And wicked was the tale;
> And every pause he always fill'd,
>     With cider, gin, or ale. (Carnell 1979: 100, verses 14–15)

The gin-filled pauses are a vivid detail. However, the carpenter resists the cooper and repents, just in time. In another broadside, "The Sale of a Wife," which is exactly contemporary, he is a drunkard pure and simple ("too fond of his beer" [line 6]), who sells his wife for ten shillings (Shields 1981: 139).

Few of the song sheets go beyond such broad strokes in depicting carpenters, and this is particularly true when it comes to the tools of their trade, a reliable signifier of occupation. These are not merely emblems but marks of identity: In the opening scene of Shakespeare's *Julius Caesar* (1599), the absence of a visible leather apron and ruler provokes confusion and irritation in those the carpenter is speaking to (*Julius Caesar*: lines 5–7). Songs are inconsistent in using these signifers. Particularly in sexual matters, carpenters are expected to use the full range of their tools. The joiner wins "The London Lady" in the face of competition from men of six other occupations by boasting,

> I have (quoth he) an Augar sharp,
>     if you'll find Board, I'll Bore it,
> I'll drive a Nale that will not fail,
>     [even] tho' there's been none before it. (Day 1987, 3:41, verse 9)

On the other hand, the joiner who helps the weaver in "Bury New Loom" makes active use of his "level and rule" in his richly metaphorical encounter with her (Harker 1980: 199).

The fact that both these cases involve a joiner may give the misleading impression that a distinction is being made, but significantly the two occupations are rarely differentiated in songs (as today in the United States). A joiner works mainly at a bench in the shop, making windows, doors, picture rails, and skirting boards. A carpenter works (often outside) on frames, joints, floors, and roofs. In *A Midsummer Night's Dream* (ca. 1595), Peter Quince is a carpenter and Snug a joiner, but only one seventeenth-century broadside known to me makes the distinction (Day 1987, 3:295). In Scots the term "joiner" is still used for both. The use of joiner or "joyner" predominates over "carpenter" in the early broadsides by a ratio of about two to one.

There are no persistent traits of character, although carpenters are often represented with happy dispositions. Rudolf Steiner wrote that "someone who knows how to make a table will always be happy," and this was evidently the case in the seventeenth-century broadside featuring "Jolly Ralph the Joiner" (Day 1987, 3:176). In Ireland, too, the stereotype persists, as in the opening lines of Tommy Makem's "Black Velvet Band":

> It was in the town of Tralee
> To the carpenter's trade I was bound;
> Many an hour's sweet happiness
> I had in that neat little town.[6]

Although Voltaire maintains in *Candide* (1759) that a carpenter's job is incompatible with honesty (Applebaum 1992: 383), there is little evidence that in England they were considered dishonest as a group. It is true that several songs like the well-known "Hard, Hard Times," sung on both sides of the Atlantic, associate them with poor workmanship:

> Then here comes the carpenter, he will build you a house:
> He will build it so snug that you'll scarce see a mouse.
> There'll be leaks in the roof, there'll be holes in the floor,
> The chimney will smoke, and it's open the door.
> [Refrain]And it's hard, hard times. (Fowke 1981: 53)

However, I have only found this verse in Newfoundland sets. In a song entitled "A Chapter of Cheats or The Roguery of Every Trade," it is said that "the carpenter will hammer in your table broken nails (Palmer 1974: 180), but this occurs in a list of more than thirty occupations, including bonnet makers and potato merchants, hardly trades that are a byword for sharp practice. Once again, the complaint seems to be directed at an individual rather than a group.

A carpenter's work was clearly thought to give a person a distinctive identity: In the great majority of cases (the main exception being "James Harris [The Dæmon Lover]," Child 273), their trade replaces their name. This is the case in the only strongly negative portrait, "The Cruel Ship's Carpenter": In Henry Burstow's 1893 version, for example, the central figure is only identified as "William," which is of course the generic name for a sailor (Broadwood 1902: 172). "The Cruel Ship's Carpenter" is often called "Pretty Polly" in the United States and is one of the most popular songs on both sides of the Atlantic to derive from an English broadside. Hugh Shields has a memorable account of a performance by Sarah Makem: "Sarah's singing…lasted 2 mins. 45 secs., during which she enters her house, boils the kettle, makes tea, lays the table, pours the tea for her husband and herself, drinks a mouthful and pronounces either the tea, or the ballad, or the confluence of circumstances 'Good!'" (Shields 1993: 176). "The Cruel Ship's Carpenter" apparently derives from a mid-eighteenth-century broadside, "The Gosport Tragedy," and as its subtitle, "The Perjured Ship-Carpenter," suggests, the carpenter is not only cruel but incapable of keeping his word. No other English songs or broadsides seem to make this association, but there is a German broadside version (ca. 1850) of the folktale of a returning son who is murdered by his parents where the father is a joiner (Cheesman 1989–90: 60–91; 1994: 92–95. The tale appears on English broadsides as "The Liverpool Tragedy").

Since "The Cruel Ship's Carpenter" is a 'Jonah,' an evildoer whose presence prevents a ship from sailing, it is tempting to link it with the known association of builders with magic and ritual. Henry Burstow's song is set in Worcester, where the carpenter promises to marry his sweetheart and introduce her to his friends before joining the king's navy. Instead, he murders her concealing the body, but the murder is revealed when the ship he is to sail on refuses to move. The ship's carpenter solemnly swears that he has not murdered anyone, at which point,

> As he was turning from the captain with speed
> He met his Polly, which made his heart bleed;
> She stript him and tore him, she tore him in three,
> Because he had murdered her baby and she. (Broadwood 1902: 173)

This must be one of the rare cases where the number of strips a revenant tears her lover into is determined by the rhyme. It is a reminder that the carpenter is by no means in control of the situation: The magic is not his, and this is true of the only other supernatural ballad to feature a carpenter, "The Dæmon Lover" (Child 243). In this ballad, enormously popular on both sides of the Atlantic, a seaman returning to his lover after many years entices her away from her husband, a ship's carpenter, with fatal results. The husband is a "homely" minor character, as Kittredge calls him, yet he seems to dominate the moral action in several ways (Sargent and Kittredge [1904] 1932: 543). It is his suicide that closes the earliest known version, the seventeenth-century "Warning for Married Women" (Day 1987, 4: 101), and as the status of the troth plighted with the seaman becomes more marginal, the carpenter's role expands. In the Appalachians and elsewhere, where ship's carpenters were not a common sight, the title "The House Carpenter" replaced "The Dæmon Lover" and has remained perhaps the most common name for the song (with a change of emphasis: As Atkinson points out, in America "the woman plainly belongs with her carpenter husband and not at all with the former lover" [1989: 605]).

Despite this enhanced role, others are still speaking for the carpenter. Unlike the jolly mood that pervades other broadsides, it is for his "distress," the predicament of what Harker calls a "respectable and timid artisan" (1992: 333), that the carpenter is known. In short he is less what his wife calls him in "A Warning for Married Women," "a carpenter of great fame" (verse 21), than a cheated husband, as much a cuckold as the superstitious carpenter of "The Miller's Tale," described by Chaucer as a "riche gnof [lout]" (Robinson 1957: 48, line 3188). "Riche" is the key word here: Artisans like the carpenter were ranked well above seamen in 1695 by Gregory King and earned about twice as much (Harker

1992: 314), so there is an element of class revenge in the way James Harris (or his dæmon) manipulates the well-born Jane Reynolds and displaces his rival.

*Speaking for Oneself*

Between 1817 and 1820, the London carpenter and builder Charles Newnham, who used to attend popular musical plays and had firsthand experience of the body snatchers, wrote an account of his life and work (Burnett 1974: 288–89). However, this is an almost unique example of a personal narrative by a carpenter which has survived. This applies most strikingly in the field of occupational song, where, as we have seen, only a handful feature carpenters. There are a number of possible reasons for this. Paradoxically, ventriloquism silences people by giving others their voice (Hansson 1998: 47). Songs of sexual preference can usually be assumed as reliable a sign that a song originated inside an occupation as today's bumper stickers which read, "Carpenters could use a few screws." Thus, "The Sandgate Girl" from Newcastle, England, a city where the carpenters had a tradition of singing, tries unsuccessfully to reject a keelman, "an ugly body, a bubbly body, / An ill-far'd ugly loon," in favor of a joiner (Lloyd 1978: 111, lines 29–30; Thompson 1971: 459; "The Sandgate Girl" was first printed by John Bell in 1812). At least until the nineteenth century, similar songs were sung by miners and navvies in the North-east and changed if they were adopted by members of other occupations (Porter 1992: 79–80)

Apart from a ribald student song sung in Michigan in 1956,[7] I have found no other examples in English of carpenters being set above others. There is also a Gaelic waulking song from Bannal where a woman extols the virtues of Calum's son, a carpenter who works with oak and a joiner with his saw, who can lay a floor so evenly:

'S e mo leannan gille Caluim  
Cairpentir an daraich thu.  
    Hé mo leannan, ho mo leannan...

[My love is Malcolm's lad  
You're a carpenter of oak!

'S e mo leannan saor an t-sàbhaibh  
Leigeadh lobht an làr gu dlùth.

My love is the sawing joiner  
Who can lay a loft floor tightly  
                    (well).

'S e mo leannan am fear dualach  
Thogaibh fonn anns an taigh chiùil.

My love is the curly haired one  
Who can raise a tune in the session  
       (literally "music house")].[8]

Eventually, though, he deserts her. Songs like these, which equate sexual desirability with the universal sense among skilled workers of the uniqueness and attractiveness of their own craft, are clearly based on an inner understanding of the carpenter's work. At the same time, such songs have a complexity of their own. The perspective throughout is a woman's, and by avoiding too much circumstantial detail, the songs manage to speak simultaneously on an individual and group level. As in most occupational songs, love and labor are fused.

The reference to the musical skill of Calum's son in the waulking song is an important indicator of the link between working with wood and making music. There are many accounts of individual carpenters singing (for an example from Arizona, see Logsdon 1989: 224). Byron left one highly circumstantial account from Venice at the beginning of the nineteenth century:

> On the 7th of last January, the author of Childe Harold, and another
> Englishman, the writer of this notice, rowed to the Lido with two
> singers, one of whom was a carpenter, and the other a gondolier.
> The former placed himself at the prow, the latter at the stern of the
> boat. A little after leaving the quay of the Piazzetta, they began to
> sing, and continued their exercise until we arrived at the island.
> They gave us, amongst other essays, the death of Clorinda, and the
> palace of Armida; and did not sing the Venetian but the Tuscan
> verses. The carpenter, however, who was the cleverer of the two,
> and was frequently obliged to prompt his companion, told us that
> he could translate the original. He added, that he could sing almost
> three hundred stanzas, but had not spirits (*morbin* was the word he
> used) to learn any more, or to sing what he already knew: a man
> must have idle time on his hands to acquire, or to repeat, and, said
> the poor fellow, "look at my clothes and at me; I am starving." This
> speech was more affecting than his performance, which habit alone
> can make attractive. The recitative was shrill, screaming, and
> monotonous; and the gondolier behind assisted his voice by
> holding his hand to one side of his mouth. The carpenter used a
> quiet action, which he evidently endeavoured to restrain; but was
> too much interested in his subject altogether to repress. From these
> men we learnt that singing is not confined to the gondoliers.
>
> (Byron 1818: canto iv, note)

However, it must be conceded that examples from England are very sparse. Literary evidence can never be ignored, although, for example, the fact that in *A Midsummer Night's Dream* Bottom the weaver says he will ask the carpenter Peter Quince to write a ballad for him called "Bottom's Dream" can hardly be regarded as conclusive evidence of singing (4. 1. 213–14).

During the period when songs were being collected from tradition bearers, collectors indisputably gave precedence to the songs of individuals over communal ones like anthems, work songs, or the songs of organized labor. This may be why no strike songs of carpenters survive in the way that the struggles of the *gesellen* (postapprenticeship carpenters) against the masters in Hamburg in the 1790s were supported by songs.[9] There is one piece of evidence, in the form of a ban, that points to carpenters in the north of England having sung together: In Newcastle in 1812, the Philanthropic Society of House-Carpenters and Joiners prohibited "disloyal sentiments" and "political songs" (Thompson 1971: 459). We may infer from this that these house carpenters sang political songs (otherwise there would be no reason for a ban). Such negative evidence suggests the way practices can be discovered from gaps in the record.

There are isolated indications of the role of song in carpenters' lives. Perhaps the greatest English traditional singer of recent years, Walter Pardon, was apprenticed at fourteen to a carpenter and worked at the trade, including his time in the army, all his life (Pardon 1977: sleeve notes). As we have seen, the novel *Adam Bede* opens with the carpenter singing, and he can be relied on to sing "Over the hills and far away" (chap. 23), but singing is not part of his social being.

None of these cases, drawn from a period of more than four centuries, suggest that carpenters sang occupational songs: I have found no songs in Walter Pardon's repertoire, for example, that deal with his work, either realistically or metaphorically. Songs by others that do deal with the work of carpenters have very little circumstantial detail. In particular technical terms, which are of course numerous in the field of woodworking, are almost entirely absent. They are a good indicator of insider songs: As Leigh Hunt remarked of the carpenter in his pastiche of Chaucer,

> termés of one craft he knew,
> Which, save of carpenters, are known of few.
> 
> (Hunt 1923: 127; see also Porter 1992: 76)

In view of the evident status of carpenters and joiners among skilled craftsmen from medieval times, and the great power and prestige of the construction unions at the height of the industrial revolution, the lack of insider songs remains puzzling. This paper has itself, of course, been an act of "speaking for," but it is above all a study of the importance of looking at lacunae in our song record. Feminist and gay studies in particular have emphasized the significance of the gaps and silences in our tradition. The known song is only the visible part of a vast network, and we must return to the countless individual narratives that make up the polyphonic discourse of the carpenters' own culture.

## Notes

1. I am grateful to Barbara Boock of the Deutsche Volksliedarchiv in Freiburg for this information.
2. Thompson 1971: 285, 260, 272, 263, 291, 346, 277, respectively. First fixers build the framework of a house, while second fixers add the details that will be visible in the finished building. Shop fitters are responsible for the work traditionally done by joiners. I am grateful to Kane Watson for this information.
3. "Chips," or today "chippie," have long been sobriquets / monikers of the carpenter. The *Oxford English Dictionary* cites 1785 for "chips" and 1913 for "chippie."
4. Ruskin 1874: 1, appendix 38; the passage was written more than twenty years earlier.
5. "He might by that means as well anoint him a Ioyner, as a Gentleman" (Briggs 1985: 113).
6. Sung by Tommy Makem at the thirtieth Cambridge Folk Festival, July 1994.
7. I wish I was a pretty little girl and I had lots of money.
   I would marry a carpenter's son; he'd be as good as any.
   He would pound and I would pump and we would pump together.
   Oh, what fun we would have, pumping one another (Cray 1992: 368).
8. Bannal, *Waulking Songs* (Greentrax CDTRAX 099, 1996: track 11a). I am indebted for this reference to T. A. McKean, who also made the translation.
9. I am grateful to Barbara Boock of the Deutsche Volksliedarchiv in Freiburg for this information.

## References

Aarne, Antti. 1961. *The Types of the Folktale: A Classification and Bibliography*. Translated and enlarged by Stith Thompson. 2d rev. ed. FF Communications, vol. 75, no. 184. Helsinki: Suomalainen Tiedeakatemia / Academia Scientarum Fennica.

Applebaum, Herbert. 1992. *The Concept of Work: Ancient, Medieval and Modern*. Albany, N.Y.: State University of New York Press.

Atkinson, David. 1989. "Marriage and Retribution in 'James Harris (The Dæmon Lover)'." *Folk Music Journal* 5, no. 5: 592–607.

Bailey, Jocelyn. 1989. *The Village Wheelwright and Carpenter*. Aylesbury, England: Shire Publications.

Bishop, Julia C. 1998. "'Dr. Carpenter from the Harvard College in America': An Introduction to James Madison Carpenter and his Collection." *Folk Music Journal* 7, no. 4: 402–20.

Briggs, Asa. 1985. *Social History of England*. Harmondsworth: Penguin.

Broadwood, Lucy E. 1902. *Journal of the Folk-Song Society* 4, vol. 1: 139–82.

Burnett, John, ed. 1974. *Useful Toil. Autobiographies of Working People from the 1820s to the 1920s.* London: Allen Lane.

Byron, Lord (George Gordon). 1818. Notes to *Childe Harolde's Pilgrimage. Canto the Fourth.* London: Murray.

Carnell, Peter W. 1979. *Ballads in the Charles Harding Firth Collection of the Unversity of Sheffield: A Descriptive Catalogue with Indexes.* Sheffield: Centre for Cultural Tradition and Language.

Cheesman, Tom. 1989–90. "The Return of the Transformed Son: A Popular Ballad Complex and Cultural History, Germany 1500–1900." *Oxford German Studies* 18, no. 19: 60–91.

————. 1994. *The Shocking Ballad Picture Show: German Popular Literature and Cultural History.* Oxford: Berg.

Cole, G. D. H., and Raymond Postgate. 1981. *The Common People 1746–1946.* London: Methuen.

Constantine, Mary-Ann. 1999. *Ballads in Wales* [Baledi yng Nghymru]. London: FLS Books.

Cray, Ed. 1992. *The Erotic Muse: American Bawdy Songs.* Urbana and Chicago: University of Chicago Press.

Day, W. G., ed. 1987. *The Pepys Ballads.* 5 vols. Cambridge: Derek Brewer.

D'Urfey, Thomas. 1719–20. *Songs Compleat, Pleasant and Divertive.* 6 vols. London: J. Tonson.

[Fielding, Sarah] By a Lady. 1744–53. *The Adventures of David Simple.* 2d. ed, rev. and corr., with a preface by Henry Fielding. London: A. Millar.

Fowke, Edith, ed. 1981. *Penguin Book of Canadian Folk Songs.* Harmondsworth: Penguin.

Grimes, Dorothy A. 1991. *Like Dew before the Sun: Life and Language in Northamptonshire.* Privately published.

Hansson, Heidi. 1998. *Romance Revived: Postmodern Romances and the Tradition.* Uppsala: Swedish Science Press.

Harker, Dave. 1980. *One for the Money: Politics and Popular Song.* London: Hutchinson.

————. 1992. "A Warning." *Folk Music Journal* 6, no. 3: 229–338.

Holloway, J., and J. Black, eds. 1975–77. *Later English Broadside Ballads.* 2 vols. London: Routledge and Kegan Paul.

Hunt, James Leigh. 1923. *Poetical Works,* edited by H.S. Milford. London: Oxford University Press.

Lloyd, A. L. 1978. *Come All Ye Bold Miners: Ballads and Songs of the Coalfields.* 2d ed. London: Lawrence and Wishart.

Logsdon, Guy. 1989. *"The Whorehouse Bells Were Ringing" and other Songs Cowboys Sing.* Urbana and Chicago: University of Illinois Press.

Morton, A. L. 1974. *A People's History of England.* London: Lawrence and Wishart.

Opie, I., and P. Opie, eds. 1951. *Oxford Dictionary of Nursery Rhymes.* Oxford: Oxford University Press.

Palmer, R., ed. 1974. *A Touch on the Times.* Harmondsworth: Penguin.

Porter, Gerald. 1991. *Singing the Changes: Variation in Four Traditional Ballads.* Umeå Papers in English. Umeå, Sweden: University of Umeå.

———— . 1992. *The English Occupational Song.* Umeå: University of Umeå.

Robinson, F. N., ed. 1957. *The Works of Geoffrey Chaucer.* 2d ed. London: Oxford University Press.

Ruskin, John. 1874. *The Stones of Venice.* London: Smith, Elder.

Sargent, H. C., and G. L. Kittredge. [1904] 1932. *English and Scottish Popular Ballads.* Reprint. Boston: Houghton Mifflin. Page references are to reprint edition.

Sharp, Cecil. 1907. *English Folk Song: Some Conclusions*. London: Simpkin.
Shields, Hugh. 1981. *Shamrock, Rose and Thistle*. Belfast: Blackstaff Press.
————. 1993. *Narrative Singing in Ireland: Lays, Ballads, Come-All-Yes and Other Songs*. Dublin: Irish Academic Press.
Thompson, E. P. 1971. *The Making of the English Working Class*. Harmondsworth: Penguin.
Wilson, F. P., ed. 1992. *Oxford Dictionary of English Proverbs*. 3rd ed. Oxford: Clarendon Press.

## *Recordings*

Bannal. 1996. *Waulking Songs*. Greentrax CDTRAX 099. Compact disk.
Pardon, Walter. 1977. *Our Side of the Baulk*. Leader Records LED 2111. Recording.
Staverton Bridge. 1975. *Staverton Bridge*. Saydisc SDL 266. Recording.

# The Servant Problem in Child Ballads

## Roger deV. Renwick

The central characters in most Child ballads are members of the gentry, often the nobility, and are even, in some cases, royalty. Because they own property, enjoy substantial income, possess unlimited leisure time, and wield significant power over others, they tend to live interesting lives—that is to say, they enjoy experiences which are the stuff of *story* and *drama,* the ballad genre's raisons d'être. Members of the employee class, on the other hand—mostly household servants of one kind or another—are seldom ballad heroes and heroines, probably because in real life such working-class folk were too busy meeting basic needs for survival to enjoy the sorts of intensified, elevated, poignant human experiences that ballads customarily describe.

While seldom ballad protagonists or antagonists, servants are quite common in supporting roles. More often than not, however, these roles are bland, homogenized, featureless work functions, like porter, kitchen helper, nurse, armed retainer, and (especially) pageboy. Moreover, the depictions of what little motivation and personality such servants do display not only are stereotypical but also appear extremely unfavorable. For example, many Child ballad servants are *not able to think for themselves.* Child Maurice's pageboy (Child 83E) can be accused of illustrating this character trait: He delivers a love letter to the object of his master's intended seduction but insists on putting it into the lady's hand in her husband's presence, even though she suggests pointedly that, surely, the letter is intended for someone else? But the messenger is completely blind to the hint. Predictably, the husband becomes suspicious, assumes an adulterous liaison, meets Child Maurice in his wife's place, and beheads his supposed rival. Similarly robbed of a chance to indulge his passion by servant thickheadedness is the protagonist of "The Broomfield Hill" (Child 43D–F), who sleeps through a visit to his love nest by the object of his desire, Fair Marjory, not because she cleverly drugged or bespelled him (as in Scandinavian cognates), but because it apparently did not occur to his servants to wake him up.

Then there are servants who *can't seem to do the job they are paid to do.* This character trait is most often implied in a well-known ballad commonplace, an employer's plaintive query, "Why can't I find any of my well-paid menials when I need one?" For example, the king in "Hind Etin" is moved to ask this rhetorical question when he discovers that his men have allowed a potential enemy into his domain: "O where are all my rangers bold / That I pay meat and fee, / To search the forest far and wide, / And bring Akin to me?" (Child 41A). A similar cry of frustration at servant inaction comes from the king in Child 114H after hearing that Johnnie Cock may be mortally wounded and dying untended in the forest. Perhaps most plaintive of all is the father's cry in "Lady Diamond" (Child 269A) after his servants have failed to stop him from murdering his daughter's kitchen-boy paramour: "O where is all my merry, merry men, / That I pay meat and wage, / That they could not withold my cruel hand, / When I was mad with rage?" These servants were evidently able neither to do the job they were paid to do nor think for themselves.

Other thoroughly unsatisfactory servants in Child ballads *do not keep their minds on their work*. Instead, they are riveted by events taking place in the household and, to make matters worse, spend far too much time gossiping about them. Such random servant gossip can bring terrible grief to others. For instance, the rumor that Mary Hamilton (Child 173) has been impregnated by the queen's husband begins in the kitchen before spreading throughout the court, resulting eventually in Mary's execution for infanticide. Similar below-stairs gossip results in the parents of Johnny Scot's pregnant love imprisoning their own daughter (Child 99C, K). A more invidious version of this type is composed of servants who not only don't keep their minds on their work but go even further and actively *mind the business of their betters*. These more-motivated, goal-directed servants can make all kinds of mischief for social superiors. For example, in "Lady Elspat" (Child 247), a page, overhearing sweet words exchanged between his master's sister and her lover, tattles to the mistress of the household, who has the lover brought before a judge. Another page, this time in "Little Musgrave" (Child 81), goes to great lengths to report his mistress's infidelity to her husband, who in a fury slays both wife and lover. An old-woman servant in "Auld Matrons" (Child 249) for no apparent reason other than busybodiness runs off to tell the sheriff that his daughter is entertaining a lover, thus putting the hero in great danger when the sheriff's men attack the house in force.

Then there are Child-ballad servants who *forget their place*. This character trait is most overtly exhibited in servant impertinence. For instance, the squire's boy in one version of "The Broomfield Hill" (Child 43F) so forgets his place as to assume moral superiority over his betters: When asked why he did not awaken his master so he could seduce a visiting maiden, the page has the cheek to reply that "in the night ye should have slept, master, / And kept awake in the day; / Had you not been sleeping when hither she came, / Then a maid she had not gone away." In Child 286A, Sir Walter Rawleigh's ship boy also has the temerity to take the moral high ground after his master refuses to carry out an earlier offer to reward the boy with his daughter's hand for sinking an enemy ship: "Then fare you well, you cozening lord," the ship boy declaims, "seeing you are not as good as your word."

Servants who forget their place normally do so temporarily or in a way that's circumscribed, so their insolence doesn't have wider, more-debilitating, or permanent effects on their employers' lives. A more-serious kind of forgetting-one's-place *does* have major consequences and is manifested in servants who *get above their station*—that is to say, try to change the ballad world's existing social structure. Typical members of this category are servants who presume to enter into love relationships with sons or daughters of the household. Examples are legion, particularly of male servants forming liaisons with their employers' daughters, as in "The Kitchie-Boy" (Child 252) and "Willie and Earl Richard's Daughter" (Child 102). These liaisons almost inevitably produce tragic results; only occasionally, when the servant proves to be truly exceptional, is the match successful, as in "Willie o Winsbury" (Child 100) and "Richie Story" (Child 232F, G), and then only after the lovers have endured significant ordeal. Perhaps the worst offenders in this category, however, are those who try to get so far above their station that they not only ape but actually impersonate their masters, as in "The Lord of Lorn and the False Steward" (Child 271). Glasgerion's servant in Child 67 may be the most prominent example of all: He impersonates his master to keep a midnight tryst with a noblewoman Glasgerion has sweet-talked into an affair.

Servants who get above themselves are just one step away from the very worst of their kind, the ones who *can't be trusted when their employers' backs are turned*. These servants go further than usurping a master's place; they more than metaphorically bite the hand that feeds them by betraying a master to his enemies—even, in some instances, by killing him themselves. Nurses are especially guilty of this character trait, as may be seen in "Sir James the Rose" (Child 213), "The Laird of Wariston" (Child 194), and "Lamkin" (Child 93), where a nurse colludes in the murders both of her mistress and the infant supposedly in her care. Servants who go so far as to slay their employers personally may be exemplified by Earl Douglas's pageboy in "The Battle of Otterburn" (Child 161B), who, like his brethren in other ballads, bears a message to his master but, unlike them, becomes so infuriated with the earl's formulaic if-your-message-be-true-I'll-reward-you-but-if-it-be-false-I'll-punish-you response that he stabs him to death.

This highly unfavorable view Child ballads apparently take of servants puzzles the folklorist. After all, a basic tenet of our discipline is that folklore is related in a fairly direct, unmediated, practical way to the social, cultural, and empirical contexts of its quotidian performance. If, as I think has generally been assumed, the Child ballad was principally a working-class cultural possession, we are moved to wonder why working people loved to sing and hear songs that presented in such a bad light characters with whom they would presumably have identified? Why, for example, would ballad collector William Allingham's contributor, "a nurse in the family of a relative in Ireland," possess in her repertoire a version of Child 93, "Lamkin," in which a nurse actively helps the villainous mason murder the baby in her care (Child 1882–98, 2: 339; Shields 1974). After all, it's not as if working-class singers "didn't know any better" (as a master or mistress might have said), since the "perfect servant" *is* represented in the Child ballad repertoire, though of course not nearly as frequently as his or her imperfect cousin. For example, the pageboy in "Lady Maisry" (Child 65A) unequivocally *does the job he's paid to do*: Ignoring the possible life-threatening harm he might suffer at the hands of his mistress's brother, he delivers Maisry's letter to her English lover, who is deeply hated by her family. In Child 244C, James Hatley resists any temptation to *get above his station*; when offered a reward of his own land and a band of retainers by the king, Hatley, knowing his place, refuses: "I thank ye, king, and I thank ye, queen, / I thank ye a', nobilitie, / But a prince's page I was a' my life, / And a prince's page I yet will be." The contributor who recited this version for folklorist William Motherwell (a Mrs. Drain of Kilmarnock) was obviously familiar with what makes a "good" ballad servant and just as obviously approved of the favorable portrayal, and there is no reason for us to think that Mrs. Drain's fellow working-class singers didn't share the same knowledge and attitude. Why, then, did they prefer to sing about "bad" servants? This apparent paradox (which in its most generalized form is a lack of logical fit between text and context) presents the ballad analyst with as big a "servant problem" as servant behavior itself poses for ballad masters and mistresses.

What are some possible answers to *this* type of servant problem? I can think of at least eight. Hypothesis One is that perhaps in the pre-modern-day period, when most of the texts in *The English and Scottish Popular Ballads* were gathered, the genre was principally a middle-class rather than working-class art form and hence indeed reflected its context by reproducing the sentiment probably common to employers of every era that "you just can't get good help anymore" (Marshall 1949: 16). Hypothesis Two: Perhaps the ballad *was* a working-class phenomenon but most common among singers and audiences who were not themselves "in service." There is evidence that servants, especially those who worked indoors, were generally disliked by the general community. To outsiders their jobs didn't seem physically demanding, and they spoke, looked, and acted in a more-genteel way than members of the nonservant working class. The unfavorable ballad representation, therefore, may reflect nondomestic working-class hostility toward domestic workers (see Maza 1983: 122–31).

Like the first two, Hypothesis Three depends chiefly on historical facts: Perhaps the singers from whom the texts in *The English and Scottish Popular Ballads* were gathered considered their songs to be archaic, by definition *not* reflective of the present but of the past; hence, they were not bothered by the apparent lack of contemporary "relevance." Indeed, ballad depiction of servants does seem in general to reflect the cultural realities of pre-eighteenth-century service, which, still exhibiting a medieval character, was built on the same patriarchal models that governed life in general. The medieval familial unit was not the nuclear or "affectionate" family of the modern era but the whole *household*, to which belonged both kin and nonkin; the servants were considered an intimate part of this household, and the family head was expected to act in loco parentis to them all, overseeing their moral, spiritual, intellectual, and physical well-being (Marshall 1949: 4–7; see Fairchilds 1984: 4–6). In fact, many servants were actual blood relatives of the manorial lord and/or lady, as reflected in "Child Maurice," "Prince Robert," and "The Earl of Errol" (Child 83D, 87C, 231E). Ballad portrayal of servants as generally immature, unreliable, lazy, impertinent, ungrateful, naturalistic, precultural creatures—often actual children and always *like* children—is consistent with this conception (see Robbins 1986: 150–52; Hecht 1980: 3–4; Goldberg 1992: 5). The bands of armed retainers appearing in several Child ballads, and to a lesser extent the many pageboys, may denote this older servant world, while the several anthropomorphized animal servants may represent the same idea metaphorically.

The next three hypotheses are less dependent on historical facts than on the psychology of ballad singers. Hypothesis Four: Perhaps singers identified not with such external attributes of ballad characters as their professions and social class but with their feelings of despair and delight, their sheer good fortune in simply having the opportunity to enjoy emotionally charged experiences redolent with tragedy and romance. In other words, perhaps ballad singers and audiences empathized with heroes and heroines, whatever their social identities (though if that were the case, then ballads would have been a form of escapism for servants and hence closer to popular culture than folklore). Another primarily psychological (and particularly Freudian) explanation is Hypothesis Five: While Child ballads usually depict a late-medieval/early modern world, the texts in *The English and Scottish Popular Ballads* come mostly from eighteenth- and early nineteenth-century sources. Perhaps these (post) Enlightenment-era bearers of ballad tradition were subconsciously dissociating themselves from their pre-eighteenth-century ancestors-*cum*-surrogate parents (perennial objects of youth hostility and antagonism) who populated the ballads' fictional landscape by embracing employers' typically deprecating views of them.

Still primarily a psychological explanation is Hypothesis Six: Real indoor servants in upper-class households were, when beginning their new lives as servants, displaced from their familiar contexts of working-class cottage culture and resituated in contexts of genteel manorial or, later, country-house culture. As an integral part of their employment, they were trained to dissociate themselves from the "commonness" of their former background and enculturated into upper-class manners, tastes, values, and worldview (see Fairchilds 1984: 101–2). But their new cultural personae had no meaningful arenas for action: Their more refined speech, clothes, deportment, or even sensibilities brought servants no significant rewards or privileges, no change in identity or circumstance. They were still, in all meaningful ways, unempowered and unprivileged. The ballad working folk they sang and heard about, however, did enjoy certain powers and privileges that *resembled* those of the leisure-class elite but were embodied in servant actions—idling, gossiping, dressing up, exercising personal power apparently on whim. Thus, the servants in "The Rantin' Laddie" who forget their place are reproducing their employers' treatment of the Earl of Aboyne's pregnant-but-unmarried love: "For her father he will not her know, / And her mother she does slight her, / And a' her friends hae lightlied her, / And their servants they neglect her" (240A). In short, to working-class singers and listeners, ballad servants may have been fantasy projections of themselves, and ballad singing and listening would have functioned psychologically as a compensatory mechanism.

Hypothesis Seven, which weds psychology to a bit of deconstruction, can be put this way: Perhaps simply singing and hearing about employers' discomfiture at servants' hands allowed working-class bearers of tradition not only to imagine but even voice discontent with their circumstances, especially the typical day-to-day indignities servants customarily suffered. Real servants had few sanctioned means of expressing grievance, for the code of conduct to which they were expected to conform mandated their silence; any complaints or contrary opinions were typically deemed examples of "talking back" or "insolence," and servants had to know how to "hold their tongues" (see Hill 1996: 1; Marshall 1949: 15). Household servants in the premodern era were thus habitually denied any voice of their own: They were urged to identify their own interests fully with those of their employers and bend to their will (Gerard 1994: 9). Singing was probably one of the few opportunities for working people to express a personal voice publicly, safely couched in that superficially innocuous form we call the "ballad of tradition." In short, ballad singing in the preindustrial British Isles may have been an act of resistance against conditions considered unjust, humiliating, and dehumanizing (see Gerard 1994: 264–68).

While this "resistance hypothesis" is attractive, it does not necessarily require us to believe that real working-class ballad singers and hearers identified with fictional servants, only that they identified with the conditions of inequity, frustration, and powerlessness service entailed. Hypothesis Eight proposes that bearers of tradition identified with *both* the conditions of ballad service *and* the imaginary characters who are ballad servants. It goes this way: perhaps the working-class singers and listeners to whom Child ballads were vital and meaningful everyday artifacts understood the motives and rationales of the servants they sang about in different ways from the ones I have already outlined. For example, from the servant point of view, Child Maurice's pageboy (Child 83) and the "merry men" serving Lady Diamond's father (Child 269), rather than not being able to think for themselves, may have been simply respecting the common employer stricture to *follow orders exactly*, while the seemingly incompetent page in "The Broomfield Hill" (Child 43) was repeating to his master that worthy's own dictum about *paying attention, keeping alert, and not sleeping on the job*. Similarly, the servants who cannot seem to do the job they are paid to do are not visible and readily available every minute one may unexpectedly need their services because they are *busy with their duties*, not loitering and enabling the devil to find work for their idle hands. As for the gossiping servants who do not keep their minds on their work, and even the interfering tattlers who mind the business of their betters, what else are they doing but pursuing the very goal of *honesty and truthfulness* that their employers repeatedly emphasize as an important virtue? After all, Lady Barnard *was* a married woman and did in fact take the initiative in seducing Little Musgrave, thus breaking her vows of fidelity to her husband (Child 81). Indeed, it can be fairly said that the servants whose gossip revealed to parents that their unmarried daughter was carrying Johnie Scot's baby were instrumental in bringing the lovers together in holy matrimony, both allowing true love to triumph and saving a child from the stigma of bastardy. The lovers themselves seemed overcome by inertia, incapable of doing anything purposeful about their situation (Child 99). Servants who forget their place and presume to offer their masters some homily like "always keep your word" are similarly acting under a moral imperative, one that was probably inculcated in them by the very employer now feeling victimized by its application, or by the sermons they were urged to take to heart (and heard at the very Sunday church services which employers insisted their servants faithfully attend).

From the masters' and mistresses' point of view, servants who get above their station are acting out of self-interest and subverting what the employer class considers the natural order of society. But servants may see such events in a different light: They may be actively modeling for their employers what is, in fact, ideal upper-class behavior. This behavior is well illustrated by "Willie o Winsbury" (Child 100) who, when his former employer finally agrees to the match between Willie and his daughter and offers to confer his personal wealth upon his new son-in-law, refuses the gift! Had Willie's motives been materialistic and self-interested he would hardly have spurned the offer of wealth and property and would not have upheld the patriarchal virtue that a husband must provide for his wife. Even those least satisfactory of servants, the ones who cannot be trusted when their employers' backs are turned to the point where they may even kill their lords, are not necessarily acting pathologically but rather, in support of cultural norms, for in every case the masters have transgressed—for example, by refusing to pay a man for his labor ("Lamkin," Child 83), which strikes against the heart of the paternalistic ethos that social obligation should counterpoint personal privilege, or by being a seducer and indiscriminate fornicator (Child 194, "The Laird of Wariston").

In short, every unfavorable servant stereotype can be revoiced to suggest that Child ballad servants are not acting destructively but constructively, appropriating values of the very "dominant discourse" that employers themselves espouse, measuring specific masters and mistresses against those standards, and revealing how unsatisfactory their behaviors actually are. In this paradigm, Child ballad servants are being as resistant as those in Hypothesis Seven but not in the obvious sense of rebelling against or subverting the "natural" order at all. In fact, they are *upholding* the traditional system of service; what they are resisting is their ballad employers' propensity to pervert that system. From this angle, then, the servant problem is not a problem at all but a solution: a solution to the master and mistress problem in Child ballads.

## References

Child, Francis James, ed. 1882–98. *The English and Scottish Popular Ballads.* 5 vols. Reprint, New York: Folklore Press, 1956–57; New York: Dover, 1965. Corrected edition prepared by Mark and Laura Heiman. Northfield, Minn.: Loomis House Press, 2002. Digital edition, with gazetteer, maps and audio CD. New York: ESPB Publishing, 2003.

Fairchilds, Cissie. 1984. *Domestic Enemies: Servants and Their Masters in Old Regime France.* Baltimore: The Johns Hopkins University Press.

Gerard, Jessica. 1994. *Country House Life: Family and Servants, 1815–1914.* Oxford: Blackwell.

Goldberg, P. J. P., ed. 1992. *Woman Is a Worthy Wight: Women in English Society c. 1200–1500.* Wolfeboro Falls, N.H.: Alan Sutton.

Hecht, J. Jean. 1980. *The Domestic Servant in Eighteenth-Century England.* London: Routledge and Kegan Paul, 1956. Reprint, London: Routledge and Kegan Paul.

Hill, Bridget. 1996. *Servants: English Domestics in the Eighteenth Century.* Oxford: Clarendon Press.

Marshall, Dorothy. 1949. *The English Domestic Servant in History.* London: George Philip and Son for the Historical Association.

Maza, Sarah C. 1983. *Servants and Masters in Eighteenth-Century France: The Uses of Loyalty.* Princeton: Princeton University Press.

Robbins, Bruce. 1986. *The Servant's Hand: English Fiction from Below.* New York: Columbia University Press.

Shields, Hugh. 1974. "William Allingham and Folk Song." *Hermathena* 117: 23–36.

# May Day and Mayhem:
## Portraits of a Holiday
## in Eighteenth-Century Dublin Ballads

Cozette Griffin-Kremer

What could be more enthralling for someone involved in calendar studies than finding ballads that appear to recount events occuring during a major holiday— May Day, in this case—and, to add to the pleasure, to hear from the source that they were sung and resung as an integral part of the holiday's celebration? This is exactly what is presented here, if somewhat obscured because the ballads examined are embedded in extensive commentary by the author of a long and detailed article that appeared in the *Dublin University Magazine* in 1843,[1] which describes life in the city some sixty years earlier. In fact, as we will see, we may describe these as "embedded ballads" in more than one way. They provide an instrument for examining the people's past as seen by the author, who is as interested in antique customs, such as riding the boundaries of the city, or the careers of its famous miscreants as in the colorful, perhaps exotic, language of the ballads themselves.

My principal objectives are threefold: one, to share my delight in finding the article in the context of a brief, general background of May Day festivities in Ireland and especially in Dublin; two, to present a pair of analyses of popular events elsewhere during approximately the same period, one concerning May Day in another urban situation, the other devoted to the use (or abuse) of bulls that is a theme common to two of the ballads in the *Dublin University Magazine* account; and three, to suggest some hypotheses about certain aspects of social evolution that may be discernible from the portraits provided by these ballads and their prose matrix.

To begin with, though, a word about the magazine, the author of the article, and several facets of the May Day custom described in the ballads. The *Dublin University Magazine (DUM)* was published monthly from 1833 to 1877, attracting major writers and editors preoccupied with forging a vision of Irishness in the framework of conservative political thought (Hall). The author of the article remained anonymous in the pages of the *DUM*, but his work was later published under his own name, John Edward Walsh, as *Ireland Sixty Years Ago* (1847), as he pursued an interest in Irish history shared by his own family and that of his wife. Walsh, in fact, became an eminent member of the legal profession, serving at one time as attorney general for Ireland and, briefly, as a Member of Parliament for Dublin University. He died in 1869 at the age of fifty-three during a visit to the Continent (Cosgrave). One of the particular dilemmas which seems to have confronted him in the article was reconciling a clear sentiment regarding the singularity, the specialness, of Irish identity with the substantial evidence of older (or not so old) customs that shocked, on the whole, the genteel sensibilities of the literate classes.

## May Day

Although May Day may be associated first and foremost with the atmosphere of a village fête, particular threads of political ideology, and, at times, the parading of military might, it is also among the most venerable of European festive days and, as a popular holiday, has continued to be observed with enthusiasm up to the present day, if less universally than it once was. We have remarkable early evidence of it in Ireland, arguably among the first in a European vernacular, in pithy notes of the late-ninth or early tenth century, written by the learned bishop/ king of Cashel, Cormac mac Cuillennain, in his glossary. There he speaks of May Day under its Irish name, *beltaine*, as one of the quarter days marking the four-part division of the year (Meyer 1912: notes 122, 149). Subsequent sources bear witness to the holiday's regular observance in Ireland, Great Britain, and over much of the European continent right through the twentieth century.

May Day celebrations in Ireland, as elsewhere in the British Isles, may well have had an apparently idyllic floral look, a distinct presence of bucolic bringing-in-of-season songs and hearty family dinners or picturesque community gatherings around a Maypole, but they were just as robustly redolent in wild and sometimes (to our eyes) cruel mayhem of several sorts, from rowdy drinking bouts, including reckless molestation of passersby, to bloody conflicts between groups of people and murderous treatment of animals, all considered fun by most of the participants. The holiday has a complex history and, as regards documentation, lies along a spectrum from benign neglect by a literate class of chroniclers to the butt of especially virulent hate campaigns and attendent oppression. If its basic elements have a tendency to crop up in nearly all accounts exhibiting a limited vocabulary of festival, nonetheless, the holiday's local avatars offer a wealth of diversity in custom, commitment, and ambiance. For our purposes, we will concentrate on a modest number of festive elements promised us by our ballads: song, strife, concern with cattle, death (this interesting subject is but a brief aside), transmission of custom in an urban environment, and commemoration as a significant instrument in the perception and construction of community.

*Song*

Needless to say, songs of the season are a hallmark of May Day festivities in most of the British Isles[2] sources, and their variety is a wonder to behold, from the pithiest of praise for nature to long digressions on the moral fiber of the universe.[3] That they were an integral part of celebrating May Day in Dublin during and before the mid-1800s, we are told by William Wilde, who speaks of them in the same breath as strife between trade communities. He also provides us with the assurance that the two songs we wish to examine, plus another we can afford but a glimpse of, were well known outside the *DUM* article, either by people who read and repeated it or independently. In his discussion of bygone customs, Wilde referred to the events that gave birth to the ballad we shall savor below, specifically to the reciprocal attempts to kidnap May bushes that concentrated all the energies and rivalries of the Dublin trade neighborhoods. It was the custom for the entire population of each neighborhood to congregate around their own bush and the nearby bonfire, as Wilde says, "to sit out the wake of the winter and spring, according to the olden usage" (Danaher 1972: 95–96, citing Wilde 1853: 59–60). Among the delights of the night, the best singers in the crowd offered numbers such as "The Nite before Larry Was Stretched," "Hie for de Sweet Libertie," or the then particularly popular "The Baiting of Lord Altham's Bull," to which we shall shortly return. But it appears that the ballad of "De May Bush" was a special favorite because of its allusions to the season and the locality. The events described must have continued to resonate through the memory of many in the city, and Wilde himself remembered a verse from what he thought was yet another song that corresponds in tone to the *DUM* version.

> Begone, ye cowardly scoundrels,
> Do ye remember de day,
> Dat yes came down to Newmarket,
> And stole de sweet May bush away? (Danaher 1972: 95–96)

We might note as an intriguing aside that one of the ballads mentioned by Wilde—"The Nite before Larry Was Stretched"—is also discussed in the *DUM* article and recounts a highly popular entertainment of the period, a public execution (1843: 664–68). There seems to be no connection between the ballad on Larry's end and May Day in the *DUM* article, although much space is devoted to describing the protagonist and his checkered career. However, we might note in passing that stories of the death of characters of heroic, if not downright mythological, proportions are often associated with the holiday, as with its mirror image on November Day. Wilde's reference to Newmarket here, along with the ballad entitled "Hie for de Sweet Libertie" in the same passage, introduces us to the two neighborhoods whose inhabitants play the central roles in the tale of the May bush conflict.

## Strife

As regards the specific case of Dublin in the late eighteenth century, Wilde cites the adversaries in the famous riots between south and north of the river, the recurrent rivalry between the Liberty Boys (the weavers inhabiting the neighborhood of the Coombe) and the Ormond Boys, the butchers whose home turf was the area of Smithfield Market. We may recall that this pattern of neighborhood and trade rivalry existed on very different scales, from little boys' "wars" to the assembled young manhood of two villages pitted against each other. In reference to the same Dublin events, Wilde adds that there was just as fierce a rivalry within each neighborhood over which street might exhibit the handsomest May bush or finest bonfire (Danaher 1972: 91). If it is easy to "plant" a bush, it can just as easily be "deplanted," and "bush-napping" from one's neighbors was often part and parcel of May Day proceedings elsewhere in Ireland. Witness a typical report referring to south County Monaghan about 1840 that all the neighbors of a locality had to "rise out" to defend their bush. This hinged on the belief that whoever managed to kidnap a bush also stole the coming year's luck from their neighbors (Danaher 1972: 92).

In fact, the May bush is but one manifestation of a portable emblem of prosperity. We have but to cast the briefest glance at Maypole celebrations throughout the British Isles and Europe to see that one significant facet of their existence is their vulnerability to theft and the logically ensuing, sometimes lightly armed, combats or, at the very least, rousing contests that characterize them.[4] The same situation applies to prizes carried off in competitions, games, races and, of course, the result of the many summer-winter battles carried on for so long and with such passion.[5] These events most usually end in general celebration and take place in a comfortable matrix of community approval. Such conflicts are sometimes explicitly said to operate as a microcosm of a macrocosmic battle on May Day, as the case with the Irish hurling matches carried on by the fairies for the prosperity of a whole province, which were paralleled by the fighting at fairs that ended in a kiss and embrace (MacNeill 1982: 204, 408; Jackson 1964–65: 84–88). This perception of conflict as fruitful and essential to the well-being of the communities involved is an evident law in a kind of elementary physics delineating the most important form of suprasocial synergy, the interrelation between human energy and cosmic order.

## Cattle

In two of the *DUM* ballads, bulls are of prime concern. In the May bush ballad, a bull is a weapon in the holiday strife, while the ballad about bullbaiting only mentions that the episode occurred on May Day. Any mention of bovines would perk up the ears of any inquirer into festival practices. People familiar with May Day anxieties about milk production, which is really getting into full swing at this time of year in preindustrial societies, are accustomed to reading about a whole panoply of practices targeting the safety of milk, butter, milch cows, and their progeny. This preoccupation with the animals' health in rural societies usually took the form of protective practices like attaching safeguards to their bodies, shelters, and fields or, as was equally familiar in people, bleeding them to promote vigor.[6] The surprise here is finding that all the attention is concentrated on bulls, and, for them, nothing healthful is going on.

## Death

There is most certainly a helping of human-generated violence in the following pages, but the only mentions of death involve animals, and this is only described in passing in these texts, where it is considered a routine part of the proceedings. Nonetheless, we will recall later that death is a significant factor in the May Day holiday and may have a distinct bearing on ways we can "read" one of our ballads, as well as the ways the subject matter of the two songs may be related to a larger complex of holiday patterns. Suffice it to say at this point that putting animals to death is a commonplace in older May Day celebrations and that the dramatic death of eminent figures, even of whole peoples, looms large in the legendary and mythological narratives in Welsh and Irish literature.

## Transmission and Commemoration

Transmission of holiday customs has been thoroughly documented in rural settings, where it is couched in an often-subtle interplay between age or work-group events, family-centered festivities, or the highly gravitational reaffirmations of identity in small communities. May Day kept villages on their toes for centuries, and there is no indication that enthusiasm for the holiday abated one whit in the atmosphere of larger towns, even a metropolis like London, although many of the customs connected with the immediacy of nature were obviously distanced. Any hypothesis of a genetic relationship between town and country custom often seems both logical and fairly difficult to substantiate, as are more broadly diffusionist theories. We can surely posit that a larger population set into the center and periphery of an urban environment multiplies work specialization and hierarchical differences, which can make negotiating holiday activities more complex. This also means that the role of commemoration as a significant instrument in the perception and construction of community may work at many levels toward a very broad, perhaps inclusive, position but may also stop abruptly at the borders established by class, age, or trade group.

The article in the *Dublin University Magazine* presents the two ballads, or extracts from them, with bull first and bush second. There are several threads common to both, and the first serves in many ways as an introduction to the second in the author's analysis. However, we will follow the article in first presenting a passing look at death (and explain why later).

*"Luke Caffrey's Kilmainham Minit"*
The presentation of this song in the *DUM* article is too detailed and complex to do justice to here, and most of the discussion lies outside both our interests in the May Day connection and bullbaiting (although the ballad does mention bulldogs). In the order followed in the article—execution, bullbait, May bush—the author mentions the ballad that William Wilde cited as a favorite in Dublin May Day neighborhood celebrations, "The Nite before Larry was Stretched," commenting that it has survived nearly all its rivals but that the song he has chosen to quote at length—"Luke Caffrey's Kilmainham Minit"—once enjoyed almost equal popularity. Walsh also cites a popular belief of the time that hanged men given to the medical profession for dissection were revived by the flow of blood. "A general belief therefore existed, that opening a vein after hanging was a certain means of restoring to life" ([Walsh] 1843: 666). Indeed, after his hanging, Luke Caffrey's cronies endeavor to "tip him a snig" in the jugular but to no avail; he is dead as a doornail. This intriguing note, and the fact that people sang about attempting a quick cure for hanging by the neck, come as an apposite reminder that, in the late eighteenth century, perceptions about blood flow were rather different from our own, as we will see was also the case with bullbaiting and running. The presence of a ballad on colorful (if not downright entertaining) death in a series of three, the last two of which either touch on May Day or are concerned with an incident that occurred then, may not be totally fortuitous.

*"Lord Altham's Bull"*

Without further ado, John Walsh proceeds to his discussion of what he calls "The Baiting of Lord Altham's Bull," a song once "in great celebrity, but now nearly forgotten." Walsh also believes it is not available in print and finds it to be the most "graphic" in its class, providing "the best specimen of the slang of sixty years ago, we subjoin a few extracts from it also" ([Walsh] 1843: 667). After all, an examination of picturesque language is stated to be the main purpose of the *DUM* article. If the ballad verses quoted in the text are but few (only six), the vocabulary for "Lord Altham's Bull" is considerably supplemented by long prose passages that alternate with the verses and are introduced by the cue "spoken."

The author begins the discussion by announcing that the subject of the song is a "bull-bait," a pastime which "the humanity of modern legislation has now very properly prohibited." Indeed, the baiting of bears, bulls, and other animals had been forbidden by Act of Parliament in 1835, only seven years before the article was published. He emphasizes that bullbaiting "was, at the time of which we speak, not merely a very common and popular sport among the lower orders, but, like prize-fighting, and the cock-pit, often keenly relished by the better classes of society," a statement with which most historical documentation quite agrees. In the detailed commentary on the vocabulary of the ballad a few columns later, Walsh notes that "his late Majesty, George IV, when Prince of Wales, was notoriously fond of bull-baiting. On one occasion, a Smithfield butcher slapped him on the back in ecstasy, crying out, with an imprecation, 'Mr. Prince, the dog that pinned the bull is my bitch!'" ([Walsh] 1843: 667, 670).

According to the author, a passion for this pastime was not only due to "the grosser tastes of the age" but to the fact that the Irish midland counties of that time were still "one great bullock walk," waving with corn to supply the armies of England. He believes that this area had long-standing ties to Spain and that bullbaiting was a degeneration of Spanish bullfighting, adding a most interesting detail about hierarchical relations in Waterford, which he knew well, and other towns that we shall return to shortly: "on the election of every mayor, he was surrounded by a mob, who shouted out 'a rope, a rope, a rope,'" and the new mayor never failed to grant their demands. "A rope two inches in diameter, with a competent leather collar and buckle, had been previously prepared" and was stored away between uses in the city-jail yard. Walsh cites an extract from the old corporation books of Waterford for October of 1714, the month when the slaughtering began, confirming that a "bull-rope be provided at the charge of the city revenue" ([Walsh] 1843: 667–68).[7]

The populace seized every bull, sometimes up to twenty animals a day during the season, and drew each to the bullring to be baited. On the rare occasions when a rope was not granted by a newly elected mayor, a bull was driven through the streets of the town in protest, an event that at times necessitated the intervention of the military to repress the rioting. This is supposed to have happened in Abbey Street in Dublin, and the mayor at the time ordered the troops to fire into the crowd rather than over their heads, an event that seems to identify the last bullbait recorded for the town as sometime before the 1798 uprising. In fact, an official enactment is said to have been published in 1779, "making it a peculiar offence to take a bull from the drivers, for such a purpose, on its way to or from market."[8] The bullbaiting was held in the Corn Market. The annotation of this detail adds that the old prison stood in this street and that the "Corn Market lay in the way from Kilmainham, to the city market, near Plunket-street, which therefore the bull had to pass through"([Walsh] 1843: 668, 670).

Even this cursory glimpse at the author's comments reveals intriguing hints that various groups could borrow a bull for diverse purposes, as is the case in the ballad not devoted to bullbaiting, "De May Bush." A bullring is verified for Dublin in 1564 as "an iron ring that sticketh in the Corn-Market, to which the bulls that are yearly baited be usually tied" (McCready: "Bull-ring" article).[9] This passage also reminds us that other sources often distinguish clearly between bullbaiting, which had its official locus in the Dublin Corn Market, and bull-running through the streets, to which we will return in a broader context. Here is a sample of the section entitled "Lord Altham's Bull," with four of the six verses and a summary of the interspersed prose recitative.

> Twas on de fust of sweet magay,
> It being a high holiday,
> Six and twenty boys of de straw
> Went to take Lord Altham's bull away.
> [The "spoken" passage refers to a hearty who rides the bull three
> times around the field, has his collarbone broken, and recovers
> under the care of a lady.]
>
> We drove de bull tro many a gap,
> And kep him going many a mile,
> Bud when we came to Kilmainham lands,
> We let de mosey rest awhile.

["Spoken" describes the bull.]

We drove de bull down sweet Truck-street,
Widout eider dread or figear,
When out run mosey Creathorn's bitch,
Hand cotched the bull be de year.

["Spoken" description of the bitch, named Nettle, and how to
protect her when she is thrown off the bull by catching her in midair,
then, at the end, giving her a sip of the warm blood.]

Lord Altham is a very bad man,
As all de neighbours know,
For driving white Roger from Kilmainham lands,
We all to Virginy must go!

The prose alternation has the last word, promising revenge on the instigator
of the deportees' plight. (Any note attempting to explain who Lord, or Lords,
Altham were would carry us into the realms of legal and literary legend.) In the
following commentary on vocabulary, the writer of the article defines "boys of
the straw" as "citizens of the straw market, Smithfield, a locality still distinguished as the residence of a bull-baiting progeny" ([Walsh] 1843: 668–70). This
is clearly a transition to the following ballad, "De May Bush," and Walsh mentions the endemic rivalry between the Liberty weavers of the Coombe and the
Ormond butchers of the Smithfield neighborhood, which was periodically enflamed
when one side stole the other group's May bush. The gleefully volunteering
combatants were not solely of trade-group extraction, as Walsh makes clear in
other passages. He especially laments that all classes were once addicted to
brawling and that, on the occasion of Liberty versus Ormond clashes, the local
gentlemen, as well as both gownsmen and fellows of Trinity College, usually
joined the weavers and their allies, the tailors. At this time also, the passion for
hurling matches between counties or districts attracted the sons of the gentry as
leaders of teams uniting all classes ([Walsh] 1843: 728, 739). Considering the
presence of the gentry standing side by side with a butcher bursting with pride
at the performance of his bitch, we may posit that Dublin bullbaiting was among
the many opportunities for vertical, if intense and brief, social relationships and
indeed the enjoyment of the sport may also have spawned faction fighting;

this certainly seems to have been one aspect of bullbaiting or running mentioned in other sources from the same period.

There is an intriguing element in Walsh's presentation of "Lord Altham's Bull"; the commentary speaks only of the month of October as the beginning of the slaughtering season, while the ballad opens with the first of May. So do any number of ballads and other narrative sources, of course; May Day as an inception point is perhaps one of the most widely honored poetic conventions in European literary history. Walsh missed commenting on this one, perhaps due to familiarity or simple lack of interest, to the fact that a bull could be slaughtered at any time in the year, or perhaps to the idea that this bull had not been intended for slaughter, which the spare content of the ballad may lead us to think. However, bullbaiting and running is associated with either life-cycle celebrations or major holidays in other places during the same historical period, and it is surely not a coincidence that the people closely associated with organizing May Day are butchers or, more exactly, butchers' boys.

Since Walsh saw the origin of bullbaiting in Spanish bullfighting, he was often tempted to perceive in recent practices a degradation of some former, usually more idealized, custom ([Walsh] 1843: 668). It is well to recall the general context of what we consider cruelty to animals associated with many celebrations and frequently with May Day or its eve, when Scottish children sought out the chicks of the Yellowhammer, a yellow-breasted finch, to kill them by a particular form of hanging (Banks 1939: 202) or the more-widespread hunt for unwary hedgehogs and hares (Danaher 1972: 110–11, E. Owen n.d.: 345). That this sort of torture was a favorite pastime in an urban setting as well, and could very easily carry over to the open pursuit of human beings, can been seen in an account of the celebration of the king's birthday in Edinburgh in the late 1700s, which we may entitle "the chase of the cats and the country bumpkins" (Chambers 1825: 162–67; also quoted in Smout and Wood 1991).

Apropos of activities we can call bullbaiting or running, it is well to remember that there is an extended spectrum in the general genre. Some sports subsumed under this heading involve cows, for instance; the participants maneuver afoot among the herd attempting to take a ribbon off a horn. (Perhaps one of the most intriguing aspects of this practice is that it is often done with very young animals over a period of years. The cows learn and remember, so they can become quite hard to catch or stalwart and dangerous to the ribbon seeker.) As we know from ancient Minoan frescoes, athletic (perhaps ritualized) events included what is usually termed "bull leaping." North American rodeos include bull riding, a trick mentioned in one of our "Lord Altham's Bull" prose sections, and the main job of rodeo clowns is breathtakingly close contact with bulls to let the riders get away with their lives. Running young bulls can simply be a preamble to catching and pinning them for branding and is a fun part of work. It was also part and parcel of butcher boys' work preceding slaughter because it was thought to tenderize very muscular meat. We have records of butchers being fined for not having the bull baited prior to slaughter, "bait" descending from the same root as "bite" (Kluge 1995: 93–95).[10]

The requirements of this sport explain nearly every detail of the physiognomy of the bulldog. A look at recent studies of the effects of oversecretion of cortisols on muscle coordination in humans might make us less sceptical on this point. Bulls, greatly weakened by stress and blood loss and subsequently killed in the ring in Spain, are dragged away so that bleeding the carcass can be completed. The resulting meat is unfit for freezing since the normal level of blood sugars that permit it have been radically reduced. It is customary to eat the meat within a day, contrary to common practice with most freshly slaughtered flesh, which is hung to let it "flavorize" (Fournier, personal communication, 2003).

We have more than ample iconography attesting to the universal popularity of bullrunning, with and without baiting by dogs, in the streets, and bullbaiting in many a local bear garden (upkeep of bears, even in herds, was an expensive proposition) and the bullring, which, as we have noted for Dublin, was a common place name within cities, near inns, at crossroads, even in quarries. Attaching the bull to a ring or other anchor was the most routine method of limiting its movement, and these facilities were specified in legal injunctions, as in 1656, when the local court ordered that the town of Thame's market cross be equipped with a pillory, a tumbrill, a bushel, and a collar and rope for bullbaiting (Thame Local History), although no ring is mentioned. We also have three-dimensional, full-color testimony to the sport in the form of fine china figurines, for example, in a handsome Staffordshire pottery piece from about 1820, labeled "bull-baiting" and including a quotation to incite the dog ("Now Captain, lad"). It shows two bulldogs at work, one having taken hold of the bull's sensitive nose (Sampson). As an aside, a byword for fair play was "one bull, one dog," but this ideal of interspecies sportsmanship does not seem to be borne out by the iconography. Shakespeare appears to be referring to bullbaiting in *Troilus and Cressida*, when Thersites cheers on both combatants, Paris and Menelaus (calling the latter "my double-horned Spartan"): "The cuckold and the cuckold-maker are at it. Now, bull! Now, dog!" (Act V, Scene vii). Perhaps bullbaiting was as rich a source of expressions in its heyday as baseball still is in North America.

Walsh notes that up to twenty bulls could be baited in a day, at least during the slaughtering season that commenced in October. In the city in 1564, bulls were baited "yearly" (McCready: "bull-ring" article). Baiting and/or running seems in many localities to have been associated with special holidays or occasions like May Day in the Dublin ballad: the Feast of the Assumption at Tutbury, connected with both a town and a religious occasion; November 13 in Stamford (*1911 Encyclopedia*); Guy Fawkes Day at Axbridge; or St. Thomas Day, December 21, at Wokingham (Bushaway 1993: 77–78), as well as at fairs and on patron saints' days. It was also an entertainment offered by the wealthy to the public to celebrate weddings, births and wakes. As a passing wink to May Day and the other hinge point articulating the half year, it is none too surprising to find bullbaiting, associated with the traditional season for animal slaughter, attached to the period near November Day, either before or after adoption of the Gregorian calendar reform (which moved the old half-year days around midmonth). It would be most interesting to see how much evidence there is of the sport being practiced also in connection with old- or new-style May Day.

Fortunately, there is a detailed study of bullrunning during and before the same period connected with Tutbury in Staffordshire, as well as other sites, to compare with the Dublin event recounted in "Lord Altham's Bull" (Bushaway 1993). A number of the points concerning bullbaiting and running already mentioned are confirmed here: For instance, the belief that bull meat should only be sold by butchers if the animal has first been baited or run is referred to—speaking of a former time—for Canterbury in 1573, along with a notice from that year stipulating that "fines are to be paid to the Chamber, for licence to kill bulls, without previously baiting them at the Bull Stake, according to the custom of those days" (Bushaway 1993: 76–77 citing Hasted 1797–1801). This wording may indicate that butchers in the sixteenth century could already pay their way out of what seems to have been a statutory rule. Whether or not the legal strictures on slaughtering had actually changed, such a note reinforces popular memory since we hear this belief was still remembered in the nineteenth century.

I already mentioned that the *DUM* account does not give particular details about the death of the bulls, and it would require a comprehensive examination of the evidence to decide if this was fairly similar wherever it was a part of slaughter. Nonetheless, an example from Axbridge offers a scenario from beginning to end and suggests—a point that is especially interesting—that the sport may at times have been followed by distribution of this "inferior" meat to the poor, something that does not seem to be confirmed in the Tutbury material. The annual bull running at Axbridge in the late-eighteenth century followed attendance at a church service by all the local authorities and thus seems to have been sanctioned, if not organized, by them. A bull was let out of the inn into the marketplace, chased by a mob, worried by dogs, and beaten with clubs through the streets, where the shop fronts were carefully barricaded; finally, it was driven out of town to a site where it was fastened to the bull anchor and beaten to death. A butcher who specialized in selling the meat of inferior animals cut up the carcass, and the flesh was distributed to the poor (Bushaway 1993: 77–78, citing Willis Watson 1920: 409–10). This occurred on Guy Fawkes Day (November 5).

A connection with an important religious holiday, the Feast of the Assumption, is at the heart of the Tutbury bull running, which seems to have been set within a complex tapestry of changing balances among several groups of players from the fourteenth to the eighteenth centuries: the commoners, who insisted on their customary rights to use the varied wood gathered in Needwood Forest; the religious of Tutbury Priory, which possessed considerable rights over Needwood Forest; and the local aristocracy, beginning in 1381, when John of Gaunt granted a charter to the minstrels of Tutbury guaranteeing they should have "a bull given to them by the Prior of Tutbury if they can take him this side of the Rover Dove" (Bushaway 1993: 80–81). This right is confirmed by an Elizabethan-period survey noting the minstrels have "by ancient custom a bull to run as well as pasture for their horses for two days" (Bushaway 1993: 84). By the late seventeenth century, Robert Plot notes they must prove to have done this by cutting some of its hair off. In this case, the bull was brought to the bailiff's house in Tutbury, where it was collared and roped to be led to the bullring in the high street and baited with dogs. After this, the minstrels were free to kill, sell, or divide it amongst themselves (Bushaway 1993: 83, citing Plot 1686). Plot indeed witnessed the running in 1680 and reported in 1686 in his *Natural History of Staffordshire* that the bull running had taken on the character of a faction fight between Derbyshire and Staffordshire men (Bushaway 1993: 82–83, citing Plot 1686). In fact, an especially bloody conflict between these two parties in 1778 led to bull running finally being suppressed (Bushaway 1993: 91, citing Edwards 1949) at a time consonant with the events in Dublin and elsewhere.

Minstrels, various forest users, religious, aristocrats are all groups that do not stand still in time; players change: The priors had disappeared, the makeup of the aristocracy had been considerably altered, and the townsfolk had become thoroughly disgusted at the mayhem produced by the bullrunning. The forest, likewise, had been drastically changed by the early 1800s, and it was, in fact, a major player in these multileveled relationships. There is no documentary evidence, but Bushaway proposes it may be assumed that the minstrels provided the music for the Assumption feast given by Tutbury Priory (1993: 82). The Feast of the Assumption was the date forest administrators gathered at Tutbury to deliberate, though the system appears to have broken down before the English Civil War and the oft-proposed plans for deforestation fell by the wayside during the Restoration (Bushaway 1993: 86–87).

In fact, there had been a long tug of war over the enclosure and deforestation of Needwood Forest, in which the commoners were not entirely helpless to resist incursion on their customary rights; they pulled down the fences in the forest in 1635, an act that provoked considerable legal ire (Bushaway 1993: 83–85). The evidence is more suggestive than exhaustive, but the demise of the bull running in 1778 and negotiation of deforestation in 1801 seem to represent the last landmarks in a long battle over the strength of local custom. Bushaway concludes that the attack on bull running was not simply an assault on brutal plebian sports but "represented a conscious dismantling of the complex ideology of custom," also crucial to the process of enclosure, which was not solely an economic measure but deliberately undermined an independent popular culture of forest dwellers. In this context, bull running had performed a multifunctional service for the region (Bushaway 1993: 92–93).

The history of relations among the same sort of players in Dublin was surely equally complex, although we cannot infer they were similar or that comparable stakes were involved without further investigation. In his section on "riding the fringes" (franchises) of Dublin, Walsh mentions a 1488 document stressing the necessity of riding the boundaries every third year to certify the town's rights against its powerful ecclesiastical neighbors. The decline of the latter's power eliminated the principal motivation for the patrols, and the custom subsequently became an occasion for the display of civic pomp in which the twenty-five corporations of the city played a prominent role ([Walsh] 1943: 655). There are a number of threads running through these various accounts to which we will return.

*"De May Bush"*
Walsh provides us with ample background to enrich enjoyment of the ballad and explain who its protagonists were, some of which we have already tasted. As an aside, we may note that the action takes place at the height of traditional tension, when the bow of a holiday is strung its tightest: not on the day itself but from the eve to May Day morning. Walsh tells us about the players and their turf; the Liberties (or Liberty) he speaks of here were an elevated tract on the western side of the city, the name arising from the privileges and immunities granted the area

occupied by trades that produced silk and woolen fabrics, many of whose members had come there after the revocation of the Edict of Nantes in 1685. It seems that around 1780 there were some thirty-four hundred looms at work in the Liberties, and in 1791, there were twelve hundred silk looms alone, a prosperity first undermined by the "woolen war" with England in the early part of the eighteenth century and then blown apart by the war with France. The coup de grâce came shortly thereafter during the insurrection of 1798, so Walsh can testify these trades had been reduced to utter beggary by the time of the Union in 1800 ([Walsh] 1843: 656).

So, in one corner, we have the tailors and weavers of the Coombe. In the other stand the Ormond boys, the butchers who lived around Ormond market, apparently supported in all endeavors by their allies, the fishwives of Pill-lane. The confrontations between the Liberty and Ormond groups were legendary in the town's annals:

> It is in the memory of many now living that the streets, and particulary the quays and bridges, were impassable in consequence of the battles of these parties. The weavers descending from the upper regions beyond Thomas-street poured down on their opponents below; they were opposed by the butchers, and a contest commenced on the quays which extended from Essex to Island bridge. The shops were closed; all business suspended; the sober and peaceable compelled to keep their houses...while the war of stones and other missiles was carried on across the river, and the bridges were taken and retaken by the hostile parties. It will hardly be believed in the present efficient state of our police, that for whole days the intercourse of the city was interrupted by the feuds of these parties. ([Walsh] 1843: 728–29)

Walsh adds that a friend watched a battle rage on Essex Bridge in which more than a thousand men were engaged, reminding us that young men of the gentry joined the frays with glee on the side of the Liberty weavers and the conflicts could turn very nasty ([Walsh] 1843: 728–29). Whoever the friend he speaks of may be, Walsh's own father was a prime contributor, equally fascinated with the history of the town and a student at Trinity himself from 1789 on (Cosgrave).

This is the context in which the specific battle of the May bush takes place. Apparently, the butchers proceeded to the usual gathering of their bush, astride which their leader was carried to the site in Smithfield, where it was set up for the festivities, one of the principal attractions being the joys of the bottle. Intense indulgence caused vigilance in guarding the bush to reach a low ebb, and the next morning, the butchers awoke to find their treasure carried off by the weavers. Bill Durham, the butchers' leader, took in the scene at a glance and loosed instant vengeance on the assailants in the form of a bull driven into the weavers' quarter. Here is the ballad of "De May Bush." As is his wont, Walsh tends to stray from the immediate subject of the ballad to colorful asides.

> We shall conclude, with specimens from one more song, very popular in its day. We have noticed in a former part of our article the feuds between the Liberty and Ormond boys. Various objects of petty display presented causes of emulation and strife. Among them was planting a May-bush—one party endeavouring to cut down what the other had set up. A memorable contest of this kind, in which the weavers cut down "the bush" of the butchers, is thus celebrated in song:—

> De May Bush.
> De nite afore de fust of Magay,
> Ri rigi di, ri ri dum dee,
> We all did agree without any delay,
> To cut a May-bush, so we pegged it away
> Riri rigi di dum dee!

> The leader of the boys was Bill Durham, a familiar corruption of Dermot, his right name, a distinguished man at that time in the Liberty riots. When the tree was cut down, it was borne back in triumph, with Bill astride on it, exhibiting a classical picture still more graphic than the gem of Bacchus astride on his ton:—

> Bill Durham, he sat astride on his bush,
> Ri rigidi, ri ri dum dee,
> And dere he kept singin, as sweet as a trush—
> His faulchin in one hand, his pipe in his mush—
> Ri rigidi, ri ri dum dee!

> "The Bush" having been planted in Smithfield, contributions were raised to do it honour; and among other contributors were the

fishwomen of Pill-lane, who, from contiguity of situation, and similarity of dealing, were closely allied to the butchers of Ormond market. A custom prevailed here, of selling the fish brought for sale, to the women who retailed it, by auction. The auctioneer, generally one of themselves, holding a plaice or a haddock by the tail, instead of a hammer, knocked down the lot to the highest bidder. This was an important time to the trade—yet the high-minded poissardes, like their Parisian sisters, "sacrificed every thing to their patriotic feelings," and abandoned the market, even at this crisis, to attend "de bush":—

From de lane came each lass in her holyday gown,
Ri rigidi, ri ri dum dee,
Do de haddock was up, and de lot was knocked down,
Dey doused all dere sieves, till they riz de half-crown
Ri rigi di, ri ri dum dee!

    After indulging in the festivities of the occasion round "de bush," some returned, and some lay about, *vino somno que supulti*; and so, not watching with due vigilance, the liberty boys stole on their security, cut down, and carried off "de bush." The effect on Bill Durham, when he heard the adversary passing on their way back with the trophy, is thus described:—

Bill Durham, being up de nite afore,
Ri rigidi ri ri dum dee,
Was now in his flea-park, taking a snore,
When he heard de mob pass by his door.
Ri rigidi dum dee!

Den over his shoulders his flesh-bag he threw,
Ri rigidi ri ri dum dee,
And out of the chimbley his faulchion he drew,
And mad as a hatter down May-lane he flew
Ri rigidi dum dee!

Wid his hat in his hand by de way of a shield.
Ri rigidi ri ri dum dee,

He kep all along crying out—never yield!—
But he never cried stop till he came to Smidfield—
Ri rigidi dum dee!

Dere finding no bush, but de watch boys all flown,
Ri rigidi ri ri dum dee,
Your sowls, ses Bill Durham, I'm left all alone—
Be de hokey de glory of Smidfield is gone!—
Ri rigidi dum dee!

Bill vows revenge in a very characteristic and professional
manner, by driving one of the bulls of Ormond market among his
adversaries:—

We'll wallap a mosey down Meadstreet in tune.
Ri rigidi ri ri dum dee,
And not leave a weaver alive on de Combe,
But rip up his tripe-bag, and burn his loom!
Ri rigidi dum dee!

«In his mush»—mouth, from the french mouche. Many words
are similarly derived—gossoon, a boy, from garcon , &c.
      «De lane.»—Pill-lane, called so par excellence, as the great
centre and mart of piscatory dealing.
      «Doused all dere sieves.»—Laid them down at their uncles, the
pawnbrokers.
      «Riz half a crown.»—The neuter verb, «rise,» is classically used
here for the active verb, "raised," a common licence with our poets.
      «Flea park.»—This appellation of Bill's bed was, no doubt,
borrowed from the account the Emperor Julian gives of his beard, "I
permit little beasts," said he, " to run about it, like animals in a
park." The word he uses is phtheires, pediculi; so that Durham's
"flea park," was evidently sanctioned by the emperor's "—park."
The Abbe de la Bletterie, who translated Julian's work, complains
that he was accused for not suppressing the image presented by
Julian; but adds very properly, *la delicatesse Francaise va-t-elle
jus'qu au falsifier les auteurs*? ([Walsh] 1843: 670–72)

Whether we are willing to accept all the author's explanations of terms (or the twist given to French grammar in his quote) is beside the point. The ballad, as it stands, purports to speak of a real historical event. The fact that Bill sets off armed to take revenge squares perfectly with Walsh's description of the nature of these recurrent conflicts, and the contributions of the fishwives correspond to the portrait of May eve and morning given us by William Wilde. Their half-crowns may well have been used for the alcoholic fuel of the festivities, but it was probably not limited to this. Wilde tells us that the Dublin folk walking about on their quest for holiday materials adorned themselves with ribbons and also solicited contributions of ribbons, handkerchiefs, and pieces of gaudy silk for the bush itself. Wilde recalls an important point here—that the Liberty and Ormond groups each had a May bush, but a bush was also the pride of even smaller neighborhood entities, the rivalry extending to which "street or district would exhibit the best dressed and handsomest May bush, or could boast the largest and hottest bonfire" (Danaher 1972: 91, citing Wilde 1853: 47–48). Remember, Bill Durham calls the butchers' bush "the glory of Smidfield." Just where the townsfolk acquired these bushes was a sore subject. If the Liberty bush had formerly been cut in Cullen Wood, the bushes were often "pegged away" from the private property of some gentleman very proud of having an especially venerable hawthorn in his garden, and there were even attempts by the civil authorities to intervene, usually to no avail. The bush could also bear candles that were lighted at nightfall and, along with its bonfire, formed the center of a gathering to sit out the wake of the winter and spring with song (Danaher 1972: 91–92, citing Wilde n.d.: 47–48, 59–60). The festivities do sound as gay as an old-fashioned wake.

Bill Durham flies down May Lane to Smithfield, whence he plans to take a bull down Meath Street to the heart of the weavers' turf around the Coombe. We have come full circle back to releasing a bull as one of the elements in the language of protest in the hierarchical relationship between the populace and the newly elected mayor, supposed to supply a rope and collar for bullbaiting. We are at the heart of a budding faction fight, and there will soon be a bull in the middle of it, but the order is backward in relation to what we have seen before, where the baiting or running provided the matrix for the conflict between groups that the townsfolk as a whole eventually rejected because of unacceptable behavior. Walsh felt that this was principally due to the civilizing influence of English refinement on Irish mores, missing the point that the same thing was happening in England, for society at this time was no more static than our own.

Prosperous trades could be wiped out within a generation by political change or technological shift, and people had to fight hard to keep on thinking anything was timeless. There were many actors jockeying for survival, economically and sociologically, as were the mighty masses of weavers with their allies in the Coombe. Earlier, I told the story of a butcher who, in the heat of a bullbaiting session, thumped the Prince of Wales soundly on the back and, we might suppose from the lack of comment, that the prince took this as it was meant: a momentarily shared passion that transcended class without threatening it. If bullbaiting, faction fighting, and hurling once unified members of different classes and groups vertically, only to see its upper-tier participants eventually shy away in favor of pastimes that took place in the parlor rather than the street, was this equally true of May bushing?

My answer is an equivocal yes. Insofar as the demise of some customs surrounding the May bush goes, the fact that a bush taken in stealth was especially valued would eventually land the thieves in hot water. We have lengthy tirades written by gentlemen whose gardens were despoiled during the same period about which Walsh and Wilde were writing (Danaher 1972: 105–6), and, in this particular area of vertical relations, we can definitely say that all did not run smoothly. As an aside, I suggest that such items as a bush may once have been freely given by their possessors. Generous contributions to May Day celebrations were once the hallmark of the most respected Welsh farmers or elegant London households lending silver to a milkmaid. I think this is probable and that we can look to a city like London for examples of the way vertical relationships were negotiated, more or less successfully, by two different trade groups in connection with May Day.

In a highly documented and subtle analysis of evolving May Day celebrations in London from the Stuart to the Hanoverian period (to which scant justice can be paid here), Charles Phythian-Adams notes that within the world's first modern metropolis the older basic unit of urban holiday interaction, the parish or street neighborhood, was no longer meaningful (1983: 94), as it definitely was in Walsh's account of Dublin. Phythian-Adams explores a successful triangular pattern of relationships where two occupational groups compete but also eventually position themselves very differently in relation to their wealthy patrons in highly imaginative ways, the milkmaids with their "garland" and the chimney sweeps with their "Jack-in-the-Green." The latter create something new and highly artificial, a custommade, walking May bush—the Jack. Between the late-seventeenth and late-eighteenth centuries, a quantum leap occurs in the size of the milkmaids' garlands—originally greenery-decked milk pails—and they mobilize the goodwill of their upper-class clientele to a remarkable degree, obtaining the loan of sumptuous silver plate to adorn the edifice their garland has become. They do not steal emblems of prosperity; they *borrow* them. In so doing, they integrate new urban symbols into a basically rural system and create a remarkable synthesis of successful class relationships. As a result, the milkmaids are genuinely treated like queens-for-a-day, effecting a relationship inversion on May Day that reinforces the status quo during the entire year. Both they and the chimney sweeps manage, in fact, to make their relationship with their patrons more complex and go on with their May Day celebrations, in the case of the milkmaids, until the end of the eighteenth century, and in that of the sweeps, until well into the nineteenth century, attaching new modes of expression to them while remaining faithful to the basic vocabulary of the rural festival inherited from a preurban past. If their festivities eventually peter out, or are transformed into a more communal panoply of holiday practices, it is mainly because their professions themselves gradually give way to the demands of modernization.

The contrast in scale between London and Dublin at this time is considerable, but the milkmaids' and chimney sweeps' innovations nonetheless provide an interesting comparison with what we can glean from Walsh and Wilde's descriptions of Dublin, where the pressures of genteel sensibilities were certainly mounting, if the weight of social complexity was perhaps less. It is clear that the identity needs of the weavers and allies and the butchers and friends were well served by this horizontal interneighborhood strife, at least in the case presented by the *DUM* article affirming that this song was a favorite subsequently sung for the May holiday. I propose that, like song, this kind of highly ritualized strife, comparable, for example, to hurling matches, is a performance genre complete with both willing and unwilling spectators and rather negative vertical relationships with town authorities. Walsh tells us that the latter were too timid (and underarmed) to intervene in the heyday of the Ormond-Liberty rivalry and that this powerlessness has since been corrected. It seems, in the meantime, that the Homeric three-F ideal of the young squire (feasting, fighting, fornicating) has also been much tempered by the inroads of gentility ([Walsh] 1843: 728–44), perhaps considerably denting the sanction for one gender, age, and class group to engage in riotous behavior in neighborhood rivalries, holiday celebration, and public bullbaiting. One of the elements in constructing this genteel ambiance was the protracted struggle for animal rights; the first bill proposed to outlaw baiting goes back to 1802, and the act that did so was passed in 1835.

This does not imply that the Dublin groups involved in both the bushing and the baiting lacked the perspicacity to find new forms for traditional practices. We know that May Day customs were faithfully observed in various forms, often green or floral, much later, eventually undergoing the varied permutations associated with the reinvention of tradition. Bullbaiting and similar blood sports certainly went underground in the first transition period but were probably largely replaced by the highly organized, usually neighborhood-bound, and eventually lucrative sport of boxing. Now we must tie up the loose threads in this exploration of song, strife, cattle, death, transmission, and commemoration.

*Song, Strife, Cattle, Death, Transmission, and Commemoration*
Here is a series of working hypotheses suggested by these ballads, described so vividly by John Edward Walsh in the *Dublin University Magazine* of 1843, that involve at first glance death, bullbaiting, and the theft of a May bush. They are first and foremost an example of the way an author can use a performance genre, the ballad, that he obviously finds delightful, to illustrate the heart of a singular, valued identity: the plain-spoken Irish dealing with the hardest facts of life (among them, violent death). Without studying other versions of the songs, we cannot say just how much of the ballads he decided to use for his analysis, but there are several reasons for remarking on their particular integral quality.

The first song, "Luke Caffrey's Kilmainham Minit," is entirely in verse; the author compares it with another ballad dealing with the same subject—a public execution—and comments extensively on the entertainment value of such events, which ties in with his deep interest in ambiguous, either quite likable or truly detestable, but always almost superhuman, miscreants. Let me say, as an aside, how particularly struck I was on first reading this material that the author could combine, in just three ballads, three of the most signal elements involved in May Day celebration: death, cattle, and strife over a May bush. Of course, William Wilde confirms this constellation of favorite songs and notes that people spoke of celebrating the *wake* of the winter and spring. It is interesting to recall that May Day, in literary traditions, is a prime time for abduction, combat, and death, but it is also the time when those who have disappeared can sometimes be found or called back. Such figures are often larger than life, for example, Mabon in Welsh tradition, but returning from the beyond may also be the luck of a more-prosaic person, perhaps a dearly beloved wife lost in childbirth. If Walsh partly disapproves of his wild characters' or convicted murderers' exploits, he presents them as exploits nonetheless, and I believe he has genuinely captured in his genteel heart the admiration of his unlettered contemporaries for people who somehow transcend the laws that strike fear into the voiceless majority.

The second ballad, "Lord Altham's Bull," is in alternating verse and recitative prose, then set in the author's abundant commentary. As for the connection with May Day in the opening lines, we could attribute it entirely to purely conventional expression. Perhaps it was as unthinking to begin the ballad this way as it is for children today to sing, "Here we go gathering nuts in May" at a time when nature does not give us many nuts. (Chances are this actually refers to nosegays of flowers.) However tentative the connection may be, I am again tempted to propose it may not be all that tenuous because of the deep preoccupation with cattle at May Day. An abiding concern for the safety and health of milch cows is typical of preindustrial societies, usually expressed in bucolic protective practices and occasionally extended to defensive guarding of a cow herd, but I think that bulls have been given too little attention until now.

Aside from any association with May Day, we have seen that in older Dublin traditions of vertical relations between commoners and the titular head of town authority, the mayor, each election initiated an intriguing demand: providing a rope to lead and then tie bait bulls to the bullring. Is this not a promise to "tie down the beast" within, a kind of truce with authority in exchange for the continuing right to practice a public entertainment that may be expensive for the whole community since bull running and baiting in city districts obviously damaged property? Dublin bullbaiting is said to have occurred yearly, although this surely refers to the slaughtering season, beginning in October, rather than to the period around May Day. The Tutbury accounts for Assumption, or the Axbridge bull running on Guy Fawkes Day, describe a privilege that granted a bull's meat to a trade group in the former case and the common folk in the latter. In both cases, the bulls were run and baited, and this meat was handled by butchers specializing in inferior animals. Even today, the meat of a bull bred for the ring in Spain is called "black" in contrast with the "white" meat of Charolais bulls bred for slaughter (Fournier, personal communication, 2003).

To develop this line of reasoning further, we would have to see what taxonomic order is meant by "inferior animals" in the Axbridge context and compare the slaughtering/bleeding practices toward cows, oxen, and calves during the same period. However, we can say a word about May Day and note that Walsh reports that the singers of his bull ballad did not see anything incongruous about beginning with a reference to the first of May. If a bull or bulls were run and baited then, and their meat perhaps once given to the poor, this would have been a godsend. If we think of May as a delightful floral period, we should remember that, for many people not long ago, it was the time of the year with the least food production. Stocks of grain and flour had long since run out, the milk-producing season was just getting into full swing, and the poor—those who had not already died of malnutrition—were often eating field plants to survive. A time when no one in his right mind would spare a cow still giving milk would be a logical occasion to gift bull meat, even if it had to be eaten immediately and not preserved some way. This tradition also confirms that brutal exercise combined with excessive blood loss while alive appears to alter the chemistry of muscles, as well as, possibly, the organoleptic properties of meat. Perhaps people once knew things about blood flow in the body that we do not.

We can also speculate in connection with May Day, but also in regard generally to cattle, that cows and bulls represent different forms of domestication, not being equally approachable. In bullbaiting, a bull's passion is aroused and quenched violently in a complex net of relationships between two domesticated animals and their humans, perhaps another type of triangular configuration à la Phythian-Adams that involves heretofore-ignored trade groups and classes. This is not the way milch cows are treated, needless to say. They are usually coddled with kindness, massaged and sung to with devotion, since these are good ways to accelerate milk production. (We need not comment on which human sex is usually responsible for which cattle sex.) We may also note that both milk and blood of bovines is used in communicating with the otherworld; we know this from the milk and blood spilled on the ground in liminal places between worlds like fairy raths. In remembering the London milkmaids and their ingenuity in finding appropriate methods for achieving smooth vertical social relationships, we must remind ourselves that blood sports also knew no class lines—a bull-pinning bitch was great whether she belonged to the butcher or the prince.

"Lord Altham's Bull" is followed by an immediate and purposeful transition to "De May Bush," presented in a different form: The ballad is interspersed in the author's textual commentary and, again, set within a background portrait. Presenting the May bush ballad as anything but a hint at the complex of customs involving vegetation would be simply dishonest. Dublin had a long-thriving Maypole tradition, and we have not even begun to delve into what sort of relationship the bushes might have had with their taller siblings, even if both forms had to weather similar storms of time. Such emblems of holiday expression are usually polyvalent, and the bush and the pole may be handled symbolically in very similar or different ways. We may recall that, in the seventeenth and eighteenth centuries, wedding practices in many areas of Great Britain involved setting up a pole or stake (also called a "bride bush") outside the house which the couple were to occupy (Phythian-Adams 1983: 89). What we have seen in the

Dublin weavers' versus butchers' battles over the May bush, decorated much as people adorn themselves for special occasions, is very comparable to a charivari and ritual abduction of a bride. This is not the place to enumerate all the examples of May Day conflicts of two suitors over a woman that reverberate through medieval literature and oral tradition in the British Isles. Still, it gives us another view of May bush strife and, perhaps, strife generally: It is a recurrent quest for a prize that is never definitively possessed.

What is more efficacious in cementing group identity than having the other side regularly remind you that your everyday, internal quarrels must be transcended? This may be a rather simplistic approach to solidarity, but it works, and we work hard to transcend differences and move on to a wider circle of "we." It would certainly be selling the Dublin butchers and weavers short to suggest they were not capable of manipulating multivalent social language, just as they were capable of the ribald, full-bodied expression in song that won the hearts of John Edward Walsh and William Wilde. The butchers' revenge in "De May Bush" consisted of utilizing an item in the vocabulary of vertical protest—driving a bull through the streets to wreak havoc—as a tool in their horizontal interaction with another neighborhood/trade group, and they certainly switched vocabulary with great glee.

As a cursory look at transmission and commemoration, we need say little more. Walsh and Wilde have detailed the many rehearsals of May bush festivities and strife of rival groups, so it is obvious no one lacked recurring examples of shared heritage and tasks that are among the building blocks of community. In fact, I think that song and strife can be seen as complementary performance genres that meet around the May bush.

Finally, we must not forget that these activities were but two threads in the vast tapestry of the holiday, which we see here within the limited, but rich, scope of a May bush, decorated with ribbons, handkerchieves, even candles, with folk dancing, drinking, and taletelling. If there was a weapon-bearing age group always ready to take up the challenge of recurrent conflict, there was likewise an intense conviviality that was surely every bit as nourishing, a congenial matrix for commemoration, remembering together.

## Notes

1. Pages 655–77 and 728–44, kindly provided to me in May of 1996 by Siobhan O' Rafferty of the Royal Irish Academy and her colleagues at the Berkeley Library of Trinity College.
2. "British Isles" is used here as a geographer's term referring to Ireland and Great Britain, including the latter's odd scattering of legally distinct islands, perhaps excepting the Channel Islands, which Normandy folk still believe firmly to be a temporary loan.
3. For the briefest of glances, consult Ifans (1983), or Wright (1940).

4.  For examples, see Deane and Shaw 1975: 172–73, or very recently in Bavaria, "Geldstrafen für Diebstahl eines Maibaums," *Frankfurter Allgemeine Zeitung*, 17 June 1997.
5.  For example, for the Dublin Maypoles, see Danaher 1972: 98–99; for the Peebles horse races, see Banks 1939: 243; for summer-winter strife, see Paton 1968: 54, or Moore 1971: 111–12; then in Wales, Trevelyan 1909: 25–26; Owen 1959: 103.
6.  For bleeding, which is a complex matter since it was also done for alimentary purposes, see Lucas 1989: chapter 6, and O' Rahilly 1977; for protection of dairy products, see Lysaght 1994.
7.  There is, however, no reference here to the corporation books of Waterford.
8.  *DUM* 668, citing statute no. 19, 20 Geo. III, e. 36.
9.  Other older street names mentioned in the ballads can be found, often with a commentary, in this McCready.
10. See the discussion of *Beil, beissen, beizen* (including *Beizjagd)*.

## References

Banks, M. Macleod. 1939. *British Calendar Customs: Scotland*. Vol. 2. London: William Glaisher.

"Bear-baiting and bull-baiting." In *1911 Encyclopedia*. Available online at <http://54.1911encyclopedia.org>

"Bull baiting and cock fighting in Thame." Available online at Thame local history website at <http://www.thamehistory.net/topics/Baiting.htm>

Bushaway, Bob. 1993. "Bulls, Ballads, Minstrels and Manors: Some Observations on the the Defense of Custom in Eighteenth-Century England." In *Aspects of British Calendar Customs*, edited by Theresa Buckland and Juliette Wood, 75–93. The Folklore Society Mistletoe Series, no. 22. Sheffield: Sheffield Academic Press.

Chambers, Robert. 1825. *Traditions of Edinburgh*. Edinburgh: W. and C. Tait.

Cosgrave, Dillon. Introduction to "Ireland Sixty Years Ago," by John Edward Walsh. Multiplex website from Ken Finlay available online at <http://indigo.ie/~finlay/60years%20ago/60intro.htm>

Danaher, Kevin. 1972. *The Year in Ireland: Irish Calendar Customs*. Cork and Dublin: The Mercier Press.

Deane, Tony, and Tony Shaw. 1975. *The Folklore of Cornwall*. London: Batsford.

Fournier, Dominique, Maison des Sciences de l'Homme, Paris. Personal communication, 6 January 2003.

"Geldstrafen für Diebstahl eines Maibaums." *Frankfurter Allgemeine Zeitung*. 17 June 1997.

Hall, Wayne E. 1999. *Dialogues in the Margin: A Study of the Dublin University Magazine*. Washington, D. C.: Catholic University of America Press. Available on the website of Shamrock Isle Bookstore at <www.shamrockisle.com/bookstore/0813209269AMUS838084.shtml>.

Ifans, Rhiannon. 1983. *Sêrs a Rybana: Astudiaeth o'r Canu Gwasael*. Llandysul, Dyfed: Gwasg Gomer.

Jackson, Kenneth. 1964–65. "Some Popular Motifs in Early Welsh Tradition." *Études Celtiques* 11, no. 1: 83–99.

Judge, Roy. 1979. *The Jack-in-the-Green*. D.S. Brewer and Rowman and Littlefield for the Folklore Society.

———. 1991. "May Day and Merrie England." *Folklore* 102, no. 2: 131–48.

Kluge, Friedrich. 1995. *Etymologisches Woerterbuch der deutschen Sprache*. Bearbeitet von Elmar Seebold. 23rd ed. Berlin, New York: Walter de Gruyter.

Lucas, A. T. 1989. *Cattle in Ancient Ireland*. Kilkenny: Boethius Press.

Lysaght, Patricia. 1994. "Women, Milk and Magic at the Boundary Festival of May." In
    *Milk and Milk Products: From Medieval to Modern Times, Proceedings of the 9th
    International Conference on Ethnological Food Research, Ireland*, edited by Patricia
    Lysaght, 208–29. Edinburgh: Canongate.

MacNeill, Máire. 1982. *The Festival of Lughnasa*. Dublin: Comhairle Bhéaloideas
    Eireann, University College.

McCready, C. T. Index of Dublin street names. Website from Ken Finlay available online
    at <http://indigo.ie/~kfinlay/index.htm> and street-name section: <http://indigo.ie/
    ~kfinlay/Dublin%20Streets/dubindex.htm>.

Meyer, Kuno. 1912. "Sanas Cormaic" [Cormac's Glossary]. *Anecdota from Irish
    Manuscripts*. Vol. 4, edited by O. J. Bergin, E. I. Best, Kuno Meyer, and J. G. O'
    Keeffe. Halle and Dublin: Max Niemeyer and Hodges, Digois and Co.

Moore, A. W. 1971. *The Folk-Lore of the Isle of Man*. Douglas, Isle of Man: Brown;
    London: D. Nutt, 1891. Reprint, [Wakefield]: S. R. Publishers.

O' Rahilly, Cecile. 1977. "The Bleeding of Living Cattle." *Celtica* 12: 183–88.

Owen, Elias. N.d. *Welsh Folk-Life: A Collection of the Folk-Tales and Legends of North
    Wales*. Oswestry and Wrexham: Woodall.

Owen, Trefor M. 1959. *Welsh Folk Customs*. Cardiff: National Museum of Wales.

Paton, C. I. 1968. *Manx Calendar Customs*. London: William Glaisher for the Folklore
    Society.

Phythian-Adams, Charles. 1983. "Milk and Soot: The Changing Vocabulary of a Popular
    Ritual in Stuart and Hanoverian London." In *The Pursuit of Urban History*, edited by
    Derek Fraser and Anthony Sutcliff, 83–104. London: Edward Arnold.

Sampson, Alistair. Alistair Sampson Antiques. HK23, English pottery, Staffordshire
    bullbaiting group decorated in exceptionally strong colors. Available online at <http://
    www.alistairsampson.com/pages/home.html> item posted as of 6 Jan 2003 under
    <http://www.alistairsampson.com/pages/hk23_bullbaiting.html>

Smout, T. C., and Sydney Wood. 1991. *Scottish Voices, 1745–1960*. London: Fontana
    Press.

Trevelyan, Marie. 1909. *Folk-Lore and Folk-Stories of Wales*. London: Elliot Stock.

[Walsh, John Edward]. 1843. "Ireland Sixty Years Ago." *Dublin University Magazine* 22:
    655–744.

Wilde, William Robert. 1853. *Irish Popular Superstitions*. Dublin: James McGlashan.

Wright, A. R. 1940. *British Calendar Customs: England*, edited by T. E. Lones.
    Publications of the Folklore Society, no. 106. London: William Glaisher.

# Malign Forces
# That Can Punish and Pardon:
# Structure and Motif

# Malign Forces That Can Punish and Pardon: Structure and Motif

Since the publication of key texts on structure and form in traditional narrative,[1] ballad scholars have sought to apply their methodology to the similar genre of narrative song. The resulting studies have concentrated on two main areas of research: the re-creation of songs using formulas or commonplaces, and Propp's ideas of function and the tale role (1968).[2] This section presents two essays on structural themes and two on particular motifs within the ballad tradition which build upon the foundations developed in the previous essays. With the recent emphasis on context and interpretation in ballad studies, aspects of performance are now being related to these structural considerations. The study of ballads in their "original" form—associated with dancing, for instance—has led to interesting conclusions about the difference between sung rhythm and the words presented on the page (on aspects of this difference, see Ives 1964: 154; also Toelken 1995: 19–21).

The first contribution, Simon Furey's "An Oddity of Catalan Folk Songs and Ballads," takes a performance-based observation as its starting point, delving into a curious situation where the rhythms of traditional dances only periodically coincide with those of the music. In most of Europe, the two genres of narrative song and dance have long since been divorced (Bronson 1959–72: ix), but there are vestiges (in Brittany, Denmark, the Faroe Islands, Catalonia) of a tradition once widespread, which illustrate a largely forgotten power, function, and, indeed, utility for the ballad tradition. Here, as everywhere in ballad studies, oral performance exposes inummerable oddities and exceptions to long-held ideas about the way traditional verse works. Multiformity is present not just in text and tune but in the very patterns we consider fundamental to our definition(s) of the genre.

Such patterns are further addressed in William B. McCarthy's essay on single-rhyme ballads in the Child corpus.[3] According to David Fowler, the Child collection (1882–98) "encourage[d] the study of ballads without respect to time and place. Not only are they considered ageless, but their characteristics are statically conceived; a ballad either has certain stylistic features or it lacks them (1968: 3). Taking a lead from this sense of frustration, McCarthy draws attention not only to an interesting feature of ballad structure but also to the way anomalous features, such as those examined by Furey, can all too easily be overlooked in songs which may have become too familiar. Structural features can be a significant indicator of date and evolutionary history. From this perspective, it becomes clear that a particular editor's, collector's, or singer's aesthetic can be a key factor in shaping our concepts of ballad form.

Motif study has been a fruitful field of research for many years, one perhaps not so long neglected as the structural anomalies just noted. Using motifs examined in classic studies (for example, Thompson 1955–58), Nicolae Constantinescu's and Larysa Vakhnina's essays explore the status and treatment of spousal murder in Ukrainian and Romanian tradition, the former through poisoning, the latter through the widespread international motif of the walled-up wife, "which has attracted the attention of many, if not most, ballad specialists in that part of the world" (Dundes 1996: x). Early work on this theme focused on conjectured origins, later work on the motif's possible ritual origins in the foundation sacrifice (x). To the debate, Constantinescu contributes a survey of its Romanian manifestations, set firmly in their regional, cultural, international contexts, throwing light on gender-based differences in singers' repertoires. As in most ballad studies, it appears that the role of the individual singer eventually influences the identity of the genre itself.

## Notes

1. These are, principally, Olrik's "epic laws" (1965, originally 1909), Stith Thompson's motif index (1955–58), Vladimir Propp's tale roles (1968, originally 1928) and Parry's and Lord's oral-formulaic theory (Lord 1964; Lord 2000). Other influential works include those of Lévi-Strauss (1963, 1969), and Bakhtin (1981).
2. Among them are Cheesman 1994: chapter 3 (functions), and McCarthy 1990; Buchan 1972; Andersen and Pettitt 1979, Atkinson 2002 (tale roles). For an examination of the interchange of plot between ballads and folktales, see Taylor 1964.
3. I use the word "corpus" advisedly because I feel "canon" gives the wrong impression.

## References

Andersen, Flemming G., and Thomas Pettitt. 1979. "Mrs Brown of Falkland: A Singer of Tales?" *Journal of American Folklore* 92: 1–24.

Atkinson, David. 2002. *The English Traditional Ballad: Theory, Method, and Practice.* Ashgate Popular and Folk Music Series. Aldershot and Burlington, Vt.: Ashgate.

Bakhtin, Mikhail Mikhailovich. 1981. *The Dialogic Imagination: Four Essays.* Edited by Michael Holquist; translated by Caryl Emerson and Michael Holquist. University of Texas Press Slavic Series, no. 1. Austin: University of Texas Press.

Bronson, Bertrand Harris. 1959–72. *The Traditional Tunes of the Child Ballads, with Their Texts, According to the Extant Records of Great Britain and America.* 4 vols. Princeton: Princeton University Press.

Buchan, David. 1972. *The Ballad and the Folk.* London: Routledge and Kegan Paul. Reprint, Phantassie, East Lothian: Tuckwell Press, 1997.

Cheesman, Tom. 1994. *The Shocking Ballad Picture Show: German Popular Literature and Cultural History.* Oxford: Berg.

Dundes, Alan, ed. 1996. *The Walled-Up Wife: A Casebook.* Madison: University of Wisconsin Press.

Fowler, David C. 1968. *A Literary History of the Popular Ballad*. Durham: Duke University Press.

Ives, Edward D. 1964. *Larry Gorman: The Man Who Made the Songs*. Bloomington: Indiana University Press.

Lévi-Strauss, Claude. 1963. *Structural Anthropology*. Translated by Claire Jacobson and Brooke Grundfest Schoepf. New York: Basic Books.

Lévi-Strauss, Claude. 1969. *The Raw and the Cooked*. Translated by John and Doreen Weightman. Introduction to a Science of Mythology, no. 1. New York: Harper and Row.

Lord, Albert B. 2000. *The Singer of Tales*. Edited by Stephen Mitchell and Gregory Nagy. 2d ed. Harvard Studies in Comparative Literature, no. 24. Cambridge: Harvard University Press, 1964. Reprint, Cambridge: Harvard University Press.

McCarthy, William Bernard. 1990. *The Ballad Matrix: Personality, Milieu, and the Oral Tradition*. Bloomington and Indianapolis: Indiana University Press, 1990.

Olrik, Axel. 1965 [1909]. "The Epic Laws of Folk Narrative." In *The Study of Folklore*, edited by Alan Dundes, 129–41. Englewood: Prentice-Hall.

Propp, Vladimir. 1968. *Morphology of the Folktale*. 2d rev. ed. with a preface by Louis A. Wagner and a new introduction by Alan Dundes. American Folklore Society Bibliographical and Special Series, vol. 9. Indiana University Research Center in Anthropology, Folklore, and Linguistics, publication 10. Austin: University of Texas Press.

Taylor, Archer. 1964. "The Parallels between Ballads and Tales." *Jahrbuch für Volksliedforschung* 9: 104–15.

Thompson, Stith. 1955–58. *Motif-Index of Folk-Literature: A Classification of Narrative Elements in Folktales, Ballads, Myths, Fables, Mediaeval Romances, Exempla, Fabliaux, Jestbooks, and Local Legends*. 6 vols. Rev. and enl. ed. Copenhagen: Rosenkilde and Bagger.

Toelken, Barre. 1995. *Morning Dew and Roses: Nuance, Metaphor, and Meaning in Folksongs*. Folklore and Society, Publications of the American Folklore Society, New Series. Urbana and Chicago: University of Illinois Press.

Una cançó vull cantar,
una cançó nova i linda,
d'un estudiant de Vic,
que en festejava una viuda.
  Bon amor, adéu-siau,
  color de rosa florida.
  Bon amor, adéu-siau.
La viuda s'hi vol casar,
el seu pare no ho volia;
l'estudiant se n'és anat
a servir una rectoria.
Quan la viuda ho va saber,
tingué llarga malaltia.
La viudeta se'n va a l'hort,
en un jardí que hi tenia,
un jardí de totes flors,
rosa vera i satalia.
A la vora del jardí
un roseret n'hi havia;
a la vora del roser,
la viuda s'hi adormia;
ja en passava un rossinyol

Fig. 1. "L'estudiant de Vic," from "Cançoner" by Joan Amades in *Folklore de Catalunya*.

Fig. 2. Musical phrasing of "L'estudiant de Vic."

# An Oddity of Catalan Folk Songs and Ballads

## Simon Furey

Catalonia lies on the Mediterranean coast, straddling the Pyrenees. Its people are very musical, and dancing in the streets is still commonplace. Anyone who has observed its national dance, the *sardana,* however, will have noticed a most peculiar feature: the dancers do not seem to dance in time to the music, yet the circles of dancers are all in time with each other. In fact, they are dancing to a rhythm that only coincides with the accompanying music after a fixed number of bars, a number which depends on the particular dance or part of it. It follows, therefore, that these dancers are likely to have a highly developed rhythmical sense. Indeed, one of the things I first noticed when I began to take an interest in Catalan folk songs was the complexity of some of their rhythms, and it is this complexity I will explore. I am not concerned here with the specificities of syllabic rhythms, which have already been dealt with in some depth by others (Aiats 1990: 93–109; Rövenstrunck 1979: 40–63), but with the rhythms and meter in relation to entire lines of text.

A case in point is the ballad "L'estudiant de Vic," a sad tale of a widow courted by a young man sent away to become a priest (Fig. 1, opposite, top). This is, of course, only a fragment of the complete song, but it is enough for our purposes. In general, every second line ends in -*a*, and the syllable count is a more or less consistent, alternating 7/8; there is nothing unconventional about the text verse structure as written. Readers unfamiliar with Catalan, and trying to work out the syllable count, should be aware that adjacent vowels are generally condensed into a single syllable (*h* and final *r* behave "invisibly" and are silent). The main exception in this text is the line, "Bon amor, adéu-siau," which is not condensed and has seven syllables.

If we turn now to the music, two features are apparent. First, the rhythm is uneven; listening to the song reveals that the mixture of 9/8 and 3/8 rhythms is only a written approximation of the actual pulse. Fig. 2 (opposite, bottom) shows the musical phrasing._We can see that the tune contains only three different musical phrases, which form the pattern *abcbcbc*. If we superimpose these phrases on the words, we get a most odd result (Fig. 3, overleaf).

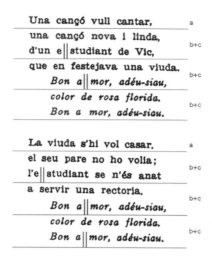

Fig. 3. Effect of musical phrasing in "L'estudiant de Vic."

If we first take the *b* and *c* phrases together in pairs, as marked by the horizontal lines in the diagram, we notice that the end of a verse does not coincide with a musical-phrase end. The chorus is simply absorbed into an extended verse. Indeed, there is no separate tune for the chorus. If we then take the *b* and *c* phrases separately, we notice that the end of the *b* phrase happens in the middle of a word: *a/mor* and *e/studiant*.

What this means is that we have a clear structure for the words and one for the tune, but they do not fit together. Indeed, we might write the metrical structure of the words as sung in the following form:

> Una cançó vull cantar;
> una cançó nova i linda d'un e
> studiant de Vic
> que festejava una viuda bon a
> mor adéu-siau
> color de rosa florida bon a
> mor adéu siau.

Part of the charm of this song, I think, is its apparent freedom. Yet it is not free; it simply has an unconventional combination of words and music. Here, perhaps, we have a song parallel to the *sardana,* but instead of the circles of dancers not following the tune, the lines of text do not. This unconventional combination can be characterized by the term "musical dislocation." The layout for the text of "L'estudiant de Vic" is a convenient, shorthand way of demonstrating it.

I originally put this song down as an oddity, having found no others quite like it among the collections published before the Spanish Civil War. However, I encountered another instance on a record produced in 1994 by the Catalan group, Clau de lluna. The song, "El pobre banya," is an amusing—and allegedly true—tale about a willing cuckold and comes from the town of Organyà in the district of Alt Urgell. It begins this way (as written in the sleeve notes):

> Déu vos guarga, l'arminguet, quina botiga n'heu muntada
> i de fil i de cotó i altra roba delicada
> Feu-li llum, feu-li llum el pobre banya, feu-li llum.

This song appears in some collections (for example, Amades 1982: 523) with a different and more-regular tune but has the same tune in volume six of *Obra del cançoner popular de Catalunya: Materials,* published in 1996. A short digression is in order here to explain the significance of this work.

In 1921 an ambitious project was undertaken to collect all of the folk songs of the Catalan-speaking lands. Small teams were sent to all points, near and far, to collect both words and music. They were successful beyond their wildest dreams and collected thousands of songs. Meanwhile, in Barcelona, another team had the unenviable task of editing the material into published volumes that contained not only the songs but background information and commentary on Catalan folk music. The editorial team was swamped, and as the years went by, the backlog of unpublished material became enormous. The situation was further complicated by political instability in the region. Collection came to a halt in 1936 with the outbreak of civil war, although a limited amount of editorial work continued during the hostilities until 1938. Over the period of the *Obra*'s activity, five books were produced, three of which contained songs collected up to 1925.

Following Franco's victory in 1939, Catalan culture was suppressed and much material destroyed. Fortunately, the unedited *Obra* papers were hidden away and preserved almost entirely. In the early 1990s, a project began at Montserrat Abbey, outside Barcelona, to publish the materials under the supervision of the eminent Catalan scholar and folklorist, Father Josep Massot i Muntaner. Publication began in 1993 at the rate of one volume per year, and Father Massot estimates that it will be nearly 2010 before selections of all of the material have been published.

## 54. DÉU LO GUARD, GALANT MINGUET

— Déu lo guard, galant Minguet,
quina botiga n'heu plantada,
ai, de fil i de cotó
i altra roba delicada.
*Feu-li llum, feu-li llum*
*al pobre banya,*
*feu-li llum.* ·
I de fil i de cotó
i altra roba delicada.
I a on teniu vostra muller,
que no la vei voltar per casa?
— Lo Lluís de l'Esquerrer,
que me la n'ha manllevada.
*Puja'l dalt,*
*puja'l dalt i gica'l caure,*

*xot-lo baix.*
Lo Lluís de l'Esquerrer,
que me la n'ha manllevada.
Me l'ha comprat per una nit,
quinze dies ja que em falta.
*Feu-li llum...*
Me l'ha comprat per una nit,
quinze dies ja que em falta,
i quon ella tornarà
jo li'n trencaré una cama.
*Feu-li llum...*
I quon ella tornarà
jo li'n trencaré una cama;
també li'n trencaré un braç
i li'n nyaufaré la cara.

Fig. 4. Beginning of "Déu lo guard, galant Minguet."

The newer publications differ from the prewar ones in one important respect. Instead of printed scores that are the result of editorial work and amendment, facsimiles of the original collected musical notations are included. The reader can analyze original field notes and see where the singer has probably varied the performance and where the collector has attempted to record these variations. The disadvantage is that mistakes, omissions, and inconsistencies caused by the method of recording are also present. Unfortunately, where uncertainties exist, it is no longer possible to ask the collectors about the right interpretation.

That said, one can only marvel at the quality of the notation, given that it was done in the field, almost entirely without phonographic recording apparatus.

Volume six of the *Obra* materials contains the notes from the field trip of Palmira Jaquetti and Maria Carbó to Alt Urgell, Pallars, and Arán undertaken between 9 July and 3 September 1925. The songs include a version of "El pobre banya" entitled "Deu lo guard, galant Minguet" (no. 54), collected in Organyà. The tune is the same as the one in the *Clau de lluna* recording, although the title is different, and the words are not quite the same (it is clearly a close variant but written down in a slightly different format than the one in the record notes). The following extract is from the *Obra* materials. It should be remembered that this version was published two years after the appearance of the recording, although collected nearly seventy years before it. It is almost certain, therefore, that the Clau de lluna version has come down through oral tradition independently of the *Obra* version, and it confirms the structure of the song as collected and notated in 1925 (Fig. 4, left). In fact, the *Obra* version seems simply to have removed some garbling from the first line of the Clau de lluna version, and it expresses the stanzaic form more clearly.

When we examine this song (or better still, listen to the recording), we sense the kind of dislocation that we noticed with "L'estudiant de Vic," and it happens in both the written and recorded versions. In this instance, there is a chorus tune, but it starts halfway through the last line of the verse, and there is another break halfway through the chorus line. Thus, if we use the text shorthand from the previous example, the chorus of the first verse is sung as follows:

> ...cada feu-li llum
> feu-li llum al pobre
> banya feu-li llum.

There is a clear dislocation between the tune phrasing and the words, in this instance half a line.

This is not the only example of such anomalies. The Jaquetti-Carbó notes contain a number of other songs that exhibit this phenomenon. Here is another, "Dona i prenda" (no. 58), a tale of a lord about to kill his fourth wife, who is saved by the intercession of her baby who miraculously speaks and pleads for her (Fig. 5, overleaf). There are all sorts of interesting things about this particular ballad which merit analysis but are outside the scope of this present investigation.

## 58. DONA I PRENDA

Dona i prenda se'n passeja
per una sala molt *grande*;
vénen les dolors de part,
que no deixaven cessar-la.

— Vés-te'n, dona i prenda,
a Castillo amb la mare. —
Dona i prenda se n'hi va,
a Castillo amb sa mare.

Fig. 5. Dona i prenda.

From a musical standpoint, some interpretation is required. The music has a triplet indicated underneath the second note of the second bar, using a short-hand notation seen elsewhere in the collection. Applying this to the entire melody (otherwise the time signature makes no sense) results in a *havanera* rhythm. The beginning has an anacrusis but one that creates a most odd result. To fit the rhythm, each line "steals" a syllable from the following one to make up the count. This is very apparent in the music. When taken into the preceding line of the melody, however, this syllable does not produce an anacrusis. Instead, the *havanera* rhythm keeps its longer note at the end of each phrase. The result is that each line, as sung, ends on the first syllable of the next line as written.

The effect in the first verse is that, instead of rhyming or creating assonance on the last syllable of a written line, assonance is created on a first syllable, thus,

Do
na i prenda se'n passeja per
una sala molt grande vé
nen les dolors de part que
no deixaven cessar-la.

Note that in Catalan, *per* is pronounced almost as *pé* and thus rhymes (or at least creates assonance) with *vé*, whereas *que* and *la* rhyme with a *schwa* vowel. At the end of the verse, the syllable loss creates a dramatic pause, which is no accidental arrangement. It would be possible to fit the words without the anacrusis and syllable shift. However, the notation makes quite clear what is happening. It is another example of dislocation, this time of a single syllable.

There are one or two other less-clear examples in the same printed collection, which contains eighty-seven songs. Thus, the phenomenon seems uncommon. It is worth pointing out that the published *Obra* materials generally contain only a small sample of the songs collected; the reader is thus at the mercy of the editor as to what is available for analysis. The total number of songs actually collected by Jaquetti and Carbó is not noted, and the frequency of occurrence is therefore impossible to ascertain from the evidence examined so far.

I have chosen to use the term musical dislocation because each tune has a structure, and the text has a structure, but it seems that the singer does not feel constrained to put the two together in the conventional manner so that the text phrasing coincides with the musical phrases. Instead, they may be combined to obtain completely different effects, as in the examples shown. Does this dislocation occur in other traditions, or is it a Catalan peculiarity? I have not found evidence of it in Castilian, French, Italian, or Provençal songs as yet, and further research is necessary before making any generalizations.

It is sometimes argued that where the words do not fit the tune, it is simply the result of a hack song peddler fitting an existing tune to some new words and doing a poor job. I do not accept that argument in this case. First, the tunes do not seem to belong to any recognizable families that have better word fits elsewhere (and Catalan folk music certainly contains tune families). I cannot be positive about this since the corpus of songs is simply too large for me to be totally familiar with it, but I think that ballad sellers would primarily have used common tunes where possible, and these are easy to recognize. Secondly, the songs are found all over Catalonia and particularly in the foothills of the Pyrenees. Until relatively recently (the 1980s), roads to some of the small villages were only dirt tracks. Indeed, the *Obra* collectors in the 1920s write of days on muleback to reach their destinations. Communication was extremely difficult; thus, I think it is unlikely that ballad sellers would have traveled to such far-flung places, especially because the people—particularly Catalan speakers—were probably illiterate anyway. In other words, we are looking at song transmission that has a high probability of being oral. The oddity is, therefore, in my view a genuine part of the Catalan song tradition, not just a clumsy accident.

In the first group, typified by "Barbara Allen" and "The Gypsy Laddie," the name or word that determines all the rhymes has a refrainlike quality. In addition to these two ballads and "Geordie," I found nine other ballads (see the list below) that utilize the same metrical form and refrainlike rhyming technique. True refrains that stand apart from the narrative lines also appear in a number of ballads, most notably the couplet ballads, but I did not count these in the single-rhyme census. I did, however, find a number of other metrical types where refrainlike narrative lines determine the rhyme scheme.

"Glasgow Peggie" (Child 228) and "Richie Story" (Child 232) constitute the whole of the second group, with feminine rhymes controlled by the names of the title characters, much as in ballads of the "Barbara Allen" type but with four beats in all four lines of the *abcb* stanza. "Lord Saltoun and Auchanachie" (Child 239), in a group by itself, is also composed in four-beat lines, but it rhymes *aabb*. The fourth line usually ends "Auchanachie," and the third rhymes with it. The ballads of the fourth group contain refrainlike last lines but are composed in stanzas of four very long lines (or eight short lines); the first and second long lines rhyme freely, but the third and fourth share a common rhyme determined by the refrainlike last half-line or line. These ballads are "Captain Wedderburn's Courtship" (Child 46), "John of Hazelgreen" (Child 293), and "Walter Lesly" (Child 296). In the fifth group are two ballads in the Middle English carol stanza of *aaab*, with all the *b* lines on the same rhyme. They are "The Gaberlunyie-Man" (Child 279 appendix) and the closely related "Beggar Laddie" (Child 280). Into a sixth group, I put a number of ballads composed in nonce stanzas with refrainlike lines that encourage a consistent single rhyme. In "Fair Flower of Northumberland" (Child 9), for example, the three-line stanza always ends with the word "Scotland" or "Northumberland." "The Golden Vanity" (Child 286) has a dozen ways to form stanzas but consistently uses rhymes on "vanity" and "lonesome sea." "Lord Randal" (Child 12), "Edward" (Child 13), and "The Maid Freed from the Gallows" (Child 95) also contain refrainlike lines that impose a common rhyme throughout the ballad.

In addition to ballads with refrainlike rhymes, I also found some with more straightforward single rhymes reminiscent of ones common in Spanish balladry. Indeed, since the most common rhyme sound in English ballads is long *e,* I expected that some ballads would rely on long-*e* rhyme throughout. Such proved to be the case. But first I should point out that some ballads, despite a marked preference for the long-*e* rhyme, at least in some versions, seem to admit stanzas with other rhymes freely enough to disqualify them as single-rhyme ballads—for example, "King Arthur and King Cornwall" (Child 30), "Young Andrew" (Child 48), and "Young Beichan" (Child 53). Quite apart from these, a large group of ballads (group seven) exhibits consistent long-*e* rhymes, regularly combined with a long meter stanza, four beats to the line. Seven of these are historical ballads, most with Percy connections: "King Henry V's Conquest of France" (Child 164), "Johnnie Armstrong" (Child 169B), "The Rising in the North" (Child 175), "The Earl of Westmoreland" (Child 177), "The Laird o' Logie" (Child 182), "Archie o' Cawfield" (Child 188), and "Outlaw Murray" (Child 305). In one of these, "The Laird o' Logie," the name must be pronounced "Low-GEE," with wrenched accent on the second syllable, and rhyme words such as "courte-SY" and "fer-RIE," must also be pronounced with wrenched accent on the last syllable. Five more magical ballads, mostly from Mrs. Brown of Falkland, are metrically identical to these historical ballads but do not rely quite as consistently on long-*e* rhymes. These five are "Kemp Owyne" (Child 34), "Allison Gross" (Child 35), "The Laily Worm and the Machrel of the Sea" (Child 36), "Thomas Rymer" (Child 37B), and "Brown Robin's Confession" (Child 57).

I found only two possible single-rhyme ballads with neither refrainlike nor long-*e* rhymes. "Erlinton" (Child 8) exhibits moderately consistent, but rather free, *n* rhymes, such as "pin"/"gane" and "wane"/"dawn." And "St. Stephen and King Herod" (Child 22) retains enough rhymes on "halle" to suggest that at one time the whole ballad may have relied on that rhyme. These two ballads constitute group eight.

Most of the categories of single-rhyme ballads, then, contain few examples. But two groups are more substantial, the initial "Barbara Allen"/"Gypsy Laddie" group and the long-*e*, long-meter group of historical ballads, mostly from Percy's *Reliques* (1765 [1996]), and magical ballads, mostly from Mrs. Brown (see Buchan 1972). The historical ballads, in particular, intrigued me at first. Apparently dating back to the sixteenth and early seventeenth century, and closely resembling late versions of romances, they seem to corroborate Fowler's thesis in *A Literary History of the Popular Ballad* (1968: chap. 4) that a minstrel ballad tradition operated into the seventeenth century. These ballads even serve to pinpoint where that minstrel tradition operated and where relics of it survived for another hundred years or more, namely, in the old Northumbrian section of northeast England and just across the border in Scotland. But survival proved to be the key element to consider. These ballads did indeed survive to be included in the Percy folio, or subsequently to be collected by Percy, but they have not survived into the twentieth century. In most cases there is only one text ever recorded for each. Four out of the five metrically similar magical ballads also survived only into the early nineteenth century. The only possible exception is "Thomas Rymer," which Duncan Williamson sings in a version (not single rhyme) that seems traditional and textually independent of the nineteenth-century versions (1987: 252–57); in other words, it is not a deliberate reworking of any of the three variations in Child. This group of historical and magical ballads may therefore constitute a subgenre, but it is essentially a dead one.

The other large group of these single-rhyme ballads, however, has not only survived but thrives, even today. Versions of "Barbara Allen," "The Gypsy Laddie," and others, have been collected in large numbers not only in England and Scotland but also in Ireland and North America, and they continue to be recorded. This group includes enough ballads, with enough common characteristics in addition to meter and rhyme technique, to warrant consideration as a living subgenre.

I found a total of twelve ballads that clearly belong in this group:

"Barbara Allen" (84)
"The Bonnie House o' Airlie" (199)
"The Gypsy Laddie" (200)
"Geordie" (209)
"The Braes o' Yarrow" (214)
"Rare Willie Drowned in Yarrow" (215)
"Andrew Lammie" (233)
"The Earl of Aboyne" (235)
"The Rantin Laddie" (240)
"The Baron o' Leys" (241)
"James Hatley" (244)
"Earl Rothes" (297)

Of these, the oldest seem to be "Barbara Allen," "The Gypsy Laddie," and perhaps "Geordie"; the newest is probably "Andrew Lammie." As one of those early ballads may well be the prototype for the subgenre, it is worth asking just how old the three are and whether they originated in England or Scotland.

The earliest reference to "Barbara Allen" is the famous entry of 2 January 1666 in the diary of Samuel Pepys: "I to my Lord Bruncker's; and there find...above all, my dear Mrs. Knipp, with whom I sang; and in perfect pleasure I was to hear her sing, and especially her little Scotch song of Barbary Allen."[1] Reading between the lines, one gathers that the song was old even in Pepys's day. But was it Scottish? Apparently Pepys did not mean to imply that. According to Hales, in an essay at the beginning of volume two of *Bishop Percy's Folio Manuscript*: "Songs and ballads of rustic and of humble life were called 'Scotch' from about the middle of the 17th century, and without any intention of imputing to them a Scottish origin, or that they were imitations." Hales adds, surprisingly, "This conventional meaning of 'Scotch' seems to have been accepted in Scotland as well as in England, for in no other sense could Allan Ramsay claim, among others, Gay's ballad, 'Black-ey'd Susan,' in the first part of 'A Miscellany of Scots Sangs'" (1867–68: xv note). The same, he says, applies to Thompson's *Orpheus Caledonius*, which includes pieces by Ambrose Phillips and other well-known Englishmen.

Sometimes, when textual evidence cannot answer questions of provenance, musical clues can suggest answers. When we look at the melodic tradition of "Barbara Allen," however, we find that the evidence is mixed. There is indeed a clear English tradition (Bronson's Group A) but also a distinctively Scots tradition (Bronson's Group B). And two further traditions (Groups C and D) are mostly American but with Scottish connections; Group C is a typically pentatonic Appalachian group with some Scots connections, while D is related to the Scots "Boyne Water" family of tunes.

To summarize the information on age and provenance: On the one hand, the earliest mention of the ballad is in England in 1666. When Pepys used the term "Scotch song," he may have meant no more than what we mean today when we, equally loosely, use the term "folk song." And there is one distinct and strong English melodic tradition. On the other hand, there is a strong Scots melodic tradition as well, and two other distinct traditions that have stronger connections with Scotland than England. The song tradition has been stronger in Scotland and Scotch-Irish parts of North America than in England and English parts of North America. And Pepys just might have meant what he said—or been more accurate than he knew—when he called the song Scotch. For "Barbara Allen," then, the evidence is ultimately ambiguous. While I strongly suspect that it is a northern song, we cannot consider the issue settled.

The case of "The Gypsy Laddie" is just the opposite: There is really no question about the provenance, but the date is unclear. The ballad seems unambiguously Scots, but the earliest known text is in the 1740 *Tea-Table Miscellany* (Child 1882–98, 4: 61). Bronson, however, feels that the connection with the house of Cassilis can show us the way to an earlier date:

The first class [of tunes for "Gypsy Laddie"] has one of the longest
traditional sequences observable in all British balladry. Its earliest
appearance is in the Skene MS., *ante* 1630; its latest is current
today. The name which it bears in the Skene MS. is "Lady Cassiles
Lilt," and Child as well as later students, failed, I believe, to note the
full implications of this fact. Child says that we have no evidence
that the ballad was associated in tradition with the Cassilis family
until the end of the eighteenth century. But this tune yields such
evidence. For it is indisputably the same tune as the one found with
our ballad in Johnson's *Museum* and in a number of recent traditional versions. The Skene tune was never translated from tablature
until Dauney published it in 1834, and anyhow it is obvious that
later variants have developed traditionally, not by derivation from
that or any other authoritative record. The most reasonable explanation of such a phenomenon is that the ballad was associated with
the family which gave its name to the tune much earlier than explicit
statements survive to show, and earlier indeed—supposing the
ballad in anything like its later form to have been circulating around
1630—by nearly a hundred years than the first extant record of the
text. (1959–72, 3: 198)

The Skene Manuscript evidence thus pushes the record of "Gypsy Laddie" back
into the early seventeenth century, a time when Gypsies had just been expelled
from Scotland and several Gypsies named Johnnie Faw were hanged for violat-
ing the interdict (Child 1882–98, 4: 63–4).

In the case of "Geordie," the evidence for age and point of origin is ambiguous. The Scots texts of "Geordie" are no earlier than the 1780s, a hundred years
or more after the earliest English texts, but Child's headnote suggests that the
historical events behind the ballad may well be traceable to 1554 and Scotland
(1882–98, 4: 124). The 1680 English broadside ballad "George of Oxford," moreover, seems to be a reworking of a traditional text to reflect events contemporary
with the broadside. It exhibits a slightly different plot and cast of characters from
the ones found in traditional versions of "Geordie." Of a second Northumbrian
"Geordie" broadside, "George Stoole," Child says that it "was printed by H.
Gosson, whose time is put at 1607–1641" (1882–98, 4: 126). He adds in a note on
the same page that "it seems to have been familiar in Aberdeen as early as 1627,"
when a Robert Gordon there collected a tune called "God Be with Thee, Geordie"

(Child received this information from William Macmath). The English broadsides are, then, earlier than any collected Scots texts but seem to be reworkings of a traditional song (or songs?), probably Scots, rather than the original forms of the ballad (see Motherwell 1827: lxxvi note; Cox 1925: 135). Child assigns the Scots form of the ballad to the main body of his entry and reserves the "George of Oxford" and "George Stoole" broadsides for an appendix.

The tunes associated with the ballad do not really clarify the question of origin. The older Northumbrian "George Stoole" broadside mentions no tune but supplies the following refrain:

> Heigh-ho, heigh-ho, my bony love,
>> Heigh-ho, heigh-ho, my bonny!
> Heigh-ho, heigh-ho, my own deare love,
>> And God be with my Georgie!

The tune Robert Gordon collected in Aberdeen in 1627, "God Be with Thee, Geordie," is surely the appropriate one, but today we have no way of knowing whether this was a Scots or an English tune. The headnote for the "George of Oxford" broadside does mention a tune, "Poor Georgie," which apparently pre-dates the broadside; this tune too, however, is otherwise unidentifiable (Simpson 1966: 136 n). Like the "Barbara Allen" evidence, the indications from "Geordie" tunes that have survived in tradition are mixed. One clear tradition (Bronson's Group B), with texts more like the broadsides, goes to an English tune. The other three traditions have Scots tunes, all also associated with other ballads (a "Gypsy Laddie" tune, Bronson's Group A; a "Barbara Allen" tune, Bronson's Group C; and a tune from the widespread Boyne Water family of ballad tunes).

After considering the evidence in each case, it seems safe to say that the three earliest identifiable examples of the "Barbara Allen"/"Gypsy Laddie" ballad subgenre were already known in the early seventeenth century. It is not as clear that the subgenre originated in Scotland. But whether this form of the single-rhyme ballad originated in Scotland or not, it was there that it took root. The three oldest of these twelve ballads exhibit strong—even if not exclusive—Scots affiliations, while the later nine are all clearly Scots in subject matter and tradition.

But what are the characteristics, besides Scots provenance, that make this a single subgenre? First, in these ballads there is a single word that determines the rhyme throughout. For five of the ballads, this word is a proper name: "Allen,"

"Geordie," "Airlie," and "Hatley," and in some texts of Child 215, "Willy." For three it is a geographical term: "Yarrow," "Gemrie," and "London." For one it is the word "lady," which is really a title, and for three more it is the word "laddie," also a sort of title. "Andrew Lammie" is anomalous in this, as in several other regards: the two names "Lammie" and "Annie" seem jointly to control the rhyme.

All of these rhyming words, "Allen," "Geordie," "laddie," "Lammie," and the rest, are two-syllable words with the accent on the first syllable. Consequently, these ballads share a feminine rhyme scheme, a feature in itself unusual in the Child tradition, which heavily favors masculine rhymes. The meter is a form of the ballad stanza, with four beats in the first and third nonrhyming lines and three beats in the second and fourth feminine-rhyming lines.

Next, the rhyme is even freer in these ballads than is usual in the Child corpus and in English/Scots folk song generally. "Yarrow," for instance, is intended to rhyme with "sorrow" and "morrow" but also with "before O," "clear O," "gude O," and "yellow." "Allen" is paired with "tavern," "token," "to him," "near him," "fell in," and "yellow," as well as with "dwelling," "falling," "growing," "hanging," or almost any other "-ing" word.

When we look at the aesthetic of these ballads, a definite lyric quality can be discerned; Pepys called "Barbara Allen" a song, and the appellation fits. The presence of this lyric quality confirms what David Fowler has to say about the aesthetic shift in ballads in the eighteenth century. He sees ballads of the preceding century or so as strongly narrative. And indeed that seems true of the long-*e* rhyming ballads with roots in the fifteenth and sixteenth centuries. But sometime around 1700, "the traditional narrative emphasis of ballads gradually became subservient to the influence of melody, which began to play a much more important part in determining ballad structure" (1968: 15–16). This movement expressed itself in intensification of narrative symmetry, development of commonplaces, and maturing of incremental repetition (1968: 16–17). In the case of the present set of ballads, we may add development of equally lyrical and haunting airs.

In discussing the lyric character of this subgenre, I will limit my examples to "The Bonnie House o' Airlie," a ballad not so familiar as others of the twelve. Parallels from the more-familiar "Barbara Allen," "Andrew Lammie," or "Gypsy Laddie" will easily come to mind.

By intensification of narrative symmetry, Fowler seems to mean both compression and increased similarity of part to part of the story, achieved, to some extent, by repetition. This symmetry is clear in "Airlie." Versions tend to run to eight or ten stanzas, with the longest in Bronson reaching only twelve. The use of repetition to forward the narrative is frequent in virtually all texts. For example, in stanza two of the text in Child's additions and corrections (1882–98, 5: 252), the men of Argyll come "For to plunder the bonnie house of Airly."

In stanza three,

> Lady Margaret looks oer her bower-window,
>     And O but she looks weary!
> And there she spied the great Argyll
>     Coming to plunder the bonnie house of Airly.

In stanza five, the great Argyll "…hath taken her by the left shoulder,/ Says, Lady where lyes thy dowry?" To which she replies, "It's up and it's down by the bonny bank-side." And in stanza seven,

> He hath taken her by the middle so small,
>     And O but she lokd weary!
> He hath laid her down by the bonny burn-side
>     Till he hath plundered the bonnie house of Airly.

This repetition is not incremental, but every line in that seventh stanza reworks at least one earlier one.

Repetition that is more truly incremental does occur in many versions of the ballad, such as the double-stanza Christie text (Bronson 1959–72, 3: 193):

> But ye'll tak' me by the milk white hand,
>     And ye'll tak me fairly,
> And ye'll lead me down to yon deep deep glen
>     That I mayna see the burning o' Airlie.

> He's ta'en her by the milk white hand,
>     But he hasna ta'en her fairly;
> For he led her up to yon high high hill,
>     Bade her look at the burning o' Airlie.

> "Ye'll bring to me a cup o' wine,
>     Ye'll bring me it frae Airlie,

> And I'll drink to Charlie the chief o' our clan,
>     And syne to my ain Lord Airlie."

Commonplaces also abound, as is clear from the preceding examples. Generally, however, they are only one or two lines in length:

> It fell on a day, on a bonny summer day,
>     When corn grew green and yellow.

> The lady looked over her own castle-wa.

> "Come down, come down, Lady Margaret," he said,
>     "Come down, and kiss me fairly."

> "I swear by the swerd I haud in my hand."

> He's ta'en her by the milk white hand.

Nevertheless, two stanzas regularly occurring in this ballad may be called proper commonplace ones, adapted to the context:

> "Gin my gweed lord had been at home,
>     As he's awa' for Charlie,
> There dursna a Campbell o' a' Argylle
>     Set a fit on the bonnie hoose o' Airlie"

and

> "Eleven bairns I ha'e born,
>     And the twelfth ne'er saw his daddie,
> But though I had gotten as mony again,
>     They suld a' gang to fecth for Charlie."

The melodious, lyrical quality of this ballad's tune is likewise typical of the subgenre. Bronson divides the main tune into two groups. The first, older group includes the authentic forms of the tune. The second includes the plagal. Many readers, although they may never have heard the ballad, nevertheless know one plagal form of the tune united to a later set of words, those of the familiar and much-loved "Loch Lomond." "The Bonnie House o' Airlie" thus exhibits not only a haunting melody but also all the traits, including intensification of narrative symmetry, commonplace development, and mature incremental repetition, that Fowler identifies with an aesthetic shift in balladry characterized by the subordination of narrative to melody. These same traits, and equally haunting melodies, are apparent in other ballads of this subgenre.

A final characteristic of this ballad subgenre is durability. Though I know of no post-Child texts of "Jamie Hatley" or "Earl Rothes," the other ten of these twelve ballads survived well into the twentieth century in oral tradition. Admittedly, for two of these ten, "Rantin Laddie" and "Baron o' Leys," the twentieth-century record is rather skimpy. But others, such as "Barbara Allen," "Yarrow," "Andrew Lammie," and "The Gypsy Laddie," continue (even as the twenty-first century gets under way) to be among the most popular of all ballads. The single rhyme, combined with the other characteristics discussed, apparently rendered these songs not just memorable but easily so.

This brief survey of single-rhyme ballads has uncovered two groups large enough to be considered subgenres within the Child corpus, in addition to a number of individual ballads and groups with distinctive rhyme and metrical schemes. The first of the subgenres, apparently from a now-extinct minstrel ballad tradition rooted in Northumberland, is characterized by long-meter (four beats to the line) stanzas with long-*e* rhymes and includes both historical and magical ballads. The second subgenre, from a still lively and widespread tradition probably Scots in origin and dating from the early seventeenth century, features lyrical romantic narratives—even when the subject matter is historical. These narratives, strongly influenced by their melodies, are framed in untypical feminine-rhyming ballad stanzas in all or nearly all of which a final word, a title ("lady" or "laddie") or a name, repeated from stanza to stanza like a refrain, determines rhyme but with considerable allowance. The melodic tunes and echoing stanzas create a lyric intensity that leads to narrative compression, enhanced by various other forms of verbal repetition, including incremental repetition, and effective use of commonplaces. As a result, these songs are not only attractive but also easy to remember, contributing, no doubt, to their unusual durability and the "perfect pleasure" that they have given listeners ever since the days of Samuel Pepys. If, as may well be the case, "Barbara Allen" was the first and the prototype of this subgenre, then we have to admit that when that hardhearted sweetheart rejected her Sweet William, she really started something. We should not be surprised, though, for we have always known that she was quite a woman.

## Notes

1. The entry can be found under this date in any edition of the diaries.

## References

Bronson, Bertrand Harris. 1959–72. *The Traditional Tunes of the Child Ballads, with Their Texts, According to the Extant Records of Great Britain and America.* 4 vols. Princeton: Princeton University Press.

Buchan, David. 1972. *The Ballad and the Folk.* London: Routledge and Kegan Paul. Reprint, Phantassie, East Lothian: Tuckwell Press, 1997.

Child, Francis James, ed. 1882–98. *The English and Scottish Popular Ballads.* 5 vols. Reprint, New York: Folklore Press, 1956–57; New York: Dover, 1965. Corrected edition prepared by Mark and Laura Heiman. Northfield, Minn.: Loomis House Press, 2002. Digital edition, with gazetteer, maps and audio CD. New York: ESPB Publishing, 2003.

Cox, John Harrington. 1925. *Folksongs of the South Collected under the Auspices of the West Virginia Folk-Lore Society.* Cambridge: Harvard University Press.

Fowler, David C. 1968. *A Literary History of the Popular Ballad.* Durham: Duke University Press.

Hales, John W., and Frederick Furnivall. 1867–68. *Bishop Percy's Folio Manuscript.* 3 vols. London: N. Trübner.

Motherwell, William. 1827. *Minstrelsy Ancient and Modern.* Glasgow: John Wylie.

Pepys, Samuel. 1985. *The Shorter Pepys.* Selected and edited by Robert Latham. Berkeley: University of California Press.

Percy, Thomas. 1996. *Reliques of Ancient English Poetry.* London: J. Dodsley, 1765. Facsimile edition edited by Nick Groom. London: Routledge/Thoemmes Press.

Simpson, Claude M. 1966. *The British Broadside and Its Music.* New Brunswick, N.J.: Rutgers University Press.

Williamson, Duncan, and Linda Williamson. 1987. *A Thorn in the King's Foot.* Harmondsworth: Penguin.

# The Motif of Poisoning in Ukrainian Ballads

Larysa Vakhnina

Poisoning for infidelity is a motif found throughout European tradition in both narratives and songs. One of the most popular ballads on this theme, "O Do Not Go, Hryts," is considered the classic example of its type and is found not only in the Ukraine but also in the ballad traditions of many other, particularly Slavic, nations. In this essay, I propose to examine versions of this song and some of the theories about its origins.

In *The Ukrainian Folk Ballad*, folklorist Oleksii Dei singles out the poisoning motif for special attention in the chapter "Love Ballads and Premarital Relations":

I–B: Witchcraft. Poisoning through witchcraft.

I–B–1: The calling of the dead lover for a date ("The Dead Lover").
The versions:
    A) The dead warrior takes his lover to the grave;
    B) The girl finds her lover's grave and talks to him.

I–B–2: The return (the defection) of a sweetheart by sorcery.

I–B–3: The boy has been poisoned with a love-potion, food and drinks.

I–B–4: The boy who loved two or three girls was poisoned by jealousy (girlfriend).

I–B–5: The girl poisons one of (the three of) those who were enamoured of her (with sorcery).

I–B–6: The girl is poisoned by sorcery at her wedding.

I–B–7: The sister poisons her brother, or the wife poisons her husband, as a consequence of her lover's calumny. (1986: 65–66)

The first print appearance of "O Do Not Go, Hryts" is in an early nineteenth-century Russian collection published by the merchant Sergei Petrov (1805: 21). Its central motif spread into Ukrainian folklore in the sixteenth to seventeenth centuries, and, by the nineteenth, the song existed in the collections of almost all the Slavic nations. Thereafter, it migrated into western Europe as well.

So popular has the ballad been that it has been translated many times, first into German. The song also appeared, with a tune, in the Lvov Catholic calendar

*Pielgrzym Lwowski* of 1822, and Austrian, German, and Hungarian musicians later borrowed the melody. In the 1840s, for example, after a tour of the Ukraine, Franz Liszt composed "The Ukrainian Ballad," whose melody is based on "O Do Not Go, Hrytsiu" (M. Fintsytski translated the text into Hungarian).[1]

When Ukrainian Poles emigrated to France and England after the defeat of November 1831, "Hryts" went with them and was subsequently cited in various essays and letters as a symbol of Ukrainian tradition and, indeed, the Ukraine itself. The ballad was also translated into French by the Polish poet Julius Slowacki, who mentions a "Cossack song" in a letter to his mother (1883: 30).

According to folklorist Hryhorij Nudha, an English version of the ballad was first published in London in Henryk Krasinski's *The Cossacks and Ukraine* (1848), a text which then appeared in various later editions. In 1916 it was published by Canadian poet F. R. Livesay under the title "The Daughter of the Witch." In 1935 it was published in a German "best songs of the world" collection after its performance by a group of Swiss musicians at the international exhibition in Brussels, where it captured the public imagination and was awarded first prize (Nudha 1967: 132).

Thus, the text of "O Do Not Go, Hryts" became the personification of the Cossack spirit in various nations of the world. Hryts was often referred to in Ukrainian ballads as exemplifying the glorious Cossack, a young, handsome man who is loved by many women at the same time:

> Oh, get up, Hrytsenku, glorious Cossack,
> Many woman are crying for you. (Dei and Iasenchuk 1987: 65)

One must note that, despite the girl's treachery, Hryts remains a hero beloved by friends; his death is often seen not as an act of revenge but as destiny. The weeds given him by his sweetheart primarily function as a love potion to bind him to the girl and turn him away from other lovers. His death is not always seen by the girl as a personal tragedy, in contrast to her mother, who asks why she poisoned him. She answers,

> Oh, mother, mother, the sorrow has no measure,
> Do not let Hryts love both at once. (Dei and Iasenchuk 1987: 66)

After his death, Hryts belongs to her alone, despite the fact that other girls constantly visit his grave. This ballad also has a kind of magical function because the text is often intertwined with the words of folk incantations.

Symbolism in the Ukrainian folk ballad is extremely rich and diversified, and it undoubtedly plays an important role in texts featuring the poisoning motif. It may be said that the female is the principal character in the Hryts ballad, despite the fact that the title bears his name. "The woman is basically the custodian of rituals and customs from the ancient days of confirmed, and already unfathomable, paganism" (Potebnia 1976: 224). In this feminist cultural conceptualization, the poisoning is not only revenge but also an echo of ancient traditions about the woman sovereign and her influence over a male's fate.

In another version, "Oyo, There's a Well in a Field," the man who wants to marry proposes that his intended poison her brother since he would undoubtedly stand in Hryts's way. She replies,

> Oh, be not daunted by my brother,
> I'll poison him myself.

And there is an unexpected symbolic comparison at the end:

> Oh, there are two guilder roses in the field,
> There were two vipers twisted together.
>                                               (Bodianski and Bodianski 1978: 188)

The girl becomes a personification of the malign forces that can punish and pardon, both loving and hating her partner, at once neglecting both her mother's advice and society's morals. Incidentally, Marusia, the heroine in most versions of "O Do Not Go, Hryts" is one of the most popular names in the Ukraine, revealing one possible sign of the character's universal appeal.

Although the Ukrainian ballad texts with this motif are relatively recent, the motif ifself undoubtedly stretches back to ancient times, when the image of the girl concocting a potion can be seen in accounts of medieval sorceresses burnt at the stake. Female images in the majority of ballads in this cycle are negative. The moral chorus tries to warn Hryts:

> Oh do not go to parties, Hrytsiu,
> 'Cause all the girls there, they are sorceresses:
> They burn straw and concoct potions
> And they will deprive you, Hrytsiu, of your health.
>                                               (Dei and Iasenchuk 1987: 65)

But Hryts neglects the warnings and continues courting the girls, inviting the tragic fate that awaits him.

It is significant that in "O Do Not Go, Hryts," as in other ballads where this motif appears, poisoning is almost always depicted as a kind of specific ritual action, where each stage of the fearful substance's preparation corresponds to a certain day of the week:

> On Sunday morning, herbs were dug,
> And on Monday the herbs were washed,
> Tuesday had come—the potion was being cooked,
> Wednesday had come—Hryts was poisoned,
> Oh, Thursday has come—and Hryts is already dead,
> And Friday has come—Hryts has already been buried.
>
> > (Dei and Iasenchuk 1987: 65)

Friday is, of course, a day of great significance in world folk belief, and in the ballad it becomes the day of the hero's funeral. In some variants, the woman realizes the irrevocability of her act and engages in a dialog with an accusatory Hryts in the otherworld:

> Oh, sweetheart, sweetheart, I sorrow for you,
> Because you are lying in the coffin deep.
> And [Hryts] replies from the depths
> With such pity, he says to his girl:
> Oh, step off, step off my tomb,
> For I lie here for little reason! (Dei and Iasenchuk 1987: 67)

In some (atypical) versions, the heroine is apparently directed by a "third" power.

It is impossible to analyze this ballad without addressing the symbolism of fire, particular in meaning in both Slavic poetry and ritual, especially Kupala. A scene in which the girls/sorceresses are "burning straw" adds a certain mood to the whole song.

Incidentally, there is an interesting parallel to the Hryts ballad in Ivan Franko's 1914 collection of *Old Scotch Ballads*, with an introduction and translations of the texts. Here we find "The Dead Sweetheart," where Lady Marjory resembles Marusia and, in a similar episode, speaks with her dead sweetheart at his tomb. There she sees three other ladies whom he loved, who have also come to his tomb (Franco 1977: 167–68).

Many academic and literary articles written on this topic since the late nineteenth century are dedicated to the geographical origins and authorship of the ballad. According to the main hypothesis, the song was written by the legendary folk poet Marusia Churay, an inhabitant of the Poltava region. She is known as an author of popular ballads, and some researchers feel that "O Do Not Go, Hryts" bears autobiographical features, even though the central female character appears in such a negative light. In recent years, the association with the poet Churay has gained great popularity in the Ukraine, especially after the appearance of the poem "Marusia Churay" by a contemporary poet. Master folk artists and professional painters now paint her portrait regularly.

Some interesting evidence regarding the connection appears in Shklyarevski's 1877 essay "Marusia Churay," where he tells of a childhood visit to the home of H. Kvitka-Osnpovyanenko, where he saw a portrait of Marusia and heard stories about her (he could not remember the details, except that a man named Hryhoriy Ostapenko had been Marusia's lover). However, Phylypovych was perfectly right in stating that Shklyarevski could have seen the portrait of Marusia in books such as Shakhovski's, where she appears with Hryts and her mother. Not all researchers agree, and many regard Marusia Churay as the same type of literary image as Natalka-Poltavka, the heroine of I. Kotlyarevski's work (which was also turned into an opera by M. Lysenko). The popularity of Marusia Churay among writers can hardly be overestimated, however, and she has become the heroine of many historical novels, narratives, and poems. The Hryts ballad itself has inspired many generations of Ukrainian writers and particularly playwrights (for example, *On Sunday Morn, Herbs Were Gathered* by O. Kobylianska).

Perhaps the mystery of the ballad's origins will never be solved since there is little contemporary evidence to associate the song with Churay. The city of Poltava, where she was born, was burnt to ashes in a great fire in the eighteenth century. There one could, perhaps, have found some documentary source material; only conjecture and hypothesis now remain. Regardless of whether the Hryts Marusia was a real historical character, the ballad has not lost its popularity. It is found in nearly thirty versions, both in the Ukraine and among the Ukrainian diaspora, and in Poland in particular. During an expedition to Podlyasze some years ago, we managed to record some variants of the song.

The motif of poisoning, as noted before, is universally found in European tradition. While creating dramatic action, it also becomes a determining factor in plot structure and development. In the Ukrainian ballad, the motif always indicates a predetermined end and its corresponding associations. The tragedy reinforces the drama, underlining the all-conquering power of love that often informs the actions of the protagonists. There are undoubtedly many similar themes in Ukrainian balladry that bear closer investigation. I hope I have shown that the motif of poisoning is one. Ukrainian tradition shares many traits with its Slavic and non-Slavic neighbors and, as such, is a rich source of comparative studies.

## Notes
1. The building where he played in Odessa is preserved and now bears a memorial plaque dedicated to the event.

## References

Bodianski, Osyp, and Fedir Bodianski. 1978. *Ukrainski narodni pisni v zapysakh Osypa ta Fedora Bodianskykh* [Ukrainian folk songs recorded by Osyp and Fedir Bodianski]. Uporiadkuvannia ta prymitky Alla I. Iasenchuk. Kyiv: Naukova Dumka [Scientific Thought].

Dei, Oleksii Ivanovych. 1986. *Ukrainska naridna balada* [The Ukrainian folk ballad]. Kyiv: Naukova Dumke [Scientific Thought].

Dei, Oleksii Ivanovych, and Alla I. Iasenchuk, eds. 1987. *Balady: kokhannia ta ddoshliubni vzaiemyny* [Ballads of love and premarital relationships]. Musical notation by A. I. Ivanytskyi. Ukrad'nska narodna tvorchist. Kyiv: Naukova Dumke [Scientific Thought].

Franko, Ivan. 1977. *Poetychni pereklady ta perespivy*, edited by O. I. Zasenko. Vol. 10 of *Zibrannia tvoriv...* [Works], edited by I. I. Bass and IE. P. Kyryliuk. Kyiv: Naukova Dumke [Scientific Thought], 1977.

Nudha, Hryhorij Antonovich. 1967. "Balada pro Otruiennia Hrytsa i Legenda pro Marusiu Churai" [Ballads about the poisoning of Hryts and the legend on Marusia Churai]. *Zhovten* 2 (October 1967), 131–38.

Petrov, Serge. 1805. *Vseobshtshyi novoizbrannyi pesennik* [A general newly selected song collection]. Moscow: Le Marchand Russe.

Potebnia, O. O. 1976. "O Nekotorykh Simvolakh v Slavianskoy Narodnoy Poezii" [On some symbols in Slavic folk poetry]. In *Estetika i poetika* [Aesthetics and poetics]. Istoriia estetiki v pamiatnikakh i dokumentakh. Moskva: Iskusstvo.

Shklyarevski, O. "Marusia Churay." 1877. *Pchela* [The bee]: 45, 711–12. Later published in *Istoricheskaya biblioteka* [Historical library] 12 (1879).

Slowacki, Juliusz. 1883. *Listy J. Slowackiego* [J. Slowacki's letters]. Vols. 38 and 39 of *Biblioteka Polska*. Lwüw [Lvov].

# Contexts and Interpretations:
# The Walled-Up Wife Ballad and Other Related Texts

## Nicolae Constantinescu

In *Cântecul epic eroic*, the catalog of Romanian verse narratives, Amzulescu listed no fewer than 211 types of heroic song and 173 of the "family ballad" (1981, 1983). Including the so-called oral journals, Fochi arrives at a total of 401 types, "the second largest stock, after Denmark, in the field of folk-epic poetry" and concludes that Romania should be added to the seven main "ballad areas" of Europe (1985: 9, 115). Although more than one hundred of these types seem to be found only in the Romanian repertoire, the epic tradition of Romania is undoubtedly deeply rooted in European and world tradition. This essay discusses the motif of the walled-up wife in its cultural context(s), taking into account, first, not only the Balkan versions of the ballad (as in most classic studies of this motif) but also its extra-European (Indian) variants, as suggested by Alan Dundes (1995); and second, not only the ballad but also other folklore forms, such as Christmas carols or winter-solstice songs, laments, legends, and contemporary legends involving the motif.

It is not simply by chance that tens, perhaps hundreds, of books and essays have been written on this old and widely distributed motif in the century and a half since the Serbian ballad was "discovered" by the renowned folklorist Vuk Stefanovic Karadjic. It captured the interest of learned men of those times, Jacob Grimm and Goethe among the earliest. In the last few years alone, two major works have appeared: Alan Dundes's *The Walled-Up Wife: A Casebook* (1996), and *Corpusul variantelor românești* (1997), the second volume of Ion Taloş's *Meșterul Manole. Contribuție la studiul unei teme de folclor european.* One may assume that Dundes's casebook and his two previous essays on this theme (1989, 1995) are better known to Western readers than the work of the Romanian-born Taloş, now a professor of comparative literature at the University of Cologne, although the content of his first book is summarized in an extended resumé (Taloş 1973: 393–412), and related studies have been published elsewhere (for example, Taloş 1981; 1983: 577–82). But, though highly praised by Mircea Eliade himself and partly known to Dundes, Taloş and his work did not feature in the *Casebook*, the language barrier no doubt playing its familiar role.

The *Casebook* contains a wide selection of studies, enlarging the territory of the ballad (traditionally confined to Europe and, even more narrowly, to south-eastern Europe or the Balkans) toward the East, specifically to India where the motif appears in connection with the construction, or digging, of a spring or well, a detail to be kept in mind by those who agree with the latest psychoanalytic interpretation ("Men fear that they may not be able to sustain an erection especially at night, a time for lovemaking" [Dundes 1995: 50]).

On the other hand, the "discovery" of the Indian variants of the walled-up wife motif led to at least two conclusions: one plainly expressed by Dundes in the very title of his 1995 article, "How Indic Parallels to the Ballad of the 'Walled-Up Wife' Reveal the Pitfalls of Parochial Nationalistic Folkloristics." The other, suggested by B. J. Gilliat-Smith and W. R. Halliday (Dundes 1996: 27–34), argues for the Indic origins for European folktales and offers "the possibility of oral transport of the tale by Gypsies" (Bottigheimer 1999: 102).

Above all, as one can see from the *Casebook*'s essays and Dundes's own concluding contribution, the most debated aspect of this ballad concerns its origins, a large group of scholars using it "to illustrate a conventional myth-ritual thesis that the story represented a survival from an actual practice of the past of offering a human sacrifice in order to appease supernatural spirits who were believed to be involved in or threatened by the proposal to build some kind of structure, for example, a bridge" (Dundes 1995: 40). Although the myth-ritual theory basically derives from the so-called anthropological or polygenetic theory, assuming multiple possible origins of a single folk motif in different places with different peoples, the walled-up wife motif, embodied in the Balkan area mainly as a *ballad,* gave birth, in the second half of the nineteenth century, to a long-lasting debate over the poem's national origin.

Dundes is right in asserting the "ethnocentric subjectivity" of those who "claim that one national version of a cross-cultural distributed folk song is more 'beautiful' or 'esthetically pleasing' than that of another nation" (1995: 45). In his turn, reviewing recent studies of the ballad which have appeared since 1973, Taloş rejects, in similar terms, the conclusions of a book by the Greek scholar G. Megas, whose work takes "a partisan stand, being conceived in the old manner of...Balkan folkloristics, obsessed by the problem of the origin and of the ways of transmission," a folklore study where "every researcher claims merits for his own people" (Taloş 1997: ix).[1]

There is no doubt that no interpretation of a folklore text can be separated from its cultural context. This is clearly reflected by the text itself. The meaning of the national or local variants comes from their intimate relationship to the national or local cultural context that generated the text. It is thus not accidental that, in the Balkan or southeastern European ballad, an edifice (bridge, stronghold, or church) is erected, while in the Indian versions a well or water tank is dug. Though this may be an apparently insignificant detail (as, it seems for some interpreters, is the fact that the interred person is the wife of the head mason, his sister, or a sister-in-law!), it cannot be set aside if one really wants to see and understand the differences.

On the other hand, the scholar's ideological stand puts its mark on interpretation as well. It is clear that in rejecting the so-called parochial nationalistic point of view, even a great scholar such as Alan Dundes cannot escape other pitfalls, although he is certainly correct in his theoretical approach: "Just as there is not one correct 'text' of an item of folklore, there is no one correct 'interpretation' of an item of folklore. Folklorists must accustom themselves to accepting multiple interpretations just as they have learned to accept the existence of multiple versions of texts" (Dundes 1995: 49–50). (The question of what constitutes a "correct" interpretation is best set aside for the moment.)

Returning to first principles, we must agree that accuracy of interpretation depends upon the number of variants/versions taken into account. As a rule, we can arrive at a better understanding of a folklore item if comprehensive materials are consulted, in other words, if *all* the variants known at a certain time are taken into consideration. At this point, it is worth mentioning that Georgios Megas, for example, makes reference to no less than 328 Greek variants of the ballad of the bridge of Arta (1976); Parpulova noted 180 Bulgarian variants (1983), while Taloş included 165 Romanian variants in his catalog (1973). Twenty-five years later, the number of Romanian variants had risen from 165 to 280, including 38 prose legends (Taloş 1997).

But what makes the difference is the fact that the texts belong to two, or even three, separate categories or genres. Usually appearing in ballad form, as an epic narrative song, the walled-up wife motif also surfaces in Romanian folklore as a *colind,* a Christmas carol or, to avoid any confusion, for the Christian content is far from obvious, as a winter-solstice song, a well-wishing song performed on the eve of Christmas or the New Year. The *colind* version is known only in Transylvania, more precisely in the northern and northwestern areas of this province, whence come most of the variants collected and published so far (Bihor, fourteen examples; Sălaj, forty-two; Lăpuş-Someş-Bistriþa, thirty-four; Năsăud-Mureş, seventeen; and so on; see Taloş 1997: 3–138).

Compared with the ballad version from southern Transylvania (twelve variants), Banat (ten), and Oltenia-Wallachia-Moldavia (sixty-seven), the *colind* version is more "primitive" or "archaic," both in structure and shape. Three master masons erect a building of unspecified type; the walls constructed by day collapse by night; the head mason informs his fellows they have to bury in the foundation the first wife who comes to the site next day; the head mason's wife comes first; he unsuccessfully tries to stop her; she is buried in the walls; her last thoughts go out to her infant, who is often left to the elements. To sum up, the main motifs or episodes of the plot are present, but, compared to the ballad, the *colind* versions are shorter, artistically less elaborated, and more direct in their cruel message. These features lead to an assumption that the *colinds* are older than the ballad version, and, consequently, as old as the most archaic variants of the ballad, those found in Greece. This may be true, and there is no reason to deny it, but this kind of judgment evokes the long-running and meaningless debate over age, the priority of one national version over the other.

I would rather not follow this path but instead suggest taking a closer look at the performance context of the *colind* version in Romanian tradition. Usually Christmas carols, or Christmas songs, performed all over the Christian world, celebrate the birth of Jesus on December 25, expressing joy at the event and praising his later life and deeds. Alongside these religious, Christian songs (called in Romanian *colinde*, from Latin *Calenda/-ae*, through Slavonic *koleda, koljada),* Romanian tradition has preserved a large stock of pre-Christian, "heathen" or "pagan" themes and motifs sung as carols at Christmas and on New Year's Eve. Among these is found "the foundation sacrifice" (no. 35 in the *Typological and Bibliographical Index of the Colinda*): "At night, the work done by some masons (very often brothers) is reduced to nothing. In order to be able to finish the construction, Siminic (Miclăuş, Manole, the Great Mason...) must bury alive his own wife. In most variants, the baby of the buried woman is left to the elements. Sweet winds will rock the orphan and does will suckle him" (Brătulescu 1981: 187–88, with twelve variants recorded, as against more than a hundred noted by Taloş in the same area [1997]).

Despite the large number of variants collected in the past forty years or so, we still have little information on how this song functioned as a *colind*. It is, however, clear that the poem was also sung in this setting, as is evident in the final formula of a Christmas variant collected by Gottfried Habenicht in 1963 (Taloş 1997: 66):

| | |
|---|---|
| Şi dând veste bună | And giving the good news |
| La tot neamu' d'împreună | To all kin |
| S-avem haznă şi folos | Let's have plenty and prosperity |
| D'e naşterea Domn[ului] Hristos E. | With the occasion of Christ's birth. |

Most contributors consider that this is a *colinda*: în Brebi-Maramureş, "o ziceau tinerii. O corindau feciori şi fete. Era tare mândră corinda" [it was sung by young people. Young boys and girls were caroling it. It was a very nice colinda] (Taloş 1997: 41). Another argument favoring the idea that this text belongs to the Christmas carol genre is the presence of the refrain/chorus, a line or verse repeated after each verse of the poem, as in, for instance, "Zuuãrel de zuã" [Little dawn of the day] (Taloş 1997: 62; see also the example of "Maria Muþiu," recorded by Habenicht in 1963).

Brãtulescu included this type in the section "Professional Colinda" (1981) and suggested that "the foundation sacrifice" carol had a "funeral function," an idea that can generally be sustained by the contributors' comments, too (see Taloş 1997: 27–28: "it is a 'sad' *colinda*," Lodovica Pop, Prodãneşti, Sãlaj; "it is a very sad one," Irina Lucaci, Ciglean, Sãlaj). It is also worth mentioning that, unlike most of the Christmas carols which are sung mainly by young men, this special *colinda* belonged to the women's repertoire: "It was sung only by women and young girls; the lads did not sing it" (Taloş 1997: 26). The addressees of the carol were women, too: "I loved this carol; I sung and I cried, too. Women cried in the house when caroling it." Although no valid general conclusions can be drawn on the basis of such scarce information, the feminist-oriented interpretation of the walled-up wife motif may count this as another sustaining argument. Long before the Yugoslav (Balkan) crises erupted, Alan Dundes provisionally stated that "if the women of the Balkan wish to cease being buried alive in a world constructed by and for men, there will have to be drastic changes in traditional Balkan social organization and in the standard roles assigned to men and women" (Dundes 1989: 163).

This "feminist-symbolic reading" of "The Building of Skadar" may be correct, but a small, but vital, fact remains to be explained. The performance context of that song shows that the ballad entered the men's repertoire exclusively—it is performed by male professional singers (Romanian *lãutari*, Serbo-Croatian *guslari*) for a male audience in special circumstances, from wedding parties to men's gatherings at coffee shops or inns. The performance context reinterprets the text and is responsible for the endless chain of individual variants of every text and the meaning of each variant. From this perspective, it is hard to find a feminine point of view in the Balkan ballad of the interred wife.

However, if we take into account the *colind* version, the perspective changes. Shorter than the ballad versions of the motif, the *colind* versions slightly change the emphasis from the masons's and master mason's deeds to the wife's acts: her determination to bring her husband's lunch against all obstacles (a wolf, heavy rain) and her responsibility to the infant left behind. All these changes in textual content can be seen as proof of the role played by the situational performance context in the continuous reelaboration of a song.

Such analysis confirms, once more, that folk-epic texts interpret their cultural context, while the performing, situational context interprets the texts, and shows how the interplay between the two environments is responsible for variations in meaning, at both the levels of myriad individual variants and local, ethnic, or national versions.

## Notes

1. Opposed to this "parochial nationalistic" perspective is the "cross-cultural interpretation"; Alan Dundes opens a door at least half opened by Mircea Eliade's earlier studies (1943, 1972), Paul G. Brewster (Dundes 1996: 35–62), and Taloş (1973) regarding the worldwide distribution of the beliefs, ritual practices, and legends connected with the building sacrifice. See *Motif-Index of Folk Literature*, S 261: Foundation Sacrifice. A human being buried alive at the base of the foundation of a building or bridge (Thompson 1955–58).

## Works cited

Amzulescu, Al. 1981. *Cântecul epic eroic*. Vol. 1. Bucureşti: Editura Academiei.

———. 1983. *Balada familiala*. Vol. 1. Bucureşti: Editura Academiei.

Bottigheimer, Ruth. 1999. Review of *The Walled-Up Wife: A Casebook*, edited by Alan Dundes. *Journal of American Folklore* 112, no. 443: 102–4.

Brătulescu, Monica. 1981. *Colinda românească* [The Romanian colinda. Winter-solstice song]. Bucureşti: Editura Minerva.

Constantinescu, Nicolae. 1986. *Lectura textului folcloric*. Bucureşti: Editura Minerva.

Dundes, Alan. 1989. "The Building of Skadar: The Measure of Meaning of a Ballad of the Balkans." In *Folklore Matters*, 151–168. Knoxville: University of Tennessee Press.

———. 1995. "How Indic Parallels to the Ballad of the 'Walled-Up Wife' Reveal the Pitfalls of Parochial Nationalistic Folkloristics." *Journal of American Folklore* 108, no. 427: 38–53.

Dundes, Alan, ed. 1996. *The Walled-Up Wife: A Casebook*. Madison: University of Wisconsin Press.

Eliade, Mircea. *Comentarii la legenda Meşterului Manole*. Bucureşti: Editura Publicom, 1943.

———. 1972. *Zamolxis. The Vanishing God: Comparative Studies in the Religions and Folklore of Dacia and Eastern Europe*. Translated by Willard R. Trask. Chicago and London: University of Chicago Press. First published as *De Zalmoxis à Gengis-Khan*. Paris: Payot, 1970.

Fochi, Adrian. 1985. *Cântecul epic tradiţional al românilor: incercare de sinteza* (summary in English, German, and French). [Bucureşti]: Editura Ştiinţifică şi Enciclopedică.

Megas, Georgios A. 1976. *Die Ballade von der Arta-Brucke: eine vergleichende Untersuchung*. Translated by Hedwig Schwent-Bertos under Mitwirkung von Vita Xanthaki-Kalopissi. Hidryma Meleton Chersonesou tou Haimou, no. 150. Thessaloniki: Institute for Balkan Studies.

Parpulova, Ljubomira. 1983. "Baladata 'Vgradena nevesta' (Kratki belejki otnosno strukturata i semantikata)." *Bălgarski folklor* 9: 20–33. Also published as "The Ballad of the

Walled-Up Wife. Notes about Its Structure and Semantics." *Balkan Studies* 25 (1984): 425–39.

Schmidt, Sigrid. 1995. "The Worker Immured in the Oker Dam in Germany." *Fabula* 36: 3, no. 4: 205–16.

Taloş, Ion. 1973. *Meşterul Manole. Contribuţie la studiul unei teme de folclor european.* Bucureşti: Editura Minerva.

———. 1981. "Einmauern." In *Enzyklopädie des Märchens,* 1271–74. Handvörterbuch zur Historischen und Vergleichenden Erzählforschung, vol. 3. Berlin: Walter de Gruyter.

———. 1983. "Menschenopfer." In *Enzyklopädie des Märchens,* 577–82. Handvörterbuch zur Historischen und Vergleichenden Erzählforschung vol. 9, no. 2. Berlin: Walter de Gruyter.

———. 1997. *Corpusul variantelor româneşti.* Vol. 2 of *Meşterul Manole. Contribuţie la studiul unei teme de folclor european.* Bucureşti: Editura Grai şi Suflet-Cultura Naţională.

Thompson, Stith. 1955–58. *Motif-Index of Folk-Literature: A Classification of Narrative Elements in Folktales, Ballads, Myths, Fables, Mediaeval Romances, Exempla, Fabliaux, Jestbooks, and Local Legends.* 6 vols. Rev. and enl. ed. Copenhagen: Rosenkilde and Bagger.

Recapturing the Journey:
Cruxes of Context,
Version, and Transmission

# Recapturing the Journey:
## Cruxes of Context, Version, and Transmission

Historical investigation is one of the classic ways of reading between the lines of ballad texts. Outside the contexts of performance and the text itself, a wealth of detail can be gained about the composers, their milieu, and, through interpolation, about the audience as well. Narrative songs, like any other cultural artifact, are products of their own time and place. Sheila Douglas's essay on "Rosie Anderson" draws us into this world—in this case, a scandalous eighteenth-century divorce—and shows how emotion, cultural ethos, and popular opinion combine to create not just the ballad text itself but an evocative, sometimes-explosive means of cultural communication.

The communicative power of ballads means that they have always adapted to changing circumstances; indeed, songs from closely related languages have crossed boundaries quite easily (Nigra [1888] 1957: 262; Nygard 1958: 13; also see Shields 1994: 607–13). For this and other reasons, a generic connection has often been assumed between songs that may, upon close inspection in their respective languages, have only a few common cognate features, for example, names, or one or two features of plot development (Nicolaisen 1992). There are difficulties in finding equivalents not only internationally but within single language groups as well, bringing into question the tacitly supposed internationality of the European ballad tradition (Nicolaisen 1991). The creation of the well-known type indexes (for example, Grundtvig, Child, Aarne, Christiansen, and Jonsson) prompted this circular problem: The types are defined with reference to the fixed set of available data; any subsequent data, then, must be inserted into these categories. "Often enough, this similitude has been so superficial that it did not even indicate a real analogy" (von Sydow 1977: 44). Certainly, songs do cross culture and language barriers but usually between languages that are linguistically or geographically very close (Shields 2000), perhaps even spoken by a single singer (von Sydow 1977: 22). This natural, common type of metamorphosis is turned on its head when a writer sets out methodically to translate a ballad tradition, as did Alexander Gray. In Larry Syndergaard's essay, the languages involved—Danish and Scots—while related, are not close, and the translator must take an overt linguistic, and consequently cultural, position with interesting repercussions for the inherent meanings explored by textualists.

David Atkinson's "'George Collins' in Hampshire" addresses problems raised by postulated genetic relationships among ballad types. Of more use, he suggests, are examinations of denotative, metaphorical, connotative, and textual detail to build up a picture of a song in its native environment, where it is at its most meaningful and resonant. But what of a song that has journeyed across time and space, "from France to Brazil via Germany and Portugal"? While the variants of "George Collins" are geographically tightly focused, we now move outward to look at the way a narrative song, "A Filha do Rei da Espanha," moves, breathes, adapts and survives in the world at large (J. J. Dias Marques). To follow the wildlife analogy a little further, we see how a song makes a home for itself as it moves, acquiring features specific to each environment, in some senses native to all and none of them.

Finally, we explore "The White Fisher," a rare ballad that touches the delicate edges of society's moral code, dealing with an illegitimate birth and its attendant difficulties. The song is only found in eastern Aberdeenshire in Scotland; could this also be the ultimate regional source for it? Julia C. Bishop's analysis of the few remaining examples yields layers of meaning and explores the subtle variations in text, even within the versions of closely related singers.

Perhaps the overarching theme of this section may be described as change and adaptation: how a flexible, multiform tradition adapts itself to differing environments—sometimes social subsets of its native territory—to ensure its own survival.

*References*

Aarne, Antti. 1961. *The Types of the Folktale: A Classification and Bibliography.* Translated and enlarged by Stith Thompson. 2d rev. ed. FF Communications, vol. 75, no. 184. Helsinki: Suomalainen Tiedeakatemia / Academia Scientarum Fennica.

Child, Francis James, ed. 1882–98. *The English and Scottish Popular Ballads.* 5 vols. Reprint, New York: Folklore Press, 1956–57; New York: Dover, 1965. Corrected edition prepared by Mark and Laura Heiman. Northfield, Minn.: Loomis House Press, 2002. Digital edition, with gazetteer, maps and audio CD. New York: ESPB Publishing, 2003.

Christiansen, Reidar Th. 1958. *The Migratory Legends: A Proposed List of Types with a Systematic Catalogue of Norwegian Variants.* FF Communications, vol. 71, no. 175. Helsinki: Suomalainen Tiedeakatemia.

Grundtvig, Svend, Axel Olrik, H. Grüner-Nielsen, Erik Dal et al., eds. 1853–1976. *Danmarks gamle Folkeviser.* 12 vols. [in 13]. København: Samfundet til den danske Literaturs Fremme and Universitets-Jubilæets danske Samfund.

Jonsson, Bengt R., Svale Solheim, Eva Danielson et al. 1978. *The Types of the Scandinavian Ballad.* Oslo, Bergen and Tromsø: Universitetsforlaget.

Nicolaisen, W. F. H. 1991."On the Internationality of Ballads." In *Gender and Print Culture: New Perspectives on International Ballad Studies,* edited by Maria Herrera-Sobek, 99–104. [Irvine, Ca.]: Kommission für Volksdichtung of the Société Internationale d'Ethnologie et de Folklore.

————. 1992. "Onomastic Aspects of Clerk Colvill." In *ARV: Scandinavian Yearbook of Folklore* 48, 31–41. Also published as *The Stockholm Ballad Conference 1991: Proceedings of the 21st International Ballad Conference, 19–22 August 1991*, edited by Bengt R. Jonsson, 31–41. Skrifter utgivna av Svenskt Visarkiv, no. 12. Stockholm: Svenskt Visarkiv, 1993.

Nigra, Costantino. [1888] 1957. *Canti Popolari del Piemonte*. Reprint, Torino: Einaudi, 1957.

Nygard, H. O. 1958. *The Ballad of Heer Halewijn*. Knoxville: University of Tennessee Press.

Shields, Hugh. 1994. "La traduction littéraire dans l'oralité: Réflexions sur des versions occitanes, et autres, de quelques chansons narratives traditionelles." In *Actes du IV Congrès International de l'association internationale d'études occitanes*, edited by Ricardo Cierbide and Emiliana Ramos, 607–13. Vitoria: AIEO.

————. 2000. "Ballads in Oral Translation between Distantly Related Languages: English and Irish." In *Bridging the Cultural Divide: Our Common Ballad Heritage/Kulturelle Brücken: Gemeinsame Balladentradition*, edited by Sigrid Rieuwerts and Helga Stein, 426–37. Hildesheim, Zürich, New York: Olms.

v[on] Sydow, C[arl] [W]ilhelm. 1977. *Selected Papers on Folklore, Published on the Occasion of His 70th Birthday*. (A selection of papers written from 1932–45.) Copenhagen: Rosenkilde and Bagger, 1948. Reprint, New York: Arno Press, 1977 (page references are to reprint edition).

# The Life and Times of Rosie Anderson

## Sheila Douglas

In his note on the ballad of "Rosie Anderson," twelve versions of which appear in his collection, Gavin Greig makes the following observations:

> Few traditional songs are so well and so widely known as "Rosie Anderson." We may take it to be about a century old, judging from the date of the events to which it refers.... Rose Anderson it seems was the daughter of a merchant in Perth and was married at the age of sixteen to another Perth merchant. As a result of certain discoveries an action for divorce was raised by the aggrieved husband, which, after much litigation, was at length granted. Lord Elgin's own first marriage was dissolved in 1808, possibly as a result of the Rosie Anderson affair.... The opinion may be ventured that only the folksinger, armed with his unconscious art, his unpretentious style and his ingenuous ethic, could well afford to handle the delicate theme. The fact is that folksong has been able to deal with many situations that literary song would hardly dare to touch, with the result that the humbler minstrelsy covers a vastly wider area of human experience. (1963: article 127)

Greig's view of folk singing in this extract, based on ideas formed before he had his eyes opened to its true nature by his collecting experience, connects it with the humbler ranks of society, the uneducated peasantry, as was common in other European cultures. He speaks of "unconscious art," "unpretentious style," and "ingenuous ethic" before admitting that "folksong has been able to deal with many situations that literary song would hardly dare to touch." But this was not because of the reasons he gives. In Scotland, folk song has never been confined to any one social class since we have ballads and songs composed by all kinds of people, from kings to ploughmen. Greig's last sentence shows that he has learned to view folk song in a different light because experience has shown him that it "covers a vastly wider area of human experience." Many ballads and songs that have been popular for generations have dealt with scandal, human frailty, and tragic relationships and have been widely sung by all kinds of people.

David Graham-Campbell, a Perth local historian, gives the following information germane to the ballad of "Rosie Anderson":

> Everyone regarded Thomas Anderson as a man of substance, and
> his daughter Rose as an heiress—an eminently suitable bride for
> the up-and-coming son of another wealthy merchant. Sure enough,
> in that year 1792, Rose Anderson was married, with the promise of a
> tocher [dowry] of £3000 to Thomas Hay Marshall, the eldest
> surviving son of another Thomas Marshall, who was very much a
> member of the Beautiful Order [the local oligarchy.]
>
> (Graham-Campbell 1985: 2)

Sadly, Marshall, whose public life had been crowned with success, was not so
happy in his marriage, a fact made clear by a petition to the Consistory Court
when Marshall sought a divorce on the grounds of his wife's adultery.

The divorce petition named two officers who had been stationed in Perth: the
Earl of Elgin,[1] who commanded the Elgin Fencibles, and Dr. Harrison, medical
officer to the Durham Rangers. The Earl of Elgin's lodgings were located across
the road from Hay Marshalls's house in Charlotte Street, and servants who were
called upon to give evidence testified that when Hay Marshall was away from
home, the Earl and Rosie "exchanged signals from their windows, sent each
other frequent notes, and…[he] visited her late at night, when they sat together
in the gloaming, refused to have candles brought and even blocked up the
keyholes so that they should not be watched" (Graham-Campbell 1985: 7). Rosie's
parents had them followed up Kinnoull Hill, a popular resort for courting couples,
where a woodcutter's son saw them disappear into a thicket. Rosie stated in her
defense that her parents had forced her into the marriage and Hay Marshall was
only interested in her money. As this was probably at least partly true, the ballad
can, like many songs, be seen as a largely one-sided version of the story.

Set amid some of the most beautiful countryside in Scotland, Perth in the
1790s was an exciting place to be. It had had city status since medieval times,
when it received its charter from William the Lion and became the capital of
Scotland and the site of the royal court, with a fine pre-Reformation church that
still stands. In the eighteenth century, the city was emulating Edinburgh, which
had become the capital, by building a New Town of fine Georgian houses. Land
for this new development was originally part of the property of Blackfriars Mon-
astery and had been purchased by a prosperous merchant, Thomas Anderson,

who had drawn up the plans for the new buildings. Anderson's son-in-law, Thomas Hay Marshall, oversaw the actual implementation of the plans.

Thomas Hay Marshall, whose statue stands outside Perth Museum with the Latin inscription "Cives Grati," was a member of one of the group of Perth families who controlled the town through a system known as the Beautiful Order. The Marshalls were well-to-do linen merchants, who also served on the council; Hay Marshall's father had been provost, or mayor, of Perth. He married Thomas Anderson's daughter Rose, who, as we have seen, was regarded as a rich heiress and proved to be rather wayward.

Thomas and Rosie occupied a house beside the North Inch, still an extensive grassy park beside the River Tay. In those days, before the New Town development, washerwomen used it as a place to bleach their clothes, but flooding has always been a problem along the River Tay and its tributaries, which together put more water into the North Sea than any other river system in Britain. When the river floods, the North Inch becomes a loch; indeed, the name Inch, from the Gaelic *innis*, suggests it may at one time have been an island. It was also, incidentally, the site of the Battle of the Clans in 1396 and is connected with ballads and legends about William Wallace.

George Penny, a Perth weaver reports that the Inch "was bounded on the north by a wall called the White Dyke, which was said to have been built by the fines levied from the brewers and bakers for fighting with the weavers; and was erected to prevent encroachments of the Muirton farmers [to the north of the city] who were in the habit of taking a few furrows, from time to time, from the common good" (1836: 7). Before the new development, the Dunkeld Road and the Town Lade ran across the Inch, but these were moved farther back from the river, the former behind the new terraced houses, and a racecourse was laid out on the Inch. The park then became a place where the townspeople walked out in their Sunday best in front of the fine houses of Rose Terrace, which looked across the Inch and the River Tay to Kinnoull, a spectacular wooded hillside with a sheer cliff, the scene of many a suicide, even to the present day.[2] At one end of this terrace is a house still called Provost Marshall's that was to have become the new town residence of Hay Marshall and his wife. The circumstances that prevented this from happening form the substance of the ballad of Rosie Anderson.

In the 1790s, Perth, being a garrison town, was full of regiments raised for the Napoleonic Wars and its streets must have been full of scarlet and blue uniforms, worn by handsome young men. Thomas Hay Marshall, already involved with the local militia, made the patriotic gesture, which proved a miscalculation as far as his marriage was concerned, of holding open house for all officers billeted in the town. He himself, being absorbed with both business and town affairs and the overseeing of the New Town development, probably had little time for the social life that his wife enjoyed; he was clearly not always present when officers took advantage of his hospitable offer to call at the house in Charlotte Street.

At this time, Perth was also a hotbed of antiwar and republican radicalism allied to the movement for Parliamentary reform. The Tree of Liberty was raised by the Friends of the People[3] on the Inch to celebrate a French victory over England. France was traditionally a friend and ally of Scotland, and not only the working people but also many of the professional classes were against the government, the war, and the gentry.

The Marshalls and Andersons, of course, like other families who owed their position to the Beautiful Order, would not have sympathized with this cause. Even a moderate radical like George Penny, whose *Traditions of Perth* refers to the order as an "abominable system, calculated for the complete subversion of the liberties of its citizens" (1836: 16), could see that reform was needed, but was not prepared to adopt violent means to achieve it. The leaders of the radical movement were often weavers, perhaps because, having a thriving trade, they were able to devote time to political agitation. The subversive activities of the reformers and republicans and the public disorder these caused, however, were another issue that preoccupied Thomas Hay Marshall in his civic role. In 1799 Rosie was in London, running up bills for fashionable clothes despite a legal injunction issued by her husband two years previously. David Graham-Campbell details examples of her purchases as "a lady's habit of superfine dark blue cloth with two rows of double gilt buttons, and a similar one of brown cloth, with three rows of gold buttons, two silk corsets and two velvet collars, two colored bonnets and two livery round hats, together with three more hats later in the year and a fur cape" (1985: 9). A divorce was granted in 1803, and Hay Marshall died five years later from "problems of ill health and overwork" at the age of thirty-eight.

Probably as a consequence of the decline in the linen trade in Perth, which was based on hand-loom weaving, Rosie's father's fortune had evaporated. Rosie claimed that that was the point when Marshall began seeking a divorce, having turned a blind eye to her indiscretions until then. Perhaps to dodge creditors, and also because of the scandal in the town, Rosie had to go with her parents and live in Edinburgh, where she continued to have liaisons with officers "from a fort or battery between Newhaven and Leith" (Graham-Campbell 1985: 9). Graham-Campbell's account concentrates thereafter on Hay Marshall's life, which ended not in the house in Rose Terrace, which he never occupied, but in another called Whistlecroft, on the other side of the River Tay in Kinnoull.

The ballad tells us that Rosie went to London, had a son, and spent time in Bedlam, or Bethlehem Hospital, the insane asylum of the time. As the ballad story closely adheres to the truth in the earlier part, it seems likely that the latter part may also be accurate. The sympathy of the balladeer, however, seems to be entirely with Hay Marshall, who was popular and respected in his own community. No doubt this had some effect on the popularity of the ballad, although the willingness of people to sing about Rosie's misfortunes also suggests an element of *schadenfreude*. This, of course, is not unusual in ballad tradition, where many older ballads probably owe their long life at least partly to the fact that people enjoy scandalous stories about the high and mighty. Certainly the use of English in the ballad suggests that it may have been a printed broadside rather than created orally and therefore easily circulated in something like this form:

Rosie Anderson [collated version by Sheila Douglas]

Hay Marshall was a gentleman as ever lived on earth
He's married Rosie Anderson, a lady intil Perth.

He's courted her, he's married her, made her his wedded wife,
And on that day I dare to say he loved her as his life.

There was an assembly intil Perth and Rosie she was there
Lord Elgin danced with her that night and did her heart ensnare.

Lord Elgin danced with her that night and he's convoyed her home
Hay Marshall he cam rushing in afore he set her down.

I'm all into surprise he said, I'm all into surprise
To see you kiss my wedded wife before my very eyes.

I did not kiss your wedded wife Lord Elgin he did say
I only brought her home to you from the dangers of the way.

Then Betsy she was sent for the truth for to relate
I would have brought my lady home, Lord Elgin took my place.

Altho you be a lord, he said, and I but a Provost's son
I'll make you smart for this, my lord, altho you think it fun.

He's tane his Rosie by the hand and led her frae the room.
I'll send you to far London till all this strife dies doon.

She had not been in far London a month but barely nine
When word came to Hay Marshall that Rosie had a son.

O wae be tae ye rose sae red, that ever I loved you!
What made you leave your own true love to tread the beds of rue?

Hay Marshall's down to far London with money in his purse
To try and find some witnesses his Rosie to divorce.

Hay Marshall's twenty witnesses and Rosie has but two.
Alas, said Rosie Anderson, whatever shall I do?

If 'twere to do that's done, she said, if 'twere to do that's done
Hay Marshall's face I would adore, Lord Elgin's I would shun.

But Spring is coming on, she said, the regiments are near
Perhaps I'll find some officer my broken heart to cheer.

Now she has got an officer and he has proved untrue
And he's left her in Bedlam her folly for to rue.

Now all ye ladies far and near a warning take by me
And ne'er forsake your own true love for any lords you see.

## Notes

1. This was the same Earl of Elgin who brought back the Elgin Marbles.
2. It was on this hillside that Patrick Geddes, one of the greatest Scottish generalists, pioneering botanists, town planners, and environmentalists, spent his childhood.
3. The Friends of the People began in Perth and grew out of an organization called the United Scotsmen.

## References

Graham-Campbell, David. 1985. *The Making of Georgian Perth*. Perth: Perth and Kinross Library.

Greig, Gavin. 1963. "Folk-Song of the North-East: Articles Contributed to the *Buchan Observer* from December 1907 to June 1911." In *Folk-Song in Buchan and Folk-Song of the North-East*, with a foreword by Kenneth S. Goldstein and Arthur Argo. Hatboro, Pa.: Folklore Associates.

Greig, Gavin, and James B. Duncan. 1997. *The Greig-Duncan Folk-Song Collection*. Vol. 7, edited by Patrick Shuldham-Shaw and Emily B. Lyle. Aberdeen: University of Aberdeen Press (cited in the text as *Greig-Duncan Collection*).

Penny, George. 1836. *Traditions of Perth, Containing Sketches of the Manners and Customs of the Inhabitants, and Notices of Public Occurrences, during the Last Century: Interesting Extracts from Old Records; Notices of the Neighbouring Localities of Historical Interest; Topographical Sketch of the County; Brief History of Perth, &c.* Perth: Dewar.

# Scholar, Antischolar:
# Sir Alexander Gray's Translations of the Danish Ballads

Larry Syndergaard

Sir Alexander Gray is already one of the most important translators of Danish ballads with his existing books, *Four-and-Forty* (1954) and *Historical Ballads of Denmark* (1958). He left unpublished a third volume called, with characteristic ironic humor, "Posthumous Ballads." With the publication of this work, Gray will arguably be the most significant of all the ninety translators of the Danish *folkeviser*. The key critical study finds that his translations work well as real ballads in Scots, a rare quality in any target language (Graves and Thomsen forthcoming).

Gray made major contributions as professor of political economy at Aberdeen and Edinburgh, as a poet in English and Scots, as a translator of folk and lyric songs into Scots, and in public service on a series of Royal Commissions and boards of review (Syndergaard 2000: 455–58, 463). Fortunately, Gray and his son John saw that his papers went to the National Library of Scotland (MSS 26009–26014), and his Danish consultant Elias Bredsdorff retained all the letters he received from Gray—all now key resources in examining his work.

In this essay, I want to consider the surprising fact that Alexander Gray maintains a tartly antischolarly stance throughout his ballad translations, reaching a peak in his "Posthumous Ballads" and letters to Bredsdorff. This is surprising from a lifelong academic, a prominent professor at prominent universities, a poet and translator whose enormous learning shows continually, and the third generation of a Scots family that rose impressively through education (Syndergaard 2000: 457, 463). Yet the archives and letters show a savvy use of scholarly resources, a penetrating understanding of scholarly problems, and the acquisition of requisite knowledge, in short: a scholarly intellect in full employ.

This curious divergence is traceable in part to Gray's own nature. But besides idiosyncracy this case also asks us to think about the nature and place of "ballad scholarship." It is a term we all use, not always remembering that its dimensions may be complex and our embrace of it ambivalent. Gray's case also lets us interrogate relationships between the translator and ballad scholarship, as well as the qualities we ask of a translator. My main goal is to understand, rather than prove a particular thesis. In discussing Gray, of course, I mean not the total man but that voice one constructs from publications, letters, archives, and interviews. I will use "we" in a rather porous way to include Danish ballad scholars but also many of the rest of us on an ad hoc basis. It may be helpful to keep in mind the opposing poles in Gray's own mantra: "I am a ballad-monger, and not a ballad-scholar" (Letter to Elias Bredsdorff, 9 November 1953; subsequent citations will include only the letter's date).

Let us begin with the evidence against "scholar" and for "monger." We have, above all, Gray's dismissive and ironic characterizations of his own work in his translation paratexts—introductions and commentaries—and his letters. As well as ballad monger, he calls himself an "ignorant amateur" (30 July 1956) "skating on thin ice" (1958: 130) and "an alien" (1958: x; 4 February 1955) committing "outrages" on the Danish material (6 October 1959). He labels his introductions as "patter" or "explanatory gossip" (MS 26012: fol. 3; 1958: 1; 19 November 1958). He insists that his translation is an "innocent pastime," a "harmless hobby," an "old man's amusement," a self-indulgence generally. His translation work occupies those marginal parts of life when he is not doing more-important things— retirement, weekends, the enforced leisure of travel (30 January 1959; 28 August 1958; 30 November 1952; 14 November 1952; 29 June 1953; 23 May 1955). In fact his *Four-and-Forty* may be the only book ever dedicated "to British Railways, who provide the ideal environment for the practice of verse-translation" (1954: v). He comes to call *Posthumous Ballads* the more-comical *Bad Boys' Book of Bloody Ballads* (6 January 1960). There is a recurring hint of false pretences.

Moreover, Gray is often ironic, humorous, or even dismissive toward the work of established ballad scholars, mainly the prominent Danish editors whose collections he owned—often calling them collectively "the commentators," "the experts," "the learned," or "austere scholarship" (1954: 140; "Posthumous Ballads": fols. 41–42, 100, 227; 1958: 72, 154). He does not exclude even the iconic Svend Grundtvig: "Of some slight interest to the historian is that the Battle of Lena was the last occasion on which the God Odin made a personal appearance in what we now call an armed conflict. It is Grundtvig who hands on this information. This may explain the slaughter of 16,982 Danes" (1958: 43).

In styling himself a ballad monger, Gray also certainly refers to his activities in the mass media. His translations regularly appeared in *The Scotsman* newspaper; he read them on the air in the BBC "Scottish Programme," and he even prepared for an early television presentation that fell through (1958: 19–20; J. Gray 1999b). He also presented his ballad translations and commentaries in what he styled "variety entertainments" or "penny readings" for interested organizations (1958: 19–20; 9 June 1957; 19 January 1959). Finally, Gray likes to dismiss his knowledge of Danish as weak and amateurish (9 January 1956 through 11 January 1958).

Many of us would probably agree that Gray's collections do not, in fact, look very "scholarly." The introductions have few footnotes; the works cited are generally restricted to source editions and other translations, and the commentaries sometimes avoid provenance, dating, diffusion, analogues, and ancient connections—favorite grist for our scholarly mills—to concentrate on the narratives themselves. In addition, the language is unpretentious in diction, sometimes humorous, and utterly, utterly clear.

But the most telling judgments on whether Gray is scholarly come in reviews of his books by Erik Dal, who must certainly be one of the two most important Scandinavian ballad scholars of the latter half of the twentieth century. Dal accepts the Scots language and the readability of Gray's translations; he accepts the irony and humor, and he appreciates Gray's feeling for the material. He partly accepts Gray's "transplantations" into Scots place names and personal names (1955: 129–30; 1959: 145; 1962: 75). But Dal's very telling reservation is that both books "have no scholarly pretensions" (1955: 129; 1959: 145). He could "very well recommend Sir Alexander Gray's light and agreeable dish, at least as an appetizer" but maintains that another translator's work, E. M. Smith-Dampier's *A Book of Danish Ballads*, remains the best general introduction for the anglophone reader (1955: 130). Possibly the same qualities of irony and humor that please Dal also tempt him to resist taking these books altogether seriously. In any event, "light appetizer" sounds more monger than scholar.

The ballad establishment had spoken, and although this criticism might seem merely to endorse what Gray himself says, he was not happy with the first review, especially Dal's preference for Miss Smith-Dampier, most of whose ballads Gray regarded as "simply lousy, smelling of being translations" (30 January 1959). Dal gets at the heart of the matter, and we will return to this. But first, what of the personal equation on Gray's side? For the manifestations of the scholarly always exist in negotiation with the rest of the self.

At the shallowest level, like the rest of us, Gray simply wants it both ways. He likes to denigrate his own efforts in a familiar defense against falling short, but throughout his poetic career, he also seeks recognition from the Erik Dals of this world. As a younger man, he keeps meticulous records of *every* review and appearance of his poetry (J. Gray, Talk: 8). He works to get his ballad-translation books reviewed (21 September 1954; 24 October 1958) and as he nears death, his distribution list for a last, honorary, anthology begins not with his family but the

British Museum (1966b). A concern with falling short of his promise regularly pursued Gray—itself ironic in such a versatile, productive man (J. Gray, Talk: 6).

But Gray's self-irony in fact runs deeper: it is a way of seeing the world in which multiple truths both coexist and undercut each other. (Such a vision is familiar to all students of Chaucer, for example.) Any scholar who seeks to resist oversimplification and the categorical in a complex world should understand Gray's irony as a more-entertaining expression of the same position. Thus, he is able both to look up to the Danish ballad scholars as being far above him in knowledge and to see their limitations, as when he likens their approach to paleontology (1958: 6).

Gray has his own scholarly adequacies and strengths, however much he calls himself a ballad monger. His command of Danish develops from marginal to good, though he never tackles the "archaic Danish" of many original texts (1958: x). He uses the National Library's imposing lexical resources, and his seeking out Danish scholar Elias Bredsdorff at Cambridge as his consultant on language and background I see not as a sign of inadequacy but as the efficient use of the ideal scholarly resource. His Danish certainly becomes good enough to let him challenge his mentor ("Posthumous Ballads": fol. 9; 1 December 1957) and see when his supposed betters, including his nemesis, Smith-Dampier, go wrong or finesse the tough spots (4 July 1954; 26 November 1957; 1 December 1957). He is more honest about insoluble problems than are most translators ("Posthumous Ballads": fol. 47). In fact, when Gray complains about his own inadequacy, one is tempted to ask, "Compared with what?" Elias Bredsdorff endorses his Danish (telephone interview, 1998), but Gray compares it with his German and Dutch, both good enough for counterpropaganda war service in "The Lie Factory" (J. Gray, Talk: 8).

"Ballad scholarship" in many minds means editing ballads, classifying them, and attempting to determine their provenance, dates, analogues, and historicity. Such studies involve examining great amounts of detailed evidence and forming hypotheses, sometimes to be disputed to near exhaustion. These are not Gray's focuses and strengths, either in translation work or, except for his first book (Davidson and Gray 1909), in economics.

Rather, Gray is that analytical scholar who sees the larger picture and cuts through to essences, in both his writing and teaching (J. Gray 1999a). He assimilates theory and can make it accessible, but he is not a theoretician. His common sense rises to the uncommon as a scholarly attribute, and he has a keen eye for imbalance and compulsions in scholarship, such as the early quest for the historical within Danish ballads (1958: 17–32, 50, 87, 128, 154–55).

Gray also has the rare scholarly ability to banish jargon, writing informally and with total clarity for a multileveled audience. If we do not see the scholarly judgment at work behind the informal diction, the limitation is ours. Gray's "mongering" in *Four-and-Forty* includes a position in an important language debate in Scotland, and in *Historical Ballads of Denmark*, he offers an insightful treatment of what we look for in so-called historical ballads—both essays significant, if limited, contributions and disarmingly clear (1954: xvi–xxvi; 1958: 1–17).

Similarly, Gray is a scholar ahead of his time in his attention to the popular media as venues for his ballad translations and commentaries. He also served on advisory boards for the BBC. If we accept "ballad monger" because of a perceived categorical opposition between the scholarly and the popular media, again the problem is ours. (Perhaps the Modern Language Association is following Gray's lead fifty years later with its new radio series, "What's the Word?") Gray is a doer, as a scholar and otherwise, not one for prolonged, inconclusive discussion: "It is so much more satisfying in every sphere of life to get on with the job…than to talk incessantly about the job, so that in the end, in the multitude of words, we all prevent each other from doing anything" (1954: xvi).

By now I believe we see the most important thing Gray reveals in his ironies: the ballad-monger/ballad-scholar opposition is a false one; ballad translations done in a scholarly, responsible way may, and should be, "mongered" to the widest audience.

Let us return to the revealing tension between the voice of Erik Dal, the ultimate ballad scholar, and that of Gray, whose ballad-monger sobriquet we now see as ironic. We may then recognize certain broader tensions among views of ballad scholarship and translation. Dal actually finds a great deal to praise in Gray, especially if we read beyond his reviews (1976: 17–18, 26). Even so, Gray's works are without "scholarly pretensions," especially because they translate from popular anthologies of redacted ballads by Danish editors and not from the great scholarly edition, *Danmarks gamle Folkeviser* (Grundtvig et al.: 1853–1976). Moreover, his sampler work *Four-and-Forty* does not include the "introduction to the world of the ballads" that Dal expects. Finally, Gray's translations do not retain some well-established formulas and incremental repetitions found in the originals (Dal 1955: 129–30; 1959: 145; 1962: 75). Dal prefers Smith-Dampier's *A Book of Danish Ballads*, certainly because it translates the "masterful introduction" in Axel Olrik's popular anthology, probably because it is simply more comprehensive (1955: 129; 1956: 375), and perhaps because she is a "trained Scandinavist" (1970: 91). Dal is asking Gray as translator to privilege the source ballads as performed in tradition, asking for stricter fidelity to Danish ballad

conventions, and asking for an introduction which digests the voluminous scholarship on Danish balladry. He is asking, in fact, for exactly the excellent features
he as editor—but not translator—gives his own *Danish Ballads and Folk Songs*
(1967).

What, from his side, does Alexander Gray want? His creative and scholarly
energies go, above all, to forming Scots ballads that work as entire poems, and
those energies certainly succeed (Graves and Thomsen forthcoming). Only sec-
ondarily is he concerned with representing Denmark, through its ballads, to the
English-speaking world. We may identify two factors here. First, for Gray,
Scotland's own balladry is a treasure poetically dependent on its life among
ordinary rural people. Thus, any ballad may get lost if enveloped in scholarship
that becomes an end in itself. (Gray's own ballad roots are in the ancestral village
of Letham.) Second, translating the Danish ballads occurs during Gray's growing emotional and intellectual focus on his Scots being, and thus he is more
driven to express what he calls the "spirit of Scotland" in these powerful ballads
than to express Danish culture (Syndergaard 2000: 455–58).

In recreating the *folkeviser* as good Scots ballads, Gray is much concerned
with narrative *consequence*, with developing coherent, internally consistent stories with organic refrains. He does not like rough edges or narrative dawdling.
Part of his scholarly effort goes into delving into the massive *Danmarks gamle
Folkeviser* to try to resolve just such perceived problems. He therefore sometimes replaces repetitive and formulaic elements that he thinks will grate on the
Scots sensibility (15 June 1959; 1 February 1963). More importantly, he tends to
choose the most straightforward (13 February 1952 to 7 August 1959), and usually the briefest, example of the narrative among his source versions ("Posthumous Ballads": fols. 122–23, 191–92; 9 June 1957 and throughout).

In this goal lies Gray's most important limitation, at least in that particular
scholarly vision exemplified by Svend Grundtvig, Erik Dal, and probably many of
us in the community of ballad scholars. In translating from redactions, not faithful editions *(Danmarks gamle Folkeviser* or Tang Kristensen), and selecting the
most "coherent" narratives, he is not privileging the cultural artifact as created in
tradition. Despite reading extensively in *Danmarks gamle Folkeviser,* he seems
not to have accepted the key paradigm established by Grundtvig in that pivotal
work. Gray also seems to want scholarship to produce "usable" results, by implication some kind of permanent gain in consensus understanding of the subject.
This is by no means what he always finds in the literature.

Gray owned all the most important redacted editions of the Danish ballads in
the twentieth century, representing an astonishing collective scholarly effort

and power. Yet their redactions for the same ballad type may be startlingly different, as are, often, their commentaries (28 March 1954; 11 April 1954; "Posthumous Ballads": fol. 54). No resolved questions here. And as Gray researches the literature to develop his introductions, he sees that ballad scholarship has its own cycles of fashion—the pursuit of antiquity, the pursuit of historicity, skepticism about historicity (1958: 2–20, 42–3, 154–55; "Posthumous Ballads": fols. 49–50, 79, 111, 218–19)—and that scholarly discussion may simply defeat itself by its own "inordinate" mass ("Posthumous Ballads": fol. 63; and throughout the letters). An ironic scholarly mind like Gray's sees both high accomplishment and futility in this great web of work, and, accordingly, his language acknowledges the scholarship yet characterizes it as an option: "The curious" may access "the literature of the learned" elsewhere ("Posthumous Ballads": fols. 218–19).

We have now explored Gray's position. What can we learn by expanding this discussion to include ballad translation and scholarship more generally?

Even if translating from redactions and not from tradition-bearers' texts is unscholarly, Gray has excellent company. In the surprisingly large collective enterprise of Danish ballad translation, only one major collection in the nineteenth century (Prior) and one in the twentieth (Dal 1967) translate from unredacted texts.

Moreover, making redacted ballads available for a broad audience is exactly what most of the giants of Danish ballad scholarship have used their learning to do: Olrik, von der Recke, Frandsen, Grüner-Nielsen, and yes, Svend Grundtvig— twice (1867, 1882)—have all produced redacted collections for general and school use. This list includes three of the four dominating editors of the ballad edition that established the scholarly vision, "All that there is, all as it is" *(Danmarks gamle Folkeviser)*. English speakers who read Gray's translations do not get the narratives as performed in Danish tradition, but neither do most Danes. To overstate somewhat, as scholars we have insisted on *recording* the poetry of the people exactly as performed, but we have *given* it to the people mainly with our considerable intervention.

What, by way of the scholarly, have we customarily asked of ballad translators? Notably, we have not usually demanded, through the marketplace nor in scholarly reviews, that they use unredacted sources. We have, on the other hand, expected an adequate command of Danish, and here the "mere ballad-monger" Gray is superior in fidelity to the majority (Syndergaard 1995: analytical tables). We have wished for "introductions to the world of the ballads," as Dal puts it, but in the other two major twentieth-century collections we have not asked that the *translator* be the scholar who generates them (Smith-Dampier 1939; Dal 1967). Unfortunately, we have not generally asked for translations that sound like ballad poetry. In other words, Alexander Gray has been asked for more of the scholarly than others. In his self-dismissive way, Gray himself has, in fact, joined this chorus. Ironically, he has hardly been asked for the poetic accomplishment that he has supplied.

I offer two final perspectives on Gray's work and the scholarly. First, a new field of scholarship, translation studies, has evolved with an empirical focus on what is created in the target text and on the translation strategy, rather than the traditional focus on the source text within a script of inevitable loss (Syndergaard 1996). *This* scholarship mandates that we examine Gray's pioneering strategy of translation into dialect, and his poetic and cultural parameters, very carefully.

Finally, studying Gray's translation work may compel us to ponder the place of the scholarly in the larger scheme of things. Gray's work on the Danish ballads begins shortly before his retirement and becomes a central focus of that period of his life. The activity gives structure; the intellectual jousting and poetic creation are satisfying. This seems to come straight from a "Have a Healthy Retirement" checklist.

But my mother-in-law tartly says, "The golden years aren't," and Gray writes that his were indeed "a bit of a swindle" (29 December 1964). The letters chronicle a diminishing curve of focus on ballad work and a rising arc of fatigue, operations, illness, frustration, with slowing, then stopped, work, and approaching mortality (30 April 1956 to 19 January 1967). Making the Danish ballads into Scots poems remains satisfying, but the obligatory scholarly work does not. Certainly some part of the aging Gray's ironic treatment of the scholarly is a reaction to having to force himself to the library or write repeatedly to Elias Bredsdorff on difficulties in reconciling "the experts" (1 December 1957). How vital is this scholarly detail work as health runs down and time becomes finite? Would we trade half the translations in "Posthumous Ballads" for introductions more "scholarly" by 25 percent?

This same irony mirrors Gray's much larger disaffection with many of the products of his academic life (26 January 1964). He finds *nothing* of his distinguished career in economics worth reprinting in the final, honorary collection, *A Timorous Civility* (7–9), and this is all part of a final retreat into, or reaffirmation of, his Scottishness (Syndergaard 2000: 455–58). Gray has always seen the limitations of scholarship that seems to pore over details, I suspect in part because he knew what it was to focus his learning toward the great national cause in the World War. In a query to Bredsdorff on yet another ballad detail, he jokes,

"By God, dont [*sic*] we waste our time and attention on awful nonsense which is of no significance whatsoever in winning the next war?" (22 November 1957). Ironic as usual, but also a reminder of due proportion: There are lesser and greater causes in this world.

What still *does* matter, in the austere reassessments of a long and productive academic and public life by this powerful, creative, and morally aware mind, is hardly the scholarly. Rather, it is identifying the "spirit of Scotland" within these kindred ballads and creating *Scots poetry* from them. That is a sobering vision for any ballad scholar to contemplate.

*References*

Bredsdorff, Elias. Telephone interview with the author, 15 July, 1998.

Dal, Erik. 1955. Review of *Four-and-Forty* by Alexander Gray. *Danske Studier*, vol. 50: 129–30.

———. 1956. *Nordisk folkeviseforskning siden 1800: Omrids af text-og melodistudiets historie og problemer især i Danmark*. København: J. H. Schultz.

———. 1959. Review of *Historical Ballads of Denmark* by Alexander Gray. *Danske Studier*, vol. 54: 145.

———. 1962. Review of *Historical Ballads of Denmark* by Alexander Gray. *Scandinavica* 1: 75.

———. 1967. *Danish Ballads and Folk Songs*. Translated by Henry Meyer. Copenhagen and New York: American-Scandinavian Foundation and Rosenkilde and Bagger.

———. 1970. "Tyske, franske og engelske oversættelser af færøkvæder." *Fróðskaparrit* 18: 77–92.

———. 1976. "Oversættelser af nordiske folkeviser." In *Samlet og Spredt om Folkeviser,* 9–29. C. C. Rafns Forlæsning, no. 4. Odense: Odense Universitetsforlag.

Davidson, John, and Alexander Gray. 1909. *The Scottish Staple at Vere. A Study in the Economic History of Scotland*. London: Longmans, Green.

Frandsen, Ernst, ed. 1937. *Danske Folkeviser i Udvalg*. 2 vols. København: Gyldendal.

Graves, Peter, and Bjarne Thorup Thomsen. Forthcoming. "Translation and Transplantation: Sir Alexander Gray's Danish Ballads." In *Frae Ither Tongues: Essays in Modern Translation into Scots*, edited by Bill Findlay. Clevedon, Avon, England: Multilingual Matters.

Gray, Alexander. "Letters to Elias Bredsdorff." Manuscript no. 11562, National Library of Scotland, Edinburgh.

———. Papers. Manuscripts no. 26009–26014, n.d., National Library of Scotland, Edinburgh.

———. N.d. "Posthumous Ballads." Unpublished manuscript, no. 26011, National Library of Scotland, Edinburgh.

———. 1954. *Four-and-Forty: A Selection of Danish Ballads Presented in Scots*. Edinburgh: Edinburgh University Press.

———. 1958. *Historical Ballads of Denmark*. Edinburgh: Edinburgh University Press.

———. 1966a. *A Timorous Civility: A Scots Miscellany*. Glasgow: Collins.

[Gray, Alexander]. 1966b. Unnumbered typescript enclosed within National Library of Scotland copy of Gray's *A Timorous Civility*.

Gray, John. N.d. Talk on Alexander Gray given to the Saltire Society, Edinburgh.

———. 1999a. Letter to the author, 6 April.

———. 1999b. Letter to the author, 11 July.

Grundtvig, Svend, ed. 1867. *Danske Kæmpeviser og Folkesange fra Middelalderen.*
    København: Gad.
———. 1882. *Danmarks Folkeviser i Udvalg.* København: Philipsens.
Grundtvig, Svend, Axel Olrik, H. Grüner-Nielsen, Erik Dal et al., eds. 1853–1976.
    *Danmarks gamle Folkeviser.* 12 vols. [in 13]. København: Samfundet til den danske
    Literaturs Fremme and Universitets-Jubilæets danske Samfund.
Grüner-Nielsen, Hakon, ed. 1925–27. *Danske Folkeviser.* 2 vols. København: Martins
    Forlag.
Olrik, Axel, with Ida Falbe-Hansen, eds. 1899–1909. *Danske Folkeviser i Udvalg.* 2 vols.
    København: Gyldendal for Dansklærerforeningen.
Prior, R. C. A., tr. 1860. *Ancient Danish Ballads.* 3 vols. London and Edinburgh:
    Williams and Norgate.
Recke, Ernst von der, ed. 1927–29. *Danmarks Fornviser.* 4 vols. København: Møller og
    Landschultz.
Smith-Dampier, E. M., tr. 1939. *A Book of Danish Ballads*, by Axel Olrik. Princeton:
    Princeton University Press and New York: American-Scandinavian Foundation.
Syndergaard, Larry. 1995. *English Translations of the Scandinavian Medieval Ballads:
    An Analytical Guide and Bibliography.* Turku: Nordic Institute of Folklore.
———. 1996. "Ballad Translation and Colonialism: The Scandinavian Ballads in
    English." Paper presented at the 26th International Ballad Conference, University of
    Wales-Swansea, 19–24 July.
———. 2000. "The Spirit of Scotland and the Danish Ballads: Sir Alexander Gray's
    Translations." In *Bridging the Cultural Divide: Our Common Ballad Heritage/
    Kulturelle Brücken: Gemeinsame Balladentradition*, edited by Sigrid Rieuwerts and
    Helga Stein, 448–63. Hildesheim, Zürich, New York: Olms.
Tang Kristensen, Evald, ed. 1868–91. *Jy(d)ske Folkeminder.* Vol. 1 Copenhagen: Iversens
    Boghandel; vols. 2, 10–11 Copenhagen: Gyldendalske Boghandel.

# "George Collins" in Hampshire

## David Atkinson

Shortly after George B. Gardiner published texts of "George Collins" collected in Hampshire (*Journal of the Folk-Song Society* 1909: 299–302), Barbara M. Cra'ster (1910) argued that the ballad should be considered more or less cognate with the Scottish "Clerk Colvill" (Child 42). Gardiner himself had compared it with "Lady Alice" (Child 85). "George Collins" does, however, include a substantial narrative unit which is not present in the texts of "Lady Alice" printed by Child. This is the opening section, where George Collins walks out on a May morning and meets a fair pretty maid washing her marble stone; she greets him and predicts that his life will not last long, and he embraces and kisses her before returning home. Subsequently, the story is comparable to "Lady Alice."

In England, this "marble stone" opening is (with one possible exception) restricted to versions of "George Collins" from Hampshire: six in Gardiner's manuscripts from southern Hampshire, dated 1906–08, and one recorded by Bob Copper farther north in the county in 1955.[1] The possible exception is a version collected later by Mike Yates in Gloucestershire, which roughly accords with the Hampshire versions but may have been influenced by the folk revival. Generally, the revival has meant that the ballad with the marble stone opening is now much more widely sung; Bob Copper himself sings it (*When the May Is All in Bloom* 1995).

Cra'ster describes the three main incidents of the Hampshire versions of "George Collins" as follows:

1. His meeting with a maiden by a stream, the maiden evidently having a supernatural nature.
2. His return home and death as the result of the meeting.
3. His true-love's realization of the tragedy through seeing his coffin, and her consequent death. (1910: 106)

These three incidents, she maintains, form exactly the main plot of "Clerk Colvill"— or, more exactly, the "Clerk Colvill" story as reconstructed on the assumption that the anglophone type is cognate with various European ballads. These include Scandinavian types (Jonsson et al. 1978: *TSB* A 63)—Danish "Elveskud" (Grundtvig et al. 1853–1976: *DgF* 47), Norwegian "Olav Liljukrans," Faroese

"Ólavur Riddararós," Icelandic "Ólafur Liljurós," Swedish "Herr Olof och älvorna"—as well as the Breton "An Aotrou Nann," francophone "Le roi Renaud," and Italian, Spanish, and other ballads. (The main arguments over presumed lines of transmission are summarized in Jonsson 1992.)

Child calls the versions of the anglophone "Clerk Colvill" "deplorably imperfect" and gives the following summary of the ballad type, much of which is actually based on inference from the European texts:

> Clerk Colvill, newly married as we may infer, is solemnly entreated by his gay lady never to go near a well-fared may who haunts a certain spring or water. It is clear that before his marriage he had been in the habit of resorting to this mermaid, as she is afterwards called, and equally clear, from the impatient answer which he renders his dame, that he means to visit her again. His coming is hailed with pleasure by the mermaid, who, in the course of their interview, does something which gives him a strange pain in the head,—a pain only increased by a prescription which she pretends will cure it, and, as she then exultingly tells him, sure to grow worse until he is dead. He draws his sword on her, but she merrily springs into the water. He mounts his horse, rides home tristful, alights heavily, and bids his mother make his bed, for all is over with him. (Child 1882–98, 1: 372)

European ballads also add the eventual discovery by the hero's wife that her husband is dead and her own resulting death. Cra'ster essentially emphasizes narrative similarities between this composite story and "George Collins," along with the seemingly similar names Colvill, Colven, and especially Colin (Child 42C), to suggest that the Hampshire "George Collins" preserves an original form from which both "Lady Alice" and the anglophone "Clerk Colvill" derived.

Subsequently, a much longer study of "George Collins" by Samuel Bayard appeared (1945). He noted American versions of the "Lady Alice" story with the "marble stone" opening, usually titled "Johnny Collins." Arguing that the hero's death presents a motivation problem in all versions of "Lady Alice," which is only compounded by the conviction that the maid washing the stone cannot be one and the same as Collins's true-love, who later sees his coffin approaching, Bayard was driven to concur with Cra'ster's argument that "Lady Alice" and "Clerk Colvill" are essentially one and the same. He elaborates the "Clerk Colvill" story by drawing on both the anglophone texts of Child 42 and its supposed European counterparts, drawing particular attention to two Italian texts where a knight encounters a washerwoman and embraces her.[2] He then goes on to identify some specific points which reveal greater or lesser similarities between "George Collins" and "Clerk Colvill" and the European ballads:

1. Washing the marble stone in "George Collins" is equated with washing clothes upon a stone in "Clerk Colvill," as in Child 42 C especially. The Italian texts also describe the woman whom the knight embraces as a washerwoman. (1945: 88–89)

2. The woman's prediction of the hero's imminent death in "George Collins" is paralleled in "Clerk Colvill." The hero of Breton and Scandinavian ballads is offered a choice between a long sickness and a quick death. The tone of this part of "George Collins" is, however, more sorrowful than in the other ballads. (1945: 89)

3. The woman at the beginning of the ballad is associated with water in both "George Collins" and "Clerk Colvill," especially Child 42 C, as well as the Italian ballad. (1945: 89–91)

4. The hero returns home to die in "George Collins," "Clerk Colvill," and the European ballads. The request to his mother to make his bed is paralleled in Scandinavian texts. (1945: 91)

5. The hero's head is bound up (presumably) to ease his pain in "George Collins," while the same action seemingly hastens his death in "Clerk Colvill" (Child 42 A, B). (1945: 91–92)

6. There is an attempt to keep the fact of the hero's death from his true-love in the European ballads, which is not present in "Clerk Colvill," but which can be compared with the latter part of "George Collins," when his true love is told that the coffin she sees approaching is that of her former lover. Her own subsequent demise also has parallels in the European ballads. (1945: 92–93)

7. Finally, there is the matter of names, Collins being compared with Colven (42 A), Colvill (42 B), and especially Colin (42 C) in "Clerk Colvill." (1945: 94)

Bayard concludes that the woman washing the marble stone in "George Collins" is a supernatural being akin to the mermaid of "Clerk Colvill"—Collins's fairy mistress (1945: 93). This then explains her prediction of Collins's death, his embracing her after she has foretold his death, and his mortal lover's subsequent uncertainty as to whose coffin she sees approaching (1945: 93–94). So "Lady Alice" and "Clerk Colvill" are considered as a single type:

> All appearances, then, seem to argue not only similarity, but identity for these two pieces. They suggest strongly that *Lady Alice* must be simply another offshoot of the ancient *Clerk Colvill* ballad—abbreviated and obscured in most texts, but still having one version ("Johnny Collins") that tells the *entire ballad story*, as it is found nowhere else in English folksong.... No two ballads in English are more closely allied. (1945: 100)

Bayard further suggests that the association of the supernatural being in the anglophone ballads with water, unlike the hills or woods of Scandinavian or Breton texts, may have been influenced by Gaelic traditions (1945: 94–100). Accordingly, he rejects the suggestion of Cra'ster (following Child) that the silken "sark," or shirt, which the mermaid is washing in "Clerk Colvill" signifies a betrothal gift and instead relates it to the characteristic activity of the banshee of Gaelic tradition:

> Her station...is generally at fords in the river; *the stone on which she folds the shirts of the doomed is in the middle of the water*; at times she is seen seated by pool or stream washing the linen of those soon to die, and folding and beating it with her hands on a stone in the middle of the water—at which times she is known as the *bean nighe*, or *washing woman*, and her being seen is a sure sign that death is near.[3] (1945: 99)

A Scottish-Irish connection would then account for the presence of "Johnny Collins" in America (1945: 98).

Harbison Parker enthusiastically embraced Bayard's arguments for allying "George Collins"/"Johnny Collins" with "Clerk Colvill" (1947). He took issue, however, with Bayard's identifying the "Clerk Colvill" mermaid and the woman washing her marble stone in "George Collins" with a banshee. Instead, he argues that the elf woman of Scandinavian ballads of the "Elveskud" kind was transformed into a mermaid associated particularly with water, as in the Scottish "Clerk Colvill," in Shetland and Orkney, where elves are much rarer in tradition. He draws comparisons with the Scandinavian ballads to elucidate further a number of the points already raised by Bayard pertaining to both "Clerk Colvill" and "George Collins":

1. In the Scandinavian ballads, the elf woman offers the hero a silken shirt. This, along with the function of a sark or shirt in other Scottish ballads like "Allison Gross" (Child 35) and "The Elfin Knight" (Child 2), suggests that the laundered sark is indeed connected with betrothal. (1947: 266–70)

2. When the woman summons the hero in "George Collins," her cries do not express grief, as Bayard believed, but represent a salutation like that of the elf women in the Scandinavian ballads. (1947: 270–73)

3. The woman's ability to predict the hero's imminent death in "George Collins" is readily explained if she is equated with the elf woman of the Scandinavian ballads and the mermaid of "Clerk Colvill," who, themselves, directly bring about his death. (1947: 273)

4. In Faroese ballads, after one of the elf women has given him a poisoned draught, she commands the hero to kiss her. This parallel may explain why the hero of "George Collins" proceeds to kiss the maid even after she has foretold his death. (1947: 273–74)

Parker also cites Grundtvig to support the onomastic transformation of Ólavur, the hero of the Faroese and Icelandic ballads, into (Clerk C)olvill (1947: 281, 283). (He is also responsible for the somewhat far-fetched suggestion that Clerk Colvill has some connection with Harry Colvile, a minister from Orkney who was murdered in Shetland in 1596 [1947: 283–84].)

Cra'ster, Bayard, and Parker effectively equate the Hampshire "George Collins" not just with the Scottish "Clerk Colvill" but with a presumed pan-European ballad type (also Forslin 1962–63; Jonsson 1992). Subsequently, there has been a broad consensus that at the very least "Lady Alice" (including the Hampshire oikotype) and "Clerk Colvill" represent one and the same ballad type. Bronson admitted the plausibility of the argument (1959–72, 2: 392). Coffin certainly accepted it (1977: 86–87). Wilgus admitted a thematic, though not necessarily genetic, link (1970: 169–72). Buchan placed the two ballads in the same "supertype" (1986: 251; 1991a: 145). It has become orthodox to write Child 42/85, and this has the added attraction that it is possible to do so without casting aspersions upon Child himself since the Hampshire "George Collins" was not available to him.

The lone voice of dissent is W. F. H. Nicolaisen, who poses a methodological objection to equating ballads from different times and places on the basis of an onomastic similarity when all that they share otherwise is the odd plot feature (1992). So he concedes that Colven (Child 42A) may readily have given rise to Colvill (42B) on the one hand and Colin (42C) on the other, while the possibility of secondary projection of the final *k* of Clerk suggests a potential precursor in *Clerk Olven, which could in turn be related to the Olav-type names of Scandinavian ballads (1992: 37). Yet beyond this, "the only feature which all the ballads which are supposed to be associated with Child 42 have in common is the statement that a son goes to his mother to tell her that he is about to die" (1992: 37). Accordingly, he maintains that it is not permissible to speak of "Clerk Colvill," "Elveskud," "Ann Aotrou Nann," and "Le roi Renaud" as all part of a single international ballad type and certainly not to designate it "Clerk Colvill" (1992: 37).[4]

The same principle applies within the anglophone ballad area. Again, there is an undeniable onomastic similarity between George, Johnny, or Giles Collins in versions of "Lady Alice" and Clerk Colin in Child 42C. All the same, a salutary lesson exists in the fact that the heroine of "Lady Isabel and the Elf-Knight" (Child 4) is called variously (May) Colvin, Colvine, Colven, Colin, Collin, or Colinn, and there is no suggestion of any genetic relationship between that ballad and "Clerk Colvill" (1992: 38). Moreover, even the onomastic evidence for a link between George Collins, as representing a putative "original" form, and the Scottish Clerk Colvill requires an awkward (though not impossible) sequence of change from Collin(s) to Colvin to Colvill(e) (1992: 39). More importantly, however, if "Clerk Colvill" is not considered cognate with various European ballads, then it is not legitimate to combine it with them to construct a hypothetical ballad which then offers points of seeming similarity with "George Collins" (1992: 39–40). In other words, if no special weight is given to the onomastic similarities alone, then "Lady Alice" and "Clerk Colvill" must be compared on their actual shared features, which amount to little more than the statement that a son goes to his mother to tell her that he is about to die. In that case, "Child was undoubtedly right in assigning these two ballads two separate numbers in his type catalogue" (1992: 40).

It is worth examining in a little more detail three of the points where "George Collins" and "Clerk Colvill" have been assumed to tell the same story.

*1. Washing her marble stone*
The encounter between the male protagonist and the woman who is washing is evidently at least partly amatory in both "Clerk Colvill" and "George Collins." The mermaid, however, is washing a "sark of silk" (Child 42A, B) or just silk (42C). Only in the last version is she described as washing it upon a stone, and even

there it is not specifically marble. In contrast, the maid in "George Collins" is washing not a piece of fabric but the marble stone itself. She might be pictured washing her doorstep or hearthstone. The meeting in "Clerk Colvill" appears to be set somewhere out in the open, by "Clyde's water" in 42C (see Nicolaisen 1992: 40–41). The meeting in "George Collins" presumably takes place at the maid's dwelling (she is usually washing *her* marble stone), even though Collins may have to cross water to reach her. On a denotative level, or as a visual image, the two male-female encounters are potentially very different.

On a connotative level, however, the two scenes do tend to converge. The sark of "Clerk Colvill" may recall those in "The Elfin Knight" and other ballads, where a sark or shirt may function as a love token but also carries allusions to death and the grave (Child 1882–98, 5: 284; Toelken 1995: 115–17). Similarly, the marble stone of "George Collins" alludes to the grave- or tombstone, as it does in rhymes from English and Scottish folktales:[5]

> Apple tree, apple tree hide me
> In case the old witch will find me
> If she do she'll break my bones
> And bury me under the marble stones. (Philip 1992: 67)

Nevertheless, while there is no denying that there is something mysterious or fey about the maid in the Hampshire "George Collins," there is a world of difference between a "fair pretty maid" and a mermaid. When the hero draws his sword on the female character in "Clerk Colvill," she turns back into a fish and vanishes. Nicolaisen (1992: 34) concurs with Buchan (1986; 1991a; 1991b: 74–75) that "Clerk Colvill" functions as an explicit (and culture-specific) warning of the dangers of amatory involvement with the supernatural world. It is very difficult to substantiate a similar claim for "George Collins."

## 2. A napkin to tie round my head

When George Collins asks a member of his family for a napkin to bind his head, it seems like a homespun attempt to relieve the pain, even though his imminent demise appears inevitable (Buchan 1994: 33). In "Clerk Colvill," however, it is the mermaid herself who invites Colvill to cut a "gare," or strip of cloth, from the sark she has been washing. She seems to delight in the increased pain that he suffers after binding the cloth around his head ("merrily laughd the mermaiden" in Child 42A) and predicts that he will endure intensifying pain until he is dead. The cloth itself could be an integral cause of his death.

Both the placing of this incident within the narrative structure, as well as the relationships between the characters involved, are different in the two ballads. Nevertheless, the connotation of imminent death attached to the action is certainly consistent between them. That connotation is perhaps best exemplified by "The Suffolk Miracle" (Child 272), where the action of a woman tying a handkerchief around her lover's head is explicitly associated with the discovery that he is dead. It is worth noting, too, that "The Suffolk Miracle" has various parallels among folktales, as well as in literary form in Bürger's *Lenore* (Child 1882–98, 5: 58–65).

### 3. Fair Eleanor (or Ellender or Helen)

If the maid "washing her marble stone" at the beginning of "George Collins" is considered analogous to the mermaid of "Clerk Colvill," it is then improbable that she can be the same character as the woman who later sees the coffin approaching. It is certainly the case that the Hampshire versions all describe at the beginning of the ballad "a fair pretty maid" apparently engaged in domestic activity, whereas Fair Eleanor sounds like a grander lady in a hall or a "room so fine," working her silk or "silver twine."

On the other hand, on his return home, George Collins requests his mother to bury him under the marble stone against Fair Eleanor's hall, wall, or home. So the two are connected by their association with the marble stone—"the sign of fair Helen" in one version (Gardiner MS H1193)—and this functions as prima facie evidence that they are one and the same character. In some American versions, their identity is even more explicit:

> Johnny Collins rode out to the fields one day,
> When the flowers were all in full bloom;
> Who did he spy but his own fair Ellen
> A-washing a white marble stone. (Davis 1929: 347–48[B])

Even Bayard was sure that some American singers identified the maid washing her marble stone with Collins's lover who later spies his coffin (1945: 80).[6]

Bayard, however, is insistent that they cannot be one and the same because then the ballad would be "utterly senseless" (and would not be cognate with "Clerk Colvill" in this regard) (1945: 79–81). His primary reason for this conclusion is that the maid foretells Collins's death, whereas his lover is seemingly uncertain whose coffin she sees. Yet this is merely a matter of interpretation, for she can surely be (fearfully) seeking confirmation of her own presentiment. Only if, as Parker claims on the basis of Scandinavian ballads and "Clerk Colvill," she directly brings about his death (1947: 273–274), does the identification of maid and true-love appear impossible (and even then not absolutely if a motive of deception can be imputed to her). The idea that a man's lover should foretell his death and be subsequently proved right gives a chilling turn to a ballad that Child (1882–98, 2: 279) described as a sort of counterpart to "Lord Lovel" (Child 75). The fair maid washing her marble stone can have a sort of second sight without being "evidently of a supernatural nature" (Cra'ster 1910: 106).

As these three cruxes illustrate, the comparative textual study of "George Collins" and "Clerk Colvill" needs to consider the ballads on at least three different levels: 1) a denotative or textual level which considers the art of storytelling in song and also the variations that affect a particular narrative; 2) a metaphorical or figurative level of connotations shared among different texts, which make up an important part of the "grammar" of balladry; and 3) a further level which comprises textual reception and draws on both denotative and connotative levels as well as extratextual factors to produce a "reading" of the text. At the denotative level, it is not so easy to maintain that "George Collins" and "Clerk Colvill" tell the same story, while at the connotative level there is certainly some shared ground. The slender evidence available from singers and others suggests that "George Collins" is considered a distinct entity. Nevertheless, a part of the dynamic of textual reception must recognize the association of the ballads, within both the Child corpus and the body of ballad scholarship that has subsequently grown up around them and has in some degree established forever the idea that there is a connection between the two types.

*Notes*

1. Gardiner MSS H327, H419, H439, H439a, H658, H1193; *Journal of the Folk-Song Society* 1909: 299–302; White 1955; Copper 1973: 246–47; *Folk Songs of Britain* 1968–71, 4; *Journal of the English Folk Dance and Song Society* 1961: 72–73; *Voice of the People* 1998, 3; *Songs and Southern Breezes* 1977. Cf. Child 85A, B, C; 1882–98, 3: 514–15, 515; Haggard 1935: 170–71; Broadwood LEB/4/179–82; R. Hook, broadside printer's catalogue (matched by title only); Sharp 1974, 1: 106–7; *Universal Songster* [1825–26], 3: 16 (a parody); Yates NSA C796/19 C4 (VWML CD 4). My thanks to Mike Yates for telling me about this last item, which is also included on *Up in the North and Down in the South* (2001).
2. Under the bridge of Rella (Diamantina) is a washerwoman. A knight passes by. The washerwoman goes into the water; the knight follows and embraces her. He goes home all wet, asks his mother to put him into bed and his horse into the stall; make him some supper and give his horse fodder; dig him a grave and bury his horse, too. He also directs bells to be rung over him and says he and his horse have many knife stabs (1945: 85).
3. Compare the figure encountered in Scottish tradition in Alec Stewart's tale of "The Shepherd and the Wee Woman" (Douglas 1987: 70–71).

4. Nicolaisen (1991) has also drawn attention to the more general problems involved in speaking of the "internationality" of ballads. Long-established trade links between Scandinavia and Scotland can perhaps reasonably be thought to have provided a channel for cultural transmission, but it is unknown whether ballads were translated from one language to another, or whether what was transmitted across geographical, linguistic, and cultural boundaries was instead a combination of narrative outline and certain motifs. Fischer takes a cautious line when discussing "Clerk Colvill" and the Faeroese "Ólavur Riddararós": "the story lines in the Faroese and Scots versions are like enough to allow some comparison to be made in how the two areas deal with a similar theme" (1998: 191). The shared ground among ballads from different regions may more readily occur at the semiotic level outlined in the analysis of Danish ballads by Jacobsen and Leavy (1988). See also de Rhett (1986).

5. For example, *"...and that's my story"* (1991: booklet, 27–29); Briggs (1970–71: part A Folk Narratives, 1: 270–71, 432–35, 441–42, 473–74); Philip (1992: 63–68, 146). Toelken (1995: 115) notes that the phrase "marble town" is common as a euphemism for the graveyard in the southern United States.

6. On the other hand, an English revival singer told me that he had always thought of the two women as different but did not, therefore, see the first as a water sprite or mermaid.

## References

Bayard, Samuel P. 1945. "The 'Johnny Collins' Version of 'Lady Alice.'" *Journal of American Folklore* 58: 73–103.

Briggs, Katharine M. 1970–71. *A Dictionary of British Folk-Tales in the English Language, Incorporating the F. J. Norton Collection.* 4 vols. London: Routledge and Kegan Paul.

Broadwood, Lucy E. Manuscript. Vaughan Williams Memorial Library, London.

Bronson, Bertrand Harris. 1959–72. *The Traditional Tunes of the Child Ballads, With Their Texts, According to the Extant Records of Great Britain and America.* 4 vols. Princeton: Princeton University Press.

Buchan, David. 1986. "Taleroles and the Otherworld Ballads." *Tod und Jenseits im Europäischen Volkslied*, edited by Walter Puchner, 247–61. 16. Internationale Balladenkonferenz, Kolympari, Kreta, 19–22 August 1986, veranstaltet von der Kommission für Volksdichtung der Société Internationale d'Ethnologie et Folklore in Zusammenarbeit mit Société Hellénique de Laographie und Orthodox Academy of Crete. Publications of Folklore Museum and Archives, no. 6. Ioannina: Faculty of Philosophy, Department of Folklore, University of Jannina.

———. 1991a. "Ballads of Otherworld Beings." In *The Good People: New Fairylore Essays*, edited by Peter Narváez, 142–154. Garland Reference Library of the Humanities, vol. 1376. New York: Garland.

———. 1991b. "Talerole Analysis and Child's Supernatural Ballads." In *The Ballad and Oral Literature*, edited by Joseph Harris, 60–77. Harvard English Studies, no. 17. Cambridge: Harvard University Press.

———. 1994. "Folk Medicine in the Scottish Ballads: A Medical Perspective." In *Images, Identities and Ideologies: Papers from the 22nd International Ballad Conference, Belfast, 29 June–3 July 1992,* edited by John M. Kirk and Colin Neilands, 31–40. Enfield Lock: Hisarlik Press. Also published in *Lore and Language* 12 (1994): 31–40.

Child, Francis James, ed. 1882–98. *The English and Scottish Popular Ballads.* 5 vols. Reprint, New York: Folklore Press, 1956–57; New York: Dover, 1965. Corrected edition prepared by Mark and Laura Heiman. Northfield, Minn.: Loomis House Press, 2002. Digital edition, with gazetteer, maps and audio CD. New York: ESPB Publishing, 2003.

Coffin, Tristram Potter. 1977. *The British Traditional Ballad in North America.* Rev. ed. with a supplement by Roger deV. Renwick. Bibliographical and Special Series published through the cooperation of the American Folklore Society. Austin: University of Texas Press.

Copper, Bob. 1973. *Songs and Southern Breezes: Country Folk and Country Ways.* London: Heinemann.

Cra'ster, Barbara M. 1910. "George Collins." *Journal of the Folk-Song Society* 4: 106–109.

Davis, Arthur Kyle, Jr., ed. 1929. *Traditional Ballads of Virginia Collected under the Auspices of the Virginia Folk-Lore Society.* Cambridge: Harvard University Press.

de Rhett, Beatriz Mariscal. 1986. "Notes on the Trans-Cultural Adaptation of Traditional Ballads." In *Tod und Jenseits im Europäischen Volkslied*, 229–45.

Douglas, Sheila, ed. 1987. *The King o' the Black Art and Other Folk Tales.* Storytellers: John Stewart, Alec Stewart, Belle Stewart, Willie MacPhee. Aberdeen: Aberdeen University Press.

Fischer, Frances J. 1998. "No Death without Warning: A Supernatural Ballad in Scotland and the Faroe Islands." In *Ljudske balade med izročilom in sodobnostjo/Ballads between Tradition and Modern Times*, edited by Marjetka Golež [Kaučič], 190–97. Proceedings of the 27th International Ballad Conference (SIEF Ballad Commission), Gozd Martuljek, Slovenia, 13–19 July 1997. Ljubljana: ZRC SAZU.

Forslin, Alfhild. 1962–63. "Balladen om riddar Olof och älvorna: En traditionsundersökning." *ARV: Journal of Scandinavian Folklore* 18–19: 1–92.

Gardiner, George B. Manuscript. Vaughan Williams Memorial Library, London.

Grundtvig, Svend, Axel Olrik, H. Grüner-Nielsen, Erik Dal et al., eds. 1853–1976. *Danmarks gamle Folkeviser.* 12 vols. [in 13]. København: Samfundet til den danske Literaturs Fremme and Universitets-Jubilæets danske Samfund.

Haggard, Lilias Rider, ed. 1935. *I Walked by Night: Being the Life and History of the King of the Norfolk Poachers, Written by Himself.* London: Nicholson and Watson.

Jacobsen, Per Schelde, and Barbara Fass Leavy. 1988. *Ibsen's Forsaken Merman: Folklore in the Late Plays.* New York: New York University Press.

Jonsson, Bengt R. 1992. "Sir Olav and the Elves: The Position of the Scandinavian Version." *ARV: Scandinavian Yearbook of Folklore* 48, 65–90. Also published as *The Stockholm Ballad Conference 1991: Proceedings of the 21st International Ballad Conference, 19–22 August 1991*, edited by Bengt R. Jonsson, 65–90. Skrifter utgivna av Svenskt Visarkiv, no. 12. Stockholm: Svenskt Visarkiv, 1993.

Jonsson, Bengt R., Svale Solheim, Eva Danielson et al. 1978. *The Types of the Scandinavian Ballad.* Oslo, Bergen and Tromsø: Universitetsforlaget.

*Journal of the English Folk Dance and Song Society* 9. 1961.

*Journal of the Folk-Song Society* 3. 1909.

Nicolaisen, W. F. H. 1991. "On the Internationality of Ballads." In *Gender and Print Culture: New Perspectives on International Ballad Studies*, edited by Maria Herrera-Sobek, 99–104. [Irvine, Ca.]: Kommission für Volksdichtung of the Société Internationale d'Ethnologie et de Folklore.

———. 1992. "Onomastic Aspects of Clerk Colvill." In *ARV: Scandinavian Yearbook of Folklore* 48, 31–41. Also published as *The Stockholm Ballad Conference 1991: Proceedings of the 21st International Ballad Conference, 19–22 August 1991*, 31–41.

Parker, Harbison. 1947. "The 'Clerk Colvill' Mermaid." *Journal of American Folklore* 60: 265–85.

Philip, Neil, ed. 1992. *The Penguin Book of English Folktales.* London: Penguin.

Sharp, Cecil. 1974. *Cecil Sharp's Collection of English Folk Songs.* Edited by Maud Karpeles. 2 vols. London: Oxford University Press.

Toelken, Barre. 1995. *Morning Dew and Roses: Nuance, Metaphor, and Meaning in Folksongs.* Folklore and Society, Publications of the American Folklore Society, New Series. Urbana and Chicago: University of Illinois Press.

*Universal Songster, or Museum of Mirth, The: Forming the Most Complete, Extensive, and Valuable Collection of Ancient and Modern Songs in the English Language.* N.d. [1825–26]. 3 vols. London: Routledge.

Wilgus, D. K. 1970. "A Type-Index of Anglo-American Traditional Narrative Songs." *Journal of the Folklore Institute* 7: 161–76.

## Recordings

*"...and that's my story": Tales, Yarns and Legends from Britain and Ireland.* 1991. Field recordings made by Ewan MacColl, Peggy Seeger, Charles Parker, Jim Carroll, Pat MacKenzie, Bob Patten, John Howson and Denis Turner. London: Vaughan Williams Memorial Library, English Folk Dance and Song Society VWML 005. Cassette and booklet.

*Folk Songs of Britain, The.* 1968–71. Edited by Peter Kennedy and Alan Lomax. 10 vols. London: Topic. Vol. 4, *The Child Ballads 1,* Topic 12T160. Recordings.

*Songs and Southern Breezes: Country Singers from Hampshire and Sussex.* 1977. Recorded by Bob Copper. London: Topic 12T317. Recording.

*Up in the North and Down in the South: Songs and Music from the Mike Yates Collection, 1964–2000.* 2001. Stroud Musical Traditions MT CD 311–12 Compact disks.

*Voice of the People, The.* 1998. Edited by Reg Hall. 20 vols. London: Topic. Vol. 3, *O'er His Grave the Grass Grew Green: Tragic Ballads,* Topic TSCD653. Compact disks.

*When the May Is All in Bloom: Traditional Singing from the South East of England.* 1995. Haughley: Veteran Tapes VT131CD. Compact disk.

White, Enos. 1955. Recorded by Bob Copper. BBC RPL 21857. Recording.

Yates, Mike. Collection of field recordings. British Library Sound Archive, London (compact disk copies in Vaughan Williams Memorial Library, London).

# From France to Brazil via Germany and Portugal:
# The Meandering Journey of a Traditional Ballad

J. J. Dias Marques

*For Samuel G. Armistead and Jackson da Silva Lima*

During research on the popularity of the Middle Ages in nineteenth-century
Portugal, I read a book published in 1848 by Gomes Monteiro, a translated anthology of German romantic poetry with a wide sampling of poems with medieval
or folk themes, among which was the following by Ludwig Uhland (Text 1):

| A Filha do Rei de Espanha | | The King of Spain's Daughter |
|---|---|---|
| A filha do rei de Espanha | | The king of Spain's daughter |
| Um ofício quis tomar, | 2 | A craft did wish to take, |
| Escolheu ser lavandeira, | | She chose to be a washer woman, |
| Quis aprender a lavar. | 4 | She wished to learn to launder. |
| | | |
| E na primeira camisa | | And the first chemise |
| Que foi ao rio lavar, | 6 | She went to the river to wash, |
| Seu anel do ebúrneo dedo | | The ring from her ivory finger |
| Deslizou, caiu ao mar. | 8 | Did slip and fall into the sea. |
| | | |
| A infanta era mimosa, | | The princess was delicate |
| E começou de chorar. | 10 | And she began to weep. |
| Cavalgava um cavaleiro | | A knight was riding by |
| Junto daquele lugar. | 12 | Near the place where she was. |
| | | |
| —Vós chorais, gentil donzela? | | —Art thou weeping, gentle maiden? |
| Quem vos pudera anojar? | 14 | Who could ever do thee harm? |
| —Um anel de ouro que eu tinha | | —The golden ring I was wearing |
| Caiu-me ao fundo do mar. | 16 | Fell deep into the sea. |
| | | |
| —Que me dareis, linda moça, | | —What wilt thou give me, pretty girl, |
| Se vosso anel for buscar? | 18 | If thy ring I seek and find? |

| | | | |
|---|---|---|---|
| —Um beijo da minha boca | | —A kiss from my mouth, | |
| Não vo-lo posso negar. | 20 | That, I cannot deny. | |
| | | | |
| Já se apeia o cavaleiro, | | From his horse the knight alights | |
| Nas ondas vai mergulhar, | 22 | And in the waves he dives, | |
| E no primeiro mergulho | | And at the first dive | |
| Nada consegue tirar, | 24 | Nothing can he find, | |
| | | | |
| E no segundo mergulho | | And at the second dive | |
| Viu no fundo o anel brilhar, | 26 | He saw the ring in the deep so bright, | |
| E no terceiro mergulho | | And at the third dive | |
| Triste se foi afogar. | 28 | Alas! The knight did drown. | |
| | | | |
| A infanta era mimosa, | | The princess was delicate | |
| E começou de chorar: | 30 | And she began to weep: | |
| —Oh! mal haja o meu mister, | | —Woe! Cursed be my craft! | |
| Oh! mal haja o meu lavar! | 32 | Woe! Cursed be my going washing. | |

(Monteiro 1848: 95–96)

At once this text brought to mind a ballad I knew from the Brazilian oral tradition, "The King of Spain's Daughter." Let us look at the oldest of its known versions, collected by Ester Pedreira in 1949 in the state of Bahia (Text 2):

| | | | |
|---|---|---|---|
| A filha do rei da Espanha | | The king of Spain's daughter | |
| Um ofício quis tomar, | 2 | A craft did wish to take, | |
| Ofício de lavadeira, | | The craft of washer woman, | |
| Foi para o rio lavar. | 4 | To the river she went washing. | |
| | | | |
| Logo à primeira camisa, | | At the very first chemise | |
| Que a donzela foi lavar, | 6 | That the maiden went to wash, | |
| O anel caiu do dedo, | | The ring fell from her finger, | |
| Foi para o fundo do mar. | 8 | Fell deep into the sea. | |
| | | | |
| A donzela, arrependida, | | The maiden was remorseful | |
| Largou-se ali a chorar. | 10 | There and then she burst out crying. | |
| Passou logo um cavalheiro | | At once a gentleman turned up | |
| Por ali a transitar. | 12 | Who was walking nearby. | |

—Por que choras, bela moça,         —Why do you cry, pretty girl?
Por que estás a chorar?     14    Why are you crying?
—Meu anel caiu do dedo,        —The ring fell from my finger,
Foi para o fundo do mar.    16    It fell deep into the sea.

—Dize o que me dás, bela moça,    —Tell me, what will you give me, pretty
Que o teu anel vou buscar.  18    For I'll fetch you your ring.    [girl,
—Um beijo da minha boca      —A kiss from my mouth
Dou-te, não posso negar.    20    I'll give you, I couldn't deny it.

Deu o primeiro mergulho       He made the first dive
E nada pôde encontrar;    22    And nothing could he find;
Deu o segundo mergulho      He made the second dive
E nada pôde buscar;    24    And nothing could he fetch;

Deu o terceiro mergulho,      He made the third dive
Foi para o fundo do mar.    26    And drowned deep in the sea.
—O mar que levou meu amor    —May the sea that took my love
Também me queira levar.    28    Take me as well.
             (Pedreira 1978: 30)

There are, of course, some differences between Monteiro's text and this one which I will examine later. Nevertheless, the version we've just seen proves beyond a doubt that the source of the Brazilian ballad "The King of Spain's Daughter" is Monteiro's Portuguese translation of the German poem by Uhland.

I decided to try and trace the journey of "The King of Spain's Daughter" from its origin until it reached the Brazilian oral tradition.[1] After some research, I arrived at the following conclusions: At the beginning of the nineteenth century, the German writer Adelbert von Chamisso lived in Paris for a while, and, since he was interested in oral poetry, he gathered some folk material for a book he had in mind (Chamisso 1839: 256–7, 262), a project that never materialized. One of the items he gathered was a French version of the pan-European ballad "The Diver,"[2] a ballad then unknown.

It so happened that, in 1810, the German poet Ludwig Uhland was also living in Paris and became friendly with Chamisso (Uhland 1911: 184). And, because Uhland was also very keen on oral poetry,[3] Chamisso showed him the French version of "The Diver," known in France as "La Fille du roi d'Espagne," he had in his collection of folk material.[4] That version is as follows (Text 3):

| | | | |
|---|---|---|---|
| La fill' du roi d'Espagne | | The king of Spain's daughter | |
| Veut apprendre un métier. | 2 | Wants to learn a craft. | |
| Ell' veut apprendre à coudre, | | She wants to learn to sew, | |
| A coudre ou à laver. | 4 | To sew or go washing. | |
| | | | |
| A la premièr' chemise | | At the first chemise | |
| Que la belle a lavé, | 6 | That the belle did wash | |
| L' anneau de la main blanche | | The ring from her white hand | |
| Dans la mer est tombé. | 8 | In the sea did fall. | |
| | | | |
| La fille était jeunette, | | The girl was very young, | |
| Ell' se mit à pleurer. | 10 | She began to weep. | |
| Par de-là il y passe | | Nearby is riding by | |
| Un noble chevalier: | 12 | A noble knight. | |
| | | | |
| —Que me donn'rez, la belle, | | —What will you give me, fair one, | |
| Je vous l' aveinderai? | 14 | If I get it back for you? | |
| —Un baiser de ma bouche | | —A kiss from my mouth | |
| Volontiers donnerai. | 16 | Willingly will I give. | |
| | | | |
| Le ch'valier se dépouille, | | The knight gets undressed | |
| Dans la mer est plongé; | 18 | And dives into the sea; | |
| A la première plonge | | At the first dive | |
| Il n' y a rien trouvé. | 20 | Nothing does he find. | |
| | | | |
| A la seconde plonge | | At the second dive | |
| L' anneau a brandillé,[5] | 22 | The ring swayed, | |
| A la troisième plonge | | At the third dive | |
| Le ch'valier fut noyé. | 24 | The knight was drowned. | |
| | | | |
| La fille était jeunette, | | The girl was very young, | |
| Ell' se mit à pleurer. | 26 | She began to weep. | |
| Ell' s' en fut chez son père: | | She went to her father: | |
| —Je ne veux plus d'métier. | 28 | —I no longer want a craft. | |

(Chamisso 1839: 258)

Uhland liked this ballad very much and, in that same year (1810), he translated it into German.[6]

In 1812 Uhland published this translation in an almanac,[7] together with a few other poems, and gave it the title "Die Königstochter." Later on, in 1820, "Die Königstochter" was published again, this time in the second edition of Uhland's *Gedichte* (Text 4):[8]

| Die Königstochter | | The King's Daughter |
|---|---|---|

| Des Königs von Spanien Tochter | | The king of Spain's daughter |
|---|---|---|
| Ein Gewerb zu lernen begann. | 2 | Began to learn a craft. |
| Sie wollte wohl lernen nähen, | | She wished to learn to sew, |
| Waschen und nähn fortan. | 4 | To wash as well as sew. |

| Und bei dem ersten Hemde, | | At the first chemise |
|---|---|---|
| Das sie sollte gewaschen han, | 6 | That she should have washed |
| Den Ring von ihrer weißen Hand | | The ring from her white hand |
| Hat ins Meer sie fallen lan. | 8 | Into the sea did fall. |

| Sie war ein zartes Fräulein, | | The girl was very delicate, |
|---|---|---|
| Zu weinen sie begann. | 10 | She began to weep. |
| Da zog des Wegs vorüber | | There rode along the way |
| Ein Ritter lobesan. | 12 | A noble knight. |

| —Wenn ich ihn wiederbringe, | | —If I get it back for you |
|---|---|---|
| Was gibt die Schöne dann? | 14 | What will you, fair one, give? |
| —Ein Kuß von meinem Munde | | —A kiss from my mouth |
| Ich nicht versagen kann. | 16 | I could not deny. |

| Der Ritter sich entkleidet, | | The knight gets undressed |
|---|---|---|
| Er taucht ins Meer wohlan, | 18 | And dives into the sea. |
| Und bei dem ersten Tauchen | | And at the first dive |
| Er nichts entdeken kann. | 20 | Nothing can he find. |

| Und bei dem zweiten Tauchen, | | And at the second dive |
|---|---|---|
| Da blinkt der Ring heran, | 22 | The ring twinkles bright, |
| Und bei dem dritten Tauchen | | And at the third dive |
| Ist ertrunken der Rittersmann. | 24 | The knight is drowned. |

| Sie war ein zartes Fräulein, |    | The girl was very delicate, |
|---|---|---|
| Zu weinen sie begann. | 26 | She began to cry. |
| Sie ging zu ihrem Vater: |    | She went to her father: |
| —Will kein Gewerb fortan! | 28 | —I no longer want a craft! |
| (Uhland 1908: 249–50) |    |    |

It was, no doubt, in Uhland's *Gedichte* that the Portuguese Monteiro read "Die Königstochter," and from there he translated the poem, together with seven other texts by Uhland, which he also included in his anthology.

This anthology was, as we have seen, published in 1848, and this was the door through which "The King of Spain's Daughter" passed into the oral tradition. The ballad was no doubt picked up from that publication (or else from a journal where it might have been republished) and then put to music, its medium of access into the oral tradition. It does in fact look likely that the traditionalization of "The King of Spain's Daughter" occurred, not because someone memorized it from a written source and then transmitted it through recitation, but rather, because the text was transformed into a song, perhaps sung with piano accompaniment in bourgeois homes and later circulated among the poorer classes.[9] To support this hypothesis, it is worth mentioning that the seven traditional versions of this poem which have music we know about are all sung to the same tune.[10] This seems to indicate that the diffusion of this ballad started with it already in song form and not simply as a text to which contributors later added a tune: If that were the case, we would surely find different tunes throughout the different versions.[11]

Before we briefly analyze a couple of the Brazilian versions of "The King of Spain's Daughter," I should mention that that this ballad probably existed first in the Portuguese tradition. This is, at least, what a small fragment collected by Leite de Vasconcellos before 1941 (the year of his death) seems to indicate (Text 5):[12]

| A filha de um rei de Espanha |    | The daughter of a king of Spain |
|---|---|---|
| aprendeu a *lambandeira* | 2 | Learned to be a washer woman |
| ................................. |    | ................................. |
|    |    |    |
| A primeira camisinha |    | The first chemisette |
| qu' ela ao mar foi *lambandar* | 4 | That she went to the sea to wash |
| ................................. |    | ................................. |
| (Vasconcellos 1960: 662) |    |    |

These lines clearly echo some from Monteiro's translation, which seems to indicate that his text had already begun to pass into the Portuguese tradition and would have reached Brazil already in its oral form. In any case, it is undeniable that it was in Brazil that "The King of Spain's Daughter" really became traditional, as it is in Brazil that it appears in several different versions.

If, as we have noticed, Text 2 is still very close to Monteiro, it is also true that we can already find some variations in it, showing the beginning of the poem's process of traditionalization.[13] Given space limitations, I will outline only one of the transformations: the added sentimentality, very typical of oral balladry, at least in the Luso-Brazilian tradition. In fact, Monteiro's translation (like the German text and, indeed, the French version) ends with the princess weeping, not for the young man's death, it seems, but *for the loss of her ring*. In Monteiro's text, therefore, only the boy appears to be in love (or at least attracted); the princess does not. On the contrary, in the oral text, the princess appears to reciprocate the youth's love and, at the end, she cries in despair, declaring her love for the knight and wishing to follow him in death:

| | | |
|---|---|---|
| —O mar que levou meu amor | | —May the sea that took my love |
| Também me queira levar. | 28 | Take me as well. |

In the other oral Brazilian versions I could find,[14] the process of traditionalization is already more advanced. I will briefly examine two versions.

Let us start with the one collected by Jackson da Silva Lima in 1974 in the state of Sergipe (Text 6):

| | | |
|---|---|---|
| A filha do rei da Espanha | | The king of Spain's daughter |
| Foi aprender a lavar, | 2 | Went to learn washing. |
| Na primeira camisa | | At her first chemise |
| Sua jóia caiu no mar. | 4 | Her jewel fell into the sea. |
| | | |
| Passando um cavaleiro, | | As a rider was passing by, |
| Ela chamou:—Venha cá, | 6 | She called:—Come over here, |
| Venha tirar minha jóia | | Come and fetch my jewel |
| Mode meu pai não falar. | 8 | So my father won't scold me. |
| | | |
| No primeiro mergulho, coitado, | | At the first dive, poor boy, |
| Nada pôde arranjar; | 10 | Nothing could he get; |

|   |   |
|---|---|
| A donzela era mimosa | The maiden was delicate, |
| Logo pegou a chorar.                     12 | There and then she burst out crying. |

|   |   |
|---|---|
| No segundo mergulho, coitado, | At the second dive, poor boy, |
| Logo foi se afogar;                      14 | There and then he drowned; |
| A donzela era mimosa | The maiden was delicate, |
| Logo pegou a chorar.                     16 | There and then she burst out crying. |

|   |   |
|---|---|
| —Ôi mar, que levou meu amante, | —Oh, may the sea that took my lover |
| Também pode me levar...            18 | Take me as well... |
| A donzela era mimosa | The maiden was delicate |
| Logo lançou-se ao mar.             20 | She jumped, there and then, into the |
| (Lima 1977: no. 43.7) | sea. |

The first feature to highlight is a well-known indicator of the process of traditionalization: the decrease in the number of narrative segments. As an example, one can see that the first two quatrains, both in Monteiro and in Text 2 (two exclusively narrative quatrains), become only one quatrain in Text 6. The second aspect is the tragic ending of Text 6: the death of both lovers. This brings to its apogee the sentimental aspect we have already noted in Text 2.

Here is another version, also collected by Jackson da Silva Lima in Sergipe, in 1979 (Text 7):

|   |   |
|---|---|
| A filha do Rei da França, | The king of France's daughter, |
| Foi tomar banho no mar,              2 | Went bathing in the sea. |
| A jóia caiu do dedo, | The jewel fell from her finger, |
| Ela se pôs a chorar.                    4 | She started crying. |

|   |   |
|---|---|
| Ia passando um cavaleiro, | A rider was passing by, |
| Deu com a mão:—Venha cá,       6 | She waved:—Come over here, |
| Venha apanhar minha jóia, | Come and fetch my jewel |
| Que está no fundo do mar.           8 | That lies in the deep sea. |

|   |   |
|---|---|
| —Se eu apanhar sua jóia | —If I fetch your jewel, |
| O que é que você me dá?            10 | What will you give me? |
| —Dou um beijo e um abraço, | —I'll give you a kiss and a hug, |
| Vamos pra o fundo do mar.         12 | We'll sink in the deep sea. |
| (Lima 1991: no. 16.2) | |

I would like to underline three elements in this version which show the poem's growing process of traditionalization: first, the adaptation of the text to the experience and world vision of the singer. In fact, the king's daughter no longer wishes to learn a craft, certainly not that of washerwoman. On the contrary, she appears at the beach, simply having fun bathing. This transformation is also present in more than half the versions of the corpus, showing clearly that the singers consider having fun at the beach a far more realistic occupation for a wealthy girl.

Second, the text in this version is abbreviated to a mere twelve lines, in contrast to the thirty-two in Monteiro's text. This reduction is managed by cutting off the final scene, among other processes, a shortening that is probably not the result of the singer's poor memory but instead the result of her wish to transform the text.[15]

The third observation concerns precisely that wish: Unlike the other versions of the ballad, this one is no longer a tragedy (ending with the young man's death), nor a double tragedy (ending with the man's death and the girl's suicide, as in Text 6). On the contrary, the unhappy love story becomes, in Text 7, a story with a happy ending. And, through the splendid last line ("We'll sink in the deep sea"), the man's mortal dive becomes a metaphorical one, not in the dangerous waves of the sea but in those of love, where *both* lovers (not only the man) will be happily lost in love.

As we have seen, the versions of "The King of Spain's Daughter" that exist in Luso-Brazilian oral tradition stem, without doubt, from Monteiro. The discovery of the proven origin of any given ballad has a relevance that transcends the scope of that one ballad. In fact, for "assessing the theories of ballad genesis and evolution," write Andersen and Pettitt, "we need...the original text of a song...as a fixed point of reference for analysis of the later versions which must all ultimately derive from it." Nevertheless, "these conditions are not fulfilled for any ballad in Child's collection, and outside it they are also extremely rare." Hence, the enormous interest, for the Anglo-Scottish tradition, presented by the "journalistic broadside ballads"— ballads published immediately after the crimes, etc., that they narrate and whose printed text is therefore without a doubt the origin of the oral versions of that ballad (Andersen and Pettitt 1985: 139).

At the time when Andersen and Pettit wrote this, debate on the nature of oral transmission of ballads was raging: Was it a memorial or an improvisational process? So, for Andersen and Pettitt, the main interest of the "journalistic broadside ballads" was precisely offering "reliable empirical evidence" (138) which could resolve that debate. In fact, they discovered the written origin of one of those ballads and, by analyzing the set of oral versions together with their original, inferred, based on firm premises, that the song "has been preserved in oral tradition by a process of memorisation rather than improvisation" (153).

Leaving aside the memory versus improvisation debate, the importance of discovering the original text of a ballad remains. Only this allows for the truly rigorous analysis of the process of textual variation. Only then is it possible to determine with absolute certainty what the oral process subtracted from and added to the original text; only then can one safely determine what makes up traditional ballad style.

The discovery that Monteiro is the source of all the oral versions of "The King of Spain's Daughter" is therefore of undeniable interest, all the more since such certainty is almost as rare in the pan-Iberian tradition as in the Anglo-Scottish one.[16] Besides, the fact that the entrance of this ballad into oral tradition cannot be prior to the second half of the nineteenth century shows that a text recently introduced can evolve according to the rules of oral narrative poetry and acquire the same traits as texts that have circulated in the tradition for centuries.

On the other hand, the meandering journey of "The King of Spain's Daughter" allows us to observe that textual transmission across political and linguistic borders can be far more complex than we sometimes assume. In fact, "The King of Spain's Daughter" is clearly the Luso-Brazilian form of the pan-European ballad "The Diver," closest, in particular, to the French form. Contrary to what one might imagine, however, "The King of Spain's Daughter" has not entered into Portugal orally from France but in written form through two successive translations of an oral text (French > German > Portuguese).

Uhland, who studied and loved oral poetry, would no doubt be happy if he knew that a ballad he liked so much became (thanks to him) traditional in Brazil, where it thrives today, nearly two hundred years after he first wrote "Die Königstochter."

*Notes*

My grateful thanks to Isabel Cardigos, who translated this paper. I am also very grateful to the Fundação Calouste Gulbenkian, the Instituto Camões, and the F. C. T. (Programa Lusitânia) for their support for my participation in the 29th International Ballad Conference.

1.  Samuel G. Armistead and Joseph H. Silverman (1978) were the first authors to study "The King of Spain's Daughter." Although they were unaware of both Monteiro's translation and Uhland's poem, and the specific version of the ballad "La Fille du roi d'Espagne" which is the origin of everything, they accurately pointed out the connection between Brazilian versions and an indeterminate written version of the French ballad.

2. On "The Diver," see Ullrich 1886. For an extensive bibliography of this ballad's versions in French, Breton, Italian, Croatian, Greek, and Lithuanian traditions, see Armistead and Silverman 1982: 236 notes 3–7, 231 note 6. A thorough bibliography of the French and Breton versions can now be found in Coirault 1996: 1723.

3. Uhland later published an important collection of old German ballads (Uhland 1844–45). At some point he also planned to organize a collection of translated French (and maybe also Spanish) songs (1911: 200, 203; 1898: 27).

4. The following note appears in Uhland's diary of 9 July 1810: "Diner mit Chamisso bei Lambert u. übriger Abend mit ihm. Die Romanze: La fille du Roy d'Espagne" [Dinner with Chamisso at Lambert's and the rest of the evening with him. The romance: 'La fille du Roy d'Espagne'] (1898: 18).

5. "Brindillé" in Chamisso's text. However, according to George Doncieux, "'brindillé' [est un] mot inexistant écrit a tort par Chamisso" (1904: 317), and it should be "brandillé." In other versions of this ballad, Doncieux notes, one can find the variants "fringué" or "voltigé," which "expriment aussi un mouvement de l'objet" and verify his proposed correction to Chamisso's transcription. According to Imbs, "brandiller" means, in fact, "'s' animer ou être animé d'un mouvement alternatif, osciller, se balancer," which makes perfect sense in this context (1975: 897).

6. In his diary entry of 25 September 1810, Uhland wrote, "Nachts Uebersetzung der altfranzösichen Romanze der spanischen Königstochter" [In the evening, translation of the old French romance of the daughter of the Spanish king] (1898: 22).

7. *Poetischer Almanach für das Jahre 1812.* I was unable to consult this book and learned that it contained some of Uhland's poems, including "Die Königstochter," through Scheffler and Bergold 1987: 79.

8. I could in fact ascertain that "Die Königstochter" does not appear in the first edition of *Gedichte* (1815). Although I was unable to consult the second edition, the list of poems that it contains (including "Die Königstochter") is available in Scheffler and Bergold 1987: 84.

9. This hypothesis for explaining the entry of "The King of Spain's Daughter" into the oral tradition was suggested by Jackson da Silva Lima in a personal letter of 26 October 1998, which I gratefully acknowledge.

10. The versions are as follows: a version from Bahia transcribed as Text 2, originally published with a musical transcription, with a sung interpretation on the CD *Brincadeiras de Roda, Estórias e Canções de Ninar* (Ramalho, Maria and Nóbrega 1983: track 9); and six versions from Sergipe, from field recordings kindly made available to me by Jackson da Silva Lima. Texts here transcribed as nos. 2, 6, and 7 were presented at the 1999 International Ballad Conference, Aberdeen, in their song form, but, for reasons beyond my control, I cannot provide musical transcriptions in this article.

11. To form a really well-grounded opinion on the subject, it would have been necessary to know the music of the eight other versions in the Brazilian corpus of "The King of Spain's Daughter," an impossibility since none of them was published with a musical transcription.

12. In Vasconcellos 1960, this version is wrongly classified and placed among the texts of the ballad "Bem Cantava a Lavadeira." It was because this version was correctly identified in Fontes 1997 that I became aware of its existence. This is the only known version of "The King of Spain's Daughter" collected in Portugal.

13. With regard to the rules behind the traditionalization of pan-Iberian ballads (probably also applicable to ballads in other languages), see Menéndez Pidal 1968: 59–80.

14. There are fifteen Brazilian versions of "The King of Spain's Daughter" known to me: two from Bahia (Pedreira 1978; Alcoforado and Albán 1996), nine from Sergipe (six in Lima 1977, two in Lima 1991, and one in Barreto 2002); one from Alagoas, though the singer was dwelling in Sergipe (Lima 1991); and three from Espírito Santo (Neves 1983).

15. That is the conclusion I have drawn, both from listening to the taped text (at the end of which the singer shows no hesitation whatsoever) and because Jackson da Silva Lima did not add any omission marks at the end of the text when he published this version, as he was careful to do in several other versions. Examples (without even leaving the corpus of "The King of Spain's Daughter") can be found in Lima 1977: 43.1, 43.4.

16. In fact, there are only three old ballads in the pan-Iberian tradition whose first text is known: "Singing Rides the Knight," "The Death of Prince Afonso of Portugal," and "Flérida." Even with ballads of recent origin (nineteenth and twentieth century), such knowledge is very rare.

## References

Alcoforado, Doralice Fernandes Xavier, and Maria del Rosário Suárez Albán. 1996. *Romanceiro Ibérico na Bahia*. Salvador: Livraria Universitária.

Andersen, Flemming G., and Thomas Pettitt. 1985. "'The Murder of Maria Marten': The Birth of a Ballad?" *Narrative Folksong: New Directions. Essays in Appreciation of W. Edson Richmond*, edited by Carol L. Edwards and Kathleen E. B. Manley, 134–78. Boulder, Col.: Westview Press.

Armistead, Samuel G., and Joseph H. Silverman. 1978. *Uma Canção Popular Francesa na Tradição Brasileira: A Filha do Rei da Espanha*. Offprint of *Ciência e Trópico* 6, no. 2 (July/December): 322–36.

———. 1982. *En torno al romancero sefardí (hispanismo y balcanismo de la tradición judeo-española)*. Madrid: Seminario Menéndez Pidal.

Barreto, Luiz Antonio. 2002. "Romances Velhos—X." *Gazeta de Sergipe* 19/20 (May): 2.

Chamisso, Adelbert von. 1839. *Werke*, 5: *Leben (1⁵ und 2⁸)—Briefe*. Edited by Julius Eduard Hitzig. Leipzig: Weidmann'sche Buchhandlung.

Coirault, Patrice. 1996. *Répertoire des chansons françaises de tradition orale*. Edited by Georges Delarue et al. Vol.1. Paris: Bibliothèque nationale de France.

Doncieux, George. 1904. *Romancéro populaire de la France. Choix de chansons populaires françaises, textes critiques,...* Avec un avant-propos et un index musical par Julien Tiersot. Paris: Librairie Emile Bouillon, Editeur.

Fontes, Manuel da Costa. 1997. *Portuguese and Brazilian Balladry: A Thematic and Bibliographic Index*. Vol. 1. Madison, Wis.: The Hispanic Seminary of Medieval Studies.

Imbs, Paul, ed. 1975. *Trésor de la langue française*. Vol. 4. Paris: C. N. R. S..

Lima, Jackson da Silva. 1977. *O Folclore em Sergipe*. Vol. 1, *Romanceiro*. Rio de Janeiro: Livraria Editora Cátedra.

———. 1991. "Achegas ao Romanceiro Tradicional em Sergipe." In *Estudos de Folclore em Homenagem a Manuel Diegues Júnior*, edited by Bráulio do Nascimento, 119–47. Rio de Janeiro and Maceió: Comissão Nacional de Folclore and Instituto Arnon de Mello.

Menéndez Pidal, R. 1968. *Romancero hispánico*. 2d ed. Vol. 1. Madrid: Espasa-Calpe.

Monteiro, José Gomes. 1848. *Eccos da Lyra Teutonica ou Traducção de Algumas Poesias dos Poetas mais Populares d'Allemanha*. Porto: Typographia de S. J. Pereira.

Neves, Guilherme Santos. 1983. *Romanceiro Capixaba*. [Vitória]: Fundação Nacional de Arte and Fundação Ceciliano Abel de Almeida.

Pedreira, Ester. 1978. *Folclore Musicado da Bahia*. Salvador: Fundação Cultural do Estado da Bahia.

*Poetischer Almanach für das Jahre 1812*. [1812]. Edited by Justinus Kerner. Heidelberg: Gottlieb Braun.

Scheffler, Walter, and Albrecht Bergold. 1987. *Ludwig Uhland (1787–1862). Dichter, Germanist, Politiker*. Mit einer Bibliographie von Monika Waldmüller. Marbach am Neckar: Deutsche Schillergesellschaft.

Uhland, Ludwig. 1844–45. *Alte hoch- und niederdeutsche Volkslieder.* Mit Abhandlung und Anmerkungen. 2 vols. Stuttgart and Tübingen: J. G. Cotta'schen Buchhandlung.

———. 1898. *Tagbuch (1810–1820).* Edited by J. Hartmann. Stuttgart: Verlag der J. G. Cotta'sche Buchhandlung.

———. 1908. *Gedichte* in *Sämtliche Werke.* Edited by Rudolf Krautz. Vol. 1. Berlin and Leipzig: Verlag von Th. Knaur Nachf.

———. 1911. *Briefwechsel.* Vol. 1, *1795–1815,* edited by Julius Hartmann. Stuttgart und Berlin: J. G. Cotta'sche Buchhandlung Nachfolger.

Ullrich, Hermann. 1886. "Die Tauchersage in ihrer litterarischen und volksthümlichen Entwickelung." *Archiv für Litteraturgeschichte* 14: 69–102.

Vasconcellos, J. Leite de. 1960. *Romanceiro Português.* Vol. 2. Coimbra: Por Ordem da Universidade.

## Recordings

Ramalho, Elba, Solange Maria and Antonio Nóbrega. 1983. *Brincadeiras de Roda, Estórias e Canções de Ninar.* São Paulo: Estúdio Eldorado.

Fig. 1. Bell Duncan. Photo courtesy of the James Madison Carpenter Collection, Archive of Folk Culture, American Folklife Center, Library of Congress (AFC 1972/001, PH097).

# "The White Fisher":

# An Illegitimate Child Ballad from Aberdeenshire

## Julia C. Bishop

The James Madison Carpenter Collection was made principally in England and Scotland during the period 1929–35. This vast unpublished field collection contains a large number of ballads and other songs from the North East of Scotland, including some rare texts and tunes. Carpenter's most prolific singer, Bell Duncan of Lambhill, in the parish of Forgue, Aberdeenshire, provided him with some sixty-five Child ballads alone, including a number of these rare songs. My encounter with her version of one such ballad, "The White Fisher" (Child 264), prompted the following examination of this little-known and seldom-studied song.[1]

"The White Fisher" has only ever been collected in east Aberdeenshire, Scotland. Francis James Child found no international analogues of the ballad, and his commentary is based on a single text. To date, only five versions are extant, four lengthy ones (one with tune) and one markedly shorter, but not necessarily incomplete, version without a documented tune. In addition, there are two stanzas, with tune, clearly deriving from "The White Fisher" but contained within a version of "Fair Ellen" (Child 63, "Child Waters") and another single stanza with tune which has recently come to light. All were documented during a period of just over a hundred years, from the time of Peter Buchan's collecting in 1816–27 to the early 1930s, when Carpenter collected the ballad (see Appendix A). These bare facts alone raise intriguing questions as to whether the ballad was more widely known within Aberdeenshire and/or beyond but for some reason was not encountered by field collectors. If not, how do we account for its limited geographical distribution and relatively short life span in oral tradition?

The intrigue of the ballad increases still further when we consider its narrative content. The basic plot, as presented in the four long versions, runs as follows: After only a month of marriage, the husband of a couple notices that his wife is pregnant and asks her who the baby's father is. She names the father (whose identity varies and will be discussed in more detail later) and implies that this man raped her.[2] Sometime later she bears a baby boy. Her husband returns to her after an absence, either at, or just after, the birth. She instructs him to drown the child in the sea, but instead he takes it to his mother and persuades her to take care of it. Returning to his wife, he finds her lamenting for the boy:

> My bonny young son is a white fisher,
> An' he's ower sune to the sea;
> And lang, lang will I think for fish
> Or he bring ony tae me. (Mrs. Annie Robb)

The husband then reveals that the child is in good hands and will be well treated. Around this basic framework of an illegitimate birth and the resolution of the difficulties which it causes, the different versions weave further refinements and subtle emphases, some of which will be explored here.

Gordon Gerould found the ballad "moving," particularly because he regarded it as quite realistic (1932: 47). The small body of critical commentary is, however, divided about the coherence and importance of its narrative and its authenticity as a traditional ballad. Most notably, Child misconstrued the plot and wrote dismissively of its narrative and stylistic detail. In this sense, then, we can view "The White Fisher" as an "illegitimate Child ballad," that is, both a Child ballad about illegitimacy and a ballad which Child only grudgingly thought had legitimate claim to be included in his compendium of genuine popular ballads. Subsequent commentators have helped validate the ballad's coherence and traditional authenticity, and some have implicitly or explicitly raised questions about its moral outlook, particularly with respect to gender roles and sexual politics.

This essay pieces together what is known of the song's history by identifying and assembling the extant verbal texts and melodies of "The White Fisher" and presenting them alongside information regarding the people who sang the song and the circumstances of its documentation. I will also make a preliminary comparison of the song's verbal and musical texts to highlight the most salient aspects of their continuity and change and review collectors' and scholars' commentaries. Given that "The White Fisher" concerns rape, illegitimacy, infanticide, and adoption, and the effect of these on marital and parental relations, the critics have often addressed the ballad's sexual politics. As we will see, closer scrutiny of these remarks often reveals implicit biases and assumptions within the secondary context of ballad scholarship itself.

*1. Verbal Texts of "The White Fisher"*
The verbal texts of the song are discussed here in the chronological order of their collection. It is worth noting beforehand that the four principal versions are

represented by remarkably full texts, given the length and complexity of the narrative, consisting of between eighteen and twenty-five stanzas (see Appendix B). Each contains four scenes:

1. The revelation of the pregnancy as a consequence of rape;
2. The labor, birth, and wife's instructions to drown the baby;
3. The negotiations between the husband and his mother concerning the care of the baby;
4. The wife's remorse over the presumed death of the baby and the husband's revelation that he has resolved the situation by getting his mother to look after the child.

Some scenes are more extended in some versions than in others, and some details come and go or alter, but the basic nature and sequence of events is the same in all the long versions.

The short (four-and-a-half-stanza) version and apparent fragments of one and two stanzas are also consistent in that they start with or are constituted by the stanza(s) containing the "white-fisher" imagery (see Appendix C). As we will see, this seems to be a particularly arresting and memorable part of the song, suggesting a regional provenance for at least these stanzas and possibly the whole ballad.

### a) The Peter Buchan version

The only version of "The White Fisher" known to Child was the one published in Peter Buchan's *Ancient Ballads and Songs of the North of Scotland* (1828) and contained in the 1816–27 manuscript on which the book was based. In this text, the wife identifies the father of the child as "a popish priest" who "vowed he would forgive my sins, / If I would him obey." When the husband takes the child to his mother, however, she initially regards it as confirmation that "that lady was an ill woman, / That ye chose for your bride." Undeterred, the husband persuades his mother to look after the child by claiming that it is really his, sent to him by "a king's daughter" over the sea. Returning home, he tries to comfort his lamenting wife with a drink, but she refuses on the grounds that, if he is capable of drowning the child, he is capable of poisoning her. After the child's true fate has been revealed, he urges her to be "a good woman," and she gratefully acknowledges that he, not she, has saved the situation.

That the woman has been raped is communicated more overtly in this version than any of the other long versions. The scenario in stanza 4 is explicitly portrayed as an act of blackmail and abuse of power by a trusted, and officially celibate, religious authority figure.

Child, however, clearly struggled to make sense of fundamental elements of the ballad's plot. He interprets the husband's invented "king's daughter" as the same person as his real wife, inferring that it is the wife's royal status which persuades the mother to change her low opinion. Child further misinterprets the final stanza as the wife declaring "if he had not been the father she should not have been the mother." He goes on, "To make this story hang together at all, we must suppose that the third and fourth stanzas are tropical, and that Willie was the priest; or else that they are sarcastic, and are uttered in bitter resentment of Willie's suspicion, or affected suspicion" (Child 1882–98, 5: 435). In other words, he thinks the stanza where she names the priest as the father and describes how he blackmailed her is somehow a figurative expression of her and her husband's sexual relationship, or else the wife resents the husband's suspicion to the extent that she pretends she has been raped by a priest. Thus, Child's commentary denies the rape of the woman altogether or sees it as her own invention.

Peter Buchan himself was under no such misapprehensions about the ballad's story. His notes to the song, which Child appears to have overlooked or ignored, indicate that he has no doubt about the identity of the rapist/child's father or the gallantry displayed by the husband. Indeed, he relishes the opportunity to deride the hypocrisy of the Roman Catholic clergy:

> Those who have read the lives of the Popes; the history of the inquisition, and of the inferior orders of the clergy of the Romish church, will be nowise surprised that the ghostly confessor should, instead of administering spiritual consolation to the lady in her husband's absence, rob her of her chastity; and betray, like an unprincipled villain, the trust reposed in him. The wicked lives and ungrateful conduct of most of the friars, monks, and priests, need no comment. (P. Buchan [1828] 1875, 1: 306)

This anti-Catholic attitude is a unique feature of Buchan's text. The internal evidence and comparison with the other versions show fairly conclusively that this is a departure from the norm. Peter Buchan's version appears at one time to have followed the pattern in other versions of incremental repetition between stanzas 2 and 3, but stanza 3 has subsequently been modified from "man of might"/"baron of high degree" to "popish priest," rather than the expected "little wee page." This and the following stanza, also unique to the Buchan version, which elaborates on this twist in the plot, inject an overt element of sectarianism into the song and are possibly the work of Buchan himself. They certainly provide a platform for his uncompromising views. Despite roundly condemning the priest, however, Buchan immediately extenuates his crime by commenting that "it would appear from the indulgence given to the lady by her husband, that he was conscious of the priest's treachery, and of her own innocence, *in as far as she was betrayed*" (P. Buchan [1828] 1875, 1: 306; emphasis added). The Catholic priest was treacherous, but Buchan is not above the suspicion that a woman may "lead a man on" to commit rape even though there is nothing in the ballad to justify this comment.

Child's aversion to the ballads collected by Buchan and his doubts about their trustworthiness are well known[3] and, in the case of "The White Fisher," these lead Child to censure the ballad still further. He writes, "We need not trouble ourselves much to make these counterfeits reasonable. Those who utter them rely confidently upon our taking folly and jargon as the marks of genuineness. The white fisher is a trumpery fancy; [stanzas] 2, 7, 8, 12 are frippery commonplaces" (Child 1882–98, 5: 435). It is clear from this thinly disguised attack on Buchan that Child believed he had inserted a number of well-known ballad formulas into "The White Fisher" and invented the stanzas containing the white-fisher imagery entirely. One wonders why Child included it in *The English and Scottish Popular Ballads* at all, given this degree of opprobrium, and still more why Child chose to adopt the ballad's name which contained the offending "trumpery fancy."

### b) The Bell Robertson and Mrs. Annie Robb versions

As with a number of ballads Child found only in Buchan's books and manuscripts, he might well have modified his view of "The White Fisher" if the two versions collected by Gavin Greig had been available to him. Alexander Keith, who first published these versions, states,

> It is not often that Child falls into error, but here he has blundered badly if not unaccountably. Mistakes, of the kind which here makes the child Willie's son, are frequent in traditional balladry, but unless they are supported by the testimony of two or three independent versions, they cannot be taken seriously. In this case Child had only a solitary, unsupported text to go upon. Further, his reading of the two lines quoted above [i.e., the final two lines] is patently untenable. The lines refer to the fate, not the paternity of the

child…. Our two versions greatly modify Child's indictment of the
ballad and of Buchan. (Keith 1925: 208)

Bell Robertson of New Pitsligo, Aberdeenshire, gave Greig the ballad in 1908,
but it is her second, more-complete version from 1912 which Keith printed in *Last
Leaves* (1925).[4] As with many of her songs, "The White Fisher" was "one of
mother's songs. I think it had been her mother's."[5] Bell Robertson was born in
1841, so this would date her version to the 1850s at the earliest, and her mother,
Jean Gall, was born in 1804, pushing her version back to around 1815 at the
earliest. Her version consists of twenty-three stanzas and, as Keith points out,
"follows Buchan's [version] at no great distance" (Keith 1925: 208).

Greig's other version of "The White Fisher" came from Mrs. Annie Robb
(née Davidson), born in Monquhitter (Porter and Campbell 2002: 577). This version is also printed by Keith in *Last Leaves*, along with the note that she "lived
'at the foot of Mormond Hill,' and d[ied] aged 88 about 1911" (1925: 208). This
makes the earliest possible date for her version around 1833. The text from Mrs.
Robb is eighteen stanzas long and was in fact given to Greig in two parts. Keith
states that Greig received stanzas 1–12 in 1908 and stanzas 13–18 in 1910, noting
that "Mrs. Robb took them to be portions of separate ballads, but Mr. Greig
recognized the connection" (Keith 1925: 208). Keith appears to be partially in
error here, however, since Greig's unpublished sixty-four volumes of folk-song
words [Gw] contain "the partial text at Gw 10.79–81 [which] ends with stanza 11
and the partial text at Gw 55.109–10 [which] begins with stanza 12."[6] Either way,
from a narrative angle, these seem odd places for the song to be divided, and one
wonders if Mrs. Robb regarded either part as a complete song in itself. Keith's
phrase "portions of separate ballads" rather than "separate ballads" suggests
that she saw each of them as incomplete. It is noteworthy, however, that "there is
no indication that Greig had any direct contact with her," and the several texts he
received came through her son, Alexander Robb (Lyle 2002: 471).

Greig immediately grasped the significance of the texts from Bell Robertson
and Mrs. Robb, and he defended the ballad and Peter Buchan against Child's
criticism. In a letter to William Walker (1912), he expresses surprise at Walker's
"harking back to Child's muddle" regarding the plot, adding, "to me the ballad is
perfectly intelligible." He goes on: "If spared to reach the 'White Fisher' I hope
to treat the matter frankly & fully in the interests of simple truth & fair play to the
ballad and to Peter Buchan, when I should be sorry to find a good man & friend
associated with Child in his hopeless position" (Greig to Walker, 5 August 1912).

Greig, alas, did not live to publish his observations on "The White Fisher," but Keith's remarks in *Last Leaves* catch something of Greig's uncompromising tone. Far from disparaging the ballad as Child had done, Keith comments that "our two versions of this ballad, particularly the first [that of Mrs. Robb], are the most interesting in our collection" (Keith 1925: 207). With the benefit of Greig's versions for comparison, he takes Child to task for misconstruing the story and condemning the ballad and Buchan. In particular, he counters Child's attack on the ballad's language and imagery:

> Child called the "white fisher" idea "a trumpery fancy." White-fishers, or line-fishers, are those engaged in inshore fishing for the home market, most of them old men and boys; and white fish are the fish caught by these inshore fishermen. "The White Fisher" is a silly title for the ballad, for the phrase in A [Mrs. Robb's version] 15 and 16 is merely a passing figure of speech. In B [Bell Robertson's version] 12 the expression, "till fite fish he fess hame" (repeated in B 20), is the equivalent to "till a' the seas gang dry," or to "till doomsday." The commonplaces in the ballad which Child designates "frippery" cannot be so peremptorily treated. (Keith 1925: 208)

Thus, Keith validates the white-fisher metaphor through regional linguistic usage and occupational practice.

Turning to the detail of the versions collection by Greig, we find that Bell Robertson's, as already mentioned, is close to Buchan's in both its plot details and diction (cf., for example, stanzas 2, 5, Buchan 6/Robertson 7, Buchan 11–16/Robertson 13–18). An important difference between the Bell Robertson and Peter Buchan versions, however, is the identity of the rapist, who in the former is the father's foot page. Here again, the rape is portrayed unequivocally, with overt emphasis on it as an act of manipulation, force, and revenge, motivated by an alleged social injustice:

> He saired my father seven years,
> And he never paid him his fee;
> But he got me in my bower my lane,
> And he made me pay the fee. (stanza 4)

This ultimately lays the blame for the situation at the father's door and also precludes any inference that the woman herself invited or colluded in the rape.

Another stanza unique to Bell Robertson's version is the concluding one, where the wife explicitly acknowledges the husband's chivalrous actions:

> My blessin's on yer cheek, your cheek,
> My blessin's on yer chin,
> My blessin's on yer red rose lips,
> For ye're aye a woman's frien. (stanza 23)

This no doubt helped prompt Keith's observation that Bell Robertson's text "emphasises all through the generous nature of the young man and the trust reposed in him by his lady" (Keith 1925: 208). Greig and Keith find this emphasis on the husband's gallantry even more pronounced in Mrs. Robb's version.

Mrs. Robb's version is distinct in a number of ways from Bell Robertson's and Peter Buchan's. Here the rape is conveyed in the formula, "he put his hand on to my shoulder/And he made me doon to fa'." This is a more-subtle suggestion of rape but still implies that she was forced to the ground. This time the rape takes place "between the kitchie and the ha'," not in the woman's bower. As in the Bell Robertson version, though, the rapist is a servant of her father, this time his "butler-boy." No reason is given for the rape, but the woman openly condemns the boy by using formulaic phrases like "And an ill death may he dee" (stanza 3) and "Oh woe be to my father's butler boy" (stanza 4). Indeed, the child's likeness to his father is cited here as the justification for drowning the boy:

> Oh ye'll tak' up that bonnie boy,
> And ye'll throw him in the sea,
> For like is he to his fause father,
> And he'll get nae mair o' me.

> Oh ye'll tak' up that bonnie boy,
> And cast him in the main,
> For like is he to his fause father
> And sair was he to blame. (stanzas 8 and 9)

There is a possible hint that the woman favored the butler boy prior to the incident, but it is ambiguous because the attribute "fause" could apply to him as a servant rather than a lover. Meanwhile, the text makes strenuous efforts to blame the rape, or possible rough seduction, on the man alone.

A particularly distinctive element of Mrs. Annie Robb's version is the absence of any explicit hostility to the wife from the mother. The husband simply persuades his mother to look after the boy and give him the best nursing and education possible. The invented "king's daughter" is also absent. However, the implication that the boy is *his* illegitimate child is retained in the injunction, unique to the versions of Mrs. Robb and Bell Duncan (below), which he gives his mother:

> An' ye'll tak' care, my mother," he said,
> "When we come here to dine,
> That ye'll kiss my son, and bless my son,
> But say nae that he's mine. (stanza 13)

Mrs. Robb moves on swiftly from this point, including the lament of the wife but omitting her suspicion that her husband could poison her, and concluding not with her acknowledgment of his saving the situation, nor her blessing him, but with his issuing the parallel admonition to his wife regarding his mother:

> An' ye'll tak' care, my lady," he said,
> "When we go there to dine,
> That ye'll kiss your son, and ye'll bless your son,
> But say not that he's thine (stanza 18).

Keith highlights these distinctive stanzas of Mrs. Robb's version, commenting that this is how the husband gets over the difficulty of what Keith terms "his lady's lapse" (Keith 1925: 208). This suggests either that Keith interprets the initial situation as rough seduction, rather than rape, or regards the woman as somehow to blame for being raped and the resulting situation.

Greig does not comment explicitly on the morality of the woman's actions. Rather, in the light of Mrs. Robb's admonitory stanzas, he focuses on the gallantry of the husband's behavior. He writes to William Walker that "Willie [is] a rare hero; nay,...the greatest hero that I have encountered in all balladry" (Greig to Walker, 5 August 1912). In a later letter, he continues to enthuse to Walker about these stanzas: "Just think of it; and it really needs a bit [of] thinking to take it all in. I have grappled with it, and am free to confess that, viewed from an ethical standpoint, the whole thing impresses one more than does any other situation which I have encountered in ballad study."[7] Thus, Greig rightly broadens the critical focus to consider the actions of the husband as well as the wife—

although he does not mention the other key character, the mother—and he underlines the uniqueness of the husband's actions from the perspective of ballad
narrative more generally. Whether or not the husband is "the greatest hero…in
all balladry," the moral outlook(s) implied by "The White Fisher" is certainly
tantalizing and worthy of further study.

*c) The Miss Annie Robb and Miss Elizabeth Robb stanzas*
Miss Annie Robb and Miss Elizabeth Robb were both daughters of Mrs. Annie
Robb (Lyle 2002: 471; Porter and Campbell 2002: 578; Campbell 2002). Eliza-
beth Robb was older, born in 1856, and Miss Annie Robb was born about 1872.
As adults they both lived in Strichen (Lyle 2002: 471; Porter and Campbell
2002: 578; Campbell 2002). They had a brother named Alexander Robb (1863–
1940) of New Deer, who was a prolific contributor to both *The Greig-Duncan
Folk-Song Collection* and the Carpenter Collection but appears not to have sung
"The White Fisher" to either Greig or Carpenter (Porter and Campbell 2002).

As can be seen from Appendix C, the stanzas contributed by both Elizabeth
and young Annie Robb contain the white-fisher imagery, and are very close to
their mother's parallel stanzas. Both are of particular interest because they were
documented with accompanying tunes and therefore provide evidence of the
ballad's melodic tradition, which will be discussed in more detail. It is difficult
at this historical distance and on the evidence available to judge how active
"The White Fisher" was in the repertoires of Elizabeth and Annie Robb. It seems
safe to assume that they both knew what they had of the ballad from their mother,
but, as noted already, she herself "knew" it as two distinct songs. Whatever the
case, Greig documented a single stanza of text from Miss Annie Robb.

Intriguingly, it appears that Elizabeth Robb may have known and sung a
fuller version of the ballad since "although no record was made of the tune [by
Greig in relation to Mrs. Robb's version], Arthur Barron [Greig's son-in-law]
mentions in a letter to William Walker of 31 August 1920…that Mrs. Robb's
daughter, Lizzie Robb, had *sung* this ballad to him the previous evening" *(Greig-
Duncan Collection* 1983, 2: 521). This tune was not documented at the time,
however, and the only available evidence of Elizabeth Robb's knowledge of the
ballad comes from the Carpenter Collection, where two stanzas of "The White
Fisher" are embedded in a version of "Fair Ellen" (Child 63, "Child Waters") she
sang to Carpenter. The stanzas occur near the end of the ballad at the point
where Lord William has gone to the stable to demand that Fair Ellen, whom he
has previously dismissed but who has just given birth to his son, open the door
to him. She replies that she cannot do so, has her son in her arms, and will be

dead before day. Then she laments, in the white-fisher stanzas, that her child has gone away and she will never see him again. This is a unique addition to this ballad as far as the textual record is concerned. The ballad concludes with Lord William breaking down the door and embracing Fair Ellen and the child, as in other versions.

The narrative implication of the stanzas is not entirely clear, and one wonders if this was an interpolation inherited by Elizabeth Robb or one she herself made, either as a consistent part of her performance or a onetime occurrence. The fact that "Fair Ellen" and "The White Fisher" were sung to basically the same melody in her family may well have facilitated the transference of these stanzas and will be discussed further. In narrative terms, the white-fisher stanzas occur in both songs immediately after the female protagonist has given birth alone, and this parallel may also have acted as a catalyst to introduce these stanzas into "Fair Ellen." That these words crossed over from "The White Fisher" to "Fair Ellen" seems certain because they are unique to Elizabeth Robb's version of "Fair Ellen" and central to "The White Fisher" in all its versions. Interestingly, Elizabeth Robb's source for "Fair Ellen" was her mother, Mrs. Annie Robb, and a further handwritten note by Carpenter states, "From gra[n]dmother. Died while Mrs. Robb was yo[un]g" (Carpenter Collection: 04836).[8] Furthermore, Elizabeth's brother, Alexander, also sang a version of "Fair Ellen," learned from his mother, for both Greig and Carpenter, but his version contains no hint of the white-fisher stanzas even though, as we will see, one of his tunes for the ballad is virtually the same as his sister's.[9]

*d) The Bell Duncan and Mrs. William Duncan versions*
The Carpenter Collection contains texts and tunes of "The White Fisher" from two singers in addition to the stanzas by Elizabeth Robb. One, consisting of four-and-a-half stanzas, was sung by Mrs. William Duncan of "Tories" (Torries?) Castle, Oyne, Aberdeenshire, and was learned from her mother sixty years earlier (ca.1870). In this version, the explicit narrative element is almost entirely absent, and the song has become a lyric, focusing on the woman's lament for a supposedly drowned son, expressed in the metaphor of the white fisher who will never return, plus the revelation of his safety and the injunction not to claim the child as her own.

Carpenter also collected a long version of "The White Fisher" from Bell Duncan. This was around 1930 when she was in her early eighties. The song was "learned from mother," Jane Hutcheon (ca. 1809–1884) of nearby Bogfouton, Aberdeenshire (Bishop: forthcoming). This version consists of twenty-four stanzas. Because of its verbal detail and inclusion of the admonitory stanzas, it has much in common with Mrs. Robb's text. It is longer, however, and has a number of distinctive features.

In particular, a number of stanzas are unique to Bell Duncan's version. In stanza 2, for example, the wife replies directly to the husband in what is, *mutatis mutandis*, a repeat of the first stanza. Stanza 7 is also unique because the husband's departure until the time of the birth is lengthier and includes a promise of his return. More extended, though not unique to Bell Duncan since it also appears in Mrs. Robb's version as a couplet, is the stanza where the wife laments that if she were bearing her husband's son, she would not be alone at the birth. The arrival of her husband immediately after this, specifically "ti ease her moan," is further dramatic proof of his sincerity toward her and the child. It is interesting to compare this with the Peter Buchan version (stanzas 6–7) and Bell Robertson version (stanzas 7–8), where the husband's goodwill, toward at least the child, is suggested by the fact that, when he learns that his wife has gone into labor, he comes home "merrily" and "singing."

Bell Duncan seems in a number of details to lay particular stress on the husband's compassionate attitude toward his wife and the illegitimate child. The text transcription, for example, indicates that stanzas 1–3, 6 and 7, which form part of the husband-wife dialogue regarding the rape and pregnancy, are sung to a melody where the final line is extended with the words "dear love," leading to a repeat of the final line:

> 'Tis a month an' 'tis nae mair,
> My dear, since I married thee,
> An' there is a baby atween thy sides,
> An I'm sure an it's nae tee me, dear love,
> An' I'm sure an' it's nae tee me. (stanza 1)

Indeed, the husband only ever refers to his wife as "my dear," "my dear love," and (in one instance) "my lily flooer," whereas other versions include variations, such as the more-impersonal "my lady" and "my gay lady." Once the child has been born, this tenderness is immediately extended to the boy, who is described as "his bonnie young son" (stanza 10). In the other versions, it is not until the next scene (the dialogue with the mother) that he calls the boy his son. Thus, Bell Duncan's version provides a particularly dramatic foil for the wife's ensuing instructions for her husband to drown the child since it places in even sharper relief her total conviction that, despite an indication to the contrary (he came home when he promised to), he is hostile to the child and therefore to her. Bell Duncan's version also intensifies the imagery of fatherly love toward the child in the third scene; he is not just "rowed...in his sleeve"/"ta'en up"/"rowd in a band" but "clasped...tee his breist."

As in Mrs. Robb's and Bell Robertson's versions, the rapist is a servant of the wife's father, this time the "kitchie boy." The reference to rape is worded similarly to Mrs. Robb's version—"he laid his han' on my shoulder, / An' he caused me bak to fa'"—making it, like Mrs. Robb's, more ambiguous than the other extant texts. Despite this and other marked resemblances to Mrs. Robb's version, however, Bell Duncan's differs from it in including, as in the other long versions, the mother's suspicion of the wife and the wife's worry that her husband could poison her.

*2. Musical Texts of "The White Fisher"*

Written in 1972, in his fourth and final volume of *The Traditional Tunes of the Child Ballads*, Bertrand Bronson's entry for "The White Fisher" noted, "Greig failed to recover a tune for the ballad, and none has yet been printed. James M. Carpenter, however, in the twenties collected one in Scotland which he may in time disclose" (Bronson 1959–72, 4: 71). Since then, it has come to light that Greig did collect a tune for the ballad and there are in fact two distinct tunes in the Carpenter Collection, which is now accessible due to its purchase by the Archive of Folk Culture, American Folklife Center, Library of Congress.

Research by the editors of *The Greig-Duncan Folk-Song Collection* (1981–2002) has led to the recent discovery that

> Greig made a preliminary attempt to note the tune under the title "White Fisher" at Argo 5.6 [a notebook] and noted it fully under the title "Lady Marrit" at Argo 5.10, giving a verse of "The White Fisher" opposite it at Argo 5.11. The tune was copied without words into Gm [Greig's volumes of "Folk-Music"] under the title "Lady Marrit" and has previously been misidentified as a version of Child 74...and was given earlier in this edition [of *The Greig-Duncan Folk-Song Collection*] as 337 "William and Margaret" B.[10]

This refers to the single stanza of text and tune provided by Miss Annie Robb (Fig. 2, overleaf):

Fig. 2. Miss Annie Robb, "William and Margaret"/"Lady Marritt"/"The White Fisher" (*The Greig-Duncan Folk-Song Collection*, 2: no. 337).

Porter and Campbell (2002) have noted the tonal ambiguity of the melody:

> A phrase that seems solidly pentatonic (based on G with a minor third above and flat leading note) concludes its second phrase on the C a fourth above. This gives the impression of both parallelism and circularity in the pentatonic conception, with a first phrase tonal structure FGB♭CD and a second phrase DFGB♭C, where the underlined note is the cadential point. (578)

There is also some uncertainty as to how Miss Annie Robb's text fits the tune as notated if the fourth note in the second complete bar is read as crossed out.

Carpenter recorded and transcribed several renditions of Elizabeth Robb's melody for "Fair Ellen," including one stanza entitled "Fair Ellen/The White Fisher" which specifically includes a stanza of the white-fisher:

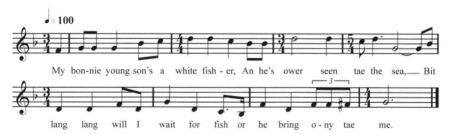

My bon-nie young son's a white fish - er, An he's ower seen tae the sea,— Bit lang lang will I wait for fish or he bring o - ny tae me.

Fig. 3. Miss Elizabeth Robb, "Fair Ellen/The White Fisher" (transposed down one tone). Courtesy of the James Madison Carpenter Collection, Archive of Folk Culture, American Folklife Center, Library of Congress (AFC 1972/001, p. 08208).

The passing note at the end of the second complete bar, not present in Greig's notation from Miss Annie Robb, accommodates all the syllables of the text. Otherwise the first half of Elizabeth Robb's tune is very similar to her sister's, although it has a slightly different metrical feel in places if we can trust Carpenter's and Greig's transcriptions. The two diverge in the second half of the stanza, in the sixth complete bar, where Elizabeth Robb's tune follows an inverted form—GDCB♭—of the first-half pentatonic pattern before returning to the cadential note G via a flat seventh and a sharpened seventh.

There are two further tune transcriptions in the Carpenter Collection, both without words, entitled "The White Fisher" and "Fair Annie (White Fisher)" respectively and ascribed to Miss E. Robb.[11] The latter melody is metrically more regular than the transcription just noted but diverges from it momentarily in pitch in the fifth complete bar.

Fig. 4. Miss Elizabeth Robb, "The White Fisher" (transposed down one tone, * appears as a flat sign in original). Courtesy of the James Madison Carpenter Collection, Archive of Folk Culture, American Folklife Center, Library of Congress (AFC 1972/001, p. 11518).

It can be seen from the melodic stanzas transcribed by Carpenter from Elizabeth Robb for the other parts of "Fair Ellen," however, that these two forms of bar 5 are characteristic of Elizabeth Robb's renditions of this melody (Carpenter Collection: 08207). Furthermore, she also employed this same tune for "Fair Annie," and the transcriptions evidence a similar variation in the fifth bar (for example, Carpenter Collection: 08204).

Carpenter documented two different tunes from Alexander Robb, the brother of Elizabeth and Miss Annie Robb, for "Fair Ellen." One is almost identical to Elizabeth Robb's but without the sharpened seventh in its penultimate bar (Carpenter Collection: 08206). The other begins in a similar manner but takes on a different melodic shape and modal character (Carpenter Collection: 08205).[12]

To summarize the tune evidence from the Robb family, it seems that both Annie and Elizabeth Robb sang "The White Fisher" to much the same tune, although with a slightly different ending. The tune was prevalent in the Robb family for a number of songs with the ending employed by Elizabeth Robb.

Bell Duncan's melody for "The White Fisher" is unrelated to the Robb family's (see Fig. 5, overleaf). It has a wide compass (a minor tenth) and is characterized by mainly stepwise movement except at the ends of the first and final lines, where the same falling fourth figure occurs. As transcribed by Carpenter, the note on

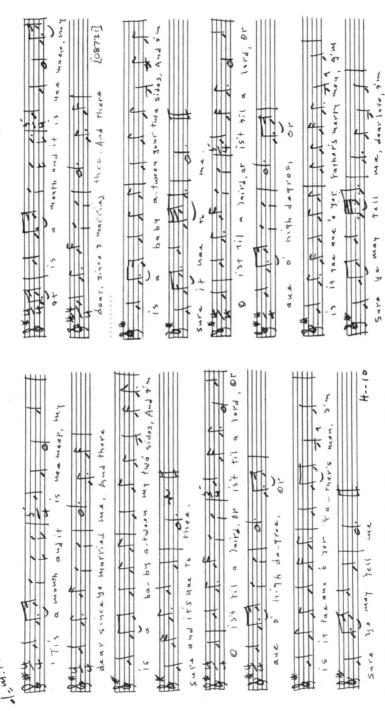

Fig. 5. Miss Bell Duncan, "The White Fisher." Courtesy of the James
Madison Carpenter Collection, Archive of Folk Culture, American
Folklife Center, Library of Congress (AFC 1972/001, p. 08731-32).
(Dotted line indicates original page break.)

which each phrase cadences (B and E respectively) tends to occur on the primary stressed beats/syllables throughout the preceding part of the phrase. As
noted already, the final line of the text is often extended by the addition of the
words "dear love," followed by the repetition of the final line. Bell Duncan easily
accomplished this within the tune by repeating the final three bars, starting from
the second beat (modified to a single D) of the sixth complete bar. It is notable
that in the two renditions transcribed by Carpenter, stanza 3 ("'O is't till a laird, o
is't till a lord'") occurs both with and without the repetition of the final line.
Likewise the verbal text which Carpenter took down from Bell Duncan's dictation
(see Appendix B) contains the repetition of the final line in stanzas 1, 2, 3, 6, and
7, whereas this only occurs in stanza 3 in the verbal text of the music which
Carpenter transcribed from his cylinder recordings.[13] These facts suggest fairly
unequivocally that repeating the last line of a stanza was a flexible practice in Bell
Duncan's renditions of the ballad, although it does seem to have been confined
to stanzas in the first scene.

*Conclusion*

The comparison of the verbal texts of "The White Fisher" has highlighted the
differences between them, but it should be reiterated that the extant "long" texts
are remarkably similar despite the ballad's narrative complexity. All retain the
four basic scenes, although, as is evident from Appendix B, the length of each
scene in number of stanzas varies. Thus, Mrs. Robb's version is evenly propor-
tioned throughout; Bell Duncan's stresses scenes 1 and 4, which center on the
husband-wife dialogues; Peter Buchan's version emphasizes scene 4, where the
problems presented in the ballad are resolved; and Bell Robertson highlights
scene 2, the labor, birth and instructions to kill the child.

In textual details, we have seen that the versions of Peter Buchan and Bell
Robertson are similar, as are those of Mrs. Robb and Bell Duncan. In musical
terms, however, the extant tunes from the Robbs and Bell Duncan are quite
different.

Even with all the known evidence before us, it is not possible to do more than
suggest possible reasons why the ballad had such a limited geographical distribution and life span in tradition. The length of the ballad and its complicated plot
may well have been a factor although this raises the question of why the ballad
was apparently not abbreviated and simplified by one or more singers who encountered it. Perhaps the ballad's moral outlook did not resonate sufficiently
with singers (who, according to the evidence, were all female apart from Peter
Buchan's source, whose sex is unknown) and/or their audiences in the North

East of Scotland or beyond. Certainly, the imagery of the child as a white fisher and the stylized portrayal of "shall never" which grows out of it in the phrase "till fite fish he fess hame" (and its variants) may have had a regional currency which limited its circulation beyond this area (although the phrase "white fish" is more widespread) (*Oxford English Dictionary*; Shields 1983). It also suggests a regional provenance for the ballad. If so, perhaps distinct social conditions in this region during this period prompted and supported the limited distribution of the ballad.

Another question raised by textual analysis is the degree to which Peter Buchan's published text may have influenced the ballad's circulation, the perpetuation of its complex narrative, and its language. In this connection, it is notable that the small amount of tune evidence for the ballad reveals two distinct melodies compatible with, though not necessarily indicative of, print distribution of the text.

Child's principal objections to "The White Fisher" stemmed from the fact that the story, as he read it, did not form a coherent narrative and the ballad had been subject to the textual meddling of Peter Buchan, especially in the "trumpery fancy" of the white-fisher metaphor, and was therefore of doubtful authenticity. However, we have seen that the ballad does form a coherent narrative, even in Peter Buchan's version, although the story is an unorthodox and complex one. The white-fisher stanzas are certainly unique to the ballad, at least as far as the Child corpus is concerned, but are probably indicative of the ballad's origins in, or at least closeness to, the culture of the Scottish North East, rather than Peter Buchan's invention. After countering Child's objections, it seems that "The White Fisher" may qualify as a legitimate member of the Child corpus after all. More importantly from the standpoint of contemporary scholarship, its in many ways unorthodox representations of rape, illegitimate birth, infanticide, adoption, and marriage, when considered in the context of the real social conditions in the North East of Scotland in the nineteenth and early twentieth centuries, make "The White Fisher" a legitimate and suggestive focus for further study.

*Appendix A: Extant versions and fragments of "The White Fisher."*

Buchan, Peter. *Ancient Ballads and Songs of the North of Scotland.* 2 vols. 1828. Reprint, Edinburgh: William Paterson, 1875. Vol. 1, 195–99 (see Appendix B). Words only.

Duncan, Bell. AFC 1972/001, pp. 05919–22 (words), 07755–57 (words, see Appendix B], 08731–32 (music with words, see Fig. 5). The James Madison Carpenter Collection, Archive of Folk Culture, American Folklife Center, Library of Congress, Washington, D.C.

Duncan, Mrs. William. AFC 1972/001, pp. 05923 (words), 07758 (words, see Appendix B). The James Madison Carpenter Collection, Archive of Folk Culture, American Folklife Center, Library of Congress, Washington, D.C. Words only.

Robb, Mrs. Annie. Keith 1925: 208–9. Reprinted in vol. 2 of *The Greig-Duncan Folk-Song Collection*, 42–43 (see in Appendix B). Words only.

Robb, Miss Annie. "William and Margaret"/"Lady Marritt"/"The White Fisher." *The Greig-Duncan Folk-Song Collection*, vol. 2, no. 337. Reprinted in vol. 8 of *The Greig-Duncan Folk-Song Collection*, 348 (see Fig. 2 and the words only in Appendix C). Words and music.

Robb, Miss Elizabeth. "Fair Ellen"/"The White Fisher". AFC 1972/001, pp. 04836–38 (words), 06924–25 (words, reproduced in Appendix B), 08208 (music with words, see Fig. 3), 11518 (music, see Fig. 4). The James Madison Carpenter Collection, Archive of Folk Culture, American Folklife Center, Library of Congress, Washington, D.C. Words and music.

Robb, Miss Elizabeth. "Fair Annie (White Fisher)." AFC 1972/001, p. 11519 (music with words). The James Madison Carpenter Collection, Archive of Folk Culture, American Folklife Center, Library of Congress, Washington, D.C. Words and music.

Robertson, Bell. Keith 1925: 209–10. Reprinted in vol. 2 of *The Greig-Duncan Folk-Song Collection*, 41–42 (see Appendix B). Words only.

*Appendix B: Correlation of Stanzas in the Long Versions of "The White Fisher"*

| Bell Duncan | Mrs. Annie Robb | Peter Buchan | Bell Robertson | Mrs. William Duncan |
|---|---|---|---|---|
| **1.** "'Tis a month an' 'tis nae mair,<br>My dear, since I married thee,<br>An' there is a baby atween thy sides,<br>An' I'm sure an' it's nae tee me, dear love,<br>An' I'm sure an' it's nae tee me." | **1.** It is a month and it is nae mair<br>My love, since I married thee,<br>And thee go with a bairnie love,<br>And ye ken it is nae to me. | **1.** "It is a month, and is nae mair,<br>Love, sin I was at thee,<br>But find a stirring in your side;<br>Who may the father be? | **1.** It's but a month, my gay lady,<br>Now sin I wedded thee,<br>Tell me fa aws the bonnie baby<br>That I see you gang wi'. | |
| **2.** "'Tis a month an' 'tis nae mair,<br>My dear, since you married me,<br>An' there is a baby atween my sides,<br>An' I'm sure an' it's nae tee thee, dear love,<br>An' I'm sure an' it's nae tee thee." | | | | |
| **3.** "O is't till a laird? Or is't till a lord?<br>Or ane o high degree?<br>Or is't tee ane o' your father's merry men?<br>I'm sure ye may tell me, dear love,<br>I'm sure an' ye may tell me." | **2.** Oh is it to a laird, or is't to a lord,<br>Or a man o' high degree?<br>Or is it to any o' your father's men,<br>My bonnie love, ye'll tell me. | **2.** "Is it to a lord of might,<br>Or baron of high degree?<br>Or is it to the little wee page<br>That rode along wi me?" | **2.** Oh, is it to a man o' micht,<br>Or a baron o' high degree?<br>Or is it to your father's foot-page?—<br>My lady, ye dinna lee. | |
| **4.** "It's nae till a laird, it's nae till a lord,<br>Nor ane o' high degree,<br>Bet it's tee my father's kitchie boy;<br>I'm sure I willna lee. | **3.** It is nae to a laird, nor to a lord,<br>Nor a man o' high degree.<br>But it is to my father's butler boy<br>And an ill death may he dee. | **3.** "It is not to a man of might,<br>Nor baron of high degree,<br>But it is to a popish priest;<br>My lord, I winna lie. | **3.** It isna to a man o' micht,<br>Or a baron o' high degree,<br>But it is to my father's foot-page<br>My good lord, I'll tell thee. | |
| **5.** "It wis my father's kitchie boy<br>Atween the kitchie an' the ha';<br>He laid his han' on my shoulder,<br>An' he caused me back to fa'." | **4.** Oh woe to my father's butler boy.<br>Between the kitchie and the ha'<br>For he put his hand on to my shoulder<br>And he made me doon to fa'." | **4.** "He got me in my bower alone,<br>As I sat pensively;<br>He vowed he would forgive my sins,<br>If I would him obey." | **4.** He saired my father seven years,<br>And he never paid him his fee;<br>But he got me in my bower my lane,<br>And he made me pay the fee. | |
| **6.** "Gang tee your boo'er, my lily flooer,<br>Till a' your months are gane,<br>An' sometimes you'll read upon a book,<br>An' sometimes sew your seam, dear love,<br>An' sometimes sew your seam. | **5.** Go to your boo'er, my lily-white floo'er<br>Or a' your months be gane,<br>And sometimes read upon a book,<br>And sometimes sew your seam. | | | |
| **7.** "An' I'll rank oot a bonnie boat<br>An' sail upon the main,<br>An' be it weet or be it dry,<br>That nicht I will be hame, dear love." | | | | |
| **8.** It fell ance upon a day<br>In travailin she fell by,<br>An' her ain gweed lord in anither room<br>He heard her thus ti cry: | **6.** But it fell ance upon a day .<br>She took her travailin'<br>If this bairn had been to my good lord,<br>I wouldna hae been here my lane. | **5.** Now it fell ance upon a day<br>This young lord went from home,<br>And great and heavy were the pains<br>That came this lady on. | **5.** Now it fell ance upon a day<br>This good lord went from home,<br>And heavy, heavy were the pains<br>The pains o' travailin'<br>That fell upon this gay lady,<br>And her good lord far fra home. | |

Bell Duncan, cont.

9. "Had my young son been tee my ain gweed lord,
He wid hae eased my moan;
Had my young son been tee my ain gweed lord,
He wid hae come an' gone."

10. It's up he rase an' in he gaes,
It wis ti ease her moan;
Up he rase an' in he gaes,
An' he saa his bonnie young son.

11. "Ye'll tak my young son in your airms
An' hae him far fae me;
Ye'll tak my young son in your airms
An' 'droon him i' the sea.'"

12. He's taen up his bonnie young son
An' clasped him tee his breist,
An' he's awa tee his mither's booer,
Faar she his laid tee rest.

Mrs. Annie Robb, cont.

7. Her good lord he was standing by,
And heard his lady's moan;
And he's awa to his lady
As fast as he can gang.

8. Oh ye'll tak' up that bonnie boy,
And ye'll throw him in the sea,
For like is he to his fause father,
And he'll get nae mair o' me.

9. Oh ye'll tak' up that bonnie boy,
And cast him in the main,
For like is he to his fause father
And sair was he to blame.

10. But he's ta'en up the bonnie boy,
To his mother's gates he ran,
Open, open, mother, he said,
Oh open and lat me in.

Peter Buchan, cont.

6. Then word has gane to her gude lord,
As he sat at the wine,
And when the tidings he did hear
Then he came singing hame.

7. When he came to his own bower-door,
He tirled at the pin:
"Sleep ye, wake ye, my gay lady,
Ye'll let your gude lord in."

8. Huly, huly raise she up,
And slowly put she on,
And slowly came she to the door;
She was a weary woman.

9. "Ye'll tak up my son, Willie,
That ye see here wi' me,
And hae him down to yon shore-side,
And throw him in the sea.

10. "Gin he sink, ye'll let him sink,
Gin he swim, ye'll let him swim;
And never let him return swim;
Till white fish he bring hame."

11. Then he's taen up his little young son,
And rowd him in a band,
And he is on to his mother,
As fast as he could gang.

Bell Robertson, cont.

6. She bolted the door without, without,
And she bolted it within,
She bolted her room round about,
None to her could win in.

7. Then word is gone to that good lord,
As he sat drinkin' wine,
Word is gane to that good lord.
And merrily cam' he hame.

8. Ye'll open the door, my lady, he says,
Ye'll open the door to me
Or I'll make a vow, and I'll keep it true.
In the fleer I'll gar it flee.

9. I'll open the door, my ain good lord,
I'll open, lat you come in,
But a' that I do ask o' you
Is it ye come in your lane.

10. Then wi' her fingers long and small
She lifted up the gin,
And wi' her arms long and wide
She embraced her good lord in.

11. Oh, ye take here this little boy,
That ye see here wi' me,
Oh, ye tak' here this little boy,
And ye throw him in the sea.

12. And gin he sink ye lat him sink,
Gin he swim, ye lat him swim,
But never lat him return again
Till fite fish he fess hame.

13. He's taen up the little boy,
And he rowed him in his sleeve,
And he is on to his mother,
At his lady he asked nae leave.

Mrs. William Duncan, cont.

Bell Duncan, cont.

13. "Ye'll open your door tee me, mother;
You'll rise an' lat me in,
For the dew fa's on my yellow hair,
An' it's weetin my bonnie young son."

14. "I taul ye afore, my son, Willie,
Fan ye gaed there ti woo,
That yon wisna a leal maiden,
An' I taul it unto you."

15. "But mither, ye ken I had anither sweetheart
Fan I wis ayont the sea,
An' this is ane o her love tokens
That she's sent hame tee me."

16. "If that be true, my son Willie,
As I trust weel it may be,
There's be nae mair ill deen tee your young son
Than ever wis deen tee thee."

17. "Fan my lady comes here," he says,
As aft she comes ti dine,
Ye'll aye be merry wi my bonnie young son,
But be sure ye dinna ca' him mine."

18. Up he rase an' awa he gaes,
As fast as he could gang;
An' fan he cam till his lady's booer,
He heard her makin her mane.

19. "My bonny young son's tee the white      [fishin,
An' he's ower young for the sea,
An' lang, lang will I think for fish
Ere he fesh hame tee me.

Mrs. Annie Robb, cont.

11. And ye'll tak' up this bonnie boy,
And gie him to nurses nine,
There'll be three to sleep and three to wake,
And three to gang atween.

12. An' ye'll tak' this bonny boy,
Learn him to write and read,
An' every other necessar'
Ye see he stan's in need.

13. An' ye'll tak' care, my mother, he said,
When we come here to dine,
That ye'll kiss my son, and bless my son,
But say nae that he's mine.

14. And he's awa' to his lady
As fast as he could gang;
But when he went to his lady
She was like to gang brain.

15. My bonny young son is a white fisher,
An' he's ower sune to the sea;
And lang, lang will I think for fish
Or he bring ony tae me.

Peter Buchan, cont.

12. "Ye'll open the door, my mother dear,
Ye'll open, let me come in;
My young son is in my arms twa,
And shivering at the chin."

13. "I tauld you true, my son Willie,
When ye was gaun to ride,
That lady was an ill woman
That ye chose for your bride."

14. "O hold your tongue, my mother dear,
Let a' your folly be;
I wat she is a king's daughter
That's sent this son to me."

15. "I wat she was a king's daughter
I loved beyond the sea,
And if my lady hear of this
Right angry will she be."

16. "If that be true, my son Willie—
Your ain tongue winna lie—
Nae waur to your son will be done
Than what was done to thee."

17. He's gane hame to his lady,
And sair mourning was she:
"What ails you now, my lady gay,
Ye weep sa bitterlie?"

18. "O bonny was the white fisher
That I sent to the sea;
But lang, lang will I look for fish
Ere white fish he bring me!

Bell Robertson, cont.

14. Open the door, my mother, he said,
Ope, lat me come in;
Open the door, my mother, he says,
And tak' in my little young son.

15. Didna I tell you, my dear son dear,
Fin ye wis gaun to ride,
Didna I tell ye, my dear son dear,
It wis nae leal virgin it ye did wed?

16. Oh, haud yer tongue, my mother dear,
Lat a' yet folly be,
A-wite it wis a king's daughter
That sent this son to me.

17. A-wite it was a king's daughter
I loved beyond the sea,
And gin my lady knew o' that
Right angry wad she be.

18. Gin that be true, my dear son dear,
As yer ain tongue winna lee,
I will tak' in yer little young son,
And gie him a nourice tee
There'll never be waur done to your young son
Than every wid done to thee.

19. Fan he gaed hame to his ladie,
And sair mournin' wis she,
Oh fat does all my gay ladie,
I pray you tell to me.

20. Oh, bonnie wis the fite fisher,
That I sent to the faem,
Lang will I mourn in bower my lane
Ere fite fish he fess hame.

Mrs. William Duncan, cont.

1. My bonnie young son's a white fisher,
Goes fishing in yonder sea,
But long, long will I think for fish
Or he return wi them to me.

Bell Duncan, cont.

**20.** "My bonny young son's tee the white    [fishin,
An' he's ower young for the main,
An' lang, lang will I think for fish
Ere fesh ony hame."

**21.** "Gang tee your bed, my dear," he says,
"Gang tee yer bed,"
"Gang tee yer bed, my dear," he says,
"An' a drink I'll mak tee thee."

**22.** "I winna gang tee my bed," she says,
"An' a drink I winna tak fae thee,
For them that wid a droont my bonnie young son,
Wid surely poison me."

**23.** "O haud your tongue, my dear," he said,
"Say nae mair ill tee me;
There'll be nae mair ill deen tee your young    [son
Than ever wis deen tee me.

**24.** "An' fan ye gang tee my mother's booer
As aft ye gang ti dine,
Ye'll aye be merry wi your bonnie young son,
But be sure ye dinna ca' him thine."

Mrs. Annie Robb, cont.

**16.** My bonny young son is a white fisher,
An' he's ower sune to the main;
An' lang, lang will I think for fish
Or he bring ony hame.

**17.** Oh haud your tongue, my lady, he,    [said,
Lat a' your folly be,
For I had your son to my mother
The day or one could see.

**18.** An' ye'll tak' care, my lady, he said,
When we go there to dine,
That ye'll kiss your son, and ye'll bless your son,
But say not that he's thine.

Peter Buchan, cont.

**19.** "O bonny was the white fisher
That ye kiest in the faem;
But lang, lang will I look for fish
Ere white fish he fetch hame!

**20.** "I fell a slumbering on my bed
That time ye went frae me,
And dreamd my young son fild my arms,
But when waked, he's in the sea."

**21.** "O hold your tongue, my gay lady,
Let a' your mourning be,
And I'll gie you some fine cordial,
My love, to comfort thee."

**22.** I value not your fine cordial,
Nor aught that ye can gie;
Who could hae drownd my bonny young son
Could as well poison me."

**23.** "Cheer up your heart, my lily flower,
Think nae sic ill o me;
Your young son's in my mother's bower,
Set on the nourice knee.

**24.** "Now, if ye'll be a gude woman,
I'll neer mind this to thee;
Nae waur is done to your young son
Than what was done to me."

**25.** "Well fell's me now, my ain gude lord;
These words do cherish me;
If it hadna come o yourself, my lord,
'T would neer hae come o me."

Bell Roberston, cont.

**21.** Oh, haud yer tongue, my gay ladie,
Lat a' yer mourning be;
There'll never be waur done to your young son
Than ever was done to me.

Mrs. William Duncan, cont.

**2.** ................
................
For those that would droont my bonnie    [young son
Would surely poison me.

**3.** Oh haud your tongue, my lady fair,
Lat a' your folly be;
For there'll nae maer come o'er your bonnie    [young son
Than ever come o'er me.

**4.** When ye gang tae rry auld mother,
When ye gang there tae dine,
There ye'll see your bonny young son
But ye'll never call him thine.

**5.** When I gang tae your auld mother,
Fan I gang there tae dine,
There I'll see my bonny young son
But I'll never call him thine.

**22.** Gin that be true, my ain good lord,
This day noo well is me;
But in't hidna come o' you, she said,
It never wad come o' me.

Bell Robertson, cont.

**23.** My blessin's on yer cheek, your cheek,
My blessin's on yer chin,
My blessin's on yer red rose lips,
For ye're aye a woman's frien.

## Appendix C: Correlation of Stanzas of "The White Fisher" Collected from the Robb Family

| Miss Elizabeth Robb | Miss Annie Robb | Mrs. Annie Robb (parallel stanzas taken from long version for comparison) |
|---|---|---|
| "My bonnie young son's a white fisher, / And he's owerseen tee the sea, / And lang, lang will I think for fish / Ere he bring any tee me. | My young son is a white fisher / And he's owre seen to the main / And lang lang will I think for fish / Till he bring white fish hame. | My bonny young son is a white fisher, / An' he's ower sune to the sea; / And lang, lang will I think for fish / Or he bring ony tae me. |
| "My bonnie young son's a white fisher, / And he's owerseen tee the main, / And lang, lang will I think for fish / Ere he bring any hame." | | My bonny young son is a white fisher, / An' he's ower sune to the main; / An' lang, lang will I think for fish / Or he bring ony hame. |

## Notes

This article has benefited from the help and advice of a number of colleagues, especially Robert Thomson, Emily Lyle, Katherine Campbell, David Atkinson, Sigrid Rieuwerts, and the staff at the Archive of Folk Culture, American Folklife Center, Library of Congress. I am most grateful to them for their time, interest, and insights.

1. For further information on Carpenter and Bell Duncan, see Bishop 1998a, 1998b, 2003.
2. Defining rape historically is difficult (Porter 1986) and, as Mitchison and Leneman warn, seduction could be rough without being termed rape (1989: 194–95). Consideration is given here to the specific ways in which rape appears to be suggested, implicitly or explicitly, in the ballad versions. That the ballad reports no dialogue or preceding encounter between the woman and the kitchie/butler boy, however, strengthens the impression that, as far as the text is concerned, this was a sudden and forceful attack, whose motivation had no pretensions to courtship and seduction of any kind. Singers, of course, may have had other interpretations.
3. See Rieuwerts in this volume; also D. Buchan 1972.
4. See the editorial notes to "The White Fisher" (version A, *The Greig-Duncan Folk-Song Collection* 1983, 2: 521), and Greig's letter of 29 July 1912 (Greig 1907–14). I am indebted to Special Collections: Rare Books, George A. Smathers Libraries, University of Florida, Gainesville, for permission to quote from this and other letters in that collection.
5. Quoted in the editorial notes to "The White Fisher" (version A, *The Greig-Duncan Folk-Song Collection* 1983, 2: 521).
6. Noted in "Supplementary Notes to Songs in Volumes 1–7," *The Greig-Duncan Folk-Song Collection* 2002, 8: 426.
7. Letter to William Walker, 17 Feburary 1913 (Greig 1907–14).
8. I take this to refer to Elizabeth Robb's grandmother, Mrs. Robb's mother.
9. Alexander Robb, "Fair Ellen" (version A, "Lord William and Lady Margaret"; *The Greig-Duncan Folk-Song Collection* 1995, 6: 429); "Fair Ellen," sung by Alex Robb, Carpenter Collection: 04834–35 (text), 06918–19 (text), 08205 (music notation), and 08206 (music notation).
10. "Supplementary Notes" (*The Greig-Duncan Folk-Song Collection* 2002, 8: 426–27).
11. The title "Fair Annie" is probably a slip by Carpenter for "Fair Ellen" since the verbal texts of "Fair Annie" (Child 62) noted from Elizabeth Robb by Carpenter have no stanzas in common with "The White Fisher." Elizabeth Robb's melody for "Fair Annie" is nevertheless almost identical to "Fair Ellen"/"The White Fisher."
12. It is clear from Carpenter's notes on this page that Alex Robb used this alternative tune for a number of ballads, including "Fair Annie" (Child 62), "The Kitchie Boy" (Child 252), "Young Akin" (Child 41, "Hind Etin") and "Edom o' Gordon" (Child 178).
13. For more on Carpenter's collecting methods, see Bishop 1998a: 407–08.

## References

Bishop, Julia C. 1998a. "'Dr. Carpenter from the Harvard College in America': An Introduction to James Madison Carpenter and his Collection." *Folk Music Journal* 7, no. 4: 402–20.

———. 1998b. "The Tunes of the English and Scottish Ballads in the James Madison Carpenter Collection." *Folk Music Journal* 7, no. 4: 450–70.

———. Forthcoming. "Bell Duncan: 'The greatest ballad singer of all time?'" Paper presented at the Folksong: Tradition and Revival Conference, University of Sheffield, July 1998 (to be included among a selection of revised papers from the conference edited by Ian Russell and David Atkinson, forthcoming 2003).

Bronson, Bertrand Harris. 1959–72. *The Traditional Tunes of the Child Ballads, with Their Texts, According to the Extant Records of Great Britain and America.* 4 vols. Princeton: Princeton University Press.

Buchan, David. 1972. "The Peter Buchan Controversy." Chapter 16 in *The Ballad and the Folk*, 205–22. London: Routledge and Kegan Paul. Reprint, Phantassie, East Lothian: Tuckwell Press, 1997.

Buchan, Peter. [1828] 1875. *Ancient Ballads and Songs of the North of Scotland*. 2 vols. Reprint, Edinburgh: William Paterson (page references are to reprint edition).

Campbell, Katherine. Personal communication, 2 August 2002.

The James M. Carpenter Collection. AFC 1972/001. Archive of Folk Culture, American Folklife Center, Library of Congress, Washington, D.C.

Child, Francis James, ed. 1882–98. *The English and Scottish Popular Ballads*. 5 vols. Reprint, New York: Folklore Press, 1956–57; New York: Dover, 1965. Corrected edition prepared by Mark and Laura Heiman. Northfield, Minn.: Loomis House Press, 2002. Digital edition, with gazetteer, maps and audio CD. New York: ESPB Publishing, 2003.

Gerould, Gordon. 1932. *The Ballad of Tradition*. Oxford: Clarendon Press.

Greig, Gavin. 1907–1914. "Letters from Gavin Greig anent matter of North Country songs and ballads." Edited by William Walker. Manuscript 821.04 W186s. Rare Books, George A. Smathers Libraries, University of Florida, Gainesville.

Greig, Gavin, and James B. Duncan. 1983, 1995, 2002. *The Greig-Duncan Folk Song Collection*. Vol. 2, edited by Patrick Shuldham-Shaw and Emily B. Lyle. Aberdeen: Aberdeen University Press; vol. 6, edited by Patrick Shuldham-Shaw, Emily B. Lyle, and Elaine Petrie. Edinburgh: Mercat Press; vol. 8, edited by Patrick Shuldham-Shaw, Emily B. Lyle, and Katherine Campbell. Edinburgh: Mercat Press (cited in the text as *Greig-Duncan Collection*).

Keith, Alexander, ed. 1925. *Last Leaves of Traditional Ballads and Ballad Airs Collected in Aberdeenshire by the Late Gavin Greig*. Aberdeen: The Buchan Club.

Lyle, Emily B. 2002. "The Formation of the Collection." In *The Greig-Duncan Folk-Song Collection*. Vol. 8, 465–529.

Mitchison, Rosalind, and Leah Leneman. 1989. *Sexuality and Social Control: Scotland 1660–1780*. Oxford: Blackwell.

Porter, James, and Katherine Campbell. 2002. "Alexander Robb." In *The Greig-Duncan Folk-Song Collection*. Vol. 8, 577–78.

Porter, Roy. 1986. "Does Rape Have a Historical Meaning?" In *Rape*, edited by Sylvana Tomaselli and Roy Porter, 216–36. Oxford: Blackwell.

Shields, Hugh. 1983. "Impossibles in Ballad Style." *The Ballad Image: Essays Presented to Bertrand Harris Bronson*, edited by James Porter, 192–214. Los Angeles: Center for the Study of Comparative Folklore and Mythology, University of California.

"White: Whitefish." In *The Oxford English Dictionary*. Available online at <http://www.oed.com/>

# Regions, Reprints

# and Repertoires

# Regions, Reprints, and Repertoires

Ballad and song collection had its main origins in the eighteenth- and nineteenth-century search for regional and cultural identities in the face of sweeping political and cultural change; there is no better barometer of this trend than the song tradition itself. Whether reflecting strong family ties, as with the Dickie and Fowlie families of New Deer in the North East of Scotland (Katherine Campbell), or the regional, quasi-national Flemish tradition (Isabelle Peere, Stefaan Top), this movement always needs futher investigation. Within themes of regionality and nationality, Stefaan Top explores the issues involved in selecting and reprinting song collections for current performers and scholars. Who exactly is the audience? What do they require in a reedition? What influence do these needs have on the collections we choose? Following on these questions, Isabelle Peere takes a close look at one of these collections, *Chants populaires flamands* (1879), suggesting that it is probably largely the repertoire of a single individual. In conjunction with Katherine Campbell's study of two related singers, it seems pertinent to remember that regional tradition is really only a fusion of several sets of personal tradition. Here ballad scholarship can repay some of the rewards it has enjoyed over the centuries, illuminating the role of the individual and, in some cases, returning repertoires to performers and enthusiasts through carefully reprinted and annotated collections.

Given the strong regional identities in song in Flemish-speaking lands and the Scottish North East, there is some mystery in the almost total lack of a solid corpus of French ballad tradition, which is addressed by Michèle Simonsen, who asks, what can we really mean by a "national" tradition in a country as linguistically and culturally diverse as France? Is any particular corpus homogeneous enough for us to make general claims? Once again, the persistent notion of individuality within regional and national traditions surfaces; the more we investigate, classify, and analyze, the more individuality emerges from ballad types, communities, and subcultures.

As touched upon in the general introduction, songs and ballads travel in oral tradition and writing with almost equal facility, each medium having its own effect on the material. The move from the oral realm to print usually comes through the efforts of an individual, collector, or printer who stands to earn something from the process, whether social or academic approbation or monetary profit. (In former days, the latter motivation was more effective, to say the least.) Songs then find their way into print in book or broadside form, where they languish or become part of the corpus of "standards" which academics know and use, or they may reenter oral tradition via an enthusiast who resurrects them (more on the theme of resurrection in the next section). But this process, as has been noted, goes both ways. Some traditional songs are recast by literary artists, and, conversely, ballads originating in the literary tradition are made traditional by oral transmission and memory (Marjetka Golež Kaučič).

Songs also travel between cultures as well as media, though, as has been noted, with less ease than often assumed by scholars. Scotland's ballad corpus, with influences ranging from the continent to the Scandinavian periphery that surrounds its northern arc, is rich and has a long history of collection, controversial editing practices, and publication touched upon later in this volume. Here Frances Fischer explores the ballad in Shetland, Scotland's most Scandinavian islands, showing how politics and history mix with national myth and legend in the creation, metamorphosis, and preservation of a tradition.

The sung tradition is the focus of Mary Anne Alburger's essay on Simon Fraser's collection of melodies for Gaelic song. Most collections and broadsides do not include music but, rather, rely on such headings as "to the tune of…," naming some song the purchaser is expected to know. Hence, Fraser's early work (1816), in concentrating on melody, is particularly interesting, given that music is a key element in the transmission and preservation of song traditions.

The work in this section addresses a rich admixture of individuality and specificity to present an overview of the ballad genre in discourse with the cultures from which the songs themselves arise.

# Ballad Singing in New Deer

Katherine Campbell

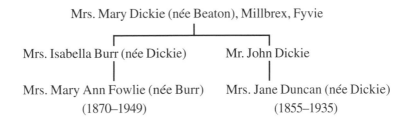

Mrs. Mary Dickie (née Beaton), Millbrex, Fyvie

Mrs. Isabella Burr (née Dickie)  Mr. John Dickie

Mrs. Mary Ann Fowlie (née Burr)  Mrs. Jane Duncan (née Dickie)
(1870–1949)  (1855–1935)

In ballad scholarship and folk-song research in general, scholars often focus on the songs themselves and their collectors, rather than the singers who contributed them. This is especially true in historical research, where it is often difficult to gather sufficient information about singers. Knowledge about these individuals—the context in which a song was sung, the identity of the singer, the singer's social circumstances, and the way the song was collected—allows a more holistic understanding of a particular song and indeed of a singing tradition at a particular point in time. Gavin Greig, the subject of this essay, who, together with the Reverend James Bruce Duncan, amassed more than three thousand texts and tunes from North East Scotland during the early years of the twentieth century, understood this better than most, noting that through folk song, "We get light thrown on the social life of the people—their occupations and interests, their amusements and recreations; while in the incidents and situations that have prompted and inspired the rustic muse local history may achieve record, or at least receive illustration" (Greig 1963a: 2).

The two singers introduced in this article, Mrs. Fowlie and Mrs. Duncan, each contributed songs to *The Greig-Duncan Folk-Song Collection*. Although they were not among Greig's most prolific contributors, their circumstances are interesting to the scholar because the two women were related and both lived in New Deer Parish, where Greig did a good deal of his collecting. As well as examining the ballads that formed part of their repertoires, this investigation aims to highlight Greig's activities as a collector.

## Mary Ann Fowlie

Mary Ann Burr Fowlie was born 8 February 1870 at Brucehill, New Deer and died 6 July 1949 at the Mill Inn, Maryculter,[1] owned at the time by her daughter Myra and her husband. She was the daughter of Peter Burr, a farm servant usually resident at Auchreddie, and Isabella Dickie, Auchmunziel, New Deer,[2] who married in 1869. As a young woman, Ann Burr, as she was commonly known, married Alexander Fowlie, a farmer. Alexander had started work early in life because his father had died young.[3] When Gavin Greig was collecting, the Fowlies were living at Ironside, Bonnykelly, Aberdeenshire. Later they moved to Mid-Culsh Farm outside New Deer, presently owned by the McConnachie family.

Fig. 1 Mrs. Fowlie. Photo courtesy of her grandson, Sandy Thow.

According to Mrs. Fowlie's grandson, Mr. Sandy Thow of Milltimber, to whom I am greatly indebted for information, she was a lady who commanded respect, "an old Edwardian type." He also noted that she had eight children who lived, out of about thirteen. It is likely that Mr. and Mrs. Fowlie had a hard and busy life running the farm and looking after the family. There was still time left over for singing, however.

Mrs. Fowlie was a relatively young woman, approximately thirty-seven years old, when Greig took down songs from her singing in August and September of 1907. One wonders how Greig originally found out that Mrs. Fowlie sang and if, in fact, she was known to him prior to his beginning work on the collection. Certainly, the couple remained in touch with him after his collecting visits. In his weekly column in the *Buchan Observer*, 4 February 1908, Greig records a donation of a "budget of songs" from Mr. Fowlie (mostly sung by his neighbor, Mr. Glennie), to whom four songs are attributed in the collection (Ob. 10[4]).

Greig was a schoolmaster at Whitehill school some three miles north of New Deer, where he remained until his death on 31 August 1914 (Shuldham-Shaw

1981: viii), and it was Whitehill where his collecting work centered. He did not
have far to travel to collect material from the Fowlies since Ironside, Bonnykelly,
is only about half a mile to a mile away as the crow flies, a distance that Greig
would probably have traveled on foot, and it is possible that he may have taken
a short cut over the fields. As with the other contributors to the collection from
whom he heard tunes, Greig did his preliminary noting of Mrs. Fowlie's material
in *sol-fa*—a system of teaching sight-singing which arose in England in the
midnineteenth century (Scholes 1944)—before transcribing the tune into staff
notation for the final copy. His collecting partner, Rev. James Bruce Duncan, also
followed this procedure in his collecting (Shuldham-Shaw 1981: x). We have a
copy of the *sol-fa* notation of "The Laird of Drum" in the case of Mrs. Fowlie,
along with Greig's fair copy of the same piece, which he entitles "I Canna Wash"
(Fig. 2).[5]

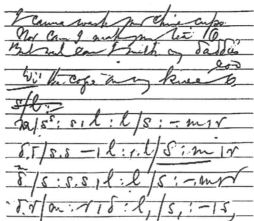

Fig. 2a. Greig's *sol-fa* notation of "The Laird of Drum" (Argo 17, p. 14).

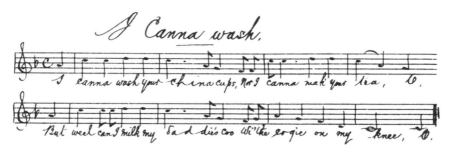

Fig. 2b. Greig's fair copy of "The Laird of Drum" *(The Greig-Duncan Folk-Song
Collection*, 4: no. 835M). Reproduced courtesy of the University of Aberdeen.

Greig, who was organist of his parish church (Shuldham-Shaw 1981: ix), clearly
had no difficulty in transcribing melodies; the books containing his *sol-fa* notation

exhibit surprisingly few deletions, indicating little doubt on his part about the notes or rhythms of tunes. Although frowned upon today by some in educational circles, tonic *sol-fa* was very much in vogue in Greig's time. His notations also correspond very closely to the final copies, indicating that they gave him a firm foundation for the later version and acted as more than just a memory aid. Greig offers some clue about the process of collecting tunes, stating, "We have to make grateful acknowledgement of the kind and patient way in which most singers have submitted to the ordeal—a necessary one in the circumstances—of singing, and singing, and singing, till every melody was duly noted" (Greig 1963b: 1; Ob. 180). Collecting folk songs may not have been altogether easy, especially if only "most" (but not all) singers submitted to the ordeal graciously.

Greig collected a total of twenty-five songs from Mrs. Fowlie, and tunes are given for all but one of them. They cover a variety of themes, but as with the entire collection, the largest proportion of them deal with love and marriage. Among Fowlie's repertoire are five Child ballads: "Binorie" (Child 10), "The Dowie Dens o' Yarrow" (Child 214), "The Gypsy Laddie" (Child 200), "The Laird o' Drum" (Child 236), and "Clyde's Waters" (Child 216), all of which have tunes, though only one verse of each is given. Although Greig was very interested in collecting ballads, noting in the *Buchan Observer* of 12 January 1909, for instance, "I like very much to get copies of the old ballads, as they are dying out faster than the songs" (Ob. 58), it is likely that neither the texts nor the tunes of these versions were particularly interesting to him since he does not comment in detail on them in his writings.

While the ballad versions that Mrs. Fowlie gave to Greig may not have been outstanding, her singing clearly was. Although without audio recordings it is difficult to tell what her vocal quality was like, we do have some descriptions of her singing. Mary Ann Crichton, a helper of Greig's who also taught at Whitehill School, described her as "a very fine ballad singer" (Keith 1925: 284) and went even further in her appraisal, noting, "Mrs. Fowlie has the genuine ballad ring in her style of rendering the songs." Crichton may be referring to Mrs. Fowlie's singing in general as having this "ballad ring," not just her rendition of ballads. Crichton continues, "She has just been singing over a few of those she gave Mr. Greig and she is splendid. One can feel the fine intervals of the real article. It took me back to the olden days when we used to go ahunting for the songs" (MS 2732/30/1, f. 5r). The use of the term "ballad ring" is interesting here. While we cannot be sure precisely what Crichton meant, I expect that it conveyed the sense she felt of both the oral tradition, of which Mrs. Fowlie was a part, and the antiquity which came through her singing. Crichton's use of the word "feel" in the context of the intervals, where one expects instead the word "hear," is also noteworthy. This, I believe, relates to the feeling one experiences when singing expressively or listening to such singing. It is difficult to put into words but is described by some Traveller singers as the "conyach."[6]

### Jane Duncan

Mrs. Jane Duncan was related to Mrs. Fowlie through their grandmother, Mrs. Mary Dickie (née Beaton), Millbrex, Fyvie (see the family tree). Mrs. Dickie is a particularly important figure as far as we are concerned because both her children, Isabella Burr (née Dickie) and John Dickie, got their songs from her.

Jane Dickie, later Mrs. Duncan, was also the daughter of a farm servant, born on 8 December 1855, fifteen years before Mrs. Fowlie, at the same place, Brucehill.[7] On 2 February 1878, she married John Duncan, at that time an agricultural laborer in New Deer. At this point she was twenty-two years old and a domestic servant at Clockhill.[8] She appears to have had a small family in comparison with her cousin; at the time of the 1891 census, four people were recorded in her home in New Deer: Jane, John Duncan (her husband, aged forty-three, a road contractor),[9] John H. Duncan (a thirteen-year-old son), and Helen Dickie, an adopted daughter, aged nine and born in Strichen. Given her surname, Helen was probably a relative.

Mrs. Duncan contributed a substantial eighty-eight songs to the collection, nineteen of them with tunes and half of them on love and marriage. The method used to collect her material was quite different from the one Greig employed with her cousin, however. Greig received the words for many of her songs from Ernest Coutts, who took down what she remembered (Keith 1925: 283). Greig does not refer to Coutts by name in his writings concerning Mrs. Duncan in the *Observer*, preferring to call him "a mutual friend." Coutts was, in fact, Greig's son-in-law and had lodged in Mrs. Duncan's home, where he no doubt heard her singing. Other songs appear to have been sent in by Mrs. Duncan herself, possibly inspired by Coutts's work; the tunes for some of the songs were written down by Greig sometime later. Interestingly, all nineteen tunes were recorded at one time, the date of collection being around 6 September 1910 (Ob. 143).

Twelve items in Mrs. Duncan's repertoire are versions of Child ballads. These are "The Mermaid" (Child 289), "Willie Grahame" (which Bronson includes in an appendix to Child 57, "Brown Robyn's Confession"), "Binorie" (Child 10), "The Young Laird o' Logie" (Child 182), "The Beggar's Dawtie" (Child 280), "The Broom of Cowdenknowes" (Child 217), "The Wee Toon Clerk" (Child 281), "Glasgow Peggie" (Child 228), "Lord Thomas o' Winchbury" (Child 100), "The Duke o' Gordon's Three Daughters" (Child 237), "The Rue and the Thyme" (which corresponds to Child 295, "The Brown Girl"), and "Fair Rosie Ann" (Child

52). These entries mostly contain several more stanzas than Mrs. Fowlie's, although tunes are given for only two: "The Mermaid" *(Greig-Duncan Collection,* 4: no. 27A) and "The Keach in the Creel" *(Greig-Duncan Collection,* 2: no. 317D).

Greig acknowledged receiving several of these, including "The Mermaid" and "Binorie," in his column (Ob. 143, 74) but does not comment in detail on her versions. He was, however, delighted to receive these ballad contributions as well as her other songs, noting, "From Mrs. Duncan, New Deer, per a mutual friend, I have got a capital budget of minstrelsy" (Ob. 71). In addition, he was happy to receive fragments as well as whole texts from her: "Some of these are complete, others are gleanings of memory, but all are very welcome and claim my sincere thanks" (Ob. 78). Mrs. Duncan's version of "The Mermaid" is a fine one and is the A version in *The Greig-Duncan Folk-Song Collection;* it also appears in Bronson (1959–72: song 289, variant 16).

When the repertoires of Mrs. Fowlie and Mrs. Duncan are compared, despite the family song connection through their grandmother, which dates some of their repertoire back to the midnineteenth century, they have surprisingly few songs in common. It has to be said, however, that valid comparisons are difficult because of the differing number of verses they give for songs. Of the eight which they have in common, there are a few textual similarities in songs such as "The Rigs o' Rye" *(Greig-Duncan Collection,* 5: no. 1054) and "The False Bride" *(Greig-Duncan Collection,* 6: no. 1198), and both tune and text are very similar in the one song which they have in common where a tune is given for both, "The Auld Gardener's Wife" *(Greig-Duncan Collection,* 6: no. 1262). In the one Child ballad that they share, "Binorie" (Child 10), there are slight similarities, although Mrs. Duncan supplies ten stanzas with no tune *(Greig-Duncan Collection,* 2: no. 213U), whereas Mrs. Fowlie offers a tune but only one stanza (213I). Mrs. Fowlie's stanza runs,

> Oh sister, O sister, give to me your hand,
> Binorie O and Binorie;
> And ye'll get the miller for your true love,
> Binorie O and Binorie.

This corresponds quite closely to Mrs. Duncan's fourth stanza:

> Oh sister, oh sister, come reach me your hand,
> Binorrie oh, an' Binnorie;
> And I'll give you all that is at my command,
> But the bonnie mullert lad o' Binorrie.

The proportion of Child ballads in Mrs. Duncan's and Mrs. Fowlie's repertoires—about one-sixth of the former's, one-fifth of the latter's—demonstrates that each had a mixed repertoire of folk song and balladry. The fact that the two singers had little in common in their overall song repertoires, however, is interesting, particularly since Mary Ann Crichton, who enthusiastically explained the family connection between the two in her notes for Alexander Keith when he was preparing *Last Leaves*, evidently expected more of a link. While this can be explained by the singers remembering songs differently, resulting in different songs being sung for collectors, it does illustrate the point that songs are often not passed from one generation to the next as one expects. Indeed, Mrs. Fowlie's daughter, Myra, Sandy Thow's mother, is a good example. Although Myra was well known as a singer in her local area, Mr. Thow did not recognize any of Mrs. Fowlie's songs in her repertoire; he said she sang a lot of Burns songs as well as popular material made famous by performers such as Vera Lynn.

Greig's collecting methods, as we have seen, were varied and included gathering material in the field, having singers come to his home, appealing for songs in his column in the *Buchan Observer,* and getting submissions through envoys such as Coutts, who greatly assisted his efforts. While many people helped him in his collecting work, Greig had rather harsh words for certain parties who did not, especially musicians. "When we began our folk-song work, we thought that our musical friends would be specially helpful in recording tunes for us. One or two have aided us much; but we have to say that, as a rule, musicians—we mean people with a good deal of technical training—have done little or nothing for the work" (Ob. 180). Volume eight of *The Greig-Duncan Folk-Song Collection* (2002) contains further notes on Greig's methods and those who contributed songs. As well as being informative for scholars, these notes are helpful to singers wishing to know more about the sources of songs, which undoubtedly helps them perform more effectively.

The fact that Mrs. Duncan and Mrs. Fowlie lived in the same parish is important in terms of *The Greig-Duncan Folk-Song Collection* as a whole, especially because Greig also lived there, which gave him ready access to local singers. In areas like Aberdeenshire, where close-knit communities are the rule and kinship ties are important, it has been possible to piece together details about the pair, particularly Mrs. Fowlie, through information from relatives and neighbors. Although there are gaps in my understanding of the singers and their singing—how often they sang, for instance—this kind of historical research, which I have only touched upon here, surely yields rich rewards, particularly in helping us understand intensely local traditions.

## Notes

1. I am most grateful to Mr. Jim Shirer, Aberdeen and North East Scotland Family History Society, for this information.
2. Marriage record 1869/225/1 (Scottish Record Office).
3. Information from Mr. Thow, Milltimber.
4. The abbreviation "Ob." will henceforth refer to the number of Greig's column, "Folk-Song of the North East," that appeared in the *Buchan Observer* from 1907 to 1911. These articles can be found in Greig 1963b.
5. Mrs. Fowlie's tunes are transcribed in the manuscript notebook Argo 17, formerly owned by Arthur Argo and now available in as originals and copies at Aberdeen University Library (MSS 3088/26/17) and at the School of Scottish Studies Archive, department of Celtic and Scottish Studies, University of Edinburgh.
6. See Harley, Ph.D. dissertation, forthcoming.
7. Birth record 1855/225/123 (Scottish Record Office).
8. Marriage record 1878/225/2 (Scottish Record Office).
9. It is probable that he took over this business from his father, Alexander Duncan, also a road contractor.

## References

Bronson, Bertrand Harris. 1959–72. *The Traditional Tunes of the Child Ballads, with Their Texts, According to the Extant Records of Great Britain and America.* 4 vols. Princeton: Princeton University Press.

Crichton, Mary Ann. Manuscript, University of Aberdeen Special Libraries and Archives, MS 2732/30/1.

Greig, Gavin. 1963a. "Folk-Song in Buchan: Reprinted from Transactions of the Buchan Field Club, Volume 9, 1906–1907." In *Folk-Song in Buchan and Folk-Song of the North-East*, with a foreword by Kenneth S. Goldstein and Arthur Argo, 2–76. Hatboro, Pa.: Folklore Associates.

Greig, Gavin. 1963b. "Folk-Song of the North-East: Articles contributed to the *Buchan Observer* from December 1907 to June 1911." In *Folk-Song in Buchan and Folk-Song of the North-East*, with a foreword by Kenneth S. Goldstein and Arthur Argo, unpaginated (articles are referred to by their original numbers). Hatboro, Pa.: Folklore Associates.

Greig, Gavin, and James B. Duncan. 1983, 1990, 1995a, 1995b, 2002. *The Greig-Duncan Folk-Song Collection.* Vol. 2, edited by Patrick Shuldham-Shaw and Emily B. Lyle. Aberdeen: University of Aberdeen Press; vol. 4, edited by Patrick Shuldham-Shaw, Emily B. Lyle, and Andrew R. Hunter. Aberdeen: Aberdeen University Press for the University of Aberdeen in association with the School of Scottish Studies, University of Edinburgh; vol. 5, edited by Patrick Shuldham-Shaw, Emily B. Lyle, and Adam McNaughtan. Edinburgh: Mercat Press; vol. 6, edited by Patrick Shuldham-Shaw, Emily B. Lyle, and Elaine Petrie. Edinburgh: Mercat Press; vol. 8, edited by Patrick Shuldham-Shaw, Emily B. Lyle, and Katherine Campbell. Edinburgh: Mercat Press (cited in the text as *Greig-Duncan Collection*).

Harley, Meredith T. Forthcoming. *"Tak It Oot Bonnie": Toward a Description of the Aesthetics and Style of Traditional Scots Singing.* Ph.D. diss., University of Edinburgh.

Keith, Alexander, ed. 1925. *Last Leaves of Traditional Ballads and Ballad Airs Collected in Aberdeenshire by the late Gavin Greig.* Aberdeen: The Buchan Club.

Scholes, Percy A. 1944. "Tonic Sol-Fa." In *The Oxford Companion to Music*, 939–45. 5th ed. London: Oxford University Press.

Shuldham-Shaw, Patrick. 1981. Introduction to *The Greig-Duncan Folk-Song Collection.* Vol. 1, vii–xiv. Aberdeen: Aberdeen University Press for the University of Aberdeen in association with the School of Scottish Studies, University of Edinburgh.

# Old Flemish Songbook Reprints

## Stefaan Top

In 1989 the reprint of Jan Frans Willems's collection *Oude Vlaemsche Liederen* [Old Flemish Songs] appeared, the first in a new series of Old Flemish Songbook Reprints. Volume five in this series appeared in 1998. The decision to reprint these old collections was made by the Koninklijke Belgische Commissie voor Volkskunde [Royal Belgian Ethnological Committee]. Three members of this committee are responsible for this particular project: Jozef Van Haver oversees the financial side, with the help of the Frans M. Olbrechts Foundation for the promotion of ethnological research in Flanders; Hubert Boone, leader of the Brabant Folk Orchestra and familiar with the Flemish folk scene, is the project's spiritual father; and I am responsible for the scholarly aspect of the project. According to Boone, folk-music ensembles in Flanders are constantly on the lookout for reliable source material, heretofore very hard to find; the reprints project will therefore fulfill an identifiable need. Because of his close contacts in these ensembles, Boone will take on the task of promoting and distributing the reprints.

Each songbook was to be situated in its cultural/historical context, along with brief assessments of content and musical qualities. At the same time, various indices would be included so that the collections would be even more accessible to the user. In selecting volumes for reprint, we took into account the age of the collections and their geographical spread, for all of the Flemish provinces had to be represented.

The inaugural selection was the collection of J. F. Willems (1793–1846), who in 1846 published a first series of forty-eight *Oude Vlaemsche Liederen* in Ghent. While working on the second series, Willems unexpectedly passed away (24 June 1846). His brother-in-arms and close friend, Ferdinand Augustijn Snellaert (1809–1872), took over publication, bringing it to a successful conclusion. Two years later, in 1848, the *Oude Vlaemsche Liederen* appeared in book form from the same publisher. The entire collection consists of 258 songs with an extensive sixty-page introduction by Snellaert.

I have previously discussed the cultural/historical context of this publication in detail, particularly Hoffmann von Fallersleben's role in it (Top 1996). Here I would like to restrict myself to looking at a few salient qualities and innovations in this remarkable and voluminous collection, especially as regards typology and public reception.

1. Snellaert's now-obsolete introduction is, by any account, monumental. He speaks of the cultural/historical value of songs and singers in the recent and more remote past. As far as the collection itself is concerned, he takes a rather critical stance, bluntly mentioning its disappointing size and claiming that Willems could have collected far more in the twenty-six years from 1820 to 1846. The new, extensive bibliography, listing national and international song collections in print and manuscript form, is very creditable (pp. xxxiv–lviii). To anyone intending a comparative or historical study of Dutch and Flemish folk songs, such information will prove indispensable. The scholarly value of the collection is therefore beyond any doubt.

2. The collection contains 258 songs; yet, in fact, we can only speak of 255 because one has been included twice (no. 15 = no. 161), and the texts numbered 78 and 97 are only pseudosongs.[1] Willems and Snellaert group their material into six categories: royal songs, historical songs, narrative songs, love and drinking songs, religious songs, and miscellaneous songs. While this classification is far from conclusive, it is at least a modest attempt to make rich and varied material accessible.

3. The philologist Willems used many different sources; almost half of the material was taken from manuscripts, printed songbooks, broadsheets, and other publications. Moreover, he received input from collaborators in France (Edmond de Coussemaker), the Netherlands, and Flanders, not all of whom, regretfully, were specific about their sources.

4. The editors added comments or annotations concerning language, melody, source, musical context, or national and international variants to nearly all the songs. This cannot but be seen in a positive light.

The book contains two true innovations: first, 106 songs, or 41.5 percent, were accompanied by musical notation, a ratio unheard of before the appearance of this collection. As mentioned before, this was a great step forward, even though contemporary commentators (for example, de Coussemaker, Van Duyse) sometimes strongly criticized Willems's transcription methods. Second was the novelty of including some thirty songs either stemming from oral tradition or taken from printed collections but still sung in Willems's and Snellaert's time. The fact that the collection occasionally includes contextual background information only heightens its ethnological value. It is obvious, therefore, that Willems's and Snellaert's edition of *Oude Vlaemsche Liederen* was a milestone in the study of Flemish folk song, as well as inspiration to international scholars.

In 1990 volume two in the series appeared: *Chants Populaires flamands avec les airs notés et Posies Populaires diverses recueillis à Bruges* par Adolphe Lootens et J. M. E. Feys. This collection was first published in the francophone Bruges journal, *Annales de la Société d'Emulation pour servir à l'Etude de l'Histoire et des Antiquités de la Flandre*, fourth series, volume two, 1878. One year later another Bruges publisher released the edition in book form; this formed the basis of the 1990 reprint.

We should note here that Lootens (1835–1884) and Feys (1819–1906) had already collaborated ten years earlier on the edition of a small, but remarkable, collection of fairy tales, *Oude kindervertelsels in den Brugschen tongval* [Old Children's Tales in the Bruges Dialect] (Brussels, 1868). Lootens copied and edited the texts and was helped on linguistic matters by Eusèbe Feys, doctor in philosophy and arts and a teacher at the Royal Athenæum at Bruges. In publishing the tales, both had gained sufficient experience to undertake a larger piece of work. Adding to their efforts were the musical contributions of M. A. Reyns, bandmaster at Bruges Cathedral and former laureate of the Brussels Royal Academy of Music, making this a very competent trio.

In contrast to Willems's work, the *Chants Populaires flamands* only contains songs and texts from oral tradition. Lootens's and Feys's eminent example was Edmond de Coussemaker, a member of the Société d'Emulation, who had collected his song material in the French arrondissements of Dunkerque and Hazebrouck, and who had, in 1856, published his *Chants populaires des Flamands de France* with the brothers F. and E. Gyselynck, Ghent, who had already published Willems and Snellaert (Top 1995). Just like their predecessors, Willems-Snellaert and de Coussemaker, Lootens and Feys stress the exclusive value and importance of material from the active oral tradition, which is much more than just a pastime. Handling such material requires expertise. In their Avant-propos (pp. i–xi), they phrase their position this way: "Leur but est purement scientifique et archéologique, et c'est à ce titre principalement que l'ouvrage a été accepté par la Société d'Emulation de Bruges, toujours disposée à encourager les publications de nature à jeter du jour sur l'histoire nationale" [Their goal is purely scientific and archaeological, and it is mainly because of this that the work was accepted by the Société d'Emulation de Bruges, which is always disposed toward encouraging publications that throw light on national history] (1990:ii).

Another argument in favor of collecting songs is their observation that "ces productions s'altèrent, s'effacent de la mémoire et tendent à disparaître entièrement, avec la vie de famille, le travail en commun, les réunions autour du foyer, les longues veillées d'hiver, le chant dans les écoles" [These productions change, disappear from memory, and tend to disappear entirely, along with family life, common labor, gatherings around the fireside, the long watches during winter, singing at school] (1990: iii). This pessimistic view is shared by many Romantic collectors devoted to popular culture during the nineteenth century.

The fact that Lootens and Feys copied down their song material from one basic source, "une dame de la bonne bourgeoisie de Bruges," is exceptional. "Cette dame d'une intelligence remarquable, douée d'une excellente mémoire, possédant le sentiment de la mélodie et du rhythme, avec un goût prononcé pour les chansons, a su retenir à peu près tout ce qu'elle a entendu" [a solidly middle-class lady from Bruges.... This lady, of remarkable intelligence, gifted with an excellent memory, with a feeling for melody and rhythm, and with a pronounced penchant for songs, has been able to retain almost everything she has ever heard] (1990:iii). This lady is probably Lootens's mother, born in Bruges in 1795 (Stalpaert 1946).

The *Chants Populaires flamands* is therefore a nineteenth-century collection which the singer had learned partly from her parents, in particular her mother, and which she repeatedly sang during her school years. This leads the authors to pay closer attention to the educational situation in nineteenth-century Bruges, and more particularly to the narrative texts children related while making bobbin lace, the so-called *tellingen,* "countings," which make up the second part of the collection.

As the title and subtitle make clear, the collection is divided into two distinct parts: 161 *Chants populaires* and 21 *Poésies populaires diverses.* Songs and items of folk poetry are not only undeniably old, but because they have been passed down in an oral tradition, they have also been molded in a remarkable way. The fact that the editors have been extremely careful in dealing with the language, rhythm, and musicality of these pieces of sung folk culture makes the collection exceptionally precious. As a result, it has been welcomed enthusiastically, both nationally and internationally.

The third volume in the reprints series is devoted to the collection *Honderd oude Vlaamsche liederen* [One Hundred Old Flemish Songs] (Namur, 1897) by the Reverend Jan Bols (1842–1921). The collection consists of the selected results of Bols's intensive fieldwork in the province of Flemish-Brabant. His informative introduction outlines the methodology he employed, and he discusses oral tradition with great expertise and appreciation. At the same time, he exhorts everyone, in particular civil authorities, major cultural organizations, journalists, and "folklorists," to pay even more attention to popular musical culture, which is threatened by the era's unfavorable cultural climate. As a child of his time, Bols does not see a bright future for popular culture. Yet he will not lay down arms and, through his edition, seeks to prove that there are still opportunities for success.

Thanks to the part played by his brother Gustaaf, Bols was able to add excellent musical annotations to each of the songs. In addition, he provides an interesting popular-cultural background to many of the songs, as well as first-hand information concerning the circumstances of performance. Moreover, since Bols, contrary to his predecessors, explicitly underlines the value of broadsheet songs and adduces evidence for his claims, his collection acquires an extra dimension.

After the West Flanders and Flemish-Brabant collections, the editors of the reprints series devoted a volume to the province of Limburg: the work of the teacher Lambrecht Lambrechts (1865–1932), *Limburgsche liederen* [Songs from Limburg]. Encouraged by the success of Lootens-Feys in Bruges and Bols in Brabant, Lambrechts built up a sizeable collection of songs from his native area from the 1890s on. After reaping the harvest, he vigorously sought publication, but while individual items were easily placed in Limburg journals, full publication was slow in coming. International interest did exist, particularly from the *Jahrbuch für Volksliedforschung*, which in 1932 published a contribution called "Flämische Volkslieder" ([Flemish Folk Songs]; the German title is somewhat misleading since the entire article was published in Dutch). This article contained eighteen songs, among which are Limburg variants of the "Heer Halewijn" [Sir Halewijn] song, and various annotations and bibliographical references.[3]

A few years after Lambrechts's death, the Committee for Old Folk Songs at last published eighty songs with annotations in two volumes (1936 and 1937), edited mainly by the committee's chairman, Professor Paul de Keyser. The criteria which led to the choice of "ballads," love songs, "comical and satirical songs," and children's songs, however, are nowhere made clear. Moreover, the fate of the unused material remains a mystery; it is likely that a considerable part of the original collection has been lost. All in all, these facts only support the case for reprinting the material.

In 1998 it was the turn of the province of Antwerp to feature in the series when volume five appeared: *Oudkempische volksliederen en dansen* [Old Campines Folk Songs and Dances] by Theophiel Peeters (1883–1949). The musically trained Peeters, son of a verger-*cum*-organist, traversed the Antwerp Campines on his bicycle between 1899 and 1910 in an attempt to track down traces of ancient popular musical culture.[4] According to direct testimonies, he had a particular musical ear and had some of his contributors repeat songs once or twice to ensure he had correctly understood both text and melody. Musicological research of the melodies has ascertained that Peeters recorded some ancient examples. Hubert Boone is consequently convinced that the Peeters collection contains exceptional pieces of popular musical culture and, moreover, includes numerous examples of the influence of liturgical modes on our popular musical patrimony (Boone 1998).

Volume five of the reprints contains four collections of *Oudkempische volksliederen en dansen* as they were posthumously published in 1952 by Jozef Nuyts for the Committee for Old Folk Songs. In all, the four collections contain 47 religious songs, 33 love songs, and 63 occasional songs, or a total of 143 songs with a wide variety of content. To this must be added thirty-one dances, described in some detail as regards style, attributes, and circumstance. As such, the collection constitutes a unique and rich sampling of the popular musical culture in the Campines, a region of distinctive cultural/historical development.

The scholarly relevance and musical quality of the five collections published so far are beyond any doubt. The oldest one (Willems-Snellaert) most accords with a nineteenth-century view of the editing of old songs, which usually do not deserve the name "folk songs." Willems and Snellaert borrowed greatly from the old Dutch and Flemish songbooks on the one hand, yet at the same time showed some interest in the song as sung. Their collection is a first step toward preserving the sort of living song material that later came to us in great numbers through the likes of Lootens-Feys, Bols, Lambrechts, and Peeters. These collectors were among the first to open their ears to the people of their native areas. Each in his own way annotated and documented his material with musical notation, giving Flanders an interesting, varied, historical, and authentic collection of musical sources.

It is all the more remarkable, therefore, that Flemish folk musicians have not greeted the reprints with great enthusiasm, despite their reasonable cost (•20–25). This has been an unpleasant surprise for the publishers, one which has prompted a number of questions: Do our modern folk musicians have no need for the material because they do not know how to handle it in a contemporary way? Are the themes of the songs obsolete or outdated? Do traditional musical qualities no longer appeal to contemporary musicians, who may be more interested in international melodies? Who can say? Whatever the answers to these questions, the reprints are a great success in academic terms, and the series continues. 2005 will see a reprint of the *Iepersch Oud-Liedbook* [Ypres Book of Old Songs], and others are in the planning stages. Academia does have its rights.

## Notes

1. It seems that these texts never have been sung. They were poems written by Hoffmann von Fallersleben, but Snellaert thought they were real songs and therefore included them in the collection.
2. I would like to thank Isabelle Peere, who has commenced a thorough study of this remarkable collection (see her contribution to this volume), and who will continue and expand this research.
3. After many disappointing attempts, Lambrechts had to concede that full publication would not be forthcoming in the foreseeable future. Even contact with Dr. Johannes Koepp, who in 1928 had published *Untersuchungen über das Antwerpener Liedbuch vom Jahre 1544* [Enquiries into the 1544 Antwerp Songbook] and who was obviously interested in Flemish song material, failed to lead to publication. See Nygard 1958 for a full treatment of "Heer Halewijn."
4. The bicycle appears to have been an essential tool to early song collectors. Consider Gavin Greig in the Northeast of Scotland in the early twentieth century (Smith 1957; ed.).

## References

Boone, Hubert. 1998. "De modale melodieën in de notaties van Theophiel Peeters" [The Modal Melodies in the Notations of Theophiel Peeters]. In *Oudkempische volksliederen en dansen* [Old Campines Folk Songs and Dances], edited by Theophiel Peeters, i–iv. Old Flemish Songbooks Reprints, vol. 5. Antwerp: K. C. Peeters-Instituut voor Volkskunde.

Nygard, H. O. 1958. *The Ballad of Heer Halewijn*. Knoxville: University of Tennessee Press.

Smith, G. E. Ley. 1957. "He Tracked Down Bothy Ballads on his Bike." *Aberdeen Press and Journal*. 28 March 1957.

Stalpaert, Hervé. 1946. "Uit de geschiedenis der Vlaamsche volkskunde. Adolf Richard Lootens (Brugge 1835–Londen 1902)" [From the History of Flemish Ethnology: Adolf Richard Lootens (Bruges 1835–London 1902]. *Volkskunde* 47, no. 1: 1–21.

Top, Stefaan. 1995. "Chants populaires Flamands de France (1856): A Contribution to Comparative Folksong Research, France/Belgium: Flanders." In *Ballads and Boundaries: Narrative Singing in an Intercultural Context,* edited by James Porter, with Ellen Sinatra, 315–24. Proceedings of the 23rd International Ballad Conference of the Commission for Folk Poetry (Société Internationale d'Ethnologie et de Folklore). Los Angeles: Department of Ethnomusicology and Systematic Musicology.

———. 1996. "The publication of Jan Frans Willems's *Oude Vlaemsche Liederen* (1848): An Expression of Flemish Nationalism?" In *Visions and Identities*, edited by Eyðun Andreassen, 9–17. Proceedings of the 24th International Ballad Conference of the Kommission für Volksdichtung (Société Internationale d'Ethnologie et de Folklore), Tórshavn, 26–30 June 1994. Annales Societatis Scientiarium Faeroensis Supplementum, no. 22. Tórshavn: Tungulist.

## Reprints in the Series

*Oude Vlaemsche Liederen* [Old Flemish Songs]. 1989. Edited by J. Fr. Willems, Ghent, 1848, with added postscript and indexes by Stefaan Top. (Herdrukken oude Vlaamse liedboeken, deel i.) Antwerp: K. C. Peeters-Instituut voor Volkskunde.

*Chants Populaires flamands avec les airs notés et poésies populaires diverses receuillis à Bruges* [Flemish Folksongs with Tunes and Other Folk Poems Collected in Bruges]. 1990. Collected and edited by Ad.-R. Lootens et J. M. E. Feys, Bruges, 1879, with added postscript and indexes by Stefaan Top. (Herdrukken oude Vlaamse liedboeken, deel ii.) Antwerp: K. C. Peeters-Instituut voor Volkskunde.

*Honderd Oude Vlaamsche Liederen* [One Hundred Old Flemish Songs]. 1992. Collected with words and tunes and brought into the light for the first time by Jan Bols, Namur, 1897, with added postscript and indexes by Stefaan Top. (Herdrukken oude Vlaamse liedboeken, deel iii.) Antwerp: K. C. Peeters-Instituut voor Volkskunde.

*Limburgsche Liederen* [Songs from Limburg]. 1995. Collected by Lambrecht Lambrechts; part one, 1936; part two, 1937; with added postscript and indexes by Stefaan Top. (Herdrukken oude Vlaamse liedboeken, deel iv.) Antwerp: K. C. Peeters-Instituut voor Volkskunde.

*Oudkempische volksliederen en dansen* [Old Campines Folk Songs and Dances]. 1998. Collected by Theophiel Peeters, four parts, 1952, with an introductory essay by H. Boone, "The Modal Melodies in the Notations of Theophiel Peeters" and postscript and indexes by Stefaan Top). (Herdrukken oude Vlaamse liedboeken, deel v.) Antwerp: K. C. Peeters-Instituut voor Volkskunde.

All page references in the text are to the reprint editions.

# *Chants Populaires Flamands* (1879):
# A Scholarly Field Collection
# and an Early Individual Repertoire

Isabelle Peere

The research project introduced here deals with performance and repertoire. While this prominent concern in modern ballad and folk-song research de facto mostly relates to synchronic tradition, personal fieldwork, and knowledge of the singer's background and personality, the Flemish repertoire described here was transcribed from the lips of a middle-class lady born in 1795 in Bruges, Belgium. Hardly more is known about her apart from the fact that she acquired most of her songs and recitations at an early age from her parents and in lacemaking school.

This rich and diversified material, published as Ad.-R. Lootens's and J. M. E. Feys's *Chants Populaires flamands avec les airs notés et poésies populaires diverses recueillis à Bruges* [Flemish Folksongs with Tunes and Other Folk Poems Collected in Bruges],[1] in 1879, is the earliest recorded individual repertoire of Flemish traditional songs, while, as an early published collection, it demonstrates remarkable insight and scholarship. All textual transcriptions of songs are accompanied by their tunes and references to Flemish and other sources, along with occasional comments on editing and performance context or style. Because of this, the *Chants Populaires flamands* provides a rare opportunity for diachronic repertoire study. Taking my lead from David Buchan's study of "Performance Contexts in Historical Perspectives" (1985) and existing ethnographic sources, I hope in future to throw light on the bygone, centuries-old, singing and lacemaking tradition of Bruges, interpreting these sung testimonies in the light of cultural and individual worldviews. Preliminary to that interpretive analysis, this essay examines the published collection and its background in an attempt to document the material at hand.

Hervé Stalpaert's devoted work on Adolphe Lootens's contribution to folklore research (1946) provides us with the only known biographical details on the major collector of *Chants Populaires flamands*. Moreover, critical study is hampered by the loss of all of Lootens's manuscripts and correspondence (Stalpaert 1946: 8), a fact which only partly accounts for the sparse attention given to his largely unknown work (Stalpaert 1979: 183).[2] Given the lack of all other primary sources, the ten-page "avant-propos" of *Chants Populaires flamands* is the collectors' only surviving testimony about their own work. It contains some clues about the genesis of the collection, the singer's background and profile, the acquisition of her repertoire, the diversified nature of the collected material, the place of singing in lacemaking, as well as some information on the collectors' editing philosophy and purpose. Yet, amid this careful information, it is surprising to find nothing on their collaboration and respective contributions.

The full title of the book leads one to believe that Lootens and Feys worked as a collecting duo, an assumption that the first-person plural in the avant-propos only reinforces. Stalpaert, however, suggests that the two men contributed in very different ways. Taking a clue from their previous collaboration on an edition of collected narratives, followed by Feys's essay on the particularities of the local dialect (Lootens [1868] 1939), Stalpaert comments that Feys's contribution probably focused on giving advice and methodological guidance on accounting, in scholarly fashion, for the linguistic variants in Lootens's native idiom (Stalpaert 1946: 15). The suggestion sounds logical enough: Feys, a teacher of Latin rhetoric at the Athénée Royal de Bruges, was a Frenchman by birth and hence was hardly apt (even as a philologist) to provide more than general linguistic comments on a language that he understood only with difficulty and hardly spoke at all (Stalpaert 1946: 9). On the same grounds, the critic implies that it was Lootens—mostly if not only—who collected and transcribed the material in the folk-song collection: Not only was he a native of Bruges but his occupation as a land surveyor would have allowed him the opportunity and leisure to devote himself to his collecting hobby (Stalpaert 1946: 5), as his regular contributions to *Rond den Heerd* suggest.[3]

Recently acquired information tempts me to qualify the basic assumption about Feys's poor knowledge of the vernacular. His family name not only has a Flemish sound and is known in Bruges but is also connected with a local Beyaert family, possibly related to Lootens's mother.[4] If so, Lootens and Feys could even have been cousins. In addition to revealing relevant details of his life and career in Bruges, the philologist's obituary suggests that his special attachment to the city, its heritage, and traditions could have a deeper basis:

> M. Feys était d'origine française. Il était né en Lorraine. Néanmoins,
> il s'intéressa toujours avec une prédilection marquée à l'histoire de
> la Flandre, et il ne négligea aucune occasion de rehausser le lustre
> du pays flamand et même de faire résonner la note patriotique, en
> célébrant les fastes historiques de notre vieille Flandre. Sous ce

rapport, on pourrait dire qu'il avait conservé une âme française, chaude et vibrante, tout en reportant sur sa patrie d'élection ses élans et ses enthousiasmes, restés presque juvéniles jusque sous les glaces de l'âge.

A la cité de Bruges aussi, il avait voué une affection toute particulière. Il aimait ses monuments, ses traditions, son histoire. N'est-ce pas lui, qui de concert avec M. Adolphe Lootens, a colligé et édité avec un soin pieux les vieilles chansons flamandes, directement recueillies, en grande partie, des dentellières brugeoises?

[M. Feys was of French origin. He was born in Lorraine. Nevertheless, he always showed a keen interest in the history of Flanders and missed no opportunity to pay homage to the Flemish country, or even celebrate the pageantry of our ancient Flanders like a patriot. On this point, one could say that, despite his warm and vibrant French nature, he never abandoned his youthful enthusiam and affection for his chosen land.

The city of Bruges he held particularly close to his heart. He loved her monuments, traditions, and history. Did he not indeed, together with M. Adolphe Lootens, in the most exact manner, gather and edit the old Flemish songs, taken down, for the most part, from the lips of the Bruges lacemakers?][5] (*Annales* 1906: 334–36)

Whether or not Feys was related to Lootens, our present data only allows us to suppose with Stalpaert that *Chants Populaires flamands* probably originated in Lootens's personal experience:

Le recueil que nous donnons aujourd'hui, a été commencé par nous il y a plus de vingt-cinq ans, sans aucune intention de le livrer à la publicité. Notre unique désir était de conserver des souvenirs de famille, de maintenir intactes les mélodies, les paroles qui avaient bercé notre enfance et charmé notre jeunesse. La collection, formée d'abord de quelques feuilles volantes, s'est accrue insensiblement. Dans la suite, le désir de la compléter nous a poussés à réunir tout ce qui était à notre portée, et alors seulement, sur les instances de plusieurs personnes compétentes, nous avons songé à l'impression. [The present collection was started more than twenty-five years ago, and with no intention to publicize it. We were merely

concerned to archive family memories, to preserve the tunes and
words which had rocked our childhood and delighted our youth.
The collection, consisting first of a few loose sheets, grew insensi-
bly. Further on, we set out to gather whatever lay at hand so as to
complete it, and then only, the advice of several knowledgeable
persons inspired us with the idea of publishing it.]

(Lootens and Feys [1879] 1990: iii)

If Lootens was the initial and major collector and transcriber of the contents,
Feys at least would have been an ideal editor. In addition to his shared interest in
local tradition, the philologist and teacher already had publications to his name
and was an effective member of the scholarly Société d'Emulation de Bruges.[6]
Incidentally, Feys, because he was fifteen years older, may have acted as a
mentor to Lootens and been the first among the "knowledgeable persons" who
encouraged him to publish his collected material.

Lootens's fond childhood memories account for the highly original quality of
the collection; its material, practically entirely, originates from a single source:

Les pièces qui composent ce volume nous ont été transmises
presque en totalité par une seule personne. Elles forment ce qu'on
pourrait appeler le répertoire d'une dame de la bonne bourgeoisie de
Bruges. Cette dame d'une intelligence remarquable, douée d'une
excellente mémoire, possédant le sentiment de la mélodie et du
rhythme [sic], avec un goût prononcé pour les chansons, a su
retenir à peu près tout ce qu'elle a entendu. Née à Bruges en 1795
de parents brugeois, elle a conservé dans son souvenir tous les
morceaux que, dans son enfance, chantaient son père et sa mère, et
ceux qui étaient sans cesse répétés dans les écoles dentellières.
[The pieces composing this volume have come to us from almost a
single source. They make up what one might call the repertoire of a
lady of the well-mannered Bruges middle-class. This lady, gifted
with a remarkable intelligence and an outstanding memory, along
with a sense of melody and rhythm, and a special taste for songs,
managed to remember practically everything she heard. Born of
Bruges parents in 1795, she had kept in her memory all the pieces
that her father and mother sang to her in her early years, as well as
those which were repeated on and on in the lacemakers' schools.]

(Lootens and Feys [1879] 1990: iii–iv)

Such a bearer of oral songs evokes Anna Gordon, Mrs. Brown of Falkland; like one of the best-known early sources for Scottish balladry, "the lady from Bruges" was not a public performer or recognized singer but someone who, through her own inclination and natural abilities, assimilated songs as part of her life experience as an educated middle-class town resident.[7]

There is likely more to this particular lady, recorded "live," than what the avant-propos reveals. Stalpaert's interview with a descendant of Lootens's convinced him that the unnamed lady, whose songs Lootens lovingly associated with his early years, was his own mother, Catherine Beyaert. As well as the birth year and family origin, Stalpaert found a similarity between the descriptions of Lootens's mother by her own family and the song source's portrait. At any rate, we can deduce that the woman was fifty-four when the nineteen-year-old Lootens, the eighth child of his family, started noting down her songs, which nicely fits with Stalpaert's suggestion of a direct affiliation between them (Stalpaert 1946: 4).[8]

Apart from her identity, the avant-propos at least throws light on the circumstances in which this middle-class lady acquired laceworkers' songs and recitations. This clue comes linked with valuable information on the working context in which singing accompanied lacemaking:

> Suivant des renseignements dignes de foi, on ne connaissait pas à Bruges en 1730, pas plus qu'il y a soixante ans, les écoles gardiennes, <u>kinder, speel ou bewaarscholen</u>. Les jeunes enfants des deux sexes étaient envoyés aux écoles ou ouvroirs de filles. Là, dans les vastes salles, ils occupaient la place laissée libre derrière les travailleuses, d'où on leur donnait le nom caractéristique de <u>achterzitters</u> (assis par derrière). La monotonie des occupations auxquelles se livraient les ouvrières, était rompue par la prière, L'enseignement de la doctrine chrétienne et le chant. Il y avait en outre, soir et matin, une heure de silence pendant laquelle on apprenait aux plus jeunes les prières, l'alphabet et plus ou moins la lecture.

> [There is trustworthy information to suggest that there were still no nursery schools in Bruges in 1750 or, indeed, until sixty years later. Both male and female infants were sent to schools or girls' workshops. There, in spacious halls, they would sit in the space left free behind the workers, hence their name as <u>achterzitters</u> (those sitting at the back). The monotony of the workers' activities was interspersed with prayer, Christian teaching and singing. Every morning

and evening, there was also an hour of silence set for teaching the younger ones prayers, the alphabet, and some reading.]

(Lootens and Feys [1879] 1990: vi–vii)

This intriguing comment follows: "Les enfants des classes aisées étaient aussi envoyés à ces écoles; à l'époque où nous parlons, les filles en général apprenaient volontairement un métier" [The better-off children were also sent to these schools; at the time we speak of, the girls would mostly and willingly learn a trade] (Lootens and Feys [1879] 1990: vii). We should be grateful for this information because neither historical nor ethnographic research about lacemaking in Flanders has taken any notice of the "social mix" in lacemaking schools in the lady's early years. The author, unfortunately, only goes on to explain:

> Quand à la fille de l'artisan, parvenue à l'âge de six ou sept ans, elle s'engageait à travailler pendant cinq ans, terme nécessaire à l'apprentissage d'un métier, pour le compte de la maîtresse de l'ouvroir. Souvent elle prolongeait son séjour à l'école jusqu'à sa quinzième ou sa seizième année. Après avoir entendu chanter pendant trois ou quatre ans, matin et soir, les mêmes morceaux, elle les chantait elle-même, sous la surveillance jalouse d'ouvrières plus âgées qui n'auraient pas souffert la plus légère altération dans le débit.
>
> [As to the craftsman's daughter, once aged six or seven, she would commit herself to working for five years, which was the time deemed necessary to learn a trade for the workshop's mistress. Yet, she would often stay on at school until the age of fifteen or sixteen. After hearing the same pieces, morning and evening, she sang them herself, under the careful supervision of elder workers, who would never have allowed the least alteration to the pace.]

(Lootens and Feys [1879] 1990: vii)

This strict watch imposed on the work, as on the singing or reciting which accompanied it, is the only explanation given by the author for the persistence of certain bizarre rhymed pieces lacking any apparent narrative coherence. Such pieces, in his estimation, went back to 1730 in an uninterrupted tradition without appreciable change. These so-called *tellingen*, in the specific sense,[9] come close to the English lacemakers' "tells" and fit Gerald Porter's description of them as "counting rhymes used in tallying the goldheaded pins used to fasten lace" (1994: 44).[10]

The corpus of *Chants Populaires flamands* essentially consists of songs the lady learned in childhood. Given her excellent memory, Lootens and Feys claim to present these songs as they were sung in 1750, before her own time ([1879] 1990: iv). She acquired a few more songs later, but these she also learned in her native town and they are easily recognizable as more recent. To her own repertoire, which constitutes the basis of the collection, a few songs were added. Though collected elsewhere, usually from elderly people, these also belong to the singing tradition of Bruges. *Chants Populaires flamands* thus amounts to a corpus of 161 songs and 21 various recited pieces, presented as "le répertoire d'une dame de la bonne bourgeoisie de Bruges" [the repertoire of an upper middle-class lady from Bruges] (Lootens and Feys [1879] 1990: iii).

While we would have been as happy—if not happier—with an accurate collection of only this lady's repertoire, one must acknowledge Lootens's and Feys's scientific intent to pass on a sociohistorical document that was as complete, representative, and rigorously defined as possible. In his effort to present not just an individual but the typical repertoire of an upper middle-class lady from about 1750 to 1850, the collector clearly was no longer engaging in a mere hobby motivated by nostalgia. He intended nothing less than to record an old and fast-disappearing oral tradition.

The appeal had come from the international authority, Edmond de Coussemaker,[11] a historian and pioneer field collector, who conceived that popular song had particular value as a unique testimony of a people's ideas and feelings (Top 1995: 319). What he had demonstrated about French Flanders motivated Lootens to contribute the fullest and most reliable evidence about his own prestigious medieval town. Though committed to preserving threatened Flemish culture, like de Coussemaker, Lootens was no more moved by romantic or nationalistic feeling than his contemporary:

> La ville de Bruges ne pouvait manquer d'apporter sa pierre à cette
> reconstitution du passé; elle devait fournir sa part de vieilles
> poésies et de vieux chants, et tel est le contenu du présent volume.
> En le publiant, l'intention des éditeurs n'est pas de procurer un
> passe-temps plus ou moins agréable aux gens désoeuvrés, encore
> moins d'offrir à l'admiration de petits chefs d'œuvre de la vieille
> muse flamande; leur but est purement scientifique et archéologique,
> et c'est à ce titre principalement que l'ouvrage a été accepté par la
> <u>Société d'Emulation de Bruges</u>, toujours disposée à encourager les
> publications de nature à jeter du jour sur l'histoire nationale.

[The city of Bruges could not but contribute her share to this
reconstruction of the past; she had to provide her part of ancient
poetry and song, hence the contents of the present volume. Its
publication intends neither to provide leisure to the idle, nor even
less to inspire admiration for the little wonders of the old Flemish
muse's imagination; the editors' ambition is solely scientific and
archeological, which accounts for the work's acknowledment by the
Société d'Emulation de Bruges, [which is] always willing to encourage publications likely to shed light on national history.]

(Lootens and Feys [1879] 1990: ii)

They thus explain the diverse makeup and barely edited form of this material
and alert us to sometimes rough, frivolous, worn out, fragmented or apparently
insignificant pieces. Regardless of any literary, aesthetic, or other concerns about
tampering with historical evidence, they claim,

Nous avons accueilli à peu près tout ce qui s'est présenté, de même
que dans les musées d'antiquités, on ne recueille pas seulement les
œuvres réellement belles, mais encore les figures grimaçantes et les
types grotesques.
[We have welcomed practically everything that came our way, just
as museums of antiquities do not just exhibit really beautiful pieces
but also grimacing figures and grotesque types.]

(Lootens and Feys [1879] 1990: ii)

Certainly, whereas most of the collected material originates from a single
person, the songs alone outnumber those which de Coussemaker collected from
fishermen and sailors in Sunday schools and lacemaking circles (Top 1995: 320).
Furthermore, although Lootens and Feys meant to present their city's old songs
and poems, the international ballad material represents neither the largest nor the
most prominent song category. The largest subgenre consists of children's songs,
which make up a good third of this corpus. In second place is a mixed category of
comic, satirical, and love songs. A third group brings together *noëls et cantiques*,
"carols and hymns." The narrative songs, sagas, ballads, and legends are the
next largest, and a last group consists of mystical and moral songs.

In a unique feature for their time, Lootens-Feys offers, in addition to songs,
various rhymed pieces derived from the choral singing of lacemakers, generically
referred to as *tellingen,* apart from the specific counting recitations already

mentioned. They also tell us that their curious mix of the various song fragments (some including odd references to ancient beliefs and practices) have been appended to the song material at the request of several scholars (Lootens and Feys [1879] 1990: viii).

The book edition of *Chants Populaires flamands*, it appears, enjoyed a unanimously warm reception. One must, however, interpret local Flemish literary reviews of this edition of Flemish songs in the context of Flanders's despised vernacular culture and language.[12] Thus, it comes as no surprise to find the work acclaimed in *Rond den Heerd*, which was already promoting Flemish language and tradition. The paper first heralded, then praised, the book, as well as proudly reproducing two eminent reviews from Holland (*Rond den Heerd* 1877–78: 161–62, 353–54). In Bruges, the first edition of songs collected from local oral tradition was acclaimed for its relevance to Flemish literary history and ethnology but also the appeal of its original, yet so familiar-sounding contents. *Chants Populaires flamands* thus created an "évènement" [*sic*] in local literary circles, where it was greeted as "a mirror of a period…reflecting the life and struggle of a whole generation,…conjuring up a full range of memories—childhood's joys and pains, simple religious faith, scenes from Flemish family life and countless other evocations of the past" (de Flou 1879: 19). Adolf Duclos, then editor of the paper, went so far as to call the collection "the most interesting work of Flemish literature to have appeared in a long time" (*Rond der Heerd* 1877–78: 72).[13]

To assess the local reception of *Chants Populaires flamands* more realistically, it is fair to cite the contemporary French folk-song collector, de Puymaigre, on the significance of Lootens's and Feys's achievement. The opening paragraph of his essay devoted to "Chants Flamands" praises their work while regretting overall ignorance of it in France, owing to limited access to Flemish:

> Il a paru à Bruges, en 1879, un recueil de chants populaires qui eût davantage excité l'attention si au texte MM. Adolphe Lootens et E. Feys eussent joint une traduction, comme M. de Coussemaker l'a fait dans un volume du même genre. Le flamand est un dialecte accessible à peu de lecteurs, et il est évident qu'avec notre mince érudition philologique, la publication de MM. Lootens et Feys devait rester en France à peu près inconnue. Elle mérite pourtant de prendre place à côté de nombreux volumes analogues que depuis quelque temps on a édités sur divers points.
> [There came out in Bruges, in 1879, a volume of popular songs which would have caught much greater attention, had MM.

Adolphe Lootens and E. Feys accompanied its contents with a
translation, as indeed was the case of a volume of a similar nature
by M. de Coussemaker. But few readers will have access to the
Flemish dialect, and given our scant philological knowledge, it is no
surprise that MM. Lootens and Feys would remain mostly ignored
in France. This, nevertheless, deserves to take a place among
numerous like volumes now available on a variety of subjects.]

(de Puymaigre 1885: 108)

The scholarly editing of Lootens's and Feys's authentic materials further
recommends their analysis. On the one hand, the genesis of *Chants Populaires
flamands* evokes the "domestic and almost pious" origin of the *Barzaz Breiz* (la
Villemarqué 1963: iv). As with the Breton pioneer collector, Lootens's interest in
popular tradition sprang from firsthand experience of his native lore. Like him
also, Lootens belonged to an educated and bilingual social elite and had been
committed since postadolescence to testifying to a native tradition which had
been relegated to a folk culture. Yet, apart from these similarities, there is evidence that Lootens and Feys, contrary to la Villemarqué, let no aesthetic or
literary influences interfere with either collecting or editing.

Lootens had demonstrated scientific rigor in his fieldwork and editing prior
to publishing *Chants populaires Flamands*. In his contributions to *Rond den
Heerd*, he insisted on reproducing not just the words but the sounds of oral
tradition exactly as he had heard them pronounced in local speech, contrary to
the views of his folklore-conscious yet literary-minded editor (Stalpaert 1968b:
204). His loyalty to the local idiom found full expression in his *Oude
Kindervertelsels uit den Brugschen tongval* [Old Narratives for Children in the
Bruges Dialect] (1868), a booklet of nine prose narratives, which, as he writes in
the preface, he printed this way: "Wij hebben deze vertelsels doen drukken zoo
als eene nauwkeurige overlevering dezelve in verscheidene huisgezinnen heeft
bewaard, zonder één woord in den tekst te veranderen, zonder ééne letter bij te
voegen of weg te laten" [We had these narratives printed exactly as one precise
transmission had preserved them identically in various households, without
changing a single word in the text, without either adding or removing a single
letter] (Lootens [1868]: 6–7).

Ironically, whereas folklore editing of the time mostly implied filtering "crude"
field data, what it meant for this early ethnographer of speech was recapturing
the live dimension of oral tradition on the page. The result looks amazing—
narratives are transcribed in an original phonetic spelling of his own creation.

The transcripts are accompanied by footnote explanations for the non-Bruges, native Flemish speaker and followed by a separate essay by J. M. E. Feys accounting for all grammatical, phonetic, and lexical variants. This modest-appearing publication resolutely sought to serve folklore study rather than attract fame or gain; its subsequent translation and full publication in the *Germania* journal the following year speaks for its scholarly quality.[14]

As Lootens treated the sounds of speech, so also did he respect the tunes of songs. We learn from Stalpaert that his love of song went hand-in-hand with that of music and he also played the cello.[15] No wonder, then, that we read in the avant-propos,

> Les airs ont été notés sous la dictée, et reproduits, comme les
> paroles, avec la plus rigoureuse fidélité. Rien n'a été ni arrangé, ni
> refait, d'après d'autres publications.
> [The tunes have been noted down from dictation and, like the texts,
> transcribed with the utmost accuracy. Nothing was either arranged
> or modified with reference to other publications.]
>
> (Lootens and Feys [1879] 1990: v)

Lootens's and Feys's *Chants Populaires flamands* was first published as the *Annales de la Société d'Emulation pour l'Etude de l'Histoire et des Antiquités de la Flandre* (1878) and as a separate book the following year. How, then, did this field collection of popular songs and poems attract the attention of the eminent society devoted to historical research? To start with, the Bruges-based national society kept contacts and exchanged annals with several other scholarly institutions, both at home and abroad (Top 1990: I). One of these was the Comité des Flamands de France [Committee of the Flemish People of France], founded by de Coussemaker in 1853 to research the history and testify to the presence of Flemish language and culture in France (Top 1995: 317–18).

The Société's minutes and correspondence further reveal that its Comité-Directeur [Executive Committee] prided itself upon the posthumous publication of an important study by that French historian.[16] Why then would they think any less of his groundbreaking folk-song collection, which attested to the source value of songs for historical study? That gives us reason to think that the Société was pleased with the chance to publish a like collection of songs from native soil (Top 1990: II) and that de Coussemaker's *Chants Populaires des Flamands de France* provided the model for Lootens's and Feys's collection, so much so, apparently, that it loaned the latter book most of its title and song categories.

The records of the Société reveal some persistent though unspecified difficulties, responsible apparently for a significant delay in publishing the Bruges
collection. At the same time, this evidence throws some light on the two authors'
respective contributions: Lootens, referred to as "l'auteur," first submitted his
manuscript in 1876. The following record, dated January 1877, reads,

> Mr Le chanoine Vandeputte [*sic*] fait le rapport sur le manuscrit des
> <u>anciennes chansons populaires flamandes</u>, présentées par Mr
> Lootens. Après une discussion à laquelle prennent part plusieurs
> membres, le comité décide d'imprimer ce travail dans ses annales
> pour l'année 1878: l'auteur sera prié d'enrichir son travail de notes
> et d'une introduction faisant connaître les publications du même
> genre faites jusqu'à ce jour, à l'étranger.
> [Canon Vandeputte reports on the manuscript containing old
> Flemish popular songs, presented by Mr. Lootens. Following a
> discussion between several members, the committee decides to
> print this work in its 1878 yearbook: The author will be requested to
> supplement notes and an introduction mentioning like works
> published abroad.] (*Soc. Pro.*: 43)

The next meeting unanimously elected Feys a member of the Société and
agreed to create "une sous-commission" [a subcommission] in charge of reexamining the manuscript:

> Puisque plusieurs membres du Comité-Directeur sont hors d'état
> d'assister régulièrement aux séances pour cause d'infirmités ou de
> changement de domicile, il est procédé à l'élection d'un quatorzième
> membre du Comité: Mr Feys, professeur de Rhétorique latine à
> l'Athénée de Bruges, est nommé à l'unanimité des membres
> présents. Sur la proposition de Mr Van de Putte [*sic*], le comité
> désigne une sous-commission composée de trois membres, à L'effet
> d'examiner de nouveau le manuscrit de Mr Lootens relatif aux
> anciennes chansons populaires flamandes, et de faire rapport de
> leur examen à la prochaine séance. Cette commission est composée
> de MM. Van de Putte [*sic*], Nelis et Verschelde.
> [Given that several members of the Executive Committee cannot
> attend sessions regularly for reasons of health or distance, an
> election is held for the appointment of a fourteenth committee

member: Mr. Feys, professor of Latin rhetoric at the Athénée de
Bruges, is unanimously elected by all attending members. On Mr.
Van de Putte's proposition, the committee designates a subcommis-
sion consisting of three members to the effect of reexamining Mr.
Lootens's manuscript relative to old Flemish popular songs and
report on their examination at the following session. This commission is composed of MM. Van de Putte, Nelis, and Verschelde.]

(*Soc. Pro.*: 45)

It is now January 1878, the year Lootens's book is due to come out, and the
Comité yet again nominates *une sous-commission,* this time including Feys among
its members:

> Le Comité nomme de nouveau une sous-commission composée de
> MM Feys, Ronde, Nelis et Verschelde, à l'effet avant-propos de
> revoir encore le manuscript des anciennes chansons populaires
> flamandes, présenté par Mr. Lootens, et d'en soigner l'impression
> au mieux des intérêts de la Société, et par les presses de la société
> de S. Augustin établie à Scheepsdaele.
> [The Committee reappoints a subcommission composed of MM
> Feys, Ronde, Nelis, and Verschelde to revise once again the
> manuscript of old Flemish popular songs, submitted by Mr Lootens,
> print it with care to befit the Société's best interest, and do so on
> the press of the Société de S. Augustin, established in
> Scheepsdaele.] (*Soc. Pro.*: 45)

In July of the same year, Feys's leading role within this commission at last
becomes explicit *and* effective:

> Mr. Feys soumet aux membres quelques feuilles imprimées de
> l'ouvrage sur les "Chants populaires de Bruges" qui est en cours
> d'impression dans l'Etablissement de St. Augustin, récemment
> fondé à Scheepsdale-lez-Bruges. L'impression de ces feuilles est
> très soignée et l'ensemble de l'ouvrage promet d'être un vrai chef-
> d'œuvre de typographie.
> [Mr. Feys submits a few printed sheets of the "Chants populaires de
> Bruges," which is with the printers of the Société de S. Augustin,
> recently established at Scheepsdale-lez-Bruges. Their printing is of

the greatest quality and the whole work promises to be a real typographical masterpiece.] (*Soc. Pro.*: 46)

The recurrent references to "le manuscrit présenté par Mr. Lootens" [the manuscript submitted by Mr. Lootens] up until 1877 (*Soc. Pro.*: 44), and the absence of any mention of Feys until the publishing stage, support the view that Lootens collected the material. If so, apart from "les instances de plusieurs personnes compétentes" [the advice of several knowledgeable persons] (Lootens and Feys [1879] 1990: ii) who recommended publication, the Société's consideration of the manuscript is also to Lootens's credit. Yet what about his manuscript's successive reexaminations? If, as it appears, its version only consisted of the textual and musical transcripts of the corpus, what did the Comité find unsatisfying, or still lacking, the second and third times? Was it not up to the Société's editing standards or de Coussemaker's model?

There are two additional clues, which in light of Lootens's personality and his conception and editing of folk materials, reveal more. The first is an arresting comment in the "Notes et Additions" appended to the published collection, referring to the "Halewijn" song, considered "the jewel of Middle Dutch literature" (Top 1993: 105). In this note, Lootens expresses regret that neither Willems nor even de Coussemaker printed their collected versions of the well-known song type as obtained from the singers, which might have helped reconstruct his own fragmented text. While reaffirming his uncompromising respect for folk materials as obtained from oral tradition, Lootens's comment also reveals a critical distance from his predecessors, de Coussemaker included. One even suspects a less-than-innocent parallel between de Coussemaker and J. F. Willems,[17] who saw no harm in rearranging texts (Top 1996: 15):

> Il est à regretter que Willems et de Coussemaker n'aient pas jugé à propos de donner cette pièce telle que le peuple l'a conservée; on serait sans aucun doute en possession de variantes remarquables, et les lacunes qui existent dans notre version, n'eussent pas manqué d'être comblées.
>
> [It is to be regretted that Willems and de Coussemaker did not judge it appropriate to give us this piece as the folk had conserved it; we would, no doubt, have had remarkable variants, and the missing parts of our version, would surely have been filled.]
>
> (Lootens and Feys [1879] 1990: 295)

Even if this comment only agrees with the statements in the avant-propos about the exact reproduction of texts and music, *Chants Populaires flamands* nevertheless clearly differs from *Oude Kindervertelsels*. The song transcripts in the latter hardly reflect the sounds of local speech, and all accompanying notes to the songs and poems are in French. This leads to the second clue: The same critic who so enthusiastically commended the special appeal of the Lootens-Feys collection regretted the suppression of all dialect variants. He even referred to an instance where the substitution of the standard spelling clearly destroyed the original end rhyme (de Flou 1879: 20). This example reveals that Lootens's original (unfortunately lost) transcripts underwent some "purifying" editing yet unaccounted for.

From all of these arguments, the following hypotheses emerge. First, I suspect that Lootens's own views on the editing of his manuscript did not agree with the Société's. The diverging views of the field collector and scientific folklorist on the one hand and his "distinguished," scholarly, yet also less folklore-aware, publisher on the other may have been the cause of the successive reexaminations. Would not the unyielding ethnographer of speech have insisted on the faithful rendering of the local dialect in song as in his narrative transcripts? Or did the earlier contributor to the Flemish culture-conscious *Rond den Heerd*, here as in his previous publications, use Flemish through and through?

Another hypothesis: If Lootens's firsthand experience of folk tradition and fine musical ear produced the best understanding and notation of songs, was the land surveyor as much a scholarly annotator, apt editor[18] and French writer? In either case, Feys eventually joining the *sous-commission* provided a welcome mediator between Lootens's and the Société's concerns about the manuscript. Would not Feys, a French native speaker, an "expert" on the Bruges dialect, and now also an executive member of the Société, have come to the aid of his collaborator and friend (or relative) to see the collection through publication?

While this exploration leaves us with more questions than answers, it is a fact that Lootens's and Feys's *Chants Populaires flamands* includes data which is both remarkable and rarely available for diachronic singing tradition. Within Flemish song scholarship, the collection offers an early and unique source on individual repertoire and local oral tradition. In addition, Lootens and Feys's sizeable corpus of work songs and rhymes, recorded with valuable contextual information, should also be relevant to other regional and less-well-documented traditions, such as those of the English lacemakers. As a nineteenth-century work, the collection presents a rare combination of fieldwork and scientific folk-lore research. Lootens's holistic attention to song derives from his early, first-hand experience within his family; both his folk-song and narrative books connect with his childhood, his mother, and his hometown and its immediate surround-ings as the three dimensions of his folklore activity.

At the same time, if both his folklore contributions display unwavering schol-arship (Stalpaert 1972), it is certainly thanks to Feys, whose collaboration and guidance (at least closer than de Coussemaker's) allowed Lootens's interests and initiatives to reach scientific excellence. Had Lootens been allowed to follow his avant-garde concept of folklore editing in this "distinguished" publication as in his "less-distinguished" booklet of narratives, we might have had a testimony truer still to life, as well as a thoroughly modern folklore edition. In spite of this, credit must be given to the Société d'Emulation de Bruges, which, in publishing the Lootens-Feys collection, played a pioneering role in Flemish folklore study (Stalpaert 1972: 265).

Strikingly, Lootens's and Feys's scholarly edition of an extensive individual repertoire transcribed from oral and rigorously defined local tradition comes closer to our modern concept of folklore study than la Villemarqué's and even de Coussemaker's collections. So one wonders why, to this day, their names remain obscure in the scholarship, if they are remembered at all. If Feys's excellence was recognized in his own field of expertise, Lootens did not receive any official recognition at all. This was perhaps partly because he was not a formally edu-cated scholar attached to an institution.[19] For the rest, we must agree with de Puymaigre that the "veil of modesty" covering the duo from Bruges and their achievement must largely be due to the fact that their material was published without French translations. Should this be the reason for the limited recognition of the pioneering Flemish field collection, it is almost ironic to see its counterpart for Brittany, the *Barzaz-Breiz*, honored on the 150th anniversary of its first publi-cation with a monolingual edition in the regional vernacular, pruned from la Villemarqué's original French translations (see Kervarker 1988[20]).

From these introductory findings, I am confident that Ad.-R. Lootens's and J. M. E. Feys's unique record of the eighteenth- and nineteenth-century repertoire of "an upper middle-class lady from Bruges" can rewardingly be analyzed and interpreted.

## Notes

I dedicate this paper with thanks to Stefaan Top, who encouraged my study of this collection. I also thank Dr. A. Vandewalle, director of the Stadsarchief of Bruges, who kindly helped access archive sources.

1. The collection is cited among "titles of collections of ballads, or of books containing ballads" appended to Child 1882–98, 5: 456.

2. Stefaan Top expresses regret at the absence of any personal appreciation of Lootens and Feys in either Florimond Van Duyse's comprehensive canon of old Dutch and Flemish songs or Maurits Sabbe's monograph on the old West Flemish song repertoire (Top 1990: VIII). This essay is a humble, but enthusiastic, attempt to compensate for this neglect.

3. *Rond den Heerd: een leer-en leesblad voor alle lieden met prenten* [Around the Hearth: An Educational Reader for All with Illustrations] was founded by the Bruges-born poet/ priest Guido Gezelle and the art historian James Weale in 1865. The paper is discussed further in this article. A detailed account of Lootens's contributions to it and critical reviews of both his folk-song and narrative editions is appended to Stalpaert 1946: 20–21.

4. See Maes 1987; the article describes the printer and publisher Georges Beyaert, son of Eugčne Beyaert (b. Roeselćre 1810, d. Kortrijk 1879) and grandson of Louis Beyaert (b. Brugge 1784, d. Kortrijk 1851) and Sofia Joanna Feys. Ongoing research is investigating the connection, if any, with Lootens's mother, Catherine Beyaert (b. Brugge 1795, d. Brugge 1879); since she belonged to "a well-respected middle-class Bruges family" (Stalpaert 1946: 4), she could be Eugčne Beyaert's sister.

5. From Feys's obituary published in *Annales*. From this, and the entry under his name in *Bibliographie Nationale*, we gather that he was born in Rambervillers, France, in 1819 and naturalized in 1853. He must have come to Bruges at the start of his career, if not earlier, for he taught at the Athénée de Bruges for thirty years. He was appointed an effective member of the Société d'Emulation de Bruges in 1873 and elected vice-president in 1882, a position which he kept until 1902. He died in Bruges in 1906. Appended to these sources is a list of his publications.

6. The Société d'Emulation was founded in 1839; it is Belgium's earliest historical society and still exists under the name of Het Brugse Genootschap voor Geschiedenis [The Bruges History Association].

7. The allusion is to Mrs. Anna Brown of Falkland (1747–1810), a most important contributor in Anglo-Scottish balladry, whose songs were highly esteemed by F.J. Child.

8. Official records reveal that Catherine Beyaert died, aged eighty-four, in 1879, the year of the collection's first publication, another likely reason for withholding her identity.

9. The same word, *tellingen* in Flemish, is used both in a specific and generic sense, the former referring to a lacemaker's counting rhyme and the latter to all songs accompanying lacemaking.

10. The *tellingen* were similarly delivered in a monotonous tone, which supports Porter's suggestion of the Flemish origin of tells, along with English lacemaking itself (1994: 38).

11. The crucial influence of de Coussemaker's *Chants Populaires des Flamands de France* (1856) on Flemish folk-song collecting, editing, and study was previously examined by Stefaan Top (1995).

12. Flanders's mostly rural population spoke Flemish, a language which orally consisted essentially of a group of local dialects. The social and educated elite, on the other hand, was mostly bilingual, using Flemish in the private context of family and friends but French in the official circumstances of public life. Incidentally, *Chants Populaires flamands,* which uses French for its title, preface, and notes, in accordance with the standard practice of its distinguished editor, the Société d'Emulation de Bruges, is illustrative of this ambiguous rapport between the "high" and "low" cultures.

13. The two quotes are my own translation from Dutch. All translations, where not attributed, are mine.
14. Stalpaert 1968b: 204; 1972: 267; Liebrecht 1869: 84–96.
15. Most biographical details on Lootens come from a relative then living in Bruges. Thus, we learn that music ran in Lootens's family—aside from his mother's fondness and talent for it, a brother wrote a study on Gregorian chant, and still another was an organ maker. While he also mentions that Lootens's father was a shipbuilder (Stalpaert 1946: 4–5), in a population census, he is registered as a *facteur*, which at the time would most likely refer to a *facteur d'orgues* ("organ maker"). (Bevolkingsregister 1830–46: A6, 135).
16. *Soc. Reg.*: 81; the work is de Coussemaker 1876.
17. Frans Jans Willems (1793–1846) is responsible for *Oude Vlaemsche Liederen* (1848), which is the first edition of Flemish folk songs collected (largely from written sources) by a native folklorist.
18. The narratives of *Oude Kindervertelsels* were accompanied with lexical notes but no scholarly annotations. These have since been provided by Stalpaert (1968a: 275).
19. Whether Lootens pursued any folklore activity at all is generally ignored. He emigrated to London in 1884, married an Englishwoman, and still made yearly visits to his hometown ( between health treatments in Germany) until his death in 1902.
20. Kervarker is the Breton translation of [Th. Hersart de] la Villemarqué. The book referred to is a modern Breton edition of la Villemarqué 1963, originally published as *Barzas-Breiz* in 1839 (see Laurent 1988).

## References

*Annales de la Société d'Emulation de Bruges*. 1906. Vol. 56: 334–36.
*Bibliographie nationale*: *Dictionnaire des écrivains Belges et catalogue de leurs publications*, no. 45. 1892. Bruxelles: Weissenbruch.
Brugge-Bevolkingsregister, vol. A6: 135 1830–46. Brugge-Stadsarchief [Bruge Municipal Archive].
Buchan, David. 1985. "Performance Contexts in Historical Perspectives." *New York Folklore* 11: 61–78.
Child, Francis James, ed. 1882–98. *The English and Scottish Popular Ballads*. 5 vols. Reprint, New York: Folklore Press, 1956–57; New York: Dover, 1965. Corrected edition prepared by Mark and Laura Heiman. Northfield, Minn.: Loomis House Press, 2002. Digital edition, with gazetteer, maps and audio CD. New York: ESPB Publishing, 2003.
de Coussemaker, Edmond. 1855–56. *Chants populaires des flamands de France*. Gand: F. et E. Gyselynck.
———. 1876. *Troubles religieux du XVIè siècle dans la Flandre Maritime 1560–1570. Documents originaux*. Brugge: De Zuttere.
de Flou, Karel. 1879. "Letterkundig Overzicht." *De Halletoren* 3: 19–21.
de Puymaigre. 1885. "Chants Flamands." In *Folk-lore*, 108–21. Paris: Perrin.
"Een Vlaamsch boek in Holland beoordeeld." 1879. *De Halletoren* 5: 62–63.
Kervarker (Th. Hersart de la Villemarqué). 1988. *Barzhaz-Breizh*. Lesneven: Mouladurioù Hor Yezh (edition in modern Breton of la Villemarqué 1963, originally published in 1839 as *Barzas-Breiz*. See Laurent 1988).
la Villemarqué, Th. Hersart de. 1963. *Barzaz-Breiz: Chants populaires de la Bretagne*. 3rd ed. Paris: Perrin.
Laurent, Donatien. 1989. *Aux sources du Barzaz-Breiz: la mémoire d'un peuple*. Douarnenez: Armen.
Liebrecht, Felix. 1869. "Vlämische Märchen und Volkslieder." *Germania* 14: 84–96.
Lootens, Ad.-R. [1868] 1939. *Oude kindervertelsels in den Brugschen tongval. Met spraakkundige aanmerkingen over het brugschen taaleigen door M. E. F.* [Old Narratives for Children in the Dialect of Bruges with Linguistic Comments by M. E.

F.]. Reprint, Brugge: De Reyghere. (The reprint has illustrations by René Depauw but lacks the appended linguistic essay. Page references are to original edition.)

Lootens, Adolphe-R., et J. M. E. Feys. [1879] 1990. *Chants Populaires flamands avec les airs notés et poésies populaires diverses recueillis à Bruges* [Flemish Folksongs with Tunes and Other Folk Poems Collected in Bruges]. (Reedited in book form from *Annales de la Société d'Emulation pour l'Etude de l'Histoire et des Antiquités de la Flandre,* 4th ser. 2 [1878]: 1–309.) Reprint, Antwerpen: K. C. Peeters Instituut voor Volkskunde, with a postscript and indices by Stefaan Top (page references are to reprint edition).

Maes, P. 1987. "Drukker-Uitgever Georges Beyaert uit Kortrijk." *Biekorf* 87: 95–96.

Peere, Isabelle. 2000. "'Chants populaires flamands' (1879) als wetenschappelijke getuigenis van een vroege individuele repertoire: een voorstudie." *Volkskunde* 101: 367–82.

———. 2001. "Le répertoire d'une 'dame de la bonne bourgeoisie de Bruges' (1879): pièces *d'identités,* traces de *mentalités.*" In *Balada şi Studiile despra Balada la Cumpana dintre Secole* [Ballad and Ballad Studies at the Turn of the Century], edited by Nicolae Constantinescu, 175–86. Proceedings of the 30th International Ballad Conference—The Ballad Commission of SIEF, 15–20 August 2000, Bucharest, Romania. Bucureşti: Editura Deliana.

———. 2002. "Comptines de dentellières brugeoises (1750–1850): entre travail, école et jeu, colère et prière." Proceedings of the 31st International Ballad Conference—The Ballad Commission of SIEF, 21–23 April 2001, Budapest, Hungary. *Acta Ethnographica Hungarica* 47: 111–26.

Pickering, Michael. 1986. "Song and Social Context." In *Singer, Song and Scholar,* edited by Ian Russell, 73–93. Sheffield: Sheffield Academic Press.

Porter, Gerald. 1994. "'Work the Old Lady Out of the Ditch': Singing at Work by English Lacemakers." *Journal of Folklore Research* 31: 35–55.

*Rond den Heerd* 5 (1869–70); 8 (1872–73): 27; 12 (1876–77): 369–70; 13 (1877–78): 105–6; 14 (1877–78): 72, 90–92, 161–62, 245–46, 353–54; 18 (1882–83): 27–28, 141–42.

Sabbe, Maurits. 1920. *Wat Oud-Vlaanderen zong* [What Old Flanders Sang]. Antwerpen: S. V. Lectura.

*Société d'Emulation: Registre de correspondance.* Vol. 1 (13 January 1839 to 30 October 1879) (cited in the text as *Soc. Reg.*).

*Société d'Emulation: Procès verbaux de ses séances.* Vol. 2 (1868 to 1886) (cited in the text as *Soc. Pro.*).

Stalpaert, Hervé. 1946. "Uit de Geschiedenis der Vlaamsche Volkskunde: Adolf-Richard Lootens. Brugge 1835–1902." *Volkskunde* 47: 1–21.

———. 1968a. "Bij een honderdste verjaring: Lootens' Kindervertelsels." *Biekorf* 69: 273–75.

———. 1968b. "Een Eeuweling: Oude Brugse Kindervertelsels." *Volkskunde* 69: 203–4.

———. 1972. "Volkskunde." In *Panorama van Brugse Geschiedschrijving sedert Duclos (1910),* 263–301. Brugge: Gidsenbond van Brugge en West-Vlaanderen.

———. 1979. "Bij een eeuwfeest: Lootens-Feys' Liederenbundel 1879–1979: een onderzoek van de passieliederen." *Volkskunde* 80: 183–98.

Top, Stefaan. [1879] 1990. Foreword to *Chants populaires flamands,* by Adolphe Lootens and J. M. E. Feys, i–viii. Antwerpen: K. C. Peeters Instituut voor Volkskunde.

———. 1993. "Sir Halewijn in the Flemish Oral and Printed Tradition." In *The Stockholm Ballad Conference 1991: Proceedings of the 21st International Ballad Conference, 19–22 August 1991,* edited by Bengt R. Jonsson, 105–18. Skrifter utgivna av Svenskt Visarkiv, no. 12. Stockholm: Svenskt Visarkiv. Also published in *ARV: Scandinavian Yearbook of Folklore* 48 (1992), 43–51.

———. 1995. "Chants populaires des Flamands de France (1856): A Contribution to Comparative Folksong Research, France/Belgium: Flanders." In *Ballads and*

*Boundaries: Narrative Singing in an Intercultural Context,* edited by James Porter, with Ellen Sinatra, 315–24. Proceedings of the 23rd International Ballad Conference of the Commission for Folk Poetry (Société Internationale d'Ethnologie et de Folklore). Los Angeles: Department of Ethnomusicology and Systematic Musicology.

———. 1996. "The publication of Jan Frans Willems's *Oude Vlaemsche Liederen* (1848): An Expression of Flemish Nationalism?" In *Visions and Identities,* edited by Eydun Andreassen, 9–17. Proceedings of the 24th International Ballad Conference of the Kommission für Volksdichtung (Société Internationale d'Ethnologie et de Folklore), Tørshavn, 26–30 June 1994. Annales Societatis Scientiarium Faeroensis Supplementum, no. 22. Tørshavn: Tungulist.

Van Duyse, Florimond. 1903. *Het oude Nederlandsche lied* [Old Dutch and Flemish Song.] 3 vols. Gravenhage: Nijhoff.

Willems, Jan Frans. [1848] 1989. *Oude Vlaemsche Liederen ten deele met de melodieën* [The Old Flemish Songs, Partly with Their Tunes]. Reprint, K. C. Peeters Instituut voor Volkskunde, with a postscript and indexes by Stefaan Top (page references are to reprint edition).

# The Corpus of French Ballads

## Michèle Simonsen

This essay aims simply to highlight some of the difficulties I encountered when trying to assess the range and importance of French traditional balladry, so I will mainly raise questions rather than suggest answers.

The first difficulty lies in the ambiguity of the very term "French ballad." Does it mean ballad in the French language, or ballad collected in the state of France? These are two very different things, if one bears in mind the particularities of French history and the creation of the French state, really a conglomerate of widely differing cultural and linguistic units. At the end of the French Revolution, when leaders faced the difficulty of turning peasants into Frenchmen, historians reckon that only 15 percent of the population had French as their native language. The rest spoke either distinct languages like Occitan, Catalan, Basque, Breton, Alsatian, Flemish, or mutually incomprehensible dialects of French, such as Poitevin or Champenois. The systematic suppression of regional languages that began during the revolution took more than one hundred years to be enforced so that, until the First World War, the great majority of the common people learned French as a second language when they started school at the age of five. Against this background, what do we make of the many collections of ballads collected and printed in the second half of the nineteenth century, such as Jean-Francois Bladé's *Chants populaires de la Gascogne*, published in French but collected in the Gascon vernacular, a dialect of Occitan? Are these French ballads or not? In fact, the richest collections of narrative songs made in France come from lower Brittany and from Flanders and are in the Breton and Flemish languages. On the other hand, the greatest bulk of folk songs in the French language, and some of the most balladic of them, have been collected outside France, specifically in French-speaking Canada.

The second difficulty lies in the fact that we have no comprehensive scholarly edition of narrative songs in the French language similar to Svend Grundtvig's for Denmark (1853–1976) or Francis James Child's for Britain (1882–98). No matter what theoretical questions these two editions may raise concerning problems of definition and delimitation, there is no denying that they testify to an awareness of the ballad as a specific genre, an awareness which they, undoubtedly, have in turn reinforced. But in France, the only "comprehensive" edition of narrative songs with scholarly ambitions is Georges Doncieux's *Le romancero populaire de la France* (1904), which contains forty-five ballad types. This edition, however, in spite of its scholarly ambitions, or rather because of them, is of very limited use in this investigation. Unlike the Grundtvig and Child editions, Doncieux only lists one version of each ballad (type), and he calls this a "version critique," that is, a reconstruction of what he considers to have been the "original" ballad. Some fifty years after Grundtvig's groundbreaking manifesto and his challenge to publish "everything there is, and as it is" (1847), Doncieux's attitude to the ballad still betrays a literary approach, blind to the specificity of oral variants. So, when looking for French ballads, we have to turn to the many regional collections of folk songs, with rather sparse source information, if any, published in the last century. We must look to two national anthologies compiled respectively by Joseph Canteloube (1951) and Henri Davenson (1957), two very learned specialists but who work for the general public. We also have at our disposal the songs submitted in response to the national campaign to collect "national popular poetries" launched in 1854 by the Ministry of Education, under the direction of Jean-Jacques Ampère, which are still mostly unpublished.

Thirdly, there is no unambiguous French term for the ballad, popular nor scholarly, and correspondingly no clear concept of the ballad as a specific subgroup of folk song. The Breton language, on the other hand, distinguishes very clearly between a *gwerz* (a narrative song) and a *sone* (a term that seems to cover all other songs). Even among ballad scholars in France, terminology is confused and confusing. *Ballade*, in reference to narrative folk songs, has sometimes been used by the Romantic poets who, following Gérard de Nerval, did much to make traditional folk songs popular among the educated classes around 1820, but it was never really adopted by French folklorists. It would also have been misleading since in French literary history, the term refers to at least two poetic genres: a medieval poem, mostly lyrical, with an intricate metrical pattern (for example, the *ballades* of Guillaume de Machaut, Charles d'Orléans, and so on), and a nineteenth-century poem with "Gothic" content and vague connotations of exotic populations (for example, Victor Hugo's *Odes et Ballades*).

French folklorists like Georges Doncieux (1904) and P. Tarbé (1863) have sometimes used the word *romancero*, in imitation of the Spanish, to designate an entire group of ballads, but only a few have adopted the Spanish *romance* to refer to a single ballad. And rightly so, since the word *romance* in French has very different connotations and usually refers to the sentimental songs that became popular among the upper classes in the eighteenth and nineteenth centuries.

The most usual word for a narrative folk song in French is *complainte*. Julien Tiersot warmly advocates the use of this word when referring to "narrative, epic, legendary and historical songs":

> Complainte...c'est bien là le nom qui convient aux chansons du
> sombre moyen-âge. La complainte en effet, dans son acception
> vraiment populaire, est avant tout un récit: elle est le type de la
> chanson narrative triste et sérieuse.
> ['Complainte': this surely is the accurate term to apply to those
> songs from the dark middle-Ages. For a complaint, in the genuine
> folk traditional sense of the term, is first of all a story. It denotes a
> sad and serious narrative song.] (Tiersot 1889: 6)

Most folklorists have followed Tiersot's example, but this is not uncomplicated, for *complainte* is also the most usual word for "broadside sheet," many of which actually start with the words: "Ecoutez la complainte...." Broadside sheets, as a medium rather than a genre, include some ballads but also literary songs and those about recent, actual events, manufactured for that particular medium. In my experience as a fieldworker, this is exactly how elderly contributors understand the word *complainte*: a song which they have acquired as a *feuille volante,* a "broadsheet," and which, for exactly that reason, relates "real" events. To add to the terminological confusion, Georges Doncieux uses *complainte* in yet another sense. He calls the forty-five songs included in his *romancéro* both *romances gallo-romaines* and *chansons lyrico-épiques* (referring respectively to their alleged (ancient) age and partly narrative content), but he characterizes each of them as either a *chanson à danser* (those with a burden, whether an independent refrain or just the second line repeated as a refrain) or a *complainte*. In his view, this is the most important distinction among traditional songs. For Doncieux then, the *complainte*, or "song to be told," is the opposite of the *ballette,* or "song to be danced to," which, after all, may have links with the original meaning of the word "ballad" (see Bec 1977).

It appears easier to talk about French ballads in English than in French. Indeed, the whole classification of French folk songs in the nineteenth century is confused. Jean-Jacques Ampère, in his official directives for the first national folk-song collecting campaign (1853), classifies them according to heterogeneous criteria, some thematic, some formal, while some have to do with origins and others with social use. When looking for ballads in the six manuscript volumes subsequently compiled, one must consult each of the following groups: *Légendes, Vies de Saints, Miracles, Poésies populaires d'origine païenne, Poésies historiques, Poésies romanesques, Chants de soldats, Chants de marins,* and *Chansons de circonstance.*

Scholars disagree not only about what to *call* ballads but also which songs are to be regarded as ballads and which are not. Thus, Doncieux's *romancero* leaves out "Le meurtre de la mie," the story of a jealous mother who forces her son to kill his true love and bring back her heart, a song that is balladic in both theme and style. Yet he includes "Les princesses au pommier doux" and "La belle est au jardin d'amour," which are not narrative at all and, to my mind, can on no account be regarded as ballads, though they do have an initial formula scene which gives them a medieval flavor. Admittedly, Doncieux died before completing the *romancero,* which was published after his death. Had he lived, the book would probably have included more ballads.

If one turns to the most recent and comprehensive catalogue of French-speaking folk songs, that of Conrad Laforte (1958), the search for ballads is not easier, for although this catalogue is very systematic, it is based upon purely formal criteria, put forward in a separate publication (Laforte, 1976). Unfortunately for this methodology, French narrative songs, unlike their Nordic and British counterparts, have no standard form or metrical pattern. Some have refrains, some do not. Some are stanzaic, some are not (at least, according to Laforte). Stanzaic ballads can have four lines, with rhymes *aabb, ccdd,* as in "La fille du Roi Louis"; they can have two lines, with rhymes *aa, bb, cc,* as in "La fiancée infidèle"; they can have three lines, with rhymes *abb, cdd,* as in "Le retour du soldat," although in performance the first line is probably repeated so that a three-line ballad turns out to be composed of quatrains. They can also have six lines, as in "Le mariage anglais"; the lines themselves vary from four syllables, admittedly very rarely, to sixteen.

Actually, the existence of nonstanzaic ballads as postulated by Laforte (1976) is more problematic, I think. He regards the difference between stanzaic and nonstanzaic songs or songs *en laisse* as the most fundamental distinction in French folk-song poetics. A *laisse* is a series of lines of the same length which end in the same assonance; it was the meter used in the medieval *Chansons de geste.* Laforte rebukes Doncieux, Nerval, and other ballad editors for writing, for example, "Les filles de La Rochelle" as a series of quatrains, where only the second and fourth lines rhyme, followed by a burden:

Ce sont les filles de la Rochelle
Qui ont armé un bâtiment [bis]
Pour aller faire la course
Dedans les mers du Levant
  *Ah! La feuille s'envole, s'envole*
  *Ah! La feuille s'envole au vent!*

La grand´voile est en dentelles
La misaine en satin blanc [bis]
Les cordages du navire
Sont de fil d'or et d'argent
  *Ah! La feuille s'envole, s'envole*
  *Ah! La feuille s'envole au vent!*

He regards the *laisse* as the primary form since each quatrain makes up a long line with the same ending throughout the song:

Ce sont les filles de La Rochelle qui ont armé un bâtiment
Pour aller faire la course dedans les mers du Levant
La grand'voile est en dentelles la misaine en satin blanc
Les cordages du navire sont de fil d'or et d'argent
L'équipage du navire c'est tout filles de quinze ans
Le cap'taine qui les gouverne est le roi des bons enfants...

Conrad Laforte may well be right in his claim that the *laisse* is the primary form from a generic historical point of view but not a folkloristic one. Folk songs, after all, are primarily oral and aural experiences; the written form must be secondary. In performance, "Les filles de La Rochelle" is, I would claim, very much a stanzaic song. The lines of the *laisse* are coupled two by two, each couplet being followed by a burden, and the second half of the first line of the *laisse* (or, if you like, the second line of the quatrain) is repeated, thus creating a sort of middle burden. Moreover, Laforte's argument takes no notice of the music, which is certainly stanzaic. I would claim that even the tunes of a ballad like "Les anneaux de Marianson" (whose text, admittedly, is stichic and without burden) are stanzaic. Marius Barbeau, who has heard as well as read the songs, characterizes them as being "toutes dans le style récitatif qui convient aux grands poèmes épiques" [all those ballads are in the chanting style characteristic of epic poetry] (1962: 135). Each line of the *laisse* is a musical stanza with a theme, a reversal, and a resolution.

A ballad which could truly be called *en laisse* would also, in performance, have every line chanted on the same few notes, infinitely repeated, without any melodic development or resolution. This is perhaps the way the *Chansons de geste* were once chanted (Gérold 1932: 79–90), but it is not the case with the ballads collected in the nineteenth century and during the twentieth in Canada, where the melody as well as the text has been collected. Even if one does not accept Laforte's distinction between stanzaic and nonstanzaic ballads, the fact remains that narrative songs in French have no standard metrical pattern.

But do French narrative songs display that special "balladic" style or structure so conspicuous in many Scandinavian and Anglo-Scottish ballads and so meticulously analyzed by studies such as David Buchan's (1972)? Here we must distinguish between the structure of the songs and their use of formula. As I have shown in an earlier essay (1987), there is an extensive use of traditional formulas in French folk songs, both narrative and supranarrative, to use Flemming Andersen's terminology (1985). But most of these formulas, including the narrative ones, apply to all sorts of folk songs. As for special balladic structure—the intricate uses of binary, trinary, and annular patterns—puzzlingly, though found in French balladry, it is restricted to a very few ballad types, mostly "La porcheronne/La porcelette," "Le Roi Renaud," and "Les ecoliers pendus." You may then think that these are isolated ballads, perhaps borrowed from alien cultural areas, but this is hardly the case. "Le Roi Renaud," for example, has been collected throughout France in many variants, all very different in diction but most with the same balladic structure. "La porcheronne" has been collected in Lorraine, Provence, and French-speaking France (Nivernais, Poitou, Forez), while "Les ecoliers pendus," which perhaps tells of a real thirteenth-century episode during the reign of King Saint Louis, has been collected both in Oc- and in Oil-speaking France, as well as Hainaut (Belgium) and Québec. Apart from these few ballad types of various origin, French narrative songs are quite linear in narrative structure.

The question of the burden is even more puzzling. In Scandinavia, the presence of the burden, repeated after each stanza of two or four lines, is almost part of the definition of the ballad. This raises the question of whether the ballad was originally a dancing song, with the added argument of the possible etymology of the word *ballata*. And while I do not refute the fact that stanzaic poetry, linked with the emergence of dancing song, may have come from France (possibly through England with the carol), we must face the fact that in French oral tradition, at least as recorded in the nineteenth century, most *rondes* or dancing songs are conspicuously nonnarrative: they are lyrical or satirical, with a clear tendency toward the nonsensical. Most narrative songs in French—"La fille du Roi Louis," "Le Roi Renaud," "La porcheronne," "Germaine," "La blanche biche," "Les anneaux de Marianson," "Renaud le tueur de femmes," "Le prince des Ormeaux"—have no burden and are very ill suited to the rhythm of the French gavotte, the chain dance that fits the *rondes*.

If we turn to the content of the songs, the picture is also quite muddled. As early as 1939, Entwistle remarked that "the ballad in France is the narrative aspect of lyrical poetry" (1939: 132). Certainly not many of the narrative songs collected in French-speaking France during the nineteenth century contain events as dramatic or epic, nor story lines as elaborate, as the Scandinavian and Scottish ballads or the romances of Spain. Supernatural ballads other than Christian legends are few: "La fille changée en cane," "La blanche biche." Significantly, "Le Roi Renaud" has dropped the initial episode of the encounter with the elf girl in France, although it does appear in the Breton versions of that ballad.

Heroic ballads are nonexistent in the French tradition. Strangely enough, the exploits of Charlemagne and his peers, which in the Middle Ages inspired the flourishing epics of the *Chansons de geste*, have left no trace at all in recorded nineteenth-century folk tradition. There are slight hints of the Crusades in the ballad type "L'escrivette" (Doncieux 1904: 125–43), which tells of a young man's search for his bride who has been stolen by the Saracens while he was away at war, and possibly in the ballad type "Germaine" (Tiersot 1903: 102–104; cf. *Mélusine* 2: 45–46; *Romania* 1: 353; Pineau 1892: 405; Barbeau 1962: 111–28). Some scholars claim that the Crusades also provide a background to "La porcheronne," in which the heroine's husband comes home incognito after having been away at war "across the seas" for seven years. The evidence is tenuous; at the very least, France has waged many wars across the seas.

There are very few historical ballads. "La prison du Roy François" tells of François I's captivity in Italy in 1525, but most of the historical songs published by Leroux de Lincy in his *Recueil de chants historiques Français* [Collection of Historical French Songs] (1841–42) are of literary origin. Again, apart from a few Christian legends, French narrative songs tell of murderous husbands and, incidentally, of revenge. They describe sea voyages and sea battles, though these appear far more often in contemporary sound recordings than published collections of the nineteenth century. This last is probably due to the fact that in earlier times fieldwork was carried out more intensively among peasants than seamen. Present-day intensive fieldwork among coastal populations will hopefully alter this distorted picture somewhat.[1]

For the most part, then, French narrative songs deal with love stories. It is worth noticing that when they end tragically and are not simply humorous stories of seduction accomplished or avoided (depending on their male or female perspective), it is usually because one of the protagonists is unloving or unfaithful, or perhaps because of the jealousy of a third party. There are not many cases of love hampered by elaborate family feuds or political events, and these songs rarely express the conflict between kin and love that characterize the majority of the knightly ballads of Scandinavia.

Perhaps we should not be surprised by the lack of a French word to designate a ballad. Three types of criteria define a folklore genre: content, form, and social use. When all three criteria merge, they are likely to create a much more self-conscious poetic genre than when only one criterion relates to that genre. The ballad in France, as a genre, seems too diffuse to define rigorously, for it has no specific form or social use. Nevertheless, many scholars have stressed the importance of France in the genesis and dissemination of the ballad. Recently, David Colbert claimed that he has pinpointed the origin of the Scandinavian ballad, narratively very elaborate, in the convergence of three elements of French medieval poetry. The French *rondeau* provided the dancing *ronde* and the burden, the *chansons de toile* supplied the formula scenes, and strophic poetry contributed the stanzaic form (1989). Lajos Vargyas considers France to be the starting point for dissemination throughout Europe of the "international ballad," the *Volkslied* type with a universal theme, less anchored in a specific social and historical context than the "Scandinavian" ballad (1983).

As I hope I have shown, the combination of elaborate narrative with a specific form (stanzaic poetry with unvarying metrical pattern) and specific poetics (special structure and uses of formulas), so characteristic of Anglo-Saxon and Scandinavian ballads, rarely appears in the same song in French. In an appendix to *Hungarian Ballads*, Vargyas lists an Index of French Ballad Types, which, on the face of it, seems impressive: 135 ballad types, as compared to the 45 ballads in Doncieux's *romancero*. Vargyas is certainly well read, and familiar with French folk songs published in books and most of those published in specialized journals; he also lists some of the unpublished material from the Ampère national collection. Nevertheless, close scrutiny of his list reveals some disturbing facts. It contains a number of ballads, which, though published in French, were collected in foreign languages, for example, Bladé's aforementioned *Chants populaires de la Gascogne.* Thirty-one of the types exist only in one version and nine in only two versions, and less than one-third of all ballad types have been collected in more than two versions. Moreover, a number of these are hardly narrative at all.

So what are we to conclude? Many French-language traditional songs have been collected, in France and Canada, over the last two centuries, resulting in the publication of many volumes of songs from all the French-speaking regions. These do contain a number of narrative songs, some collected in many variants. Some belong to the international repertoire—"The Diver," "The Maiden on the Shore," for example—and yet, as a genre, the ballad in France is diffuse and invisible; is is submerged in the body of other kinds of traditional song. In those that can be found, their content is hardly epic, their narrative extension minimal, and their tone usually lighthearted rather than tragic or serious.

I see at least two possible explanations for this fact. First, there may have been, at some stage, a flourishing balladic tradition in French-speaking France, a tradition of more elaborate plots with narrative structures more specific to orally composed poetry. This tradition has left no trace in earlier written literature, its poetic too alien to literate people and therefore despised. It had already faded away by the second half of the nineteenth century, when the large-scale collecting of folklore began.

Second, alternatively, France has contributed to international balladry only isolated elements: strophic poetry, end rhyme, burden and chain dance, a few formulaic scenes. These elements merged into the ballad genre once they left France, where apposite historical and cultural context could provide specific, elaborate story plots. In that case, if France can be said to be the cradle of the ballad, the baby started to thrive long after leaving the cradle.

*Notes*

1.  See Barbeau 1962, and the series of recordings, *Anthologie des Chansons de mer*, made by the *Chasse-Marée* (Douarnenez), an association which also publishes an eponymous review of maritime folklore.

*References*

Ampère, Jean-Jacques. 1853. *Instructions relatives aux poésies populaires de la France.* Section de Philologie du Comité de la langue, de l'histoire, et des arts de la France. Paris: Imprimerie impériale.

Andersen, Flemming G. 1985. *Commonplace and Creativity: The Role of Formulaic Diction in Anglo-Scottish Traditional Balladry.* Odense University Studies from the Medieval Centre, vol. 1. [Odense]: Odense University Press.

Barbeau, Marius. 1962. *Le rossignol y chante: le repertoire de la chanson folklorique francaise au Canada.* Musée national du Canada, bulletin no. 175. Ottawa: Musée national de l'Homme.

Bec, Pierre. 1977. *La lyrique française au Moyen Âge (XIIe–XIIIe siècles): Contribution à une typologie des genres poétiques médiévaux. Etudes et textes.* Paris: Editions A. and J. Picard.

Buchan, David. 1972. *The Ballad and the Folk.* London: Routledge and Kegan Paul. Reprint, Phantassie, East Lothian: Tuckwell Press, 1997.

Canteloube, Joseph. 1951. *Anthologie des chants populaires français, groupés et présentés par pays ou provinces.* Vol. 1, Provence, Languedoc, Roussillon, Comté de Foix, Béarn, Gascogne, Corse. Paris: Durand.

Child, Francis James, ed. 1882–98. *The English and Scottish Popular Ballads.* 5 vols. Reprint, New York: Folklore Press, 1956–57; New York: Dover, 1965. Corrected edition prepared by Mark and Laura Heiman. Northfield, Minn.: Loomis House Press, 2002. Digital edition, with gazetteer, maps and audio CD. New York: ESPB Publishing, 2003.

Colbert, David. 1989. *The Birth of the Ballad: The Scandinavian Medieval Genre.* Skrifter / utgivna av Svenskt Visarkiv, no. 10. Stockholm: Svenskt Visarkiv.

Doncieux, Georges. 1904. *Le romancéro populaire de la France: choix de chansons populaires françaises.* With foreword and musical index by Julien Tiersot. Paris: E. Bouillon.

Entwistle, William J. 1939. *European Balladry.* Oxford: Clarendon Press.

Gérold, Théodore. 1932. *La musique au Moyen-âge.* Les classiques français du moyen âge, no. 73. Paris: H. Champion.

Grundtvig, Svend. 1847. *Prøve på en Udgave af Danmarks gamle Folkeviser for Samfundet til den Danske Litteraturs Fremme. Andet oplæg, med Aftryk af Planen, samt Tillægsbemærkninger.* Kjöbenhavn: Samfundet for den danske Litteratur Fremme [The Society for the Promotion for Danish Literature. (Contains revised manifesto based on the first version of February 1847: *Plan til en ny Udgave af Danmarks gamle Folkeviser af Svend Grundtvig.*)

———. 1881. *Elveskud, dansk, svensk, norsk, faerøsk, islandsk, skotsck, vendisk, bømisk, tysk, fransk, italiensk, katalonsk, spansk, bretonsk folkevise.* Kjøbenhavn: [Thieles bogtrykkeri].

Grundtvig, Svend, Axel Olrik, H. Grüner-Nielsen, Erik Dal et al., eds. 1853–1976. *Danmarks gamle Folkeviser.* 12 vols. [in 13]. København: Samfundet til den danske Literaturs Fremme and Universitets-Jubilæets danske Samfund.

Hugo, Victor. 1828. *Odes et ballades.* [city and publisher missing]

Laforte, Conrad. 1958. *Catalogue de la chanson folklorique française I–VI.* Publications des Archives de folklore, Université Laval. Québec: Presses Universitaires Laval.

———. 1976. *Poétique de la chanson traditionnelle française: Classification de la chanson folklorique française.* Les archives de folklore, no. 17. Québec: Presses Universitaires Laval.

Leroux de Lincy, Adrien Jean Victor. 1841–42. *Recueil de chants historiques français: depuis le XIIe jusqu'au XVIIIe siècle.* Paris: Charles Gosselin.

*Mélusine: Revue de mythologie, littérature populaire, traditions et usages.* Edited by H. Gaidoz and E. Rolland. No. 2 (1877) (cited as *Mélusine* in the text).

Pineau, Léon. 1892. *Le Folk-lore du Poitou.* Paris: E. Leroux.

———. 1898–1901. *Les vieux chants populaires scandinaves (Gamle nordiske folkeviser).* Paris: Libraire Emile Bouillon, editeur.

*Romania: Recueil trimestriel consacré à l'étude des langues et des littératures romanes* No. 1 (1872). Paris: Honoré Champion (cited as *Romania* in the text).

Simonsen, Michèle. 1987. "French Traditional Ballads." In *UNIFOL Årsberetning 1986,* 17–56. Københavns: Institut for Folkemindevidenskab, Københavns Universitet.

Tarbé, P. 1863. *Romancéro de la Champagne.* 2 vols. Reims: Brissart-Binet.

Tiersot, Julien. 1889. *Histoire de la chanson populaire en France.* Paris: E. Plon, Nourrit, et Cie.

———. 1903. *Chansons populaires recueillies dans les Alpes françaises (Savoie et Dauphiné.)* Grenoble: Moutier.

Vargyas, Lajos. 1983. *Hungarian Ballads and the European Ballad Tradition.* Translated by Imre Gombos. Budapest: Akadémiai Kiadó.

# The Slovenian Folk and Literary Ballad

Marjetka Golež Kaučič

For European folklorists, the definition of the term "ballad" has been more or less fixed since 1966, when it was codified by researchers in Freiburg as a narrative song with dramatic emphasis, irrespective of the ending, tragic or otherwise (Kumer 1998: 31). One always has this technical meaning in mind when using the word, though it is not generally used by traditional singers themselves (Brown 1998: 47–48). Numerous, roughly equivalent terms exist throughout Europe, of course, the most widely used being "narrative song" *(Erzähllied* in German, *ballade* in French, *balada* or *pripovedna pesem* in Slovenian). Others include "women's songs" (Croatian), *žalostne,* "sad," or *stare,* "old," songs (Slovenian); *byline* (Russian); *dume* (Ukrainian); *vise* (Scandinavian); and *romance* (Spanish). Nevertheless, ballad has been accepted as the preferred term for professional, international use through its adoption in German folklore studies and the defining canons from northern Europe, particularly those of England, Scotland, and Scandinavia (Kumer 1976: 131). Research has shown that the narrative songs of other European nations do not completely comply with this type, however.

In Slovenia, ballad came to be used in literary historical studies for shorter narrative songs about unusual, dramatically tense, sometimes-terrifying events from the world of fairy tales, myths, history, and also modern times, where epic components are linked with dramatic and lyrical ones. Some ballads may also, therefore, be lyrics (Kos 1987: 173–74). Slovenian literary practice also began to differentiate between the folk romance and the ballad, following the model of literary poetry, though it is well known that, in Spanish tradition, "romance" applies to a shorter epic/lyric song of Spanish origin, similar to the ballad in motifs and themes but different in spirit, mood, style, and composition and with a particular verse form. Slovenian academics have therefore classified some folk ballads as romances, rather than true ballads, by analogy with the more-cheerful, less-tragic literary romances, "Kralj Matjaž" [King Mathias] and "Pegam and Lambergar" (Kos 1996: 269–70), for example. In contrast with the literary ballad, whose emphasis is mainly on content, the folk ballad concentrates on narration. The criteria on which we classify a song as a ballad should therefore be its level of drama. In comparison to the epic song, the ballad is shorter, its narration is more condensed, and the level of drama is intensified so that dialogue is foregrounded. There are more than three hundred types of narrative song in Slovenian tradition, with ballads the most numerous.

In Slovenia, the term "folk ballad" is defined very differently in academic and literary tradition, resulting in confusion when discussing ballads in relation to folk and literary poetry. A typical heroic, narrative song such as "Pegam and Lambergar" is thus, according to literary historians, a romance because of its light nature and description of the time of the knights, while according to folklorists, it is a typical heroic narrative song or ballad (Kos 1979: 70).

Literary historians have used the term ballad to describe similarly structured narrative folk songs—"Desetnica" [The Tenth Daughter], "Rošlin and Verjanko," and so on—which has had a powerful influence on the subsequent development of the ballad in Slovenian art literature. Within the literary establishment, a ballad is an exclusively tragic song, gloomy and dramatic; all songs without such endings are called romances. Accordingly, the typically balladic "Godec pred peklom" [The Fiddler outside Hell] should be called a romance and not a ballad, which is absurd. It is equally ridiculous to classify "Kralj Matjaž" [King Mathias] or "Zvesta deklica" [The Faithful Girl] as romances solely because they end happily. Slovenian folklore studies, led by Zmaga Kumer, therefore use the more generally applicable term "narrative song," thereby including romances and avoiding taxonomic confusion.

Folklorists maintain that the term ballad, in its meaning of narrative song, was brought into art literature by Bürger in *Lenore* [Lenora] in 1770. This became the role model for the static, literary ballad of Enlightenment writers throughout Europe, who enthusiastically translated the German pre-Romantic ballads of Bürger, Goethe, and Schiller.

The pioneer of the literary ballad in Slovenia was our national poet, France Prešeren, who translated *Lenore* in the nineteenth century (Kos 1979: 131). Soon after, he wrote the first Slovenian literary ballad, "Povodni mož" [The Water Man], which, like Bürger's poem, was also modeled on a folk tradition about a proud girl from Ljubljana who rejected all dancing partners except one; he turned out to be a river man who swept her into the currents of the Ljubljanica. Prešeren probably based the poem on a written report by the polymath Valvazor, which tells of the abduction of Urška Šefer during a dance under the linden tree in Stari Trg (the Old Market) in Ljubljana, but a folk ballad about the water man already existed, "Hudič odnese plesalko" [The Devil Carries Off the Dancer]. We may assume that Prešeren was familiar with the song, which describes a similar event, but the reason the dancer was spirited away by the devil was because the sign of the cross was not made before the dance began (SLP 1, no. 25; Š 1, nos. 82, 83b; this ballad is supposed to be originally Slovenian[1]). Prešeren presumably also knew of another song, "The Water Man" (SLP 24; Š 1, nos. 81, 89; Kumer et al.

1970: 143–46), which was familiar in Germany as well ("Wassermanns Braut"), though it was confined to the west of the Elbe and Saale Rivers, the area of the Old Slavs. It is also known in Croatia (HNP 5, no. $11^2$), but there the girl is abducted by a dragon instead of the water man. So, even in the earliest period of the Slovenian literary ballad, clear connections with folk ballads existed.

Prešeren was also engaged in the poetic reworking of folk songs, medieval ballads in particular. *Lenore*, of course, already had its folk version, "Mrtvec pride po ljubico" [The Dead Man Comes to Get His Lover]. Bürger himself drew on the folk motif, so it may be said that the literary version of the ballad reflects the romantic tendencies of the time to delve into the folkloric, original, and popular. The same holds true for Prešeren's poem, which became popular with the public; it was set to music, and singers embraced it as their own, though this was probably due to the influence of schools. The Slovenian archives contain three versions of this ballad (twenty-five out of thirty-six stanzas). Since the poem was long and hard to understand, the story was not amenable to the folk process of condensation and fragmentation and therefore did not spread as widely as the more-concise folk ballad "The Dead Man Comes to Get His Lover," which exists in the archives in several tens of versions, the last recorded in 1982 in Dolenjska.

The differences between the folk and the literary versions are obvious. The folk version consists of condensed narration, dramatic story, lyrical elements, and a refrain which is not gloomy, perhaps even cheerful. A folk singer would therefore have no reservations about using a cheerful melody. Most singers probably learned the literary "Lenora" in school; its melody belongs to a semiliterary, semifolkloric creation of the modern period. A similar tune can be heard in several semiliterary, religious songs (particularly Christmas carols and those with eight-line stanzas (Kumer et al. 1970: 327). The literary reworkings are only discernable in some variants; the literary text became shorter until it was completely replaced by the folk version, sung even today and certainly more well known than Prešeren's. These ballads represent the beginning of the so-called series of folk/literary ballads, which intertwine elements of the two (see figures overleaf).

Fig. 1. "The Dead Man Comes to Get His Lover."

Fig. 2. "Lenore."

"Lenore," and the folk song "The Dead Man Comes to Get His Lover," are associated with a number of Slovenian literary authors, who have established new semantic and formal relationships with the theme.

> The subject, which draws on the idea that the dead cannot rest peacefully in their grave if their relatives mourn them excessively, and that the dead person therefore returns and takes the mourner with him, has its roots in mythology. This subject is preserved as the memory of the old family custom that a wife is not allowed to outlive her husband; this custom is believed to have been first recorded in the early twelfth century in the Hindu collection *Vetala's Twenty-Five Tales*. The idea has survived throughout the centuries and has been reflected in works by all Indo-European nations, sometimes in poetic creations and sometimes in prose. Nations have changed its content according to their own individualities; on the basis of this, we are justified in talking about the Germanic, Roman, and Slavic Lenore (Trdina 1938: 125).

The story itself is incorporated into both poetry and prose as part of the folk-literary tradition across Europe (AT 365) in the motif of a dead rider who appears in a series of ballads where the dead person returns and takes away his wife, child, or lover. (Examples include the Greek "Constantine and Arete" or "The Dead Brother's Return," the English "The Suffolk Miracle" (Child 272), and the Scottish "Sweet William's Ghost" (Child 77) (Leach 1949: 108, Harmon 1949: 299).

Let us now examine a series of texts derived from two different treatments of the same subject—"The Dead Man Comes to Get His Lover" and the translation, or poetic recreation, of Bürger's *Lenore*—one a folk ballad, the other a literary creation. The latter's popularity in tradition is not difficult to fathom because it tells the same story using the same metric and rhythmic patterns as the folk ballad, but through investigating intertextual relationships and transformations of motif and character, we may also explore issues of meaning and social function. In addition, while the print-based literary ballad keeps changing, the literary ballad in oral tradition has remained relatively static, a reminder of the active nature of the relationship (Golež Kaučič 1993: 168).

"Lenora," or "The Dead Man Comes to Get His Lover," has come to us through different literary poems at different times; as a result, its original meaning has been enlarged as it has evolved. The comparative texts presented here are part of a series of independent variants, based on the same motif and category, which have changed their genre and central idea during different literary/ historical periods. Though its language has changed considerably, the content and genre of the folk ballad has been very stable. In fact, though it has been in oral tradition for many generations, the folk ballad has, paradoxically, changed much less than the literary ballad, with the result that stable versions still exist today in certain places. Conversely, no version of Prešeren's deliberately innovative "Lenore" has been found in oral tradition since 1965.

| Mrtvec pride po ljubico | The Dead Man Comes to Get His Lover |
|---|---|
| 1. Po vrtu je špancirala<br>hojladrija, hojladrija,<br>in drobne rožce zbirala,<br>hojladrija, drija drom. | She wandered around the garden<br>hojladrija, hojladrija,<br>and picking small flowers,<br>holadrija, drija drom. |
| 2. "Po pušelc bom pa res pršu<br>če živ ne bom, bom pa mrtu." | "I will come for a bouquet,*<br>if I am alive, I will be dead." |
| 3. Urca enajst je udarila<br>Anzelj na okno potrklja. | The clock struck eleven,<br>Anzelj knocked on the window. |

*She asks him first whether he would come for a bouquet if he were alive or dead. The singer left out this stanza.

4.  "Oh Micka, al si ti doma,            "Oh Micka, are you home
    da bodeš z mano rajžala?"            to travel with me?"

5.  Urno na konja jo položi             He swiftly placed her on the horse
    in hitro hitro v noč zbeži.         and quickly disappeared into the night.

6.  "Oj Micka, al te je kaj strah?"     "Oh Micka, are you afraid?"
    "Oj kaj bo, kaj bo mene strah!"     "Well, what is fear to me!"

7.  Ko pa do britofa prideta            When they drew near to the cemetery,
    hiter gor zajašeta.                 they quickly mounted.

8.  En grob se urno odvali,             A grave swiftly opened,
    Anzelj se vanjga položi.            Anzelj lay down inside.

9.  Micka je dol se zgrudila            Micka collapsed to the ground,
    in svojo dušo zdihnila.             and her soul sighed.

10. Naša, naša luba Gospa               Our dear Lady,
    le prosi ti za rajnca dva.          we only pray to you for two deceased.

In its variants, the story of "Lenore," or "The Dead Man Comes to Get His Lover," has been reduced due to the challenges of memory. The story has become denser, while individual details have been lost. "The Dead Man" and "Lenore" have merged into a single central motif which is tapped by poets. So the series of ballads that begin with a folk ballad (Š 1, no. 61A) and Prešeren's "Lenore" (1830), on which the popular ballad "The Dead Man" (SLP 1, no. 60) is based, is simply a continuation of a trend of artistic recreation, drawing on diverse aspects of content and style.

The first ballad to follow Prešeren's lead is Simon Jenko's "Knezov zet" [The Duke's Son-In-Law] (published 1860), a transformation of the folk ballad "Graščakov vrtnar" [The Gardener of the Lord of the Castle] combined with the motif of the dead man who comes to get his lover. The central theme is social inequality, which condemns the love between the duke's daughter and a gardener; this merges with the power of love, since that is what enables the girl to raise her beloved, executed by the duke, from his death dwelling. The story goes through a number of deviations, inversions, stylizations, and a complete transformation of genre and content.

Next is Anton Aškerc's "Vojakova nevesta" [The Soldier's Bride] (1890), featuring the central motif of a soldier returning to get his lover. The poet merged the method of storytelling in folk songs with the central part of Bürger's *Lenore*.

The third poem is "Lenorina pesem" [Lenore's Song] (1963) by Gregor Strniša. In four four-line assonant stanzas, Strniša creates a ballad mood, while with a single syntagma—"he's coming from the black soil riding a horse"—he conveys the essence of the story, a poetic attempt to interrelate love and death in the cosmos.

The fourth is a poem written by Svetlana Makarovič: "Lenora" (1972). An intense lyricism is also present in this poem; the first verse immediately transfers us to the dark world of the afterlife:

> When the moon rises above the mountain,
> The graves open,
> And my beloved will come to me,
> To make me feel even sadder.

The fifth poem, also by Gregor Strniša, is called "Želod" [Acorn] (1972).

> The great dead man rides
> Armoured from his grave.

This formal structure combines the assonantal characteristic of the older Slovenian folk ballad with the four-line stanzas characteristic of folk love songs. Strniša uses the ballad to elevate the dead man into the cosmos, where the poet is no longer limited by space or time or confined to tragic love between two people; rather, the poem switches between day and night, and life and death.

The fifth author is Franci Zagoričnik, whose "Sveder" [Drill] (1983) is written in pure blank verse; the only similarity with *Lenore* is the so-called ballad mood and the heroine's name. On the other hand, Milan Vincetič develops his "Lenora" in seven variants in assonantal four-line stanzas (1988). He uses the motif of Lenore to create a song about seven nights the dead man spends with his (living?) lover in his grave.

This series of texts demonstrates an alteration of genres in the direction of genuine ballad structure; lyric and epic elements blend with dramatic ones. Strniša, Makarovič, and Vincetič, for example, use only ballad mood, whereas Zagoričnik's works are ballads in name only, the genre being evoked by the title (Golež Kaučič 1993: 170–79). While the poems, structurally speaking, are not genuine ballads, they nevertheless contain concealed dramatic and epic elements. Each is reminiscent of the folk ballad's nature and motifs and thus awakens half-forgotten meanings by analogy. The texts, therefore, represent a cultural shift and the recreation of meaning using traditional themes (Juvan 1990: 30).

The Slovenian literary ballad is an individual's intimate and deliberate creation. It often evokes folk balladry but remains a literary invention with its own particular niche in literary history. Though derived from the traditional form, it soon becomes a hybrid where two distinct poetic forms merge, as we have seen in the Lenore texts. Under the high-cultural surface, the folk ballad suffuses the literary ballad, providing important parallel developments of themes.

There are, however, a few more features which separate the folk ballad from the literary one. The folk ballad is dense and concise, melodic; it is sung mostly as a part song, frequently by individual female singers; in addition, it plays a particular role in people's lives, offering an opportunity to sing while working together or protecting or watching over the dead. Group work—the wine harvest, weeding, husking, spinning, shelling peas, for instance—was always accompanied by singing, which included ballads. And since, in Slovenia, folk songs were performed collectively, *everybody* took part in the singing as long as they knew the words and the melody, a fact which has contributed to the preservation and popularization of the genre as a whole. Some parts of Slovenia continue to practice the custom that, until the funeral, the corpse lies at home on a bier, where relatives and friends gather to sing, giving the ballad an additional dimension as a lament. This custom, too, has no doubt assisted in preserving some ballads. (This category includes ballads on the death of the bride on her wedding day, the widower with his child at his wife's grave, the doomed soul,and the death of a girl who marries far from home.)

The ballad can also be a ritual song: from the Karst region, we have the "Three Magi" carol, whose central part is the ballad of "Marija in brodnik" [Mary and the Ferryman]. It can also be a lullaby, such as "The Ballad of the Maid," where a servant's child is murdered by the wife of the lord of the castle. The ballad has also been preserved as a dance song in Bela Krajina in southern Slovenia, where on 27 December each year the local population organizes a winter bonfire and dances the *kolo*, a kind of round dance, and sings a fairy-tale ballad about a shepherd whose heart was torn out of his chest by three witches (his mother, sister, and lover) while he was sleeping. The dance step can be compared to the Faroe Islands ballad dance. It used to be strictly ritual, but today it is part of the program performed by the Predgrad folklore group.

In terms of thematic content, folk ballads do not differ substantially from their literary counterparts. Love and family ballads prevail, followed by legendary and mythological ones, while social, heroic, and jocular examples are fewer. Poets from the nineteenth century mostly dealt with historical, heroic, and love themes, while contemporary poets have created ballads according to their own individual tastes, with the exception of poems which draw on folk ballads. In these cases, the poets create a double poetic layer, reflecting both folk meanings and their own ideas. Folk ballads can be described as largely characterized by moral themes whereby folk justice demands punishment for any bad deed committed. People understand and forgive human weaknesses, but they do not forgive social sins—refusal of hospitality, vanity, infidelity, hard-heartedness, oppression of the poor, fraud, and the like. The folk ballad also differs from its literary cousin because it is sung very rhythmically and rarely recited. The most common types of verse are the lyrical decasyllabic, three-part octosyllabic, trochaic septisyllabic, two-part octosyllabic, and octosyllabic and septisyllabic distichs. This type of ballad often has a chorus, while older ones lack even rhyme. Harmonic singing, so characteristic of Slovenian folk song in general, also appears in ballads, which may be sung in two or three parts by women, and mostly in three parts by men with the lead vocal in the middle (Kumer 1976: 132–47).

The folk ballad is a closely-packed narrative song, sometimes with a stressed dramatic and dialogic structure. Slovenia's literary ballad tradition, first emerging in France Prešeren's nineteenth-century work, has naturally varied in popularity, reaching its peak in contemporary creations that have often destroyed its classic form. We must distinguish between the literary ballad based on folk tradition and the one which has no connection with it whatsoever. By comparing texts, we have seen how literary ballads incorporate content and sometimes even the form of the folk ballad, while adding contemporary meanings and ideas, in the process changing the method of narration. Contemporary works are often ballads which retain folk motifs and verse patterns, thereby functioning as palimpsests. These are the easiest to identify the relationships between folk and literary elements. Throughout all literary periods, the Slovenian folk ballad has had mixed fortune, undergoing reinvention while often preserving its fundamental form, which is alive among traditional singers even today.

## Notes

1. 'SLP' and 'Š' refer to the standard reference works on Slovenian ballads: *Slovenske ljudske pesmi* (Kumer et al. 1970) and *Slovenske narodne pesmi* (Štrekelj 1898-1923).
2. 'HNP' refers to the standard reference work on Croatian folk songs: *Hrvatske narodne pjesme* (1909).

## References

Brown, Mary Ellen. 1998. "Ballad." In *Encyclopedia of Folklore and Literature*, edited by Mary Ellen Brown and Bruce A. Rosenberg, 47–48. Santa Barbara, Denver, Oxford: ABC-CLIO.

Buchan, David. 1972. *The Ballad and the Folk*. London: Routledge and Kegan Paul. Reprint, Phantassie, East Lothian: Tuckwell Press, 1997.

Emerson, O. F. 1915. *The Earliest English Translation of Bürger's 'Lenore': A Study in English and German Romanticism*. Cleveland: Western Reserve University Press.

Espinoza, M. Aurelio. 1950. "Spanish Ballad." In *Funk and Wagnalls Standard Dictionary of Folklore, Mythology and Legend*, edited by Maria Leach, 1058–60. New York: Funk and Wagnall.

Golež [Kaučič], Marjetka. 1993. *Slovenska ljudska pesem in sodobna slovenska poezija*. Ph.D. diss. Ljubljana: Filozofska fakulteta.

Golež [Kaučič], Marjetka, ed. 1998. *Ljudske balade med izročilom in sodobnostjo* [Ballads between Tradition and Modern Times]. Proceedings of the 27th International Ballad Conference—The Ballad Commission of SIEF), 13–19 July 1997, Gozd Martuljek, Slovenia. Ljubljana: ZRC SAZU.

Harmon, Mamie. 1949. "Dead Rider." In *Funk and Wagnalls Standard Dictionary of Folklore, Mythology and Legend*, edited by Maria Leach, 299. New York: Funk and Wagnall.

HNP. 1909. *Hrvatske narodne pjesme*, edited by Nikola Andriæ. Vol. 5. Zagreb: Matica hrvatska.

Juvan, Marko. 1990. O obliki in smislu v medbesedilnem nizu (na primeru Krsta pri Savici), 59-74. 26th *seminar slovenskega jezika, literature in kulture*. Ljubljana: Filozofska fakulteta.

Kos, Janko. 1979. *Pregled slovenskega slovstva*. Ljubljana: Dražvna založba Slovenije.

———. 1987. "Balada." In *Enciklopedija Slovenije*, 173–74. Ljubljana: Mladinska knjiga.

———. 1996. "Romanca." In *Enciklopedija Slovenije*, 269–70. Ljubljana: Mladinska knjiga.

Kumer, Zmaga, Milko Matičetov, Boris Merhar, Valens Vodušek, eds. 1970. *Slovenske ljudske pesmi*. Vol. 1. Ljubljana: Slovenska matica (cited in the text as SLP).

———. 1976. "Slovenska ljudska balada." *Zbornik Predavanj*, 131–47. 12th seminar slovenskega jezika, literature in kulture. Ljubljana: Filozofska fakulteta.

———. 1988. "Die Ballade im Volksleben der Slowenen (Zur Frage des Verhältnisses zu anderen Gattungen)." In *Ballads and Other Genres/Balladen und Andere Gattungen*, edited by Jerko Beziæ et al., 21–26. Proceedings of the 17th International Ballad Conference in Rovinj, 1987. Zagreb: Zavod za istraživanje folklora.

———. 1998. "Pogledi na dosedanje delo baladne komisije [An Overview on the Work of the Ballad Commission to Date]." In *Ljudske balade med izročilom in sodobnostjo/ Ballads between Tradition and Modern Times*, edited by Marjetka Golež [Kaučič], 31–35. Proceedings of the 27th International Ballad Conference (SIEF Ballad Commission), Gozd Martuljek, Slovenia, 13–19 July 1997. Ljubljana: ZRC SAZU.

Leach, MacEdward. 1949. "Ballad." In *Funk and Wagnalls Standard Dictionary of Folklore, Mythology and Legend*, edited by Maria Leach, 106–11. New York: Funk and Wagnall.

Prešeren, France. 1830. "Lenore." *Kranjska Čbelica* (1830–34).
Štrekelj, Karel, ed. 1898-1923. *Slovenske narodne pesmi*. Vols. 1–4. Ljubljana:
    Slovenska matica (cited in the text as Š).
Trdina, Silva. 1938. "Lenorina snov v slovanskih literaturah, Narodna Lenora." In
    *Slovenski jezik*, vol. 1, no. 1–4: 125–29. Ljubljana: [n.p.].

# Scotland's Nordic Ballads

### Frances J. Fischer

That traces of Scotland's Nordic ballads could still be found in the last days of the nineteenth century is surprising, but there is nothing "commonplace" about the story of their texts, contexts, and what we know of them more than one thousand years after the Northmen came to Scotland.

The area in question includes the Orkney and Shetland Islands, north of the Scottish mainland at approximately sixty degrees north latitude, about halfway between Norway and the Faroe Islands—or one third of the way from Norway to Iceland. In this essay, I will discuss how this geographic position combined with historical developments to bring us Nordic ballads. Using that foundation, I will then consider each of the songs in greater detail: how it was discovered and what links there are to other Nordic members of the genre. This is not quite as arduous a task as it seems because the corpus is sadly slim.

Our northern islands of Orkney and Shetland were among those North Atlantic areas subject to invasion from the eighth century on, when that great wave of Nordic migration swept around Europe. The nature of the islands' native population is not clearly known, although some, if not all, were apparently Pictish. It appears there were also Irish religious hermits, if we can judge from such residual place names as Papa Westray and the similar situation in the Faroe Islands.

Farther to the south, the Viking invaders controlled the Scottish western isles and much of the western coast until they met defeat at the Battle of Largs in 1263. That area was ceded to the crown of Scotland by the Treaty of Perth in 1266. In this same treaty, the only islands exempted from transfer to Alexander III, king of Scots, were the Orkney and Shetland archipelagos, "which were specially reserved to Norway" (Anderson 1981: lii). Farther to the east, "The Orkneyinga Saga" tells us that by 875 the Norse had conquered as far south as the Ekkialsbakki—the River Oykel. But Norse power retreated north. By the midthirteenth century, only the lowland sections of Caithness and the northern islands remained occupied by the Norse aristocratic families, who were by then intermarried with the natives and increasingly hard to distinguish from similar Scottish families. As the political and cultural boundaries moved north, so also did the use of the local variant of the West Scandinavian language, which became known as Norn. In 1308, Norway and its colonies (the Faroe Islands,

Iceland, Orkney, and Shetland) came under Danish rule, but direct administration did not pass to Copenhagen until 1536.

Before that time, however, the Orkney and Shetland Islands were transferred to Scottish control when they were offered as surety in 1468–69 for the dowry of Princess Margaret, daughter of King Christian I, when she married James III, king of Scots. In Orkney and Shetland, few, if any, changes occurred before the 1560s because it was generally expected that the islands would be redeemed by the payment of the sum due. This did not happen, and Scottish sovereignty continued. This was probably as much an exercise in realpolitik as finance: It was unlikely that the Scandinavians could have continued to control distant islands whose leading families also owed fealty to the Scottish king for estates held on neighboring mainland Scotland. Surrender of sovereignty did not include property rights, however, and the "Lords of Norway" continued to own property in Shetland. In 1611, Shetland and Orkney were integrated into Scotland, and Scots law and statutes were adopted.

The latest date we have for a surviving Shetland legal document in a Scandinavian language is 1607, and the language is Danish—the language of administration (Renaud 1992: 217). The legal use of Scandinavian appears to have ended considerably earlier in Orkney, where a more fertile landscape had attracted greater numbers of Scots-speaking settlers.[1] The use of Norn, however, lingered on. The expected return to Scandinavia was the earliest factor encouraging the native islanders to cling to their Nordic heritage. In 1539, a priest newly transferred to the Shetland island of Unst was sent to Norway to learn the language because his congregation could understand no other (Scott 1928: 298). But the language was pushed ever north by lowland Scots-English spoken by the settlers and the language choice of the rest of the population. Norn became one language among many. During the sixteenth and seventeenth centuries, Dutch was the second language of Lerwick because of the enormous size of the fishing fleets from the Low Countries. In the eighteenth century, we know little about the use of Norn in Orkney, but we do know more about the situation in Shetland. In 1773, Thomas Gifford of Busta wrote that everyone spoke English with a good accent but many still spoke Norn among themselves (Gifford 1879: 31–32). Brian Smith, the Shetland archivist, has estimated that Norn was the language of the people until the balance began to shift in the late seventeenth century. By the early years of the eighteenth century, "Norn was on the way out: not because of oppression, but because the Shetlanders, especially younger Shetlanders chose not to speak it. They turned their attention elsewhere. It's as simple as that" (Smith 1996: 35).

Shetland was turning to Scotland. Contacts with Scandinavia remained, but the previous focus on the Northlands diminished. Fewer people continued to sing the old songs, but they did not disappear without a trace. George Low, an early traveler, gave an account of his 1774 journey to the islands,[2] where he noted that most of the remaining Norn fragments still in circulation were "old historical ballads and Romances, this kind of poetry being more greedily swallowed and retentively preserved in memory than any others, and most fitted to the genius of the Northerns" (Low 1879: 107). On this same page, Low quotes his contributor, William Henry, a farmer at Guttorm on the isolated Shetland island of Foula. Henry claimed that there were three kinds of poetry in Norn that were repeated and sung by the old men: the "ballad" or "romance," the verse then commonly sung to dances, and the simple song. What he called the ballad or romance seems to have been valued chiefly for its subject matter and was sung by the fire during the long winter evenings. They were probably similar to the extended adventure tales or epics which are famously present in the Faroese corpus.

The dance in Shetland at the time of Low's visit was described this way: "...then would a number of the happy sons and daughters of Hjaltland [Shetland] take each other by the hand, and while one of them sang a Norn viseck, they would perform a circular dance, their steps continually changing with the tune" (Hibbert 1891: 563). This form of dancing was the local variant of the chain and ring dances known throughout Europe in the medieval period and still danced (although self-consciously) in the Faroe Islands. But the language was going, and the round dance and its accompanying songs were making way for the Scottish reels and the playing of the fiddle.

What I have described so far has been the history and social context of a Nordic ballad society in the throes of change. Now I would like to turn my attention to what we know of the ballad fragments.

The first text that we hear of—though sadly we have no written record—involves a minister on the Orkney island of North Ronaldsay, who, in 1770, read to his older parishioners Gray's ode "Fatal Sisters" (an interpretation of the "Darraðarljóð") because it was a poem which "regarded the history of their own country." In return, they pointed out to him that they already knew this work in their own language (Norn) and had recited it to him in the past (Scott 1871: 460–61). Some scholars have maintained on linguistic grounds that this "Song of Darrad" was actually written on Orkney and there are good reasons for believing that other Norse poetry, such as the "Krákumál" [Lay of Kráka] and the

"Málshattákvædi" [Proverb Poem] were also products of this same area (Olsen 1932: 147–53). These works now exist only in Icelandic texts.[3]

Let us, however, return to George Low's 1774 journey. Concerning the northern islanders, Low wrote, "Most if not all of their tales are relative to the history of Norway, they seem to know little of the rest of Europe but by names; Norwegian transactions they have at their fingers' ends" (Low 1879: 114). Our good fortune is that he provided an example. He took down from William Henry the text of thirty-five verses of a Norn ballad concerning the relationship between Hildina, a Norwegian princess, and an earl of Orkney. Low wrote the text in his journal under the heading of "Foula," and this manuscript is now in the library of the University of Edinburgh. Low did not understand the words he heard, but he interpreted the sounds as any Scot might and attempted to use standard English orthography to reproduce phonetically the Norn of an eroded dialect. He did, however, know the story and called his text "The Earl of Orkney and the King of Norway's Daughter."

Here is a brief summary of the story. The earl [jarl] of Orkney abducts Hildina, daughter of the king of Norway, during her father's absence. The king comes in pursuit. Hildina persuades her husband the jarl to make peace with her father, and her father accepts the jarl as a son-in-law. After the meeting, however, Hilluge, a jealous courtier who lusts after Hildina, reignites the king's anger. A general battle gives way to a duel between the jarl and Hilluge. The latter cuts off the jarl's head and throws it into Hildina's arms while taunting her. Hildina must now return with her father to Norway. Hilluge seeks Hildina's hand, her father presses the suit, and the lady agrees after being granted the right to serve the wine at the wedding feast. Hildina drugs the wine and, after all fall asleep, has her father removed from the house. At that point, the house is set on fire, and Hildina gains her revenge by preventing Hilluge's escape. She, in fact, grants him just the same mercy that he gave to the jarl.

The ballad received some attention before the publication of Low's manuscript, but this was virtually limited to the reproduction of Low's text. The actual publication occurred when, for a variety of social and political reasons, islanders' interest in their Nordic heritage began growing. This change in attitude also attracted the interest of the linguists Jakob Jakobsen and Marius Hægstad (who gave the ballad the name "Hildina"). Hægstad's monograph "Hildinakvadet" (1900) goes through Low's text thoroughly, pointing out where Low made changes. He stresses the fact that the linguistic problems are difficult to untangle, and, in addition to poorly distinguished line and verse divisions, there are problems with Low's handwriting. For ballad scholars, this may appear less than crucially important, but I must point out that Hægstad was also trying to determine the structure of the Norn language.

The first three verses of the "Hildina" text (Low 1879: 101) are:

1. Da vara Iarlin d'Orkneyar
   For frinda sin spur de ro
   Whirdì an skildè meun
   Our glas buryon burtaga.

2. Or vanna ro eidnar fuo
   Tega du meun our glas buryon
   Kere friendè min yamna meun
   Eso vrildan stiendi gede min vara to din.

3. Yom keimir cullingin
   Fro liene burt
   Asta vaar hon fruen Hildina
   Hemi stu mer stien.

This ballad has been poorly served by translators, although the initial work was done by Hægstad himself in his Danish monograph. An additional Hægstad translation (1901) into Nynorsk[4] was freer since the author needed slight alterations to accommodate a rhyme scheme. W. G. Collingwood published the only existing complete translation into English, and his aim was to present the ballad in "readable English without sacrificing rhyme and metre to literal translation" (Collingwood 1908: 211). Some sample stanzas indicate the general tenor:

1. It was the Earl of Orkney
   Of his friend has taken rede
   Whereby to bring a maiden
   Forth of her perilous need
   From the Broch of glass to save her.

2. "Take ye the maid from the Broch of glass
   Dearest friend of mine,
   And aye as long as the world may stand
   Shall be told this deed of thine."

3. Homewards comes the noble kin
   From the hostings as he rides,
   But gone is the lady Hildina;
   At home her step-dame bides.

9. "Now shalt thou take thy horse in hand
   And down to the water wend,
   And greet my father fair and blithe;
   He will gladly be thy friend."

Here is a more-literal (but not poetic) translation of the first verse:

It was the Earl of Orkney,
he asked his kinsman for advice,
whether he ought to take the girl
away from her suffering, and away from Castle Glass.

There is no equivalent to this entire ballad narrative in Scottish tradition, but individual motifs do occur. "Earl Brand" (Child 7), for instance, also concerns the abduction of a willing young noblewoman and the inevitable pursuit. The pleas for mercy, however, are quite different. Where, in the middle of battle, Hildina calls out to save her lover,

"Father for the sake of humanity
don't waste more men's lives" (verse 20).

Lady Margaret cries,

"O hold your hand Lord William!" she said,
"For your strokes they are wonderous sair;
True lovers I can get many a ane,
But a father I can never get mair." (Child 7B: 7)

Hægstad made this same point when he wrote in 1901, "I have neither seen or heard any song which is quite like this one in any other country" (1901: 9) He then commented on a long series of Scandinavian ballads about abduction, rescue, and revenge—such as the Faroese "Kappin Illhugi" and its Scandinavian counterparts listed under E 140 in *The Types of the Scandinavian Medieval Ballad* (Jonsson et al. 1978). Others have extended this search for parallels and suggest that the first part of "Hildina" resembles the legend of the Battle of Hjadninga as told in both "Younger Edda" and "Sørla Þáttr" [Saga of Olav Trygveson], both dating perhaps to the thirteenth century (Hægstad 1901: 11–12). Such is the zeal of scholars on the trail. Be that as it may, there is no doubt that this text from Shetland is firmly embedded in Nordic rather than Scottish tradition.

Jakob Jakobsen is an important figure in the study of Norn—historically, if perhaps not theoretically. He was a Faroese philologist who went to Shetland in 1893 and remained there for two years recording Norn remnants. He submitted this work as his doctoral thesis in 1897, and it was published as *Det Norrøne Sprog på Shetland*. He made two further brief visits to Shetland in 1905 and 1912 but did his major collecting during his first visit. His other publications, as far as Shetland Norn is concerned, are *The Place Names of Shetland* (1936) and the extraordinary two volumes of the *Etymologisk ordbog over det norrøne sprog på Shetland* (1908–21), which was translated and published in 1928–32 as *An Etymological Dictionary of the Norn Language in Shetland*. This work lists ten thousand individual words and fragments of Norn (Barnes 1998: 2–3). Unfortunately, there is no detailed record of his interviewing techniques, and the Norn fragments are sometimes left without comment (Barnes 1998: 4).

Among these "fragments" are small pieces of songs and a ballad. Neither Liestøl (the Norwegian folklorist) nor Child mention Norn songs, other than ballads, that survived in Shetland. Jakobsen, however, noted the existence of two lines of a cradle song, some fragments of an eagle song from Foula, and a boat song with some varying lines now known as "The Unst Boat Song" (Jakobsen 1928, 1: lciv, cxii–cxiii).

The ballad fragments involve two scraps, one of two lines and another of four. Jakobsen suspected that the two shreds might be related but was unable to identify the ballad because so few lines survived. It was the mid-1930s before the Norwegian Knut Liestøl confirmed that suspicion and demonstrated it in the Faroese canon (Liestøl 1936: 80). Jakobsen recorded the four-line section phonetically and then reconstructed it in what he thought was the original Norn. Alongside it I have placed the fifth verse of "Hústrú og Bóndi" (*CCF* 179).

| Norn | Faroese |
|------|---------|
| Ek hef malit meldra mín (or meldrann), | Bádi havi eg kýrnað, |
| ek hef sópat husin; | og feiað havi eg hús, |
| ennflá sefr (søfr, liggr) flat sœta lín | statt nú upp, kæra hustrú |
| (hin sœta mín), | mín, |
| ok dagrinn er komin í ljós. | og nú gerst dagurin ljús! |
| (Jakobsen 1897: 19) | (*CCF* 179: 5) |

| | |
|------|---------|
| [I have ground my corn, | [I have both churned and |
| have swept the house; | swept the house; |
| yet my wife is still sleeping, | get up now, dear wife, |
| when daylight is dawning.] | for dawn is breaking.] |

The two-line fragment is more difficult to duplicate because Jakobsen did not transcribe it from the phonetic notation.

> Idla jå'lsa swa'rta tap,
> skala fə'rte håŋga. (Jakobsen 1897: 153)

The text apparently concerns the care of a black-crested hen which gave the husband many problems. To help interpret this two-line segment, Liestøl pointed out that, in Jakobsen's own Norn dictionary, the expression "Idla jålsa" can be translated as "Devil take her" and the second line appears to mean that the creature ought to be hung. In a similar manner, verse 10 of the same Faroese ballad offers us,

| 'skamm faí tú, reyða toppa, | Confound you, redcrest, |
|------------------------------|-------------------------|
| tað mundi eg av tær notið | this happened because of you. |

The following first two (of twenty-three) verses indicate what might have been sung in Shetland some four hundred years ago.

| 1. Árla var um morgunin, | It was early in the morning, |
|--------------------------|------------------------------|
| høsini tóku at gala, | roosters were starting to crow, |
| hústrú vekir upp bónda sín, | the wife wakes up her husband, |
| biður hann fara at mala. | bids him start grinding (corn). |

2. Tað var Jógvan stolti,                    It was proud Jogvan,
   snippar og hann grætur:               he cried and lamented,
   'skamm faí tín høsn,                      "Confound your chickens,
   ið tiðliga gala um nætur."             that crow so early at night."

A distant parallel to this is "The Wife of Auchtermuchty," although this is not included in the Child collection.[5] In the Scottish case, however, the role reversal is caused by the husband, who considers his wife has an easy life inside the house while he slaves away at the farm work in all weather. At the end, the farmer admits that his assumptions are all wrong and he is willing to return to his own work:

> Quoth he, Dame, I sall hald my tung,
> For an we fecht I'll get the war,
> Quoth he, When I forsuke my plewch,
> I trow I but forsuke my skill:
> Then I will to my plewch again;
> For I and this house will nevir do weil. (Herd 1973, 2: 129–30)

There is here, however, no sign of the unending public shaming that is an essential part of the Faroese "Hústrú og bóndi" or its Danish cognate "Den huslige bondeman" [The House Husband]. Here again, the Shetland ballad is firmly part of a Nordic tradition.

The only other possible remnants of Nordic balladry are an Odinic ballad found in Unst and the debased Norn burden of Child 19, "King Orfeo." The eight lines found in Unst during the nineteenth century are interesting: Turville-Petre gives the text in Shetlandic Scots as

> Nine days he hang   pa de rütless tree;
> for ill was da folk     in' güd wis he.
> A blüdy mael           wis in his side—
> made wi' a lance—    'at wid na hide.
> Nine lang nichts,      i' da nippin rime,
> hang he dare            wi' his naeked limb.
>         Some, dey leuch;
>         but idders gret.[6] (Turville-Petre 1964: 43)

More importantly, it was the knowledge of this text that encouraged Child to expect to find ballads in Shetland. His only discovery there was the fascinating "King Orfeo," and scholars have been busily trying to determine its significance and authenticity ever since (Fischer 1996).

The corpus of Nordic ballads in Scotland is very small and usually overlooked. We should not forget it, however, as it is a link to important aspects of Scottish history.

## Notes

1. But the matter is hard to judge because of the vagaries of document survival.
2. This was not actually published until 1879.
3. The "Darraðarljóð" recounts that Darrað had a vision in Caithness on Good Friday of 1014 concerning the Irish Battle of Clontarf which took place that same year. The eleven stanzas of the "Darraðarljóð" are found in *Njal's Saga* (Magnusson and Pálsson 1960: 349–50).
4. Nynorsk, formerly Landsmål, is a literary form of Norwegian, created in the later nineteenth century as a purer language (more closely based on Old Norse) than the usual Dano-Norwegian, known as Riksmål or Bokmål (ed.).
5. It is, however, listed in Wehse (1979: 372) as no. 248.
6. While recognizing the Christian ambiguities of this text, Turville-Petre points out its similarity to the "Rúnatals Þáttr" in the *Hávamál* (1964: strophs 138–45).

## References

Anderson, Joseph, ed. 1981. *The Orkneyinga Saga*. Edinburgh: Edmonston and Douglas, 1873. Reprint, Edinburgh: Mercat Press.

Barnes, Michael P. 1998. *The Norn Language of Orkney and Shetland*. Lerwick: Shetland Times.

Chesnutt, Michael and Kaj Larsen. 1996. *Føroya Kvæði: Corpus Carminum Færoensium.* Vol. 7: History, Manuscripts, Indexes. Universitets-jubilæets danske samfunds skriftserie, no. 540. Copenhagen: C. A. Reitzel (see Matras, Djurhus et al. 1941–72).

Child, Francis James, ed. 1882–98. *The English and Scottish Popular Ballads*. 5 vols. Reprint, New York: Folklore Press, 1956–57; New York: Dover, 1965. Corrected edition prepared by Mark and Laura Heiman. Northfield, Minn.: Loomis House Press, 2002. Digital edition, with gazetteer, maps and audio CD. New York: ESPB Publishing, 2003.

Collingwood, W. G. 1908. "The Ballad of Hildina." *Orkney and Shetland Miscellany*. Orkney and Shetland Old Lore 1, edited by Alfred W. Johnston and Amy Johnston, 211–16.

Fischer, Frances. 1996. "A King among the People: 'King Orfeo' (Child 19) in the Shetland Islands." In *Visions and Identities*, edited by Eyðun Andreassen, 94–100. Proceedings of the 24th International Ballad Conference of the Kommission für Volksdichtung (Société Internationale d'Ethnologie et de Folklore), 26–30 June 1994, Tørshavn. Annales Societatis Scientiarium Faeroensis Supplementum, no. 22. Tørshavn: Tungulist.

Gifford, Thomas. 1879. *Historical description of the Zetland Islands in the Year 1733*. Edinburgh: n.p.

Hægstad, Marius. 1900. *Hildinakvadet: med uitgreiding um det norske maal paa Shetland i eldre tid*. Christiania [Oslo]: Jacob Dybwad.

———. 1901. "Hildinakvadet." *Syn og segn* (1901): 1–14.

Herd, David. 1973. *Ancient and Modern Scottish Songs, Heroic Ballads, &c.* Edinburgh: Martin and Witherspoon, 1769. Reprint, Edinburgh: Scottish Academic Press (page references are to reprint edition).

Hibbert, Samuel. 1891. *A Description of the Shetland Islands, Comprising an Account of Their Scenery, Antiquities and Superstitions.* Edinburgh: printed for Archibald Constable and Co.; London: Hurst, Robinson and Co., 1822. Reprint, Lerwick: T. and J. Manson (page references are to reprint edition).

Jakobsen, Jakob. 1897. *Det norrøne sprog på Shetland.* Copenhagen: W. Prior.

————. 1908–21. *Etymologisk ordbog over det norrøne sprog på Shetland.* Copenhagen: V. Priors kgl. Hofboghandel.

————. 1928. *Etymological Dictionary of the Norn Language in Shetland.* 2 vols. London: Nutt.

————. 1993. *The Place Names of Shetland.* London: Nutt, 1936. Reprint, Lerwick: Shetland Library.

Jonsson, Bengt R., Svale Solheim, Eva Danielson et al. 1978. *The Types of the Scandinavian Ballad.* Oslo, Bergen, and Tromsø: Universitetsforlaget.

Liestøl, Knut. 1936. "Ei folkevise på norn-mål frå Shetland." *Maal og minne* (1936): 79–82.

Low, George. 1879. *A Tour through Orkney and Schetland, Containing Hints Relating to their Ancient, Modern and Natural History, Collected in 1774 by George Low.* Kirkwall: W. Peace and Son.

Magnusson, Magnus, and Hermann Pálsson, tr. 1960. *Njal's Saga.* London: Penguin.

Matras, Christian, Napoleon Djurhus et al., eds. 1941–72. *Føroya Kvæði: Corpus Carminum Færoensium.* 6 vols. Copenhagen: Munksgaard (D. B. K.) (cited in the text as *CCF*; see Chesnutt and Larsen 1996).

Olsen, Magnus. 1932. "Orknø-Norn og norrøn diktning på Orknøene." *Maal og minne* (1932): 137–153.

Renaud, Jean. 1992. *Les Vikings et les Celts.* Rennes: Editions Ouest-France.

Scott, Hew. 1928. *Fasti Ecclesiæ Scoticanæ.* Edinburgh: Oliver and Boyd.

Scott, Walter. 1871. *The Pirate.* Edinburgh: Cadell, 1831. Reprint, Edinburgh: Adam & Charles Black.

Smith, Brian. 1996. "The Development of the Spoken and Written Shetland Dialect: A Historian's View." In *Shetland's Northern Links: Language and History*, edited by Doreen J. Waugh, 30–43. Edinburgh: Scottish Society for Northern Studies.

Turville-Petre, Edward O. G. 1964. *Myth and Religion of the North.* New York: Holt, Rinehart and Winston.

Wehse, Rainer. 1979. *Schwanklied und Flugblatt in Grossbritannien.* Frankfurt-am-Main, Bern, Las Vegas: Lang.

# Simon Fraser's *Airs and Melodies* [1816]:
# An Instrumental Collection as a Source
# of Scottish Gaelic Songs

Mary Anne Alburger

From the Highlands and Islands of Scotland to Nova Scotia, collectors of Scottish Gaelic[1] songs, such as Francis Tolmie (1998), Margaret Fay Shaw (1955), and John Lorne Campbell (1990), had the singer and the song as the focus of their attention. As their publications have shown, these songs, some of which originated hundreds of years ago in Scotland, remained part of an oral tradition still vigorous during the twentieth century.

One of those who collected music for Gaelic songs many years earlier was fiddler and composer Simon Fraser (1772/3–1852), born in the parish of Abertarf, near Loch Ness, Inverness-shire, the only son of Captain John Fraser, late of the 78th, or Black Watch, regiment, and his wife.[2] In 1794–95 he published his first collection of music, *Thirty Highland Airs, Strathspeys, &c* (Edinburgh), mostly his own compositions. In February 1795 he joined the Fraser Fencibles, a local Highland regiment raised to fight in Ireland and active during the rebellions of the United Irishmen, remaining until it was disbanded in 1802. He rose to captain and was particularly successful at recruiting, "his enthusiasm as a Highlander and his passion for the native Celtic music being highly captivating" (*Inverness Courier*, 22 July 1852: 1). Following military service, he returned to a tenancy at Knockie, near his father's family home, where he became a sheep farmer. Poor advice led to financial ruin around the time *Airs* was published. By then he and his wife, Jane, had three young children. Simon also had an older illegitimate son, Angus (or Æneas) Fraser, or Watson, (1800–72), born to an Inverness servant girl. After twenty-five years in the Army, he was discharged on medical grounds as unfit for service. He went to live with his father, and spent the rest of his life trying to get Simon's remaining manuscript music and compositions published.

During the late-eighteenth and early-nineteenth centuries, when Simon was preparing his collection, scholarly interest in Highland traditional song focused on the words (the poetry), or the music, but, unlike Tolmie, Shaw, and Campbell, seldom on both. Simon Fraser's *Airs and Melodies Peculiar to the Highlands of Scotland and the Isles* (hereafter *Airs*) [1816] was always intended to display the music, not the words. Although Fraser included some of his own compositions in the 232 tunes, and referred to contemporary as well as older Gaelic songs in his endnotes, the collection was essentially instrumental, set for violin, piano, and cello.[3] Fraser made a conscious choice not to publish Gaelic words for the melodies, for, as he saw it, "many of the words attached to these airs are known to be objectionable in point of delicacy or loyalty, or frequently both;—indeed, numbers of them are unworthy of notice but for the melody" (Fraser 1816: 4).

Despite this declared stance and although he never claimed to be a singer, Fraser's introduction and comments on the tunes, and the music's Gaelic and English titles, have enabled me to find many of the poems referred to in Fraser's texts, and, in this ongoing research, to recover examples of the song repertoire (largely no longer current) by fitting these words to his melodies, which were originally presented as he probably played them on the violin. The information in *Airs* also demonstrates his father's and grandfather's varied song repertoires (dating to at least the beginning of the seventeenth century), as well as Fraser's own eclectic tastes. Examples include a wide variety of song types, several in the older stressed meters (where the melody varies rhythmically to meet the requirements of the poem's structure), and one which seems to have been designed to be declaimed at pitch, rather than sung to a recognizable melody.

*Gaelic Song*

Ballad scholars are no doubt aware that Gaelic songs are not usually included in ballad study. The songs, their form and function, share little, if any, of the Anglo-Scottish ballad tradition. As Anne Dhu Shapiro wrote, there are "undeniable differences in the total text and music complex of Gaelic and Lowland songs. The rhythm, syntax, and accentuation of the two languages are different; the poetic and conceptual heritage of the two linguistic traditions differs as well" (1985: 407).

James Ross, writing in 1957, was more specific: "While much of Gaelic song, particularly from the earlier period, shares features that we find in the ballad, such as 'stress on the crucial situation,' and 'letting the action unfold itself in event and speech,' it lacks the important third constant of telling the story 'objectively with little comment or intrusion of personal bias.'" The story, Ross explained, "may be recognized as a classical ballad plot, but it is told not by a detached observer, but by a participant" (127; the widely known "A' Bhean Eudach" [The Jealous Woman], parallels "Binnorie" [Child 10] and is usually considered the most complete example of a ballad plot in Gaelic song).

Nevertheless, the songs discussed in this essay do share with ballads the common features necessary for oral transmission as formulated by Cecil Sharp:

variation, through the musical variants which Fraser recorded of songs still known; continuity, through the music for songs he recorded which are still sung; and selection, through those he recorded which no longer exist in tradition. This article follows Bertrand Bronson's approach, exemplified in *The Ballad as Song*, but widens it to include other poetry, not only ballads, which "had been traditionally sung" (1969: vii). Although the elements of "song," and "poetry" as understood here may be discussed separately, it is important to remember that they seem to have been originally considered inseparable, one and the same.

## Gaelic Poetry

The complex and strict metrical rules of the early "classical" poetry of the literate professional (*filidh*), the often archaic language, and the internal and end rhymes of poems such as the eulogy, the elegy, the panegyric, and the complaint do not have direct English equivalents—traditional or otherwise—nor do they seem to have been melodies as they are usually understood. Because of their complexity—there are "about three hundred" metrical systems (Watson 1976: xvii)[4]—it is generally thought that these compositions were declaimed at varying pitches as surviving musical examples, one of which is included, seem to indicate.

By the early seventeenth century, when the seat of political power moved to London with James I and VI (of England and Scotland, respectively), the role of the *filidh* had already begun to diminish, as had the effectiveness of the clan system. New poets emerged who, though they might know and follow many of the constraints of the rigorous older poetry, began to use less complex rhyme schemes and were prepared to abandon the arcane meters and archaisms, along with the old orthography shared with Irish Gaelic.

This newer style of vernacular poetry, accounting for the texts of the majority of the song melodies Fraser collected, is referred to as "modern" Scottish Gaelic poetry (although many of the old features, such as strong assonance and internal rhymes, remained important), which flourished "between 1640 to about 1830" (Watson 1976: xix). Some of these songs are still found in oral tradition, although it is increasingly likely that their production may have been influenced by secondary communication, the reinforcement of text or music directly or indirectly by manuscript or printed sources, or aural sources, such as recordings and other mechanical media.

## Words without Songs

The major scholarly works on Gaelic poetry edited and published during the nineteenth and twentieth centuries understandably concentrated on trying to interpret the language and decipher obscure texts. Music was of no concern. The main exceptions are studies by the late William Matheson, School of Scottish Studies, University of Edinburgh, himself a singer, and Colm Ó Baoill, University of Aberdeen. More typical was the approach of William Watson, who, in *Bàrdachd Ghàidhlig* ([1918] 1976), ignored performance elements, such as choruses, vocables, and rolling stanzas, which had they been considered, would perhaps have shed light on the texts in question.

Paralleling the work of the early Anglo-Scottish ballad collectors, much of the Gaelic scholars' research focused on the work of those who had created early manuscripts of Gaelic poetry, helping to preserve the language and art by writing down the words which they and their friends knew or by copying others' manuscripts. Written Gaelic was nonstandardized well into the nineteenth century, always in flux, a language which could be as individual as each writer and his dialect—even today standard orthography is not acceptable to all. During the eighteenth century, individuals, by necessity, had to create their own orthographies, however curious. In the older poetry, they also had to deal with a vocabulary of archaic words, many of which still puzzle scholars.

By the time Fraser's *Airs* was published, some of the collected Gaelic poetry which relates to his work was already in print, for example, that of Alasdair Mac Mhaighstir Alasdair (1751) and collections by his son, Ronald MacDonald of the Isle of Eigg (1776), James Gillies (1784), Alexander and Donald Stewart (1804), and Patrick Turner (1813), among others. As with Percy's and Herder's eighteenth-century compilations (1996, 1990), the words lacked music, either because it was thought immaterial, or because the music was in common circulation.

*Signposts to Tunes and Service Tunes*

In the Gaelic-speaking world, from the time of the first published songs, sources of suitable music were provided alongside the poetry. Alasdair Mac Mhaighstir Alasdair, whose *Ais-eirigh* (Mac-Dhonuill 1751)[5] was the first published book of Gaelic poetry, set a precedent by suggesting melodies already in print to which twenty-one of his own poems could be sung. These were mostly English and Scottish airs, some from William Thomson's two-volume *Orpheus Caledonius* ([1733]); others were popular song melodies arranged for violin and continuo by the Edinburgh violinist and composer William McGibbon (ca. 1697–1752). Mac Mhaighstir Alasdair does not seem to have chosen the music because the English title or lyrics expressed a similar sentiment or the melodic line was attractive, but because it had a rhythmic pattern to serve as a model for the performance of the song. For his poem "Oran Morair Mhic-Shiomoin" [An Elegy on Lord

Lovat], for example, he suggested the tune "Hap Me with Thy Petticoat," found in Thomson's *Orpheus Caledonius* (1972, 1: 21), which may seem a puzzling choice but one which suits the poem's meter (Campbell 1984: 106–15, 300).

After Patrick MacDonald's *A Collection of Highland Vocal Airs* appeared in 1784, later poetry collections commonly gave exact page numbers and titles from MacDonald as sources for the song melodies. Alexander and Donald Stewart's *Cochruinneacha* (1804) prefaced Màiri nighean Alasdair Ruaidh's poem "Luinneag Mhic Leòid" with "for the air, see Mr. MacDonald's Collection of Highland Vocal Airs, page 28, [number] 163." In MacDonald the melody is given simply as "A Skye Air," with the title "Hithi-ùil-agus Ò-hithil-Ò-hòrino," which corresponds to the vocables of the chorus as they appear in the Stewarts' version of Màiri's song. In other cases, the MacDonald reference acted as a service tune, citing music for another song by another poet, as with another poem by Màiri nighean Alasdair Ruaidh, directed to be sung to the tune for quite a different poem, one by Rob Donn.

Simon Fraser's name appears in the subscribers' lists of several books of Gaelic poetry, so he may have had easy access to printed texts while he was working on *Airs*, although I have as yet found no evidence that he actually used any of the printed poems as sources of titles for the melodies in his collection. A list of other books (which date from 1770) to which he could have had access can be found in his son Angus Fraser's papers at the National Library of Scotland (Fraser: Papers).

*Printed Sources of Music for Gaelic Songs Prior to Airs*
The first traditional Gaelic melodies (including "MacIntosh's Lament," a version of a pibroch dated about 1526), some with transliterated Gaelic titles, were published in London by Scottish musician and composer James Oswald in *The Caledonian Pocket Companion* from the 1740s on. These had probably been picked up from passing singers or musicians, in what could be considered an informal type of fieldwork.

Music publishing in Scotland had only recently begun , with music for songs from Allan Ramsay's *Tea-Table Miscellany* (Stuart 1726–27).[6] As public balls and dancing assemblies became increasingly popular, published collections of dance music increased, with hundreds appearing during the boom years from the 1780s through the 1820s. Many were what I describe as "first-generation" collections (those containing music published for the first time) from native Gaelic speakers, such as Donald Dow's *A Collection of Ancient Scots Music* (1778) and the hundreds of arrangements of Gaelic songs by Gaelic-speaking musicians as dance sets, particularly those by Niel Gow (1727–1808) and his son Nathaniel, starting in 1784.

*Early Fieldwork-Based Printed Collections of Music for Gaelic Songs*
*A Collection of Highland Vocal Airs* (1784) was the first specifically of Gaelic songs. (At the time, 'Highland' was used to describe anything having to do with Scottish Gaeldom.) The music was collected through fieldwork and from correspondents by Argyll-based Rev. Patrick MacDonald (1729–1824) and his brother Joseph (1739–1763).[7]

The breadth of interest can be seen in the *Highland Vocal Airs* subscribers' list, which includes James (Ossian) Macpherson, Dr. Charles Burney, Mrs. Boswell of Auchinleck, Professor Gordon of King's College, Aberdeen (whose daughter Anna is better known as Mrs. Brown of Falkland), Dr. James Beattie, Aberdeen (later professor of moral philosophy at the University of Edinburgh), "Mr. Cramer" and "Mr. Abel," "musician, London" (highly regarded players and composers), and nobles including the Duke of Buccleuch and the Duke of Atholl, alongside others in the forefront of artistic and intellectual pursuits.

It was more than thirty years later that the words and music of Gaelic songs were published together, concurrently with Simon Fraser's *Airs*, in Alexander Campbell's *Albyn's Anthology* (1816, 1818). Gaelic-speaking Campbell, assisted and encouraged by his onetime music pupil the author Walter Scott, had traveled, like the MacDonalds, to collect the material for his book, assisted by a grant from the Highland Society of Scotland. A case could be made for Campbell being the first Scottish ethnomusicologist since, when he undertook his fieldwork, he followed the guidelines of the society's Music Committee:

> The Committee shall furnish Mr. Campbell with such instructions in regard to the mode of proceeding in the Collection as may appear proper....
> 1. Should not interfere with any thing already published by [Rev. Patrick] Macdonald;
> 2. Nor with Captain Fraser [who had also applied to the society for funding];
> 3. Should go through the district of Argyle Inverness & as many of the accompanying islands as possible;
> 4. To collect unknown tunes and give them without improvement or alienation;
> 5. To record any historical notes collected with the tune;

6. To note the place where the tune was got and the person from whom it was got;

7. The instrument on which the tune is played;

8. To note down the words adapted to the tune (Royal Highland and Agricultural Society of Scotland Archives; henceforth RHASSA[8]).

Valuable as it was, his publication was marred by poor production values: inelegant music notation and ill-set Gaelic, due in part to his having commissioned alternative poems in English which took precedence over the Gaelic melodies, whose text settings appear as rather hasty afterthoughts.

*Songs without Words*

Although Simon Fraser had also contacted the Highland Society for funding and presumably been issued similar guidelines, he provided notes as requested on "where the tune was got and the person from whom it was got," and "historical notes collected with the tune," but not "the words adapted to the tune." He may have honestly believed that the Gaelic words were "objectionable in point of delicacy or loyalty" (Fraser 1816: 4), but there may be a simpler explanation.

According to the records found thus far of his communications with the Highland Society, he first contacted them for financial support in 1815 (RHASSA, 28 February 1815). By that time his father John, the main source of the vocal music in *Airs*, had been dead for five years. Simon's large collection must have been started well before his father's death, and, since he was a violinist, it is likely that, from the beginning, he only recorded the music since that was what he intended to publish, along with his own compositions. By the time he saw the guidelines, it was too late, and any opportunities he may have had to collect the words for songs he had not troubled to learn had been lost.

This situation is similar to the one which Hugh Shields found in his study of nineteenth-century ballad fieldwork in Ireland (1993), which may shed light on the way Fraser and other musicians viewed their involvement:

> Serious amateurs with archival instincts may lack the very rudiments of technology and, though certainly literate, it is unusual for them to be literate enough in music to write down airs. On the other hand collectors of the past, when they *could* write music, sometimes took interest in it which so far outweighed their interest in words that they overlooked the words or perhaps commented on them only...to complain. (Vallely 1999: 131)

*The Singers*

Fraser's main access to his song repertoire was through his father, John, who died on 14 April 1810 (*Inverness Courier*, 20 April). Simon recalled a night that he and his father spent with his uncle, who sat "with one or two select friends, exhorting from [John] the songs and anecdotes of which this work [*Airs*] consists, and the party in the highest glee imaginable. That very night added considerably to the work" (Fraser 1816: 2).

In turn, John's principal informant was his father, Angus Fraser (ca. 1707–77). Angus was "one of the most extensive graziers and cattle-dealers in the North" (Fraser 1816: 2), who was in partnership with his cousin, MacKay of Bighouse, in Sutherland, for a time the landlord of the Gaelic poet Rob Donn. A successful businessman, Angus brought cattle from Sutherland, in the far north, to be fattened on good grazing near Loch Ness before being driven to markets in the Lowlands. Through his travels, which included his work as a justice of the peace, Angus was acquainted with a wide number of other Gaelic-speaking men who were also singers.

Fraser wrote of his predecessor Angus Fraser,

> that in point of song, independent of being a man of good education, [he] stood almost unrivalled (the late Alex. Fraser of Culduthel, the most sprightly singer of Highland song known in the North, alone excepted). They were, however, inseparable, as the best deer hunters and sportsmen of their day, and remarkable for a social and convivial disposition, anxious and interested to acquire a notion of the peculiarities and sentiments...of the different districts through which the one so frequently traveled, as well as to obtain the music and words of their best songs. (Fraser 1816: 1)

Throughout his work, Simon emphasized the paramount importance and veracity of the oral tradition of which he was part. Writing again of Angus, Simon said, "The nature and magnitude of his business led him to every corner of the Highlands and Islands...[and] the airs were sung and retained with great accuracy by my father, who added very considerably to the collection through contact with brother Caledonians from every quarter of the North, while on service during the first American war" (Fraser 1816: 2). It was Angus Fraser's friends, though, whom Simon mentioned most often and whom he considered, along with his grandfather, most influential, whose song versions became a "standard, formed a century ago, by three neighboring gentlemen of Nairnshire, eminent performers, Mr. Rose of Kilravock, Mr. Campbell of Budyet, and Mr. Sutherland of Kinsteary" (Fraser 1816: 107). Other gentlemen included Alexander Fraser of Leadclune and Lachlan MacPherson of Strathmashie.[9]

The association of traditional Gaelic songs with the landed gentry would have been perfectly familiar to Gaelic mother-tongue speakers, who were aware that their singers and poets came from all social classes, but might have surprised some Anglophone antiquarians, who at this time associated traditional song most closely with "the illiterate of the preceding age" (Withrington and Grant 1982: 345).

*The Poets*
Unlike Anglo-Scottish ballads, the Gaelic repertoire still includes the names of many of the poets who contributed to the genre, some from as early as the sixteenth century. It is also possible to date many of the poems from internal evidence. Some can be identified with battles or other historic events, or with the dates of the chieftains whom the poets praised, satirized, or mourned. Fraser often gave a précis or paraphrase of the poem and recorded the names of some of the best-known poets, among them:

- Alasdair Mac Mhaighstir Alasdair (Alexander Macdonald), ca. 1700–ca. 1770, a literate, well-read scholar who prepared the first Gaelic/English vocabulary for schools in 1739, held a commission in Prince Charles Edward Stewart's Jacobite army, and was a cousin of Flora MacDonald, who helped save the prince's life after the Battle of Culloden.
- Donnchadh Bàn Mhic-an-t-Saoir (Duncan Ban MacIntyre), 1724–1812, an Argyllshire forester who served in another's place on the Jacobite side in the 1745–46 rebellion (the '45), and later joined the Edinburgh City Guard.
- Màiri nighean Alasdair Ruaidh (Mary MacLeod, of Skye), ca. 1615–1707, thought to have been a nurse to the children of the clan chief.
- Rob Donn 1714–1778, a cattleman in Sutherland.

Lesser poets include Dughall Bochannan (Dugald Buchanan), 1716–1768, a Perthshire-born catechist and hymnist, whose judgment-day poem, "Laiodh an t-Slaighnear" [Praise to the Savior], may be the longest modern poem in Scottish Gaelic, and Lachlan MacPherson of Strathmashie, ca. 1723–ca. 1798, of whom Fraser wrote, "the world is indebted for suggesting, urging, and aiding his friend [James Macpherson] in the publication of the Poems of Ossian" (Fraser 1816: 2).

*Simon Fraser's* Airs *as a Source of Melodies for Songs.*
Unlike Patrick MacDonald's collection, Simon Fraser's repertoire never became a
popular resource for song melodies. The most obvious drawbacks to using it this
way were made clear by the antiquarian William Stenhouse: "In Captain Fraser's
Gaelic Airs, lately published, a set of this tune ["An Gilleadh dubh"] appears in
two strains [sections], loaded with *trills*, *crescendos*, *diminuendos*, *cadences
ad libitum*, and other modern Italian graces. This gentleman professes, however,
to give the airs in their ancient and native purity, but *ex uno disce omnes*! [*sic*]"
(Stenhouse 1853: 131). Fraser was naturally trying to present the traditional melodies in what he thought was the most up-to-date violin style, although, to be fair,
the florid decorations which Stenhouse so disliked were already behind the times.
Fraser (or his arranger) also tried, time after time, to force basically pentatonic
melodies into classical, harmonically correct, major or minor keys to which they
were quite unsuited. This, in turn, led to unmusical harmonizations, which distort
and haunt many of the settings. Fraser may have had assistance from Nathaniel
Gow (son of the famous fiddler Niel Gow, 1727–1807), violinist and publisher, for
whom he wrote "Mile taing' an Udair" [The Editor's Thanks to Mr. Nathaniel
Gow[10]] found in *Airs* (Fraser 1816: 103).

Nevertheless, a few scholars have used music from *Airs*, among them Adam
Gunn and Malcolm MacFarlane (*Orain agus Dàin le Rob Donn Mac-Aoidh*,
1899); John Lorne Campbell (*Highland Songs of the Forty-five*, 1984); and Colm
Ó Baoill (*Bàrdachd Shìlis na Ceapaich* and *Gàir nan Clàrsach*, 1972 and 1994),
while William Matheson referred to *Airs* but chose to use music from the Angus
Fraser manuscript (Matheson 1970) thought to have belonged to Simon's son.

*Fitting the Words to the Music*
The common-sense method William Matheson describes takes for granted that
the editor will have to make some alterations to the music, beginning with the
need to find the true bar lines of the melody, those which will be appropriate to
the stress of the poem:

> When the position of the barlines is identified, the task of setting
> syllables to related notes presents no great difficulty. It need only
> be remarked that, to accommodate the words, some dotted crotchets
> require to be replaced by two or three notes, as the case may be, of
> the same total time-value. The opening bars of the second and
> succeeding stanzas [of "Thriall bhur bunadh gu Phàro," the poem
> being discussed], as so often happens, are different from the

corresponding bars of the first stanza. The latter has seven lines, but some other stanzas are shorter, and it is a question of determining by ear which phrase or phrases in the music should be left out. There are also some eight-line stanzas, and here the only recourse is to think of a variation on the existing musical phrases that chimes with the rest. (1983: 131)

The major editorial problems for someone working with the music in *Airs* arise from the difficulties Fraser had when he attempted to transcribe music which was not the same in each verse, where the rhythm needed to change as the stress of the poetry altered. This aspect of oral transmission, basic to Fraser's collection, was of course allied to whatever skills he had as receiver and transcriber. He at least had what seems like optimum facilities in which to work. At home at Knockie, he could listen to his father or other visiting singers, active sources,[11] with his violin at hand, along with an organ (perhaps played by his wife),[11] lined paper on which to write, his aural memory, and his musical literacy. Presuming that Fraser learned the tunes on his violin first, how easily he learned and transcribed the songs depended on how familiar he already was with the melodies and perhaps how well the singer could repeat the same song until he was satisfied that the tune was correct. Whatever the present editorial puzzles, it is clear that Fraser did the best that he could.

The music used in my editions is based solely on that found in *Airs* (see appendix). Wherever possible, the words fitted to the music come from poems printed earlier than *Airs* [1816]. This provides texts which are contemporary with Fraser's own song sources. Although there are a few poems which I have only been able to find in print later than 1816, it is certain that poems published after *Airs* could have had no effect on Fraser's descriptive notes to the songs, or on his music. The music examples given below are, as far as possible, as printed in *Airs*. Only the first two verses of each song are provided here. Any editorial alterations are summarized in Notes to the Music, at the end of this article.

## The Range of the Repertoire

Gaelic songs are difficult, if not impossible, to categorize scientifically. Perhaps emulating those ballad scholars who have tried to develop thematic catalogues, James Ross made a credible attempt (1957), but such research can produce more problems than it solves since the poets' intentions and methods of achieving them are, by their very nature, multipurpose and overlapping. There is a wide choice of subjects and types of songs in Fraser's collection. Here is a small selection:

| | |
|---|---|
| Complaints | Lullabies |
| Dialogue songs | Martial songs |
| Drinking songs | Panegyrics |
| Elegies | Religious songs |
| Eulogies | Rowing songs |
| Historical songs | Satirical songs |
| Humorous songs | Sentimental songs |
| Laments | Songs associated with hunting |
| Love songs | Songs associated with marriage |

*Evidence of Oral Transmission*

Of the poets mentioned here, only Mac Mhaighstir Alasdair was literate. The others, as far as is known, were nonliterate Gaelic speakers. Their poems were circulated orally/aurally or written down directly from a spoken or sung source— what I will call a transforming interaction, one where the medium of communication is altered—or copied from someone else's manuscripts, either to be kept for the writer's own reference, passed on to others, or used as the basis for publications. Rob Donn's poems, for example, were written down by Rev. Æneas Macleod, minister of Rogart, Sutherland, and by a daughter of the nearby Durness minister, Rev. John Thomson (Morrison, 1899: xliv). After appearing individually in many books of Gaelic poetry, his poems were finally collected and published in 1829, more than fifty years after his death.

Simon Fraser's personal repertoire of Gaelic songs was the matching half, the music, rather than the words, collected from his father, and his friends. As he described the melodies he had collected, "it is well known that I never left my own or my father's house to acquire them, as no exertion of mine could equal the deposit left with me" (Fraser 1816: 3). His music, although not printed with the words, can still be considered part of a living source connecting his present and past vocal repertoire with our present and past, which has ultimately produced a printed artifact, representing his musical and linguistic knowledge, sensibilities, likes and dislikes, caught at the moment in time, 1816, when *Airs* was published. As the writer of the best-known quotation about Fraser said, perfectly describing his role in relation to traditional Gaelic music, "I never knew anyone who could make the fiddle speak Gaelic so beautifully" (MacKay 1874).

*Appendix: Some Songs from Fraser's* Airs

Of the first song, "Bodhan airdh 'm braigh Rannoch," Fraser wrote, "The shealing in the braes of Rannoch is also [as is his song number 53] given as acquired from the same gentlemen [his father John Fraser, grandfather Angus Fraser and his friends], and more recently sung by Colonel John Ross of the 86th regiment" (Fraser 1816: 108). A sheiling was a temporary wooden hut, thatched with heather, built each spring in the higher pastures where the cattle were moved for better grazing. The song describes the beauty of the setting and is nostalgic about the life shared there. The chorus comes from Watson, 1976: 192; the verses, Gillies, 1786: 242.

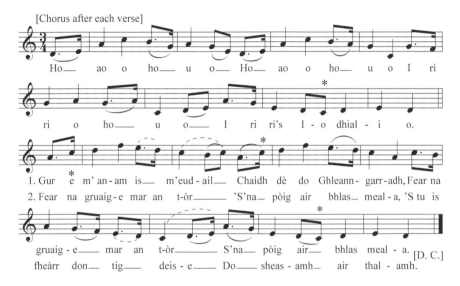

Fig. 1. "Bodhan airidh 'm braigh Rannoch" (Fraser 1816: 29, no. 54).

"Eiridh na Finnacha' Gaelach," which Fraser describes as "The Rebel War Song" (see Fig. 2, overleaf), is a political song associated with the Jacobite rising of 1715 by the Isle of Eigg poet Iain Dubh mac Iain mhic Ailein (John MacDonald, ca. 1665–ca. 1725). The words are from Ó Baoill, 1994: 23–24. Fraser's note reads, "There are few collections of Gaelic songs but begin with this rebel war song, so that it is well known, and contains a verse in praise of the virtues and valor of each of the Highland clans who joined in the rebellion, but anticipating more than they seemed capable of performing" (Fraser 1816: 108).

Fig. 2. "Eiridh na Finnacha' Gaelach" (Fraser 1816: 11, no. 2).

The third song, "Mi m' shuidh n' deireadh Bata" [Sitting in the Stern of a Boat], is one which Fraser obviously knew well: No. 161 is the composition of the Reverend Mr. M'Leod, who, the Editor [Fraser himself] thinks, was minister of Bracadale, in the Isle of Skye, before the last incumbent, and afterwards removed to Argyllshire, being an adieu to his native country. The Editor's father was extremely fond of this air, as characterizing two friends in early life, very partial to him, and whom he highly esteemed, Major M'Leod of Balmeanach, and Colonel MacLeod of Talisker. The composer gives a most poetical description of his sailing from Skye, whilst every well-known object, one by one, gradually recedes from his sight, till, at last, no trace of Skye is visible, except the "Bhan Bhein," or white mountain, and, when it vanishes in the misty vapor, he concludes with a benediction on all he has left behind him, worthy of a genuine poet (Fraser 1816: 114–15). The words are from R. MacDonald, 1776: 341.

Fig. 3. "Mi m' shuidh n' deireadh Bata" (Fraser 1816: 76, no. 161).

## Notes

1.  Henceforth, "Gaelic" refers to Scottish Gaelic.
2.  All information about Simon Fraser, his collection, and his family, if not otherwise referenced, may be found in Alburger 2001.
3.  The original title page is usually missing from *Airs,* having been covered over or removed when the volumes were leatherbound. The title in current use is from the frontispiece, which reads, The Airs and Melodies Peculiar to the Highlands of Scotland and the Isles, communicated in an original, pleasing & familiar style, having the lively airs introduced as medleys, to form a sequence to each slower movement, with an admired plain harmony, for the piano forte, harp, organ, or violoncello, intended rather to preserve simplicity, than load with embellishments. It is unusual that he does not mention the violin, which he played, although the melodies perfectly suit the range of the instrument, and he includes other technical instructions relevant to the violin.
4.  See Watson for more information about "classical" poetry.
5.  Gaelic personal names are often allied with patronymics, or other means of distinguishing people of the same name. The poet known as Alasdair Mac Mhaighstir Alasdair [Alasdair son of Master (or Teacher) Alasdair] is the same person as Alastair Mac-Dhonuill, usually translated into English as Alexander MacDonald.
6.  The Aberdeen publication of Forbes's "Cantus" in the seventeenth century was an anomaly; see Alburger 1996: 17.
7.  Joseph's seminal work, *A Compleat Theory of the Scots Highland Bagpipe,* also collected in the field, vanished at his death in India in 1763, but was rediscovered and published by his brother Patrick (of *Highland Vocal Airs*) in 1806; see Alburger 2004.
8.  The Highland Society (now the Royal Highland and Agricultural Society of Scotland) volumes are identified by title.
9.  The designation "of," as in "of Strathmashie," indicates which property the person held, usually as tacksman or wadsetter, whose land was gifted by the clan chief, and signaled someone of the landed gentry; the name of the property often remained associated with the person as a courtesy even if the property (Knockie, in Simon Fraser's case) was no longer held.
10. The titles of Fraser's melodies are given here as originally printed with the music, rather than as they appear in his index. His English versions of the titles follow in brackets.
11. Fraser's note to this song (no. 157) mentions that "Mrs. Fraser, wife of the Editor, frequently performed it [the song] on the organ" (Fraser 1816: 114).

## Notes to the Music Examples

Fig. 1. "Bodhan airdh 'm braigh Rannoch". The melody has been transposed down a fourth. The original key signature had two flats. The slurs are editorial; grace notes, pauses, and repeats are omitted. Notes with asterisks were originally a semitone higher.

Fig. 2. "Eiridh na Finnacha' Gaelach". Syllables within brackets are epenthetic vowels, pronounced, but not written, between certain consonants. They, and the notes to which they are sung are editorial, included here since they influence the rhythm of the poetry, and thus the music.

Fig. 3. "Mi m' shuidh n' deireadh Bata". The original slurs have been altered without notice. Notes above the staves show where the original rhythms differ from this edition.

## References

Alburger, Mary Anne. 1996. *Scottish Fiddlers and Their Music*. London: Gollancz, 1983. Reprint, Edinburgh: The Hardie Press.

————. 2001. *Making the Fiddle Sing Gaelic: Captain Simon Fraser and His Airs and Melodies Peculiar to the Highlands of Scotland and the Isles*. Ph.D. diss., University of Aberdeen, Aberdeen, Scotland.

—— ——. Forthcoming 2004. "Patrick and Joseph MacDonald." In *The New Dictionary of National Biography*. Oxford: Oxford University Press.

Bronson, Bertrand Harris. 1969. *The Ballad as Song*. Berkeley: University of California Press.

Calder, George, ed., and tr. 1912. *The Songs of Duncan Ban MacIntyre*. Edinburgh: Iain Grannd.

Campbell, Alexander, coll. and arr. 1816, 1818. *Albyn's Anthology, or, A Select Collection of the Melodies and Local Poetry Peculiar to Scotland and the Isles Hitherto Unpublished....* Edinburgh: Oliver and Boyd.

Campbell, John Lorne, ed. and tr. 1984. *Highland Songs of the Forty-five*. Scottish Gaelic Text Society, no. 15. Revised edition. Edinburgh: Scottish Academic Press.

————, ed. 1990. *Songs Remembered in Exile*. Aberdeen: Aberdeen University Press.

Fraser, Angus. Manuscript. Edinburgh University Library, Edinburgh, Scotland, EUL MS GEN.614.

Fraser, Angus. Papers, National Library of Scotland, Edinburgh, Scotland, Adv. MS.73.1.5 f.ir.

Fraser, Simon. 1816. *Airs and Melodies Peculiar to the Highlands of Scotland and the Isles*. Edinburgh: Printed and sold for the editor (cited in the text as *Airs*).

Gillies, John. 1786. *Sean Dain agus Orain Ghaidhealach*. Perth: Printed for John Gillies.

Gunn, Adam, and Malcolm MacFarlane, eds. 1899. *Orain agus Dàin le Rob Donn Mac-Aoidh*. Glascho [Glasgow]: Iain Mac-Aoidh [J. Mackay].

Herder, Johann Gottfried. 1990. *Volkslieder; Übertragungen; Dichtungen*. Edited by Ulrich Gaier. Werke in zehn Bänden, Johann Gottfried Herder, vol. 3; Bibliothek deutscher Klassiker, 60. Frankfurt am Main: Deutscher Klassiker Verlag.

*Inverness Courier*.

Mac-Dhonuill, Alastair. 1751. *Ais-eiridh na Sean Chánoin Albannaich; no, An Nuadh Oranaiche Gaidealach*. [The Resurrection of the Old Scottish Tongue; or, The New Gaelic Songster]. Ris am bheil coimh-cheangailte, eider-theangair am mineachadh ann am Beurla gach cruaigh fhacall a tharlas anns an leabhar. [Included in which is a dictionary with English meanings for every difficult word in the book]. Duneidiunn [Edinburgh]: Go feim an ughdair [For the author].

MacDonald, Ronald. 1776. *Comh-chruinneachidh Orannaigh Gaidhealach*. Duneidiunn [Edinburgh]: Vol. I.

MacKay, William. [1874]. Preface to *The Airs and Melodies Peculiar to the Highlands of Scotland and the Isles*, by Simon Fraser. Edited by Angus Fraser and William MacKay. Inverness: The Highland Society of Scotland, Hugh MacKenzie.

Matheson, William, ed. 1970. *An Clàrsair Dall: The Blind Harper: The Songs of Roderick Morison and His Music*. [Orain Ruaidhri Mhic Mhuirich agus a Chuid Ciùil]. Scottish Gaelic Text Society, no. 12. Edinburgh: Clark.

Morrison, Hew, ed. 1899. *Songs and Poems in the Gaelic Language by Rob Donn. Containing Several Poems Never Before Published, with English Notes and a New Memoir of the Poet*. Edinburgh: J. Grant.

Ó Baoill, Colm, ed., and Meg Bateman, tr. 1994. *Gàir nan Clàrsach—The Harps' Cry*. Edinburgh: Birlinn.

Ó Baoill, Colm. 1994. *Iain Dubh*. Obar-Dheathain [Aberdeen]: An Clò Gàidhealach.

Percy, Thomas. 1996. *Reliques of Ancient English Poetry*. London: J. Dodsley, 1765. Facsimile edition edited by Nick Groom. London: Routledge/Thoemmes Press.Ross, James. 1957. "A Classification of Gaelic Folk-Song." *Scottish Studies* 1: 95–151.

Royal Highland and Agricultural Society of Scotland Archives, Ingliston, Scotland.
    Volumes consulted: "Sederunt Books: 1815–18"; "Draught of Minutes &c. 1815–
    1818," containing "Minutes of Sub Committee of The Highland Society, 28th
    February 1815 (cited as RHASSA in the text; volumes have no manuscript numbers
    but are identified by title).
Shapiro, Anne Dhu. 1985. "Regional Song Styles: The Scottish Connection." In *Music
    and Context*, edited by Anne Dhu Shapiro, 404–17. Cambridge: Harvard University
    Press.
Shaw, Margaret Fay. [1955]. *Folksongs and Folklore of South Uist*. London: Routledge
    and Kegan Paul.
Shields, Hugh. 1993. *Narrative Singing in Ireland: Lays, Ballads, Come-All-Yes and Other
    Songs*. Dublin: Irish Academic Press.
Stenhouse, William. 1853. *Illustrations of the Lyric Poetry and Music of Scotland*.
    Reprint, Edinburgh: W. Blackwood.
Stuart, Alexander. 1726–27. *Musick for Allan Ramsay's Collection of Scots Songs*. Vol. 1.
    Edinburgh: Printed and sold by Allan Ramsay. (The second volume was never
    published.)
Thomson, Derick, ed. *The MacDiarmid MS Anthology*. Edinburgh.
Thomson, William. 1972. *Orpheus Caledonius: A Collection of Scots Songs*. 2nd ed,
    London: For the Author, 1733. Reprint, two volumes in one, Edinburgh: James Thin
    (page references are to reprint edition).
Tolmie, Frances. [1911] 1998. *One Hundred and Five Songs of Occupation from the
    Western Isles of Scotland*. Reprint, Felinfach: Llanerch. Originally published in the
    *Journal of the Folk-Song Society* 16, vol. 4, part 3, 1911.
Vallely, Fintan. 1999. *The Companion to Irish Traditional Music*. Cork: Cork University
    Press.
Watson, William J. 1976. *Bàrdachd Ghàidhlig*. 3rd ed. Inverness: An Comunn
    Gaidhealach.
Withrington, Donald J., and Ian R. Grant, eds. 1982. *Inverness-shire, Ross and Cromarty*.
    Vol. 15 of *The Statistical Account of Scotland, 1791–1799*, edited by Sir John Sinclair.
    Wakefield, England: EP Publishing.

"Purement scientifique

et archéologique":

The Mediating Collector

## "Purement scientifique et archéologique":
## The Mediating Collector

The work of ballad collectors is many faceted and, answering F. J. Child's aspiration that he "should wish to sift that matter thoroughly" (Hustvedt 1970: 248), this section addresses their diverse legacies. There has always been an element of resurrectionism in ballad studies, with collectors using words reminiscent of anatomists exhuming corpses ("Leur but est purement scientifique et archéologique"; see Lootens and Feys [1879] 1990: ii), reflecting, in a nutshell, the basic agendas of the time: excavation and the creation of the national and regional identities explored in the previous section.

Not only did ballad traditions apparently require excavation, but innumerable collectors also charged themselves with restoring their former glory. One such was Peter Buchan, one of Scotland's best and most notorious collectors. "Peter as usual…managed somehow (we wish we always knew how) to attain that completeness which is the despair of other ballad collectors," wrote Gavin Greig, "*They* may be 'fashed' with blanks; *Peter* never is" (1963, article 157). While collecting was ostensibly undertaken for scientific and literary interest, it was also socially and financially profitable and earned Buchan a substantial fortune. Greig admired Buchan's tenacity and success as a collector while chiding his penchant for filling in the gaps himself, though, fortunately, he was quite good at it. As Kenneth S. Goldstein noted, in relation to anthropological and folklore fieldwork,

> The collector chooses types of problems that need solving,
> informed by training in culture theory and based in part on his
> aesthetic.... The existence of the collector's aesthetic is a fact—a
> fact that comes into frequent play in the collector's communications
> with informants. In response, the informant's selection of the song
> or ballads to be performed is tempered by his knowledge of the
> collectors's taste. Simply put, collectors, intentionally or uninten-
> tionally, pass on such information to their informants who in turn
> sing ballads or songs they believe will please the collector.
>
> (1989: 367–68)

Subsequent editors must, of course, reach their own conclusions about the extent of the fieldworker's influence. Sigrid Rieuwerts's essay deals with exactly this issue in the context of F. J. Child's troubled attitude toward Peter Buchan's reliability; even that great editor was not able to come to any firm conclusions. Over and above various gradations of forgery, mediators of traditional song, as they are fashionably called, have been accused of cultural appropriation and worse. The collector as invader is an idea that has become more popular in the postcolonial era. Valentina Bold's essay offers a reflexive look at a fieldworker's place in the centuries-old procession of collectors to and through the Borders and North East of Scotland, surely one of the most heavily mined areas of ballad tradition anywhere in the world.

Finally, this section offers an academic and personal appreciation, from James Porter, David Engle, and Roger deV. Renwick, of the wide-ranging contribution of the late D. K. Wilgus to international ballad scholarship: his emphasis on the texts and related contextual information; his ideas of cataloging by narrative and thematic units, rather than whole ballads types; and his magnificent achievement of summarizing the complex, sometimes ill-tempered debates in a century of folk-song scholarship since the death of Francis James Child (see Wilgus 1959: chaps 1, 2).

## References

Goldstein, Kenneth S. 1989. "The Collector's Personal Aesthetic as an Influence on the Informant's Choice of Repertory." In *Ballades et Chansons Folkloriques*, edited by Conrad Laforte, 367–71. Actes de la 18th session de la Commission pour l'Étude de la Poésie de Tradition Orale (Kommission für Volksdichtung) de la Société Internationale d'Ethnologie et de Folklore [SIEF]. Actes du Célat, no. 4. Québec: Célat, Université Laval, 1989.

Greig, Gavin. 1963. "Folk-Song of the North-East: Articles Contributed to the *Buchan Observer* from December 1907 to June 1911." In *Folk-Song in Buchan and Folk-Song of the North-East*, with a foreword by Kenneth S. Goldstein and Arthur Argo. Hatboro, Pa.: Folklore Associates.

Hustvedt, Sigurd B. 1970. *Ballad Books and Ballad Men*. Cambridge: Harvard University Press, 1930. Reprint, New York: Johnson (page references are to reprint edition).

Lootens, Adolphe-R., et J. M. E. Feys. [1879] 1990. *Chants Populaires flamands avec les airs notés et poésies populaires diverses recueillis à Bruges* [Flemish Folksongs with Tunes and Other Folk Poems Collected in Bruges]. Reprint, Antwerpen: K. C. Peeters Instituut voor Volkskunde, with a postscript and indices by Stefaan Top (page references are to reprint edition).

Wilgus, D. K. 1959. *Anglo-American Folksong Scholarship since 1898*. New Brunswick, N.J.: Rutgers University Press.

# The Case against Peter Buchan

## Sigrid Rieuwerts

It is a well-known fact that the North East of Scotland is particularly rich in traditional songs and ballads. In *The English and Scottish Popular Ballads*, almost one-third of Child's A texts—those he considered the oldest and best examples of a specific ballad type—come from this area. One of Aberdeenshire's chief and most voluminous collections of traditional ballads in the nineteenth century was undertaken by Peter Buchan (1790–1854). He not only edited important collections like *Gleanings of Scarce Old Ballads* (1825) and *Ancient Ballads and Songs of the North of Scotland* (1828) but also left invaluable manuscript collections of songs, ballads, and tales.

And yet, far from being held in great honor and esteem, Peter Buchan has been the most criticized ballad collector ever. In his lifetime, he was generally regarded as a forger, and Scottish scholars (among them William Walker, Gavin Greig, Alexander Keith, and David Buchan) have been trying to clear his name ever since. Instead of rehearsing old arguments, I will discuss the case against Peter Buchan by focusing on F. J. Child's changing view of the Aberdeenshire ballad collector and editor.

When Child published his first, eight-part ballad collection, *English and Scottish Ballads*, in 1857–59, he meant it to be the most comprehensive collection of these ancient narrative songs that had ever appeared. Thus, he explained in his preface, any traditional ballad was to be included in the collection, however mutilated or void of aesthetic value. He felt, however, obliged to justify the inclusion of what he felt to be particularly bad examples, namely those from Peter Buchan's ballad compilations, by adding the following footnote: "Some resolution has been exercised, and much disgust suppressed, in retaining certain pieces from Buchan's collections, so strong is the suspicion that, after having been procured from very inferior sources, they were tampered with by the editor" (Child 1857–59, 1: ix).

In the second, substantially revised edition of 1860, this footnote has been withdrawn, and Child—for the first time in his career as a ballad collector and editor (see Rieuwerts 1994: 8–10)—employs the distinction between the "poetry of the people" and the "poetry of art." No longer is disgust expressed at Peter Buchan's traditional ballads but rather, at the lowest form of art poetry, namely broadsides of the Roxburghe and Pepys type.

For his third and ultimate collection of traditional ballads, Child felt at a loss about Peter Buchan. He took Svend Grundtvig's *Danmarks gamle Folkeviser* as his model but surprisingly did not accept his friend's advice on the Scottish collector/editor. In his first letter to Child, Grundtvig pointed out that Buchan's "much abused but very valuable collections" might appear spurious but were nevertheless genuine. "I am able to prove, through a comparison with undoubtedly genuine Scandinavian ballads, the material authenticity of many of those pieces, which consequently may safely [be added] to the English ballad store" (Grundtvig to Child, 17 February 1872, quoted in Hustvedt 1970: 244). So close is the connection with traditional Scandinavian material that Grundtvig chose many of Buchan's texts (in addition to those of Motherwell and Scott) for his translations into Danish. The collection appeared in 1842 under the title *Engelske og Skotske Folkeviser med oplysende Anmærkninger fordanskede af S. G. Kjöbenhavn.*

Grundtvig was very much aware of the fact that English scholars had slighted Peter Buchan. Years after the Percy Society had published *Scottish Traditional Versions of Ancient Ballads* in 1845, he took issue with the editor, J. H. Dixon, for not giving Buchan the credit he deserved. After all, the Percy Society's publication was based on two of Buchan's manuscript volumes, containing ballad versions taken from oral tradition in the north of Scotland, yet not a word was said about Peter Buchan's own ballad collections. Why was it, Grundtvig asked, that "it is not even mentioned, that this same Mr. Buchan has published three different collections of traditionary songs, and, in fact, is the man who has rescued, and for the first time published, more traditionary ballad versions than any other antiquary in Great Britain that we know of? (Grundtvig 1855: 21). Grundtvig pointed out that two-thirds of the texts published by the Percy Society had already appeared in print. As it was a printing society devoted to making unpublished material available to its members, this fact would have caused an outcry. At the time, Grundtvig placed his defence of Peter Buchan in *Notes and Queries* on 14 July 1855; however, the Percy Society had already been dissolved for three years.

What he could not have foreseen, and what would have infuriated Grundtvig even further, was the fact that Dixon's Percy Society publication was to be reissued two years later by Robert Bell as part of his *Annotated Edition of the English Poets.* (Note the word "English.") All references to Peter Buchan or Scotland were eliminated and the full title ran *Ancient Poems, Ballads, and Songs of the Peasantry of England, Taken Down from Oral Recitation, and*

*Transcribed from Private Manuscripts, Rare Broadsides, and Scarce Publications, Edited by Robert Bell.*

This book, incidentally, sparked Child's first ballad collection of 1857–59. Asked to model an American series of British poetry on Bell's rather successful *Annotated Edition of the English Poets*, Child copied many parts of the British publication. The only place where he thought he could do better was the anonymous poets of the British Isles. He regarded Dixon's and Bell's collections as dreadful and, instead of reissuing a very similar, if not identical, collection, he printed his eight volumes of *English and Scottish Ballads*. In trying to put his stamp on his edition, Child directed his criticism at Peter Buchan's ballads, the very material Dixon and Bell had used without acknowledgment. He felt, as he wrote time and again, disgusted by the sheer vulgarity of Buchan's versions, differing in quality and markedly longer than the ones Child regarded as the genuine ballads of the people. Child wrote to Grundtvig (26 March 1872) in response to his Danish friend's endorsement of Buchan's texts: "From the internal evidence, the extraordinary *vulgarity*, especially, of many of his ballads, I should think that he must have tampered very extensively with his originals, if even he did not invent out and out. I should wish to sift that matter thoroughly" (quoted in Hustvedt 1970: 248). Grundtvig did not want to let the matter rest and took issue with Child over Buchan's presumed "vulgarity."

> The extreme elegance and exquisite taste exhibited in many of
> Scott's texts is to my eyes a strong direct proof of their want of
> genuineness, while on the other hand what you term the "vulgarity"
> of the Buchan texts is to me the best proof of their material
> authenticity;...very often what now to delicate eyes and ears may
> seem "vulgar," is in fact of the old stamp.
> (Grundtvig to Child, 2 June 1872, quoted in Hustvedt 1970: 249)

Still, Child felt on sure ground, for he had one proof that old Peter Buchan was a cheat.

> Dr. John Hill Burton testifies that a part of the ballad called *Chil Ether*
> was drafted by a friend at his bedside when he was recovering from
> an illness and was sent to Buchan, with the intention of taking the
> measure of his honesty. Peter was so happy as to be able to supply
> all that was missing *from the recollections of the peasantry.*—I had

reason to believe in Buchan's dishonesty before, but I wanted explicit
proof. (Child to Grundtvig, 1 July 1873, quoted in Hustvedt 1970: 257)

Child was right: "Chil Ether" was indeed a forgery. Only a note can be found in
Buchan's manuscripts that he printed the text from a different source. Joseph
Robertson and John Hill Burton, later George Kinloch's and Robert Chambers's
coworkers, passed on their ballad to the unsuspecting Peter Buchan. Furthermore, they were abetted by Dean Christie, who claimed later that he had found
the tune of that "popular" ballad.

Grundtvig was undoubtedly familiar with these accusations, as they were
reiterated in *Notes and Queries* by J. C. R. and T. G. S. (1855: 95, 135) in response
to his praise of Buchan in that journal. He seems to have accepted Buchan's
failings, but he still holds out hope that the publication of Buchan's manuscripts
will clear his name: "What now ought to be done is this, that the whole ballad
portion of Mr. Buchan's MSS. should be published from the MSS., but with all
the additions and variae lectiones of the published collections of Mr. Buchan
thrown into the notes" (Grundtvig 1855: 22). Therefore, he is extremely interested
in Child's passing remark that Buchan's papers are now in the British Museum
and he will have copies made. What Child does not tell Grundtvig is that he was
instrumental in arranging their deposit at a public library. Just before Buchan's
sudden death in London on the 19 September 1854, at the age of sixty-four, he
had sold the rights to his manuscripts to the publishers Ingram and Co., who
subsequently left them to their broker, the poet Charles Mackey, who used them
for his *Illustrated Book of Scottish Songs*.

As is well known, Child was very eager to have all the genuine old ballads of
the English language in their authentic versions, not touched up by editors.
Having the use of the ballad collector's and editor's original manuscripts was
therefore of paramount importance. And in tracing the various manuscripts Child
employed one of the most industrious scholars of the time, the ever-helpful
Frederick James Furnivall. At Child's request and insistence, the latter had earlier
secured Percy's folio manuscript, often described as the foundation document
of English ballad lore. Furnivall, again being Child's agent, now persuaded Mackey
to sell the two volumes of Buchan's manuscripts to the British Library. Thus,
they were deposited in 1873, and, in the summer of that same year, Child was able
to consult them in London.

Naturally Grundtvig was very anxious to learn what Child had found in the
manuscripts and also added in his letter to Child, "The impression (or the proofs)
you have got, as to the trustworthiness (or untrustworthiness) of the editors, for

instance, Peter Buchan" (25 March 1874, quoted in Hustvedt 1970: 261). Having made up his mind about Peter Buchan, Grundtvig did not even want to wait for Child's response, for he enclosed in the same letter a long series of generally favorable comments on individual ballads in Buchan's *Ancient Ballads and Songs*.

Taking his friend's advice on all matters but Peter Buchan, Child could not lay the matter to rest: "Now it is a very serious question what to do with Buchan" (quoted in Hustvedt 1970: 264). The copies of the British Library Buchan manuscripts did nothing to dispel his doubts. It became clear, after close examination, that Buchan's manuscript sources from which the ballads were supposedly printed differed considerably from the printed versions. Quite a number of the ballads from Buchan's 1828 ballad collection were in the manuscript, but since only minor alterations between handwritten and printed copy were detectable, the manuscripts could not be used as proof against Peter Buchan. They did nothing to clear his name, either, for some of the material was as vulgar as Child had predicted.

Child, as he confessed to Grundtvig, was now at a complete loss about the Scotsman. Buchan's texts were so different from all the other versions Child had that he could not use the texts for collation only. Should he therefore print them in smaller type? Child knew that he had to print the whole of Buchan's collection if he wanted to abide by his principle that *The English and Scottish Popular Ballads* should contain "every bit of genuine ballad lore, and consequently all that may be genuine, and...all that has been so" (Child to Grundtvig, 25 March 1874, quoted in Hustvedt 1970: 260). Buchan's style of expression was, he said, far from "volksmäßig," and therefore it was more likely that the ballads came from a man and not a class of people. He could not understand that similar ballad collections from the North East of Scotland (for example, Kinloch's), did not exhibit the same artificial vulgarity. On the other hand, Child did not believe that Buchan had "enough wit" to forge a complete ballad.

Always eager to print from manuscripts or oral tradition, Child planned to get to the bottom of the Buchan problem by probing into the Scottish ballad tradition. Encouraged by recent finds of traditional ballads by a Danish schoolmaster, he sent an appeal to about two thousand schoolmasters and ministers in Scotland, asking them to note every bit of traditional songs and ballads. He was seriously considering going to Scotland himself in the summer of 1877, but Murison, English master at Aberdeen Grammar, advised against it. He and his wife collected for Child instead. From Child's Christmas letter to Lowell, we learn of his utter disappointment: "I have had an Aberdeen man, rather his wife, noting down what can now be collected in Old Deir, and such trash I get! Better work the mines of Spain & Denmark" (Child to Lowell, Christmas 1877, quoted in DeWolfe Howe and Cottrell 1970: 31). Two years later, he still had not given up on the idea of going to the North East of Scotland: "There must be ballads there:—how else have the people held out against poverty, cold & darkness?" (Child to Lowell, 21 December 1879, quoted in DeWolfe Howe and Cottrell 1970: 45). Not wanting to delay the publication of *The English and Scottish Popular Ballads* even further, he eventually began to print without having been able to judge the situation in the North East of Scotland for himself.

When the first installment of Child's major work came out in 1882, he was immediately taken to task in a review for including "freakish" and "monstrous" verses, and the reviewer added, "…even some whole ballads from the collection of Peter Buchan, as well as from some less heinously offending collections." From that reviewer's perspective, Buchan's collection was one of the worst possible examples of ballad lore:

> It contains many genuine and precious fragments of old ballads; but these are so mixed up with bald doggerel, either written by the collector himself or palmed off on him by some one having as little feeling as himself for the true ballad style, that it is almost worse than useless. It will never be of any value until some person with the proper qualifications, goes over it thoroughly and separates the chaff and tares from the sound grain. (Davidson 1909: 468)

In fifteen pages, the review went to extraordinary lengths in dismissing any claims Peter Buchan's collection might have on representing the genuine ballads of the people in the North East of Scotland. Child should have been more careful in admitting the work of such a forger, he argued. Child's A text of "Leesome Brand" (Child 5), for example, was described as a fabrication. The author of the review lent particular weight to his accusations by adding that he had grown up in Aberdeenshire, spoke the dialect, and even sang some of the ballads mentioned.

Child, always eager to receive advice, did not take issue with any of these accusations in public, perhaps because the author of the review was Thomas Davidson, an American scholar of Scottish extraction who had become a friend a couple of years earlier. We learn more about Davidson from one of Child's letters:

Is it not odd that, after having flooded Scotland with circulars
addressed to schoolmasters & ministers, with scarcely a perceptible
effect, I should find a man in this very town whose mother knows
(as he says) 164 ballads? This man is a scholar, & knows whereof he
is talking. His mother lives in Old Deer. I have tried to make him
abandon all worldly business and go back to Aberdeenshire—
where others, I think, besides his mother still retain ballads—and
collect all that he can find. In default of willingness on his part to
come up to this manifest duty, I have accepted his mediation with
two persons three thousand miles nearer the source and I hope that
good may be the result. The same gentleman thinks that he may be
able to get some light concerning P. Buchan's proceedings.

(Child to Murdoch, 2 February 1876, Murdoch MSS. no. 21;

see also Lyle 1976: 137–38)

Thomas Davidson clearly felt strongly about Buchan. Since Grundtvig had died
just after the first installment of *The English and Scottish Popular Ballads*,
Child became heavily dependent on Davidson in all matters relating to
Aberdeenshire. His influence was substantial, for he gave Child not only invaluable information on his home county but also supplied him with contacts in
Aberdeenshire and, last but not least, with ballads. Davidson firmly believed
that Peter Buchan was a cheat. He felt particularly insulted by Buchan's claim
that his ballads were derived from oral tradition.

With Grundtvig dismissing the case against Buchan, and Davidson strenu-
ously trying to prove it, Child sat on the fence, feeling less well equipped to be a
judge on these matters than his two friends. He could not dismiss the ballads
outright, as Furnivall, Ebsworth, Chappell, and other English editors had done.
He did, however, feel their disgust at the vulgarity of some of Buchan's texts. He
printed them, nevertheless, unlike Kittredge, who deliberately omitted them from
his later one-volume edition.

One of the oft-quoted pieces of evidence against Peter Buchan was his letter
to the Earl of Buchan, published in Motherwell's review of *Ancient Ballads and
Songs of the North of Scotland*. In this letter, Peter Buchan described how his
ballad collection of 1828 came about.

The Ballads and Songs were all taken down from the recitation of
very old people, during a ten or twelve years siege that I stormed

their straw-covered citadels, and by many good judges they have
been considered the most original and best collection hitherto
published, having been given in their primitive truth and order. The
task was really laborious and expensive, as I kept a wight of
Homer's craft, an old Senachial veteran, constantly in pay,...still it
has come short of rewarding me for the time, trouble, and expense I
have been at in *creating it out of a chaos of rude materials.*
(Buchan, quoted in Motherwell 1828: 648; emphasis mine)

The choice of the word "creating" was seen as an indictment against the authenticity of his published versions. At the time, however, the prevailing attitude was
that incomplete or mutilated copies from tradition had to be improved by collation with versions obtained from different quarters. Filling in missing verses, or
improving existing ones, was common practice among singers, and it was difficult for editors to refrain from doing the same. Since Peter Buchan worked in the
broadside trade and boasted more than once of the great stock of ballads he had
accumulated in print, it was reasonable to assume that some stanzas had been
lifted from these sources.

The source Buchan named, "a wight of Homer's craft" he kept in constant
pay, was seen as further proof. James Rankin, a blind beggar, had been a colorful
contributor indeed, and not even Buchan trusted him completely. In his note to
"The Scottish Exile" in the manuscript, Buchan says Rankin has "deceived him
again" (see Walker 1887: 59, 166).

Although Motherwell and Buchan were both field collectors, they also employed people to collect ballads. The quality—and definitely the authenticity—
of the ballad collected depended to a large extent on these intermediaries.
Exchanges between collectors were frequent, and thus James Nicol's ballads, for
example, appear not only in Peter Buchan's manuscripts but also in the collections of Motherwell, Maidment, Sharpe, and Scott (for further details, see Buchan
1972: 223–43). James Nicol was probably a middleman who sold ballads he had
abstracted from a great variety of sources. Child describes him in his note on
"Young Bearswell" (1882–98, 5: 178) as "a respectable voucher." And while
Motherwell's collector Thomas McQueen is also above suspicion, James Rankin
was largely responsible for bringing Peter Buchan's collection into disrepute. In
sum, Peter Buchan was to Child anything but the ideal ballad collector/editor.

The only thing that would have decided the case against Peter Buchan one
way or the other was a publication of all his manuscripts—Grundtvig was right.

When Buchan was forced to sell his library in 1837, a great number of ballad manuscripts were listed, among them "about twelve or more volumes of Manuscript Scottish Ballads and Songs exactly as taken down from the singing and sighing of the old Dames and Carles amongst the mountains and glens in the North Countrie, Scottish Straggling Ballads, of the last century, from Oral Tradition, scarce MSS. and old printed copies, containing about 400 pages" (*Catalogue* 1837: 41–42). Only a couple of these are accounted for, and I am surprised that nobody has ever tried to trace the others. Why, for example, should the Glenbuchat manuscript not be one of the missing Buchan documents? In my view, this is a possibility and worth investigating.[1]

Summing up, it is really no wonder that Child and his contemporaries were confused about the different Buchan manuscripts. The one deemed original extends from 1816 to 1827. Buchan gathered in one huge folio volume (about 1,112 pages) all the songs and ballads he intended for publication: 220 items in total. It passed through many hands and was offered to Child several times, but having seen Buchan's manuscripts in the British Library, he gave them little importance (C. K. Sharpe had testified that everything was faithfully recorded in the copies after the first sixteen pages).

When Child mentioned to William Macmath, on 29 June 1892, that he would still like to see David Scott of Peterborough's Buchan manuscripts, despite their modernized and "stylized" spelling, Macmath was intrigued. He and Murdoch had had the chance to buy them. Apparently, on that missed occasion, Scott bought one Buchan volume at an auction in Edinburgh for twenty pounds; Murdoch had offered eighteen for it. According to both of Child's main Scottish correspondents, it was not worth more than that. To Macmath, it seemed that all the pieces were in the printed book, and furthermore, he said, there was the question whether the printed book, or the manuscript, came first. In any case, he concluded, the manuscript was not a copy from tradition, and thus Child was led to believe that there was no great loss in not having it. (For Child's correspondence with his Scottish friends, see: Child MSS.)

Unlike Motherwell's own manuscripts, the Buchan manuscript is not a working copy. It gives very little insight into the oral tradition from which he was gathering. Only a few of the contributors are named, and the circumstances of collection—the singer's identity and the time and place—remain unrecorded. A field notebook, like the one Motherwell kept, does not seem to have survived, if indeed it ever existed. Furthermore, Buchan did not focus on songs and ballads from oral tradition as much as Motherwell did, instead collecting at random from broadsides, periodicals, and earlier songbooks. But since he wanted to give his collection a distinctly "northern" touch—balancing Sir Walter Scott's Border collection—his attention inevitably turned to the yet uncollected stores of ballad lore in the North.

William Walker eventually secured the Buchan manuscripts for Harvard College Library, but Child did not live to see them. I doubt, however, that the manuscripts—valuable as they might have been to him—would have changed his mind. They would have answered many of his philological questions, and certainly he would have seen for himself how much (or rather how little) Buchan's *Ballads of the North of Scotland* differed from the manuscript versions (see Child to Walker, 19 November 1891, in Walker 1930: 6–7). This manuscript alone, however, cannot answer the crucial question as to whether Buchan's recordings of traditional ballads are trustworthy.

Child, in the end, gave Buchan the benefit of the doubt, but he was far from James Dingwell Walker's estimation of Peter Buchan as "the saviour of the ballad minstrelsy of the north" (1887: 388). To the very end, what Child confided to Grundtvig at the beginning holds true: "When I come to Buchan, I am in difficulty. I must confess that my treatment of his ballads both seems and was capricious" (Child to Grundtvig, 8 May 1874, quoted in Hustvedt 1970: 264).

## Notes

1. The Glenbuchat manuscript was being prepared for publication by the late David Buchan; the work is being extended and completed by James Moreira.

## References

Buchan, David. 1972. *The Ballad and the Folk*. London: Routledge and Kegan Paul. Reprint, Phantassie, East Lothian: Tuckwell Press, 1997.

*Catalogue of the Private Library of Peter Buchan*. 1837. Aberdeen: Chalmers.

Child, Francis James. Correpondence and Papers Relating to Ballads, with Many Ballad Versions. 33 vols. Harvard College Library, 25241l.47* (cited in the text as Child MSS).

Child, Francis James, ed. 1857–59. *English and Scottish Ballads*. 8 vols. Boston: Little, Brown and Company.

Child, Francis James, ed. 1882–98. *The English and Scottish Popular Ballads*. Boston: Houghton, Mifflin. 5 vols. Reprint, New York: Folklore Press, 1956–57; New York: Dover, 1965. Corrected edition prepared by Mark and Laura Heiman. Northfield, Minn.: Loomis House Press, 2002. Digital edition, with gazetteer, maps and audio CD. New York: ESPB Publishing, 2003.

Davidson, Thomas. 1909. "Prof. Child's Ballad Book." *American Journal of Philology* 5: 466–78.

DeWolfe Howe, M. A., and G. W. Cottrell, eds. 1970. *The Scholar-Friends: Letters of Francis James Child and James Russell Lowell*. Westport, Conn.: Greenwood.

Grundtvig, Svend. 1855. "Buchan's Scottish Ballads: Percy's Reliques." *Notes and Queries* 12 (14 July): 21–22.

Hustvedt, Sigurd B. 1970. *Ballad Books and Ballad Men.* Cambridge: Harvard University Press, 1930. Reprint, New York: Johnson.

Lyle, E. B. 1976. "Child's Scottish Harvest." *Harvard Library Bulletin* 25: 125–54.

Motherwell, William. 1828. "Ancient Ballads of the North of Scotland." *The Paisley Magazine* 13 (1 December): 639–66.

Murdoch, James Barclay. n.d. Correspondence. Harvard College Library, MS Am 1319/ *53m–101 (cited in text as Murdoch MSS).

R., J. C. 1855. "Buchan Ballads." *Notes and Queries* 12 (1855): 135.

Rieuwerts, Sigrid. 1994. "'The Genuine Ballads of the People': F. J. Child and the ballad cause." *Journal of Folklore Research* 31, nos. 1–3: 1–34.

S., T. G. 1855. "Buchan Ballads." *Notes and Queries* 12 (1855): 95.

Walker, William. 1887. *The Bards of Bon-Accord 1375–1860.* Aberdeen: J. and J. P. Edmond and Spark.

Walker, William. *Peter Buchan and Other Papers on Scottish and English Ballads and Songs.* Aberdeen: Wyllie & Sons, 1915.

[Walker, William]. 1930. *Letters on Scottish Ballads from Professor Francis J. Child to W. W[alker].* Aberdeen: Bon-Accord Press.

# Ballad Raids and Spoilt Songs:
# Collection as Colonization

Valentina Bold

I would like to start this discussion of collection as colonization with a quote
from Jock Duncan, a singer from North East Scotland, talking about local
songmaker Geordie Thomson and Gavin Greig as a collector:

> Geordie wis assistant chemist at New Deer, he wis trainin there. An
> he wrote sangs at amazin speed. He wid hae written a sang a nicht,
> bit far are they aa? There's nae mony left. He niver took life seri-
> ously, ye see?...
>
> Geordie likit the drink, ye see, an he took e train intae Aiberdeen
> ae Settirday nicht. The bobbies hidnae much tae dee at at time; they
> arrested him for drunk, for bein drunk an disorderly. Geordie wid
> niver have been disorderly.
>
> Somebody must hae lettan Gavin Greig ken, cause he gaed in, he
> gaed in, he took the train an peyed is fine an took im hame wi him.
> An e says, "Now George, hae ye ony o that songs, A want that
> sangs, A wint them for ma collection!"
>
> (Bold and McKean 1999: Song section)

Greig's fanatical desire to accumulate songs—"I want that sangs, I wint them
for ma collection"—reminds one of Walter Scott's violent-sounding "ballad raids"
into the Scottish Borders, which resulted in the "spoilt songs" which so of-
fended Margaret Laidlaw. Greig's direct action, making order from the some-
times-drunken, if not disorderly, behavior of Thomson, exemplifies the
phenomenon of collection as colonization.

The colonization begins with the collector/colonizer's desire to conquer the
territory, or intellectual property, of the native/performer who is, implicitly, incapable of managing it. The territory itself may be "new" (unfamiliar to the collector), or others may have previously surveyed it. Reaching the territory may
involve a journey through space, or an even more arduous one through cultural
and class barriers. People, too, can be colonized, from a small identifiable group
to a larger group (for example, the Travelling people of Scotland) or an entire
nation.

Subsequently, if the work is done properly, the territory—preferably containing large deposits of natural resources, ballads in this case—can be mapped into blocks, using a system of numbers or themes. Subsequent waves of settlers often follow the colonist. The success of Gavin Greig in North East Scotland, for instance, encouraged further forays into this area, including the research programs of the Elphinstone Institute, University of Aberdeen, established in 1995.

I do not mean to suggest that ballad collecting is wholly about domination by the collector. Singers are active contributors to the creation of colonized spaces. Equally, prominent local collectors, like Greig, strive to assert locally generated identities through a form of micronationalism on behalf of locals. Paradoxically, though, Greig discovered that many North East songs were actually of Irish origin. The intellectual and physical borders of colonial space are often in dispute, and collecting, even by sympathetic colonizers with friendly collaborators, is frequently based on profound, sometimes disturbing, imbalances of power. These are rarely explicitly mentioned, largely for fear of offending the dedicated and well-motivated people engaged in collecting.

Scotland has experienced centuries of ongoing colonization as a ballad space. I want to look, in particular, at two regions or, in this context, colonial provinces, the North East and the Borders, and focus on three varieties of collectors-as-colonizers. First is the incomer colonizer, the international, transient collector, resident for the purposes of collection. Next comes the colonizer from within, whether indigenous or a regional migrant and, lastly, the cross-cultural team, which blends both types. For this last group, experiences of the exotic culture are mitigated by local guides: the figurative "native bearers" (or amanuenses, to be polite).

Modern colonial theory has an immediate bearing on understanding collecting processes as colonization. V.G. Kiernan, for instance, draws attention to the so called civilizing mission of the colonizer (1996, 1969). In song collecting, of course, the mission may be overtly the opposite: to seek a countercultural balance to modern civilization or return to a precivilized age, as in the case of James Macpherson's collection of Ossianic material (see Macpherson 1996). Even so, the desire to impose order on this material for a literate age can be seen as a type of civilizing mission.

Collecting as colonization is most visible in the work of the colonizer from without. Bear in mind Said's distinctions while reading a familiar passage from Kenneth Goldstein's *A Guide for Field Workers in Folklore* in which the "us" and "them" division is obvious. This is from the section entitled "Locating Living Quarters":

> The first of the collector's activities in the community necessarily
> involves his finding a place to settle.... His headquarters should be
> centrally located (permitting easy access to all parts of the commu-
> nity) and situated so that the collector's activities will be as
> conspicuous as possible. A large part of rapport establishment
> involves the collector's being seen frequently enough by the
> inhabitants for them to become used to his presence and to begin to
> accept him as a natural part of the local scene.... In selecting a place
> to settle, the collector may obtain assistance from some of the
> inhabitants of the community.... It will also aid in rapport establish-
> ment if the collector makes it plain by seeking such aid that he is
> dependent upon the local citizenry. If they have a part in his very
> first steps in the community, they are likely to feel responsible for
> him from that point on. (1964: 48–49)

In the relationship between collector and collected, a "them" and "us" distinction may, of course, be desirable. Cultural allegiances related to points of
origin must be considered, along with the practical considerations of how much
territory is actually manageable. Just as the colonist focuses on target areas in
the short term, so must the collector.

Goldstein's suggestions make practical sense, but this view of fieldwork
planning does seem to indicate a colonial mindset. There is the notion of being
seen and seeking out a local guide, similar to the way the colonizer makes preliminary moves and finds trusted collaborators. Then there is the advice to find a
suitable "headquarters," like a military base of operations. The very notion of
entering the field suggests a military campaign to gain new territory by collecting
its cultural materials.

Goldstein goes on to advise the collector on cultural camouflage or blending
in with the natives. The collector should not take a "grand" house or move "to
the wrong side of the tracks" but select a house "which represents the average
mode of existence for the community." The transportation section calls for similar circumspection: "to travel around in a new, mile-long Cadillac or fancy sports
car will immediately type the collector as a show-off, a vacationer, or worse. An
inexpensive old model auto, plain luggage, and a minimum of supplies and equip-
ment will help to type the collector as a reasonable kind of fellow" (1964: 51).

Goldstein advocates adapting to local ideologies. In North Carolina, "it could
have been disastrous to my project had I indicated that I was connected with...any
educational institution." On the other hand, "Northeastern Scotland...offers no

difficulties whatsoever over the educational affiliations of collectors. The Scots countryman admires education and learning" (1964: 33).

To reverse perspective, we may ask how the collector/colonizer is perceived by these local guides? Does camouflage work? Elizabeth Stewart, in her teens when Goldstein was working with her family in the North East, has a sophisticated understanding of collection as colonization. When Tom McKean and I were talking with Elizabeth about her experiences as a Traveller in her childhood, we got on the subject of how being collected affected her, and her family's, self-image.

> A aye wantit tae be noticet for ma playin. Nae fur showin aff...but fur folk tae listen til't, cause A got *so* much enjoyment out o it, A wantit other people tae enjoy it. Tae realize, understand fit A wis daein, it's great tae get a bit o encouragement.
>
> Before [my aunt and mother] started [being collected] they were very modest and very shy. Even though my mother was a musician and out in the public, she was still very shy, and for someone to come and invade their private lives for a start was a wee bittie, they were a wee bittie wary. But then when Kenny showed interest in the music, an things, ken fit A mean, more interest in the music really, they likit to play, they would hae playet tae anybody for nothin, ken fit A mean, it wis jist somethin they liked daein.... It took a lot fir Lucy to start, for she wis very very shy, very modest. Ma mither, playin fir ma mother, that wis OK fur her, an she played tae Kenny an a'...she played on the box.[1] (Stewart 1997)

Elizabeth's use of the word "invade" really intrigued me, as did her description of people coming out of their shell through encouragement and responding to this benevolent form of colonization. She continued,

> We were excited that somebody wis wantin tae listen, A wis very young when Peter Kennedy came, but it's exciting that somebody's wantin tae ken yir music, especially you as a Traveller, and wantit tae ken that, and wantit tae ken yer lifestyle, but we were a bit wary fur whit were they wantin tae ken our lifestyles for? Ye ken fit A mean? An ye dinnae ken fa ye've got. An people comin fae America, comin fae London, till a wee place like Fetterangus.... We

> were a bittie bad mindet, ye ken, a bittie backward in comin forwart,
> because o livin awa out in the country, out in the hills campin an
> things fur years, jist keep tae themsels, ken?
>
> (Elphinstone Institute field recording 1997.021)

The reaction of the indigenous people to the outsider, then, seems to have been a mixture of pride in having their traditions valued, coupled with suspicion of the nonnative colonizer.

Elizabeth also explained the way those not interviewed perceived the collectors' interests locally. The noncolonized natives, apparently, "couldnae care less, some o them thought it was stupit, because they wir ignorant o fit wis happenin, they had nae interest in the academic side o things.... Nothin wis goin tae change them.... Some people can be nice tae ye but it aye comes oot." Elizabeth was equally aware that the colonial listener was not always alert to the range of cultural nuances bound up in a lifetime's appreciation and learning about indigenous culture. The colonizer lacked what could be termed "brocht up learning"; musically, as Elizabeth said, "they hear it in a different wey. They dinna understand it right."

Even so, being colonized can be a positive experience with its own rewards. The interest in Stewart, as a native bearer of traditions, has given her four tours of America, beginning with an eighteen-state visit in 1972. For her music, she is a willing participant in cultural colonization: "I got so much enjoyment out o it, I wanted other people to enjoy it." The same can be said of those colonized in Scotland in earlier generations, like James Hogg, whose creative career began with his role as an agent for Walter Scott's *The Minstrelsy of the Scottish Border* (1801–03), a product of Scotland's age of empire. Coincidentally, one of Scott's most active native guides, John Leyden, later died while fulfilling a real colonial role, as a surgeon in the British expedition to Java. In his introduction to the *Minstrelsy*, Scott sets out his agenda: to reclaim a regional territory of Scotland in the past through ballads and reform it for the present.[2] His aim is, specifically,

> to contribute somewhat to the history of my native country; the
> peculiar features of whose manners and character are daily melting
> and dissolving into those of her sister and ally. And, trivial as may
> appear such an offering, to the manes of a kingdom, once proud and
> independent, I hang it upon her altar with a mixture of feelings,
> which I shall not attempt to describe. (1801: cxxxii-cxiiii)

Such passionate involvement and political engagement with his material is typical of Scott and the other indigenous colonizers from within. Of course, Scott, though indigenous, was also of a different class from many of those from whom he collected. Those of the same class, like Anna Gordon, objected to being cited in print, perhaps because of Scott's unconscious violation of colonial rules. Equally, as David Buchan stressed in *The Ballad and the Folk*, Scott used a great deal of North East material, and because of this, he was a covert, as well as overt, colonizer for his own ends.

James Hogg, as one of Scott's major sources from the second volume of the *Minstrelsy* on, responded to this enthusiasm and experienced the same tempered wariness that Elizabeth Stewart expresses:

> One fine summer day of 1801 [actually July 1802], as I was busily engaged working in the field at Ettrick House, Wat Sheil came over to me and said, that "I boud gang away down to the Ramseycleuch as fast as my feet could carry me, for there war some gentlement there wha wantit to speak to me.... I'm thinking it's the Shirra an' some o his gang." I was rejoiced to hear this, for I had seen the first volumes of "The Minstrelsy of the Scottish Border," and had copied a number of them from my mother's recital, and sent them to the editor preparatory for a third volume. I accordingly went towards home to put on my Sunday clothes, but before reaching it I met with THE SHIRRA and Mr William Laidlaw.... They alighted and remained in our cottage for a space better than an hour, and my mother chanted the ballad of Old Maitlan' to them.... I remember he asked her if she thought it had ever been printed; and her answer was, "Oo, na, na, sir, it was never printed i' the world. For my brothers an' me learned it frae auld Baby Mettlin, that was the housekeeper to the first laird o' Tushilaw." "Then that must be a very auld story, indeed, Margaret." "Ay it is that! It is an auld story! But mair not that, except George Warton and James Steward, there was never ane o' my songs prentit till ye prentit them yourself, an' ye hae spoilt them a'thegither. They war made for singing, an' no for reading; and they're nouther right spelled nor right setten down." (quoted in Bold 2000: 116)

Like Stewart, Hogg recalls this from a distance of several decades; in the interim he had become a well-known authority on traditional culture. However, the way he presents the episode, with its physical "ride-out" for ballads and the invading "gang," its implicit power imbalance, the need to find his Sunday clothes, and so on does suggest some real discomfort with the casting of himself, and his family, as colonial guides.

Scott sought virgin territory for colonization (unprinted ballads), and Margaret Laidlaw, though not quite shy, was certainly not comfortable with the way her songs had been treated. Hogg's relatives seem to have felt that Scott did not properly understand the context of the texts. There is a sense of hurt family pride in this well-known anecdote, reflecting the experience of having their texts appropriated for public consumption without a full acknowledgment of either their lineage or meaning to the family. No matter how benevolent and politically appropriate, this is a form of collection as colonization.

Margaret Laidlaw, according to her son, continued, "Ye hae broken the charm noo, an' they'll never be sung again" (quoted in Bold 2000: 116). This anecdote reminds me of a point North East tradition bearer Stanley Robertson made. Stanley was telling us that a student had been misdirected in interpreting Jeannie Robertson's instruction to "bring a sang oot bonnie." The tutor had explained that this meant to sing "prettily" when the emphasis should have been on the "oot": The song goes in, complete with its understanding, and appreciation of its source, and should be brought out the same way (Robertson 1999).

Perhaps the ballad raider, without a direct understanding of the material of the tradition bearer, can never transmit the full value and experience of the items collected. It is likely that this is what is so disturbing to the culturally colonized. To cite Stanley Robertson and Elizabeth Stewart as sources again, Traveller culture involves intense discussions of ballads (and stories): Children are advised directly about the moral and metaphorical meanings of songs and encouraged to analyze the precise meanings, with particular relevance to Traveller culture. Naturally, those who produce "spoilt" songs lack the inside understanding of the colonized. The colonizer, therefore, acclimatizes the culture to his or her own standards. Just as curry, acquired colonially, is Scotland's second national dish, so, too, ballads are conquered in print or performance transmissions. They conform to the collector's cultural conventions and notions of proper presentation and order.

A variation on Scott's experience appears in the collecting work of Hamish Henderson and the School of Scottish Studies, University of Edinburgh, in the North East. As a representative regional migrant, Henderson is well placed to explore and conquer: familiar with the cultural ground rules and able to engage in a form of economic colonization by mining the territory for songs, like gold.

Henderson, writing about the "Folk-song Heritage of the North East" in *The Glasgow Herald* in 1981, remarks, "Aberdeenshire has continued to supply collectors with fine folk-song of every description, as the archives of the School of Scottish Studies amply testify" (1992: 132). Henderson's work has contributed immensely to the valuing of a national tradition as the colony becomes subverted to reclaim our territory nationally, as Scots. As one would expect from his political background, Henderson is alert to the needs of the colonized. Nevertheless, the desire to accumulate ballads and songs, like colonial booty, in precisely located places is evident in his recollections of collecting occasions such as "the marathon recording sessions of 1954, during which the entire travelling community of Aberdeen seems to be passing in never-ending relays through Jeannie's house in Causewayend," providing huge quantities of songs (1992: 167).

Quantity and place are two elements often present in collectors' work, and I do not mean to suggest this has wholly negative effects; obviously, bulk collection produces significant, and lasting, materials for scholars and singers. However, the cultural interpolations of the colonizers construct intellectual colonies despite their best intentions.

Having accused some of our greatest collectors of being colonists, I must reveal I am also a humble practitioner of colonialism by exposing the virtual colony of the Elphinstone Institute's *Northern Folk* CD-ROM. This is a result of cross-cultural colonization: a collaboration between the incomer colonizer (Tom McKean from the United States) and the colonizer from within (me from Fife).

*Northern Folk* maps out the territory of the North East of Scotland very explicitly and makes it possible to access the information wholly territorially through the map option. We have divided the traditions of the area into three main sections: Work, Recreation, and Community. However, the CD-ROM's strength as a resource, and where we hope it transcends its colonial framework, is in offering users a holistic cultural complex, where they can, at least partially, experience what people feel about tradition as a whole, not just, say, ballads. Four hundred text screens of interview and print extracts are all illustrated with still and moving images accompanied by a half-hour soundtrack. Our aim was to create as few power imbalances as we could, to be as postcolonial as possible. Making a CD-ROM with its one-minute audiovisual edits, however, led to a great many colonial negotiations.

At its best, the CD-ROM allows a colonized person to reclaim his or her territory. I conclude with Jock Duncan talking about "The Battle o' Harlaw" (Child 163). Jock was our first "native guide," and he sang the song sitting on the battlefield itself. Here he maps the song on the ground for his audience, providing contextual information he considers necessary:

> It must hae been a fair battle for aa that. Ye canna sing is sang sae good as ye can sing't up here. It gies ye that, A don't know, feelin within yoursel, ye see. Far mair feelin singin't up here, far the actual battle took place, oh aye, absolutely.
>
> A wis brocht up an hearin the first glimmerins o the "Battle o Harlaw." Especially nae far fae ma birthplace. Even at the school, we thought this wis good, ye see, studyin the [battle]. The Dominie wis good in history, he wis affa good in history an he brought the battle tae life an aa, ye ken? An ye niver forget it. [We were] fourteen, fifteen mile as the crow flies, richt ower here, look. Practically due North o Harlaw. And many were the tales aboot it in my young day. Although a lot o them were pretty far fetched, ye know....
>
> This isn't the true story an yet it's a popular sang. Ye widn't be very popular at all, I suppose, if ye changed the theme o't. If [ye hid] somebdy else killed instead o Lord Donald, no, no. It doesn't sound well at all, ye see. Perhaps they didn't have a good *balladeer* amonst them at the time that could have recorded the *true* story of what actually happent at the battle. I think they probably got fed up [hearin] the story....
>
> It probably only lastit a few hours. I *don't* suppose either there wis a heavy loss o life. I mean it speaks aboot "fifty-two gaed hame," no. Bit *maybe* there's quite a heavy loss o life. There cuidha even been a thousand people killed on both sides, bit they hid tae *retire*.... As for *sackin*, we don't know. There's nobdy can tell us if they killed the people *out o hand*, I *don't think* they did.
>
> Ony time A'm up here, A niver fail tae stop here an hae a look around mi. Lookin oot at Bennachie. It's jist fu o story an history an legendary tales, put it that way. Tremendous. A canna sing this sang naewey else sae good as A wid sing't up here. No. Nothing like it.
>
> I'd an uncle sung it, ye see? My uncle Charlie Duncan; he likit singin. He hid a wee croft on the Hill o Bennagoak most o his days, although he wis foreman at the great fermtoon o Netherton o Millbrex.... That wis the era o singin. My father's generation, ma granfather's generation, ma granmither's; that wis the era o singin,

fin I wis a bairn. Singin aa the time. Within a space o twinty year it
seemed tae disappear fae the countryside, the big ballad singers,
*completely* disappear.

(reordered from Bold and McKean 1999: Song section)

## Notes

1. Quotations from Elizabeth Stewart are taken from archive recordings held at the
   Elphinstone Institute, University of Aberdeen. Fluid movement between Scots and
   English is typical of Scots language speakers generally [ed.].
2. Scott's use of balladry to reclaim geographical and cultural territory continues today,
   e.g. Lesley Stevenson's "Traditional Song and the Tourist Gaze in Dumfries and Galloway"
   (forthcoming).

## References

Bold, Valentina, and Tom McKean. 1999. *Northern Folk: Living Traditions of North East
    Scotland*. Aberdeen: Elphinstone Institute.

Bold, Valentina. 2000. "'Nouther Right Spelled nor Right Setten Down': Scott, Child and
    the Hogg Family Ballads." In *The Ballad and Scottish History*, edited by Edward J.
    Cowan, 116–140. Phastassie, East Linton: Tuckwell.

Buchan, David. 1972. *The Ballad and the Folk*. London: Routledge and Kegan Paul.
    Reprint, Phantassie, East Lothian: Tuckwell Press, 1997.

Clifford, James. 1988. *The Predicament of Culture: Twentieth-Century Ethnography,
    Literature, and Art*. Cambridge: Harvard University Press.

Goldstein, Kenneth S. 1964. *A Guide for Field Workers in Folklore*. Hatboro, Pa:
    Published for the American Folklore Society by Folklore Associates.

Henderson, Hamish. 1992. *Alias MacAlias*. Edinburgh: Polygon.

Kiernan, V.G. 1969. *The Lords of Human Kind: Black Man, Yellow Man, and White Man
    in an Age of Empire*. Boston: Little, Brown.

———. 1995. *Imperialism its Contradictions*. Edited by Harvey J. Kaye. London:
    Routledge.

Macpherson, James. 1996. *The Poems of Ossian and Related Works*. Edited by Howard
    Gaskill. Edinburgh: Edinburgh University Press.

Robertson, Stanley. 1999. Personal Communication.

Said, Edward. 1994. *Culture and Imperialism*. London: Vintage.

Scott, Walter. 1801–03. *The Minstrelsy of the Scottish Border*. Kelso: James Ballantyne.

Stevenson, Lesley. Forthcoming. "Traditional Song and the Tourist Gaze in Dumfries and
    Galloway." In *Proceedings of the 2003 International Ballad Conference of the
    Kommission für Volksdichtung, Leuven, Belgium*. Trier: Wissenschaftlicher Verlag.

Stewart, Elizabeth. 1997. Recorded interview, EI 1997.021. Elphinstone Institute
    Archive, University of Aberdeen.

# The Contribution of D. K. Wilgus
# to Ballad and Folksong Scholarship

David G. Engle, James Porter, and Roger deV. Renwick

D. K. Wilgus was a staunch member of the Kommission für Volksdichtung for many years. Donald Knight Wilgus died on Christmas morning, 1989, in Los Angeles, where he had served as professor of English and Anglo-American folk song at the University of California, Los Angeles, from 1963 till his retirement on June 30, 1989. His participation in the conferences of the Ballad Commission spanned more than twenty years, from its first meetings in the mid-1960s to the late 1980s. For this reason alone, it is fitting that an assessment of his work should appear in this volume. This look at his scholarly contribution to ballad and folk-song studies melds the perspectives of two former students and a longtime colleague, all working in the field of folk song and balladry. What follows is not an encomium but rather, as D. K. himself would have wished, a professional evaluation of his work by some who knew it intimately.

The facts of Wilgus's life are straightforward: He was born in 1918 in West Mansfield, Ohio, and graduated from East High School, Columbus, in 1935. He attended Ohio State University, graduating with a B.A. (1941), M.A. (1947), and Ph.D. (1954), the last under the direction of Francis Lee Utley. He served as an administrator at Purdue University during 1941–42 and then with the U. S. Army from 1942 to 1945. While finishing his doctorate, he taught English at Ohio State, leaving there in 1950 for Western Kentucky State University, where he was associate professor from 1950 to 1961, then professor of English from 1961 to 1963. During this period, he founded of the *Kentucky Folklore Record* (1955), acting as editor until 1961. He was named a fellow of the Guggenheim Foundation for 1957–58, and in 1963 he left for UCLA, where he was formally a joint member of the departments of music and English.

During his period at Kentucky State, he undertook fieldwork in Cumberland River County with his student, Lynwood Montell, resulting in the article, "Clure and Joe Williams: Legend and Blues Ballad," which was later published in the *Journal of American Folklore* (1968) and established the blues ballad as a distinctive subgenre in North American tradition. He explored this topic further in an extensive article coauthored with Eleanor Long, his second wife (Wilgus and Long 1985). Wilgus also did fieldwork in Ireland in the 1970s, recording (with

Tom Munnelly) the Traveller John Reilly, who sang for them "The Well Below the Valley," a version of the rarely found ballad, "The Maid and the Palmer" (Child 21; see Munnelly 1972). Wilgus had by that time founded the Folklore and Mythology Program at UCLA in 1965, serving as its chair for seventeen years. He also built an archive of eleven thousand commercial recordings and more than fifty thousand manuscript items. Elected a fellow of the American Folklore Society in 1960, he served on its Executive Board from 1964–69 and was elected president in 1971–72. His presidential address, entitled "The Text Is the Thing," was a lively response to the current fashion in the field for performance studies (1973). He was also president of the California Folklore Society, and, from 1970 to 1975, he assumed the editorship of its journal, *Western Folklore*. There he also published his Archer Taylor Memorial Lecture on connections between the Irish *aisling* [vision poem] and Anglo-American balladry (1985).

Wilgus's major achievement in the field of folk-song studies, however, was his *Anglo-American Folksong Scholarship Since 1898*, published in 1959. This magisterial account of folk-song scholarship in Britain and North America since the death of Francis James Child is a stirring narrative of fractious disputes and clashes among scholars with radically different theories on the origin and nature of folk song. Besides this authoritative critical study, Wilgus was a productive scholar and published several other books, including an edition of Josiah Combs's *Folk-Songs of the Southern United States* (Combs 1967), more than four dozen scholarly articles, countless papers and reviews—especially record reviews, for he was record-review editor for the *Journal of American Folklore* from 1959 to 1973. Because of his encyclopedic knowledge of the country and bluegrass traditions, he was one of the first to propose that hillbilly music be studied like any other folk genre (1971).

Although the last twenty-seven years of his life were closely tied to the growth of folklore and mythology studies at UCLA, it was as a ballad scholar and regular member of the Kommission that Wilgus will be remembered. He attended its meetings from the first one in Freiburg (1966) almost every year until his death. Through all these years, he was concerned with devising an ambitious classification scheme—as distinguished from a cataloguing "arrangement," as he once described it—for English-language ballad texts, a task which was the raison d'être for the Kommission's founding in the first place. Indeed, his knowledge of the basic topics of Anglo-American balladry was unrivaled, except possibly for that of his hero, Phillips Barry, from whom he took both his methodological inspiration and the idea of "ballad themes." As a balancing factor to the difficult and far-reaching goal of classifying ballads by theme, he studied single topics, such as the "Lord Leitrim" or "Titanic" ballad complexes and, in a more general way, the Irish ballad corpus as a whole. In this last he saw vital connections with North American balladry, and his analyses always had a strong historical bent, one he was careful to disassociate from historical/geographical studies of ballad origin and diffusion.

### *"The Text Is the Thing"*

"The Text Is the Thing" is the title which made D. K. Wilgus famous in many circles, but that fame is in many ways both unfortunate and unearned. Wilgus— and we—would be better served to recall the true center of his work, which is not to view some "mere" text as being the "only thing" but rather, take the songs as a whole: their singers, their performances, their contexts, and yes, also their texts. Of course, Wilgus received his formal training in English (it was at the time New Criticism was blossoming), and the area where he did the majority of his publishing was the study of song texts, narratives, and international parallels.

Wilgus was one of the first college-campus performers of folk music, and it was he who reminded generations of students to respect the folk who sang the songs. His master's thesis was the first academic treatment of American hillbilly music, showing its indebtedness to traditional folk song, and today we recognize that it was Wilgus, above all, who legitimized the study of popular hillbilly and country-and-western music for folklorists. In this pursuit (dare we call it a crusade?), it was Wilgus who brought the art of the record review—as opposed to a book review—and liner notes to legitimacy and then stature. Wilgus was an avid collector of folk music, and as such he was groundbreaking in his inclusivensss, seeking out not only venerable pieces canonized by Professor Child but attempting to record what the folk were actually playing and singing, as well as how they were doing it.

We can recall, for instance, his insistence that many "fragments" (as they are often labeled in published collections) are created by the collector, who only records a portion of the piece. Others are, of course, just the last shreds of memory, but many are only "short" pieces, fragments to the scholar but not to the performer. Labeling such a short piece a fragment does violence to the collected piece and the performer. If it was Bertrand Bronson who taught us that the folk ballad is song, D. K. Wilgus taught us that the ballad was sung by this individual and that friend. One case in point is his pioneering study, years in the making, of Andrew Jenkins, a performer who can be categorized as both professional and folk (Wilgus 1981: 109–28).

Wilgus was always on the cutting edge of scholarship, for it was his insistence on looking at the whole tradition which brought new insights; in discussions of ballad classification, he pointed out that many *aislingi* cite a narrative without recounting it. He coined the term "blues ballad" to refer to a ballad sung in blues style—without stable text and often without a stable narrative (both improvized each time)—but nevertheless balladesque since the events in the ballad "celebrating" them are stable and known to both singer and audience. Such insights are not born from a "simple" concentration on text.

In exhorting us to take the "text" as the "thing," Wilgus was asking that we concentrate on the artifacts within their performance and traditional contexts, rather than lose sight of them. He was exhorting us to inspect the data, engage it, and not ignore it. This idea was typical for Wilgus, who was a model of humility when it came to confronting the material or recognizing the hard work of others. He worked hard, and he demanded that his students do the same. If one advanced an idea not thought through, Wilgus could offer dozens of examples to question it. Above all, Wilgus's emphasis on the text is basically an expression of his fundamental and radical honesty: to the performer, the study of folklore methodology, the music, and the text.

*Ballad Classification*

Of particular interest is Wilgus's role in ballad classification, the scholarly task which gave rise to the Kommission für Volksdichtung. When ballad scholars gathered in Freiburg in 1966 to develop a ballad index which would stimulate ballad research within a pan-European context, Wilgus was there. He was dissatisfied with the "Freiburg proposal," though, because he thought its arrangement of whole ballads in a largely predetermined (or "procrustean," as he termed it) list hid more ballad relationships than it revealed. His proposal, developed in conjunction with Eleanor Long and promulgated at numerous ballad conferences, was to classify the ballads analytically according to the themes in their plots. Thus was born the valuable notion of "narrative theme," a concept which informed Wilgus's work thereafter, eventually called "thematic units" (Wilgus 1970a, 1979b, 1986b; Wilgus and Long 1985).

It was Wilgus's contention that the ballads themselves should provide the key to any classification system, and so he worked inductively on the project from the ground up. He always searched for common narrative themes (or plot ideas) which occurred in more than one ballad text. Such themes should serve to bring ballads together. Unlike the Freiburg proposal's "whole ballad method,"

Wilgus's concentration on small themes allowed songs that had similar sections to be combined on that basis while recognizing at the same time that other portions of the songs could be radically different. By being able to classify song parts, then, Wilgus's idea began to do justice to ballad "contamination," crossing, hybridization, or even "reworkings." That "adaptability" was the true giant step forward and is what separates Wilgus's classification work from previous collections, lists, and static arrangements. In fact, it was the only way to work with the manifold relationships between "broadside" and "traditional" (let alone "bluesy" and "fragmented") textual treatments of a single "ballad idea."

Wilgus adopted this approach by wrestling with the texts, as his 1972 presidential address to the American Folklore Society encouraged us to do, and certainly his struggle was not limited to text alone. Of all his services to the Kommission für Volksdichtung, we should perhaps list first his coining the term "narrative unit," but we should also emphasize his honesty and aggressively investigative approach toward well nigh all aspects of ballad singing. Naturally he does not stand alone in having such an approach, but he has nonetheless been a beacon to several generations of scholars. To reduce Wilgus to the status of a "textualist" would be a major disservice to folklore study. Wilgus himself would have eschewed such reductions.

## Idealism and Realism

D. K. Wilgus contributed seminally to the study of hillbilly music and Irish-American song. He was convinced that individual song histories and a diachronic focus are central to the future of folk-song study. This diachronic approach was inevitably combined, in his view, with a comparative approach, particularly in analyzing the textual traditions of a single song. Summing up his position in a 1983 paper, he pinpointed the need for a balanced analysis of text and context:

> The comparativist is not one who denies the validity of other approaches and indeed can and should utilize any results that contribute to the understanding of the ballad as a product of humankind, just as the contextualist needs comparative evidence to prevent errors in interpretation. Although the comparative approach was designed to deal with far-flung items about which there existed too little contextual data, it can and has been applied successfully to more restricted traditions and has made use of contextual data available from current fieldwork. (1986b: 23)

The careful analysis of song texts, comparatively and diachronically, was not only vital to Wilgus's methods but also central to the idea of "Anglo-American" folk-song study as a whole. Although he believed that data on singers, context, the transmission process, and cultural meanings had relevance, for him they were secondary to the ballad idea, narrative themes, or texts as objects worthy of study in and for themselves. This does not contradict what has been said, for attention to singer, performance and context was part of that "textual" centrality, not separate from it. A focus on themes in particular could provide the basis for ballad classification in the form of a type index. In general, he espoused a rationalistic or "hardheaded" approach to scholarship—"the dispassionate, objective, and historical investigation of the phenomena of folk song as a self-contained study," and by this he meant primarily the study of texts (1964: 36).

Admiration for Phillips Barry led Wilgus to declare that Barry had gone to the heart of the matter in balladry by identifying "themes" or "manifestations of folk ideas" by which to list ballads, thus extending the boundaries of ballad histories beyond textual filiation (1986b: 6–8). Wilgus was undoubtedly following Barry's view that "folksong is in reality an idea, of which we can get but the process of actualization, traceable as a history" (Barry 1911: 333). Barry constantly argued for a more holistic view of balladry than the "ballad aristocracy" offered by Child and his followers. Barry saw song formation as a dynamic process "by which a simple event in human experience, of subjective interest, narrated in simple language, set to a simple melody, is progressively objectivated" (Barry 1913: 5). From an appreciation of song content, Barry later moved toward a psychosocial analysis of folk song that included the creativity of singers, their families, and their communities (Barry 1936, 1937, 1961). In Barry's mind, the real dominated the ideal, whereas with Wilgus, the duel between the real and the ideal was ongoing and dialectical.

Wilgus derived his position directly from Barry, but with Wilgus the balance between the study of texts and the enactment of tradition shifted markedly toward one of Barry's early interests—verbal thematics in folk song—rather than his later concern with singers and performance. Although Wilgus maintained, as already noted, an interest in folk performers and composers such as Andy Jenkins, the issue of ballad themes, and what he termed a "convergence model," animated his later comparative work. This model does not take a single text as its "original" of a ballad tradition, "but at most a narrative theme that has been manifested in structures otherwise unrelated except in the norms of the tradition in which structures are produced" (1986b: 19). Such a model includes the possibility that, in a given geographical area, different structures with the same theme may lead to enough mutually related versions of a song that a scholar may be tempted to apply the other alternative, a "divergence model," one that notes departures from a hypothetical original text. Anne Cohen's treatment of the murdered-sweetheart tradition in relation to the Pearl Bryan ballads used this approach. *Convergence* stresses the *theme* as central to the evolution of a particular ballad tradition; yet determining what the theme is in many ballads often demands the dialectic of negotiation (Engle 1985).

Wilgus's thinking, then, is representative of a fundamentally realistic or materialistic viewpoint in North American scholarship that has on occasion moved into the idealistic territory of ballad types and ballad themes. But even as he became associated, roughly in midcareer, with what has been dubbed the "rationalistic" or "rational" approach (at the time of a 1961 symposium juxtaposing literary, anthropological, and comparative approaches that were termed variously "eclectic," "pragmatic," or "rationalistic"), Wilgus pointed out that the lineage of his approach stretched at least from Joseph Ritson to G. Malcolm Laws, Jr. (1964: 30). One can argue that Wilgus, like the philosopher G. H. Mead, was a realist and rationalist because he believed in a world that is experienced and exists separately from cognition and perception. In his folk-song analyses, Wilgus held that experience confronts us with phenomena that lead to conflicting attitudes, problems that call for reconstructions and new meanings. He was, in short, an empiricist working within the American pragmatist tradition deriving essentially from William James, John Dewey, Charles Peirce, and Mead, although Wilgus is a not usually associated with an explicitly Meadian "sociological" approach to folk-song analysis. Rather, his "common-sense" approach links him to this tradition (Abrahams 1985; see also Porter 1993).

*Roger deV. Renwick Remembers Studying with D. K. Wilgus*
While D. K. Wilgus's published work, especially the definitive *Anglo-American Folksong Scholarship Since 1898*, and even unpublished research like his ballad index, was famous throughout folklore circles, he also exerted palpable influence on the discipline through the activities of people he taught. For over the three distinct decades of the sixties, seventies, and eighties, we find his name prominent in the acknowledgment sections of books by former students—books like *The Maid and the Hangman; Poor Pearl! Poor Girl!* and *Warrior Women and Popular Balladry 1650–1850*, whose high quality is widely recognized among Anglo-American folk-song cognoscenti (Long 1971; Cohen 1973; Dugaw

1989). Roger Renwick's assertion, in *English Folk Poetry* (1980), that D. K. "more than anyone [was] responsible for whatever may be praiseworthy" in that volume is profoundly heartfelt. Roger relates his own experience:

> His standards were extremely high, and a student had to earn his or her way into D. K.'s esteem and eventual mentorship: good intentions, an amiable personality, even the possession of substantial factual knowledge, were not enough. As a beginning graduate student taking D. K.'s Anglo-American folk-song course during my first quarter in the master's program in folklore and mythology at UCLA, I experienced firsthand the difficulties of achieving a student-professor bonding, of becoming "one of D. K.'s students." Having had the benefit of several years of off-and-on informal reading in folk-song scholarship before entering UCLA, I was in the unusual position for a new student of being already familiar with many versions of the very songs D. K. used in his lectures, and more than once found myself correcting my professor's factual errors in on-the-spot examples—on the meter of "Chevy Chase," on the traditional status of "The Maid and the Palmer." But each time, D. K. seemed to become more irritated than admiring! While this reaction may have stemmed in part from a certain insecurity one often finds in folklorists, there is no doubt that D. K. also thought this new-to-the-program student was superficially "smart," whereas to form a serious, long-term relationship with him, you had to be truly committed.
>
> A breakthrough came when I found, quite by chance, the tune "Rose Connolly" in Bunting's 1840 collection, *The Ancient Music of Ireland*, and immediately shared the discovery with D. K. I knew that he had long thought the murder ballad of the same title, so popular in the U.S. South, was in fact Irish in origin and not a "native" American ballad as G. Malcolm Laws, Jr., had characterized it. Here was the first piece of hard ethnographic evidence that D. K. might be correct! My excitement, which just about matched his, must have shown: for the first time, D. K. seemed to suspect that the neophyte might have a genuine folk-song scholar's sensibility and be worthy of his mentorship. (And as we know, D. K.'s hypothesis was later validated when Tom Munnelly found a version in the

Irish Folklore Commission's archival holdings that had been collected in Galway in 1929; see Wilgus 1979b.)

Once he'd decided on that pedagogical commitment to me, D. K. was unstinting in his attention. He soon made me his research assistant, a job which lasted eighteen months and which, for sheer self-satisfaction, I would state unequivocally, was unmatched by any I had before and remains unequaled since. As research assistant, I synopsized, coded, and entered folk-song texts into D. K.'s two major databases, the huge Anglo-American ballad index (organized by narrative themes) and the anglophone Irish one, with its simpler topical organization.

Just a few weeks after I started, D. K. charged me with a major task: extracting and arranging into appropriate subcategories all ballads from the Anglo-American database fitting the Freiburg catalogue system's category X (*fabliau* ballads) for a presentation to the Ballad Commission at its 1970 meeting at Kloster Utstein, Norway (Wilgus 1970). I did what I thought was an excellent job, and the boss did indeed compliment me; but just before leaving for the conference, D. K. showed his research assistant the final list for his presentation, and while he'd kept all the material I had given him, he had increased the number of songs by at least a third. He used the opportunity to explain in detail to the fledgling folklorist (now indisputably "one of D. K.'s students") some of his favorite scholarly principles, ones he constantly reinforced both inside and outside the classroom: the necessity of thoroughness in data gathering, the importance of inclusivity as opposed to exclusivity, the intrinsically intertextual nature of folk songs, and the privileged place induction should hold over deduction in developing valid ballad constructs and theories. All of these principles are embodied in what D. K. told me after I lamented that a study of "The Bold Fisherman" was leading into what were surely quite-unrelated song types, such as the murdered sweetheart: namely, that once you start looking at any one folk song, you will end up looking at them all.

And just as he'd employed a hands-on mentorship with his brand-new research assistant on the *fabliau*-ballads project, D. K. actively involved himself with all his students' term projects, trying to get them to understand, appreciate, and practice these principles.

For example, he constantly made sure they had checked for versions in readily accessible but easily forgotten places, such as Child's "Additions and Corrections," or volumes four and five of the *Frank C. Brown Collection of North Carolina Folklore*, where the presence of many song texts, not found elsewhere, is disguised by the volumes' deceptive titles: "The Music of the Ballads" and "The Music of the Folk Songs" (see Schinhan 1952–64). D. K. went much further and even photocopied texts not accessible to students, with college library help—for instance, texts from ephemeral songbooks and broadsides he had in his personal collection. Without being asked, he taped for students copies of acoustic versions from his extensive collection of phonograph records, even personally transcribing and typing up the words himself.

Long after I had finished my UCLA master's degree in folklore and mythology, I tried to remain true to these principles of thoroughness, inclusivity, interrelatedness, and respect for what the texts had to say, even tried to emulate the hands-on method of making obscure versions accessible to students. Though many other teachers provided me with other worthy principles that I also tried to incorporate into my scholarly sensibilities, neither their personalities nor their maxims were ever as starkly omnipresent in my consciousness as D. K.'s. Truth to tell, I never wrote anything in my later years as a doctoral student at Penn and, later still, as a member of the professoriate without being very, very sensitive to whether it would meet D. K.'s standards. In fact, more than a decade after his death, I still don't.

*Relation to Contemporaries*

D. K. Wilgus tenaciously followed his instincts in a field of folk-song scholarship that was shrinking in importance, declining in the prestige it had enjoyed in North American folkloristics since the turn of the twentieth century. The revival of the fifties and sixties had revitalized public as well as scholarly interest in folk song, but in the seventies, folkloristics took a new turn with performance studies (often oriented toward linguistics or communal enactment rather than singing) and an interest in the ethnography of everyday life (Porter 1986). Folk song is, after all, a specialized study that requires total devotion because of the large amount of data available to scholars in English-language folk song alone. It is not a subject for part-timers or dilettantes. Here Wilgus shone within the American Folklore Society, not only for his devotion to his chosen subject but his unrivaled knowledge of Anglo-American folk-song traditions and their evolution. While contemporaries working in the same area espoused idealist positions, pet theories of ballad origins, or performance studies, Wilgus steadfastly maintained his position as the champion of comparative and historical case studies in folk song. Generally speaking, he steered clear of political discussions, and his affection for populist culture did not take him in the direction of ideological critique. But like any scholar worth his salt, he had his critics: for his down-to-earth view of historical ballad icons like Child, for instance, or his defence of classification as a contemporary principle in folklore studies (see Bell 1980; Porter 1980).

But for all that, he will be remembered for positive achievements: first, his masterly grasp of the field of Anglo-American folk song as a whole; second, his development of an ambitious classification system of ballads based on narrative themes; third, his work on the connections between Irish and North American folk-song textual traditions; fourth, his recognition of the value of hillbilly song tradition; fifth, his identifying the blues ballad as an important subgenre in American balladry; and last but not least, his inspired and unfailing support for his students and colleagues (even when he disagreed with them on matters of interpretation). These generous attributes sat easily with a discriminating, clever, restless mind and complex personality. As an individual, he was approachable and kind, but also shy and unaggressive; he had his demons, of course, and wrestled with them while at the same time finding the energy to run a lively university program, engage in exacting field studies, prepare his own and others's publications, address conferences, assume official professional duties, or attend tiresome faculty meetings. His varied accomplishments mark him as a major scholar in the field of folklore and American cultural tradition, and his well-earned retirement was full of unfinished projects: an annotated index of Irish ballads, books on songs about "Lord Leitrim" and the Titanic, an ambitious study of Kentucky beliefs and superstitions. It is comforting to know that his widow, Eleanor Long, is working to bring these projects to fruition.

*References*

Abrahams, Roger D. 1985. "Pragmatism and a Folklore Experience." *Western Folklore* 44: 324–32.

Barry, Phillips. 1911. "Irish Folk Song." *Journal of American Folklore* 24: 332–43.

———. 1913. "An American Homiletic Ballad." *Modern Language Notes* 28: 1–5.

――――. 1936. "On the Psychopathology of Ballad-Singing." *Bulletin of the Folk-Song Society of the Northeast* 11: 16–18

――――. 1937. "Notes on the Ways of Folk Singers with Folk Tunes." *Bulletin of the Folk-Song Society of the Northeast* 12: 2–6.

――――. 1961. "The Part of the Folk Singer in the Making of Folk Balladry." In *The Critics and the Ballad*, edited by MacEdward Leach and T. P. Coffin, 59–76. Carbondale: Southern Illinois University Press.

Bell, Michael J. 1988. "'No Borders to the Ballad Maker's Art': Francis James Child and the Politics of the People." *Western Folklore* 47: 285–307.

Cohen, Anne B. 1973. *Poor Pearl! Poor Girl! The Murdered-Girl Stereotype in Ballad and Newspaper*. Austin: University of Texas Press.

Combs, Josiah H. 1967. *Folk-Songs of the Southern United States*. Edited by D. K. Wilgus. Austin: University of Texas Press. (First published as *Folk-Songs du Midi des Etats-Unis*. Paris: 1925.)

Dugaw, Dianne. 1989. *Warrior Women and Popular Balladry, 1650–1850*. Cambridge: Cambridge University Press.

Engle, David. 1985. *A Preliminary Catalogue and Edition of German Folk Ballads*. Ph.D. diss., University of California, Los Angeles.

Long, Eleanor R. 1971. *"'The Maid' and 'The Hangman': Myth and Tradition in a Popular Ballad*. Folklore Studies, no. 21. Berkeley: University of California Press.

――――. 1986. "Ballad Classification and the 'Narrative Theme' Concept Together with a Thematic Index to Anglo-Irish-American Balladry." In *Ballad Research: Dublin 1985*, edited by Hugh Shields, 197–213. Dublin: Folk Music Society of Ireland.

Munnelly, Tom. 1972. "The Man and His Music: John Reilly." *Ceol* 4, no. 1: 2–8.

Porter, James. 1980. "Principles of Ballad Classification: A Suggestion for Regional Catalogues of Ballad Style." *Jahrbuch für Volksliedforschung* 25: 11–26.

――――. 1986. "Ballad Explanations, Ballad Reality, and the Singer's Epistemics." *Western Folklore* 45: 110–25.

――――. 1993. "Convergence, Divergence, and Dialectic in Folksong Paradigms: Critical Directions for Transatlantic Scholarship." *Journal of American Folklore* 106: 61–98.

Renwick, Roger, deV. 1980. *English Folk Poetry: Structure and Meaning*. Philadelphia: University of Pennsylvania Press.

Schinhan, Jan P., ed. 1952–64. *The Music of the Ballads*, vol. 4, and *The Music of the Folk Songs*, vol. 5 of *The Frank C. Brown Collection of North Carolina Folklore*, edited by Newman Ivey White. Durham, N.C.: Duke University Press.

Wilgus, D. K. 1955. "Ballad Classification." *Midwest Folklore* 5, no. 2: 95–100.

――――. 1959. *Anglo-American Folksong Scholarship Since 1898*. New Brunswick, N.J.: Rutgers University Press.

――――. 1964. "The Rationalistic Approach." In *Folksong and Folksong Scholarship: Changing Approaches and Attitudes*, 29–39. Dallas: Southern Methodist University Press.

――――. 1970a. "A Type-Index of Anglo-American Traditional Narrative Songs." *Journal of the Folklore Institute* 7: 161–76.

――――. 1970b. "Anglo-American Narrative Songs Classified by the 'Freiburg System' of Fabliau Ballads *(Schwankballaden)*." *3. Arbeitstagungen über Fragen des Typenindex der europäischen Volksballaden*, edited by Rolf W. Brednich et al., 27–30. Berlin: Staatliches Institut für Musikforschung.

――――. 1971. "Country-Western Music and the Urban Hillbilly." *The Urban Experience and Folk Tradition*, edited by Américo Paredes and Ellen J. Stekert, 137–59. Austin: University of Texas Press.

――――. 1973. "The Text Is the Thing." *Journal of American Folklore* 86: 241–52.

――――. 1979a. "'Rose Connelly': An Irish Ballad." *Journal of American Folklore* 92:

172–95.

———. 1979b. "Thematic Units in Traditional Narrative Songs of Social Conflict." *9. Arbeitstagung über Fragen des Typenindex der europäischen Volksballaden*, edited by Rolf W. Brednich, Jürgen Dittmar, David G. Engle, and Ildikó Kriza, 138–55. Budapest: Ethnographisches Institut der U. A. d. W.

———. 1981. "Andrew Jenkins, Folk Composer: An Overview." *Lore and Language* (special issue) 3, nos. 4–5 (January/July): 109–28.

———. 1985. "The *Aisling* and the Cowboy: Some Unnoticed Influences of Irish Vision Poetry on Anglo-American Balladry." *Western Folklore* 44: 255–300.

———. 1986a. "The Catalogue of Irish Traditional Ballads in English." *Ballad Research: Dublin 1985*, edited by Hugh Shields, 215–27. Dublin: Folk Music Society of Ireland.

———. 1986b. "The Comparative Approach." In *The Ballad and the Scholars: Approaches to Ballad Study,* 3–28. Los Angeles: William Andrews Clark Library.

Wilgus, D. K., and Eleanor R. Long. 1985. "The Blues Ballad and the Genesis of Style in Traditional Narrative Song." In *Narrative Folksong: New Directions*, edited by Carol L. Edwards and Kathleen B. Manley, 437–82. Boulder, Colo.: Westview Press.

Wilgus, D. K., and Lynwood Montell. 1968. "Clure and Joe Williams: Legend and Blues Ballad." *Journal of American Folklore* 81: 295–315.

# Acknowledgments

I would like to thank my colleagues—the members of the Kommission für Volksdichtung scattered round the world—for their friendship, a common obsession with ballads, and for their patience.

Particular thanks go to all the authors, of course, but also to Barre Toelken, to John Alley of Utah State University Press along with Barbara Bannon for her patient, uncannily thorough copyediting. A special debt of gratitude goes to Ian Hamilton of MacAber, to Malcolm Reavell, and to Kathy Scherdt at Edwards Brothers for help with the images and file transfers, to Mary Anne Alburger for typesetting the music examples, and to Ian Russell and Alison Sharman of the Elphinstone Institute, University of Aberdeen, for their help and advice.

Thanks also to Barbara Boock, of the Deutsche Volksliedarchiv, Stefaan Top, David Engle, along with Bill Nicolaisen, Gerald Porter and David Atkinson for bibliographic help along with stylistic and scholarly advice during the long editing and typesetting process. I am especially grateful, also, to the three external readers for their scrutiny of the manuscript and for their helpful comments. Lastly, my thanks to L. D. K. and R. L. M$^2$ for a combination of help, understanding and forebearance.

All authors can be contacted through the Kommission für Volksdichtung website <http://www.KfVweb.org>.

Thomas A. M<sup>c</sup>Kean

# Notes on Contributors

Thomas A. McKean is a folklorist researching the social function of song, particularly that of the Scottish Highlands, the Scots speaking North East of Scotland, and his native New England. He lectures on traditional song, custom and belief, and methodology at the Elphinstone Institute, University of Aberdeen, where he is also archivist. His book, *Hebridean Song-maker: Iain Macneacail of the Isle of Skye* (1997), is the first full-length study of a Gaelic township poet.

Mary Anne Alburger studies the music and dance traditions of Scotland, concentrating on the fiddle from its construction to its use. A musician recently involved in the reconstruction of the "Mary Rose fiddle" from Henry VIII's flagship, she is also the author of *Scottish Fiddlers and Their Music* (1983) and has recently completed a Ph.D. dissertation on Simon Fraser's *Airs and Melodies Peculiar to the Highlands of Scotland and the Isles*.

David Atkinson is the author of *The English Traditional Ballad: Theory, Method, and Practice* (2002), and a member of the editorial board of *Folk Music Journal*.

Julia C. Bishop has researched and published widely on British and Newfoundland ballads, in addition to running several major research projects on childlore and the production of the James Madison Carpenter Collection Online Catalogue, now available at <http://www.hrionline.ac.uk/carpenter/>.

Valentina Bold is senior lecturer and head of Scottish studies at the University of Glasgow's Crichton Campus in Dumfries. She established and runs an interdisciplinary program in Scottish Studies with three main strands: literature, history and ethnology (oral traditions) and is currently introducing a new undergraduate program in Heritage and Tourism. Her latest book is *Nature's Making: James Hogg and the Autodidacts* (2003).

Dr Katherine Campbell is a British Academy Research Fellow at the Elphinstone Institute, University of Aberdeen, where she is preparing *The Performance Edition of* The Greig-Duncan Folk-Song Collection and formerly AHRB Research Fellow in the Creative and Performing Arts at the department of Celtic and Scottish Studies, University of Edinburgh. As author, scholar and performer, she is involved in promoting Scottish music on many levels, and was a joint editor of volume eight of *The Greig-Duncan Collection*. Other publications include *The Fiddle in Scottish Culture* (forthcoming) and *Traditional Scottish Songs and Music* (with Ewan McVicar, 2001).

Nicolae Constantinescu is professor of folklore at the University of Bucharest, also teaching in cultural anthropology and ethnology. He has published extensively on Romanian traditions in including foodways, custom and belief, and contemporary legend.

Luisa Del Giudice is director of the Italian Oral History Institute, visiting professor of Italian Folklife at the University of California, Los Angeles (1995–2001), and president of the Kommission für Volksdichtung (KfV) of the Société Internationale d'Ethnologie et de Folklore. She has written extensively on Italian traditional song and on Italian and Italian American folklife.

Sheila Douglas is a folklorist, singer and composer who also lectures on the Scots language for the traditional music program at Glasgow's Royal Scottish Academy of Music and Dance. Among her publications are *The Sang's the Thing: Voices from Lowland Scotland* (1992) and *The King o the Black Art and Other Folk Tales* (1987).

David Engle is professor of German and Folklore at California State University, Fresno. He recently founded the Central California Folklore Archives and is assistant editor of the web-based *Traditional Ballad Index*.

Frances J. Fischer is a folklorist and historian focusing generally on Scandinavian and Scots language areas. Her dissertation, *A comparison of ballads in Scotland and the Faroe Islands* will be published in Tørshavn.

Simon Furey is a computing consultant, singer and Morris dancer with a Ph.D. on Catalan folk music. His publications include *Bon cop de falç!: Traditional Songs from Catalonia and the Balearic Islands* (1992) and a commentary on the Dance of Death from the village of Verges in northern Catalonia (1997).

Vic Gammon is senior lecturer in music at the University of Leeds, specializing in the popular, traditional and vernacular musics of Britain and North America. Recent publications include "Cecil Sharp and English folk music" in *Still Growing: English Traditional Songs and Singers from the Cecil Sharp Collection* (2003).

Marjetka Golež Kaučič, senior lecturer, is director of the Glasbenonarodopisni inštitut ZRC SAZU (Institute of Ethnomusicology SRC SASA), Ljubljana, as well as vice president of the KfV. She writes, edits, broadcasts and presents widely on Slovenian song, particularly on animal motifs in the ballad.

Pauline Greenhill teaches Women's Studies at the University of Winnipeg. Her research interests centre on Canadian traditional and popular culture and feminist folklore theory. She is coeditor, with Diane Tye, of *Undisciplined Women: Tradition and Culture in Canada* (1997) and numerous journal articles.

Cozette Griffin-Kremer researches the folklife of Great Britain, Ireland and France, specializing in popular calendar systems and the history of preindustrial technologies. She is currently a research associate at the Centre de Recherches Bretonne et Celtique, Universite de Bretagne Occidentale, Brest.

William Bernard McCarthy is professor of English at Penn State University, DuBois campus and also teaches courses in religion and mythology. Publications on traditional narrative and the ballad include *Jack in Two Worlds: Contemporary North American Taletellers* (1995) and *The Ballad Matrix: Personality, Milieu, and the Oral Tradition* (1995).

J. J. Dias Marques has been studying the Portuguese oral tradition for more than twenty years, concentrating on the ballad, which was the focus of his Ph.D dissertation. He teaches oral literature at the University of the Algarve, Faro, and is assistant editor of *Estudos de literatura oral.*

Isabelle Peere, vice president of the KfV, lectures at the Facultés Universitaires Saint-Louis, Brussels. Her doctoral work dealt with the revenant in Newfoundland versions of Child ballads. She has since been investigating *tellingen*, the work songs and rhymes of the Flemish lacemakers, and issues of literacy.

Gerald Porter is senior lecturer in English at the University of Vaasa in Finland. He has written extensively on political and vernacular song, his *English Occupational Song* (1992) being the first full-length study of the subject. Other areas of interest include literary studies, society and culture and language studies.

James Porter is Professor Emeritus, University of California, Los Angeles, and Honorary Professor, University of Aberdeen. He has published widely on Scottish folklore, traditional music, and song, including studies of traditional singers, and was a founding editor of *The Garland Encyclopedia of World Music* (10 vols., 1999–2002). He is currently executive editor of The Music of Scotland, a project to publish manuscripts of early Scottish music, sponsored by the universities of Aberdeen and Glasgow.

Roger deV. Renwick holds an M.A. in Folklore and Mythology from the University of California, Los Angeles and a Ph.D. in Folklore and Folklife from the University of Pennsylvania. His most recent publication is *Recentering Anglo/American Folksong* (2001).hhh

Sigrid Rieuwerts lectures at the Seminar für Englische Philologie, Johannes Gutenberg-Universität Mainz. Extracurricularly, she specializes in the life and work of Francis James Child, as well as oral tradition and gender.

Michèle Simonsen taught French Language and Literature, and Folklore Studies, at the University of Copenhagen from 1971 to her early retirement in 1997. Her main research interests are oral literature and festive traditions and popular rituals, past and present.

Larry Syndergaard is professor emeritus of English and member of the Medieval Institute, Western Michigan University, Kalamazoo, and organizer of ballad sessions at the annual International Congress on Medieval Studies at Kalamazoo. Research interests include Scandinavian and British traditional ballads, ballad translation, and oral-traditional literature and culture.

Stefaan Top lectures at the Catholic University, Leuven and is honorary president of the KfV. A driving force behind much current research into Flemish folk culture, he is closely involved with the Vlaams Centrum voor Volkscultuur songbooks reprint series.

Larysa Vakhnina lectures in Ukrainian culture and ethnology at the University of Kiev. She lectures widely on Eastern European folklore matters.

Lynn Wollstadt is a researcher in Anglo-American folk song.

# General Index

# Song Title Index

This index cites instances where songs are discussed, rather than simply mentioned in examples or citations. Capitalization follows respective language customs.